THE
SECRET LEGACY
OF JESUS

"Many books are informative; this remarkable book is also important. Rev. Bütz traces an 'underground stream' of Jewish-Christian (Ebionite) affirmation of the humanity of Jesus—from his family and original apostles through nearly two millennia, culminating in Freemasonic traditions of the Founding Fathers who wrote the Constitution of the United States."

MARGARET STARBIRD, AUTHOR OF
MAGDALENE'S LOST LEGACY AND
WOMAN WITH THE ALABASTER JAR

"I just read Jeffrey Bütz's latest brilliant work and am more convinced than ever that America is the New Jerusalem. Bütz lays out clearly and convincingly that the original teachings of Christ, as handed down by Jesus's brother James, impacted Freemasonry. When the Freemasons threw their support behind Thomas Jefferson, Benjamin Franklin, and others, they were able to manifest the greatest expression of a democratic republic this planet has ever seen: the U.S. Constitution. This book is superb!"

ROBERT R. HIERONIMUS, PH.D., AUTHOR OF
FOUNDING FATHERS, SECRET SOCIETIES AND
UNITED SYMBOLISM OF AMERICA

THE
SECRET LEGACY
OF JESUS

The Judaic Teachings That Passed from
James the Just to the Founding Fathers

JEFFREY J. BÜTZ

Inner Traditions
Rochester, Vermont • Toronto, Canada

Inner Traditions
One Park Street
Rochester, Vermont 05767
www.InnerTraditions.com

Library of Congress Cataloging-in-Publication Data

Bütz, Jeffrey J.
 The secret legacy of Jesus : the Judaic teachings that passed from James the Just to the Founding Fathers / Jeffrey J. Bütz.
  p. cm.
 Includes bibliographical references and index.
 ISBN 978-1-59477-307-5 (pbk.)
 1. Jewish Christians—History—Early church, ca. 30–600 2. Jesus Christ—Miscellanea. 3. Christianity—Miscellanea. 4. Secret societies—Religious aspects—Christianity. 5. Freemasonry—Religious aspects—Christianity. 6. James, Brother of the Lord, Saint. I. Title.

 BR195.J8B88 2010
 281'.1—dc22
                                                                              2009033664

Printed and bound in the United States by Lake Book Manufacturing

10 9 8 7 6 5 4 3 2 1

Text design by Jon Desautels and layout by Peri Swan
This book was typeset in Garamond Premier Pro with Trajan and Gill Sans used as display typefaces

Unless otherwise indicated, all scripture quotations are from the New Revised Standard Version of the Bible (copyright 1989, Division of Christian Education of the National Council of the Churches of Christ in the U.S.A.); all quotations from the Qur'an are from the translation by N. J. Dawood (New York: Penguin, 1999); and all quotations from the church fathers are taken from *The Early Church Fathers* on CD-ROM (Salem, Oregon: Harmony Media, 2000).

To send correspondence to the author of this book, mail a first-class letter to the author c/o Inner Traditions • Bear & Company, One Park Street, Rochester, VT 05767, and we will forward the communication.

Dedicated to the memory of
Dr. Hugh J. Schonfield
(1901–1988)
scholar, humanitarian,
and Nazarene prophet

CONTENTS

FOREWORD

On the face of it, the thesis of Reverend Jeffrey Bütz's new book might strike one as far-fetched if not downright absurd, namely that the "true teachings" of Jesus were passed in some underground fashion, down through the ages, and ended up shaping the vision of the Founding Fathers as they forged the principles and ideals of the United States of America. Over the past decade the bookstores have been full of new titles claiming to reveal at last some lost, forgotten, suppressed, hidden, "underground" stream of Christianity, with connections to various esoteric traditions within Western history. The titles speak for themselves: *Holy Blood, Holy Grail, The Da Vinci Code, The Hiram Key, The Templar Revelation.* Few of these works have received the attention, much less the academic endorsement, of mainstream historians, and probably for good reason. They are often long on speculation and short on hard evidence. It would be a mistake for readers to classify Bütz's latest work in this genre. In contrast, it is a serious work, in touch with mainstream scholarship, and characterized by full references to original source materials.

Admittedly the trail Bütz follows, from Jesus to Jefferson, is a faint one, with many dead ends, twists, and turns. After all, groups such as the Ebionites, the *Desposyni,* the Elkesaites, and the Cathars are hardly household names. Bütz's imaginative but careful consideration of evidence pays off and results in a fascinating thesis that informs the very roots of our American culture.

My first contact with the scholarly work of Rev. Jeffrey J. Bütz was through his earlier book, *The Brother of Jesus and the Lost Teachings of Christianity* (2005). I had devoted much of my academic career to research on the little-known history and influence of James—the little-known and mostly forgotten brother of Jesus—and the movement that scholars call "Jewish Christianity." I found Bütz's work to be a thoroughly reliable but altogether accessible treatment for the general public of this vital but neglected area of study. Bütz has the rare gift of presenting the complex findings of historians and scholars in a clear and engaging way, while at the same time exploring his own insights and evaluations of the evidence in ways I have found consistently stimulating and enlightening. In *The Secret Legacy of Jesus,* Bütz has honed these skills to a fine point.

The book is divided into three parts. Parts 1 and 2, making up about two-thirds of the whole, deals with the roots and history of Jewish Christianity. The term refers to those original Jewish followers of Jesus, led by James the brother of Jesus, who continued in their Jewish beliefs and practices, rejected Paul and the Nicaean Church, and according to most scholars continued into the late fourth century, particularly in areas east of Palestine. These followers of Jesus valued the royal "bloodline" of the Jesus family, whether that of Jesus himself, if he was married with children, or that of his brothers and immediate family. Indeed, Bütz argues that these successors of Jesus and his brother James can properly be viewed as a type of "Caliphate," in many ways similar to the Shiite branch of Islam. Bütz further argues that these "Nazarenes" set up a provisional government with their own Sanhedrin led by James as high priest, and the Twelve apostles as a kind of inner ruling cabinet. Bütz further locates the operations of this sectarian "government" on the southwest hill called Mt. Zion where both Armenian and Catholic traditions place the "throne" of James, the "Upper Room," and the house of Mary and the Jesus family.

By far the majority of scholars who have dealt with this branch of Jewish Christianity have tended to trail things off in the late fourth century where most of our records seem to terminate. Bütz takes things much farther, and herein lies the special value and contribution of his work. Not only does he pick up on the "Ebionite" trail through an obscure sect of southern Mesopotamia known to us as the Elkesaites, but in part 3 of his treatment he convincingly traces the key characteristics of this original Jewish Christian perspective into early Islam as well. Although the chapter on Islam is somewhat of an excursus, Bütz returns to his more linear story line as he moves from the Elkesaites through the Cathars, and thus to the Templars and earliest roots of Freemasonry. It is in these last one hundred pages of his book that Bütz truly offers the reader, and in my estimation, the academic world as well, the skeletal framework of a wholly new perspective on the ideas that were most influential upon our Founding Fathers. Here I have in mind specifically the ways in which they imagined America as a sort of New Jerusalem/Promised Land. Other historians have touched on this sort of biblically based idealism, but I think Bütz might be the first to suggest there is an actual current or stream of influence running back into antiquity. I for one find it rather convincing. The history of ideas always remains a tenuous enterprise with no definable *terminia post/ad quem*, but as Jonathan Z. Smith, the most eminent history of religions scholar used to put things—even an exaggeration in the direction of the truth is progress. I believe that Reverend Bütz has provided us with new perspectives waiting to be tested with subsequent review and consideration. I for one am grateful to him for the opportunity to consider this innovative approach to understanding the roots of our American founding and its ideals.

JAMES D. TABOR

James D. Tabor is chair of the Department of Religious Studies at the University of North Carolina at Charlotte, where he has taught since 1989. He is the author of numerous scholarly articles and four books: *Things Unutterable, A Noble Death, Why Waco? Cults and the Battle for Religious Freedom in America* (with Eugene Gallagher), and the international bestseller *The Jesus Dynasty: A New Historical Investigation of Jesus, His Royal Family, and the Birth of Christianity.*

Tabor has combined his work on ancient texts with field work in archaeology at a number of sites in Israel and Jordan, including Qumran, Wadi el-Yabis, Masada, Sepphoris, and the "Suba" cave, west of Jerusalem. He is codirector of the Mt. Zion Archaeological Expedition and also serves as main editor of the Original Bible Project, an ongoing effort to produce a new translation of the Bible. He is presently working on a new book on the apostle Paul due out in early 2010.

ACKNOWLEDGMENTS

I first wish to acknowledge the research and original insights of all the scholars I quote in this book. It is they who have done the difficult "meat and potatoes" work, which I have been blessed to be able to popularize for the general public and help expose to the light of day. As in my first book, *The Brother of Jesus and the Lost Teachings of Christianity* (2005), I consider myself not so much an original researcher as a popularizer, who has been given the privilege of synthesizing the detailed research and findings of world-class scholars and forming it into a bigger philosophical picture.

I wish to dedicate this book to the memory of Dr. Hugh J. Schonfield (1901–1988), a true Jewish prophet, sadly maligned by conservative Christians, who foresaw so much of what has now become widely accepted in the third quest for the historical Jesus. Dr. Schonfield may have been the first to fully understand the Jewish nature of Jesus and his mission, and certainly he was the first to understand the vital role of Jesus's family in his ministry. Nominated for the Nobel Peace Prize for his services toward international humanity, Dr. Schonfield was a true Nazarene who embodied in his life's work Jesus's great high priestly prayer that "they may all be one" (Luke 17:21).

I owe a huge debt of thanks to Dr. James D. Tabor for his enthusiastic support of my work almost from the moment my first book was published, and for his willingness to take time from an incredibly busy schedule to grace this new book with his foreword. When his groundbreaking book, *The Jesus Dynasty* (2006), appeared a year after mine, we were both amazed at how, working totally independently of each other (not knowing of each other's work at all), we had arrived at astoundingly similar conclusions.

I wish to thank Dr. Shimon Gibson and his associates on the Mt. Zion Archaeological Expedition, Rafi Lewis and Mareike Grosser, for teaching me field archaeology in what has to be the most exciting place in the world to dig. While in Jerusalem, I was blessed to receive the help of the Rev. Fr. Pakrad Berjekian, director of the real estate department of the Armenian Patriarchate, who made it possible for me to go on a V.I.P. tour of the Cathedral of St. James with Archbishop Nourhan Manougian, Canon Sacrist, who graciously allowed me to take photographs, which have never before been published.

I owe a big debt of gratitude to Keith Akers, author of *The Lost Religion of Jesus,* for graciously sharing with me his yet unpublished manuscript on the Ebionites. Keith's highly detailed work and fresh insights greatly enhanced my chapter on Ebionite theology. A big thank-you as well to Brian Fegely, a Freemason and truly top-notch amateur historian, who confirmed my suspicions about a link between the Ebionites and Freemasonry, and who shared some astounding insights into Masonic ritual through the seemingly unlikely lens of Jesus's brother, James. (Now get your own theories out there in book form, Brian!)

There are a number of fellow authors I need to thank for their inspiration and support: Dr. James Gardner (for his unceasing questioning of sacred cows), Dr. Bob Hieronimus (for a fantastic radio interview), and Kathleen McGowan and Margaret Starbird (for much-needed theological renewal). I also must thank two of my students at Penn State University: Charles Kuttruff (for his years of wisdom and providing me with insights on the Christianity of the Founding Fathers), and Kimberly Luckey for her astute proofreading of my manuscript (and corrections to bad Latin and misunderstandings of Catholicism!).

I sincerely thank everyone I have worked with at Inner Traditions International, who make publishing a book feel like you are working with family and friends: Ehud Sperling, Jon Graham, Rob Meadows, Patricia Rydle, Cynthia Fowles, Bill Pfau, and especially my editors, Jeanie Levitan, Mindy Branstetter, and Abigail Lewis, and art director Peri Swan for making both of my books look so great!

Finally, on a personal note I wish to thank all of my parishioners at Grace Lutheran Church in Nazareth, Pennsylvania, for their unfailing Christian love and support, and my many pastoral colleagues in the Northeastern Pennsylvania Synod of the Evangelical Lutheran Church in America for their open-minded support of my work. Most especially, I could not do what I do without the love and support of my sisters Joan and Edy (especially for their public relations work!), and my long-suffering, patient wife and soulmate, Kathy, and the two amazing children she helped me bring into the world—Rachel and David. And, of course, thanksgiving *ad majorem Dei gloriam* to Messiah Jesus and his forgotten brothers.

INTRODUCTION
The Quest for the Grail

Thanks mainly to Dan Brown and his record-breaking bestseller, *The Da Vinci Code,* and the accompanying movie directed by Ron Howard, there is presently an incredible amount of interest in all things related to what has been called for centuries the "Quest for the Holy Grail." The roots of this current fascination with the Holy Grail can be traced back to a 1982 nonfiction bestseller—*Holy Blood, Holy Grail*—which is the real source of all the current mania. The historical roots of the idea of a quest for a Holy Grail go back to the end of the twelfth century and a cycle of hugely popular tales of the time, written by the medieval author Chrétien de Troyes, concerning the legendary Knights of the Round Table and their quest for the cup used by Jesus and his apostles at the Last Supper. It is said that Joseph of Arimathea caught the blood of Jesus in this cup as he hung on the cross.

Thanks to both *Holy Blood, Holy Grail* and *The Da Vinci Code,* the Grail has come to be widely understood in a different sense—as a symbol or metaphor for the sacred marriage of Jesus and Mary Magdalene, and more specifically, for the bloodline they produced. A veritable theological movement, and even a seminal new sect of Christianity, has arisen around this controversial and highly disputed belief, spearheaded by scholarly works such as Margaret Starbird's *The Woman with the Alabaster Jar,* as well as the fictional bestseller *The Expected One,* by Kathleen McGowan. These books, along with a host of others, have clearly tapped into the collective subconscious yearnings of a huge number of people who are spiritually starving in today's secular, post-Christian world. The great father of psychoanalysis, Carl Jung, would see this current fascination with the Grail as a classic example of an enduring archetype; in this case, a symbol of suppressed religious knowledge that moves people and history at a subconscious level. If Jung were alive today he undoubtedly would be extremely interested in it all.

The main attracting force of this archetype would seem to be the conspiracy theory that lies at its center: the belief that an underground stream of heretical theological knowledge has clandestinely existed beneath the mainstream of Christianity for the past two thousand years, despite the best efforts of the Christian Church to eradicate it. This is obviously—simply based on the huge number of books sold—a very powerful idea, and a whole new category of literature, sometimes called "alternative Christianity," has arisen around it.[1] The purported heretical knowledge that has been the source of this widespread appeal is the belief that a royal Davidic bloodline issuing from Jesus and Mary Magdalene gave rise to the "holy blood" of some of Europe's most ancient and powerful dynasties. The story goes that this knowledge has been protected for two millennia by a clandestine cabal composed of some of history's brightest and most enigmatic luminaries, including Isaac Newton, Robert Fludd, Victor Hugo, and, of course, Leonardo Da Vinci, who is supposed to have hidden clues within his most famous artwork. This is heady stuff, and it is no wonder so many have become fascinated by it, whether in a literal, allegorical, or fictional sense.

Within the following pages we shall take a serious look at a theory that presently lies on the outer fringes of mainstream academia, with multiple facets that have been researched by such "alternative historians" as Michael Baigent, Richard Leigh, and Henry Lincoln, authors of *Holy Blood, Holy Grail* (1982); Robert Knight and Christopher Lomas, authors of *The Hiram Key* (1996); and Lynn Picknett and Clive Prince, authors of *The Templar Revelation* (1997). These works, more than any others, represent the early seedbed in which the ideas expressed by Dan Brown in *The Da Vinci Code* germinated. Ever since the release of *The Da Vinci Code* in 2003, what was once a cottage industry has turned into a mega-industry, and sales of both fiction and nonfiction books on topics ranging from Gnosticism to the Knights Templar to Freemasonry have gone through the roof. The astonishingly high level of interest in books on these and other highly esoteric topics by the average person on the street is sociologically quite remarkable. There is obviously great spiritual appeal in the idea of a hidden lineage of Jesus.

While conspiracy theories are scoffed at by most scholars, we shall see within these pages that there are indeed things that can be kept quiet and preserved for centuries by patient and determined people protecting highly treasured beliefs. The thesis of this book is that an underground stream of alternative Christian belief representing the true teachings of Jesus as preserved by the descendants of his family has, in fact, existed clandestinely beneath the mainstream of Christianity for the past two thousand years. This "underground stream" has gone by various names throughout the ages; its adherents have been called by names such as Nazarenes, Ebionites, and Elkesaites, but perhaps the most useful umbrella term that captures this underground stream in all of its many changing facets is "Jewish Christianity." While this is a somewhat loaded term and not without inherent problems (including, as we shall see, the danger of a latent anti-Semitism, or subtle Christian "supersessionism"),* it remains the most apt and useful description for those earliest followers of Jesus of Nazareth and their descendants, who never relinquished their Jewish beliefs and practices. They resolutely resisted falling in with the emerging Roman Catholic Church, and considered its beliefs and practices to be heretical distortions of Jesus's original teachings.

The book you are about to read is a history of Jewish Christianity

---

*While a number of scholars have recently begun raising objections to the use of the term "Jewish Christianity" and suggesting new terms such as "Christian Judaism," this has led to a lot of unnecessary confusion. I agree with F. Stanley Jones that the long-accepted Jewish Christianity remains the most useful term. An excellent discussion of the problems associated with the use of the term Jewish Christianity can be found in a new collection of papers on the subject, *Jewish Christianity Reconsidered*.[2]

from its beginnings in first-century Galilee up to the modern day. While most Christian scholars have considered Jewish Christianity to be a heresy, thankfully that understanding has been rapidly changing in the past few decades; and while most scholars have supposed that Jewish Christian sects such as the Ebionites and Elkesaites died out by the fifth or sixth centuries, I will present evidence to the contrary. We will come to see that the Jewish Christians were not heretics, but rather the torchbearers of original orthodoxy; their beliefs never died out, but continued to exert an often remarkable influence on the rise of other religious groups and movements throughout history, such as the religion of Islam, the Cathar "heretics" of medieval France, the Knights Templar, and modern Freemasonry.

These are obviously radical claims to make, and as the late astronomer Carl Sagan once rightly said in regard to the search for extraterrestrial life, "Extraordinary claims require extraordinary evidence." The presentation of the extraordinary evidence for these extraordinary claims will be found in the pages that follow. Because such a thesis will require impeccable research and documentation, the evidence presented herein will come almost exclusively from mainstream historians and theologians, both ancient and modern; the research of current popular writers and researchers outside the mainstream of academia (some of which is, in fact, quite valuable) has for the most part been intentionally set aside. We shall see, however, that many of the theories of the so-called alternative historians who have written about descendants of Jesus and Mary Magdalene are not all that far off the mark, although they have largely mistaken the clandestine existence of Jewish Christian thought and practice for a secret cabal of Jesus's physical descendants. If, as conspiracy theorists claim, there are actually any hidden documents buried beneath Rosslyn Chapel in Scotland or Father Sauniere's Magdalen Tower in France (something the Dead Sea Scrolls scholar Robert Eisenman takes quite seriously), they are likely Jewish Christian scriptures rather than family genealogies.

While the premise of this book may at first seem perhaps ludicrous, there is a wealth of reliable scholarly evidence presented within these pages to support it. And as history has shown time and time again, the presiding paradigm of scholarly consensus has been repeatedly overturned when what was once considered heresy becomes the new orthodoxy overnight. Five hundred years ago, the prevailing orthodoxy of an Earth-centered solar system was replaced by the "heresy" of a Sun-centered solar system; and in just the last century the entire solar system has been displaced to a remote fringe of one ordinary galaxy among trillions of other galaxies. Moving in the other direction, within the last century the prevailing paradigm of a world composed of physical building blocks called "atoms" has been replaced by the new paradigm of quantum physics, in which everything we thought was solid and physical has turned out to be composed of subatomic particles, which are not solid at all but pure energy, and which defy every known law of Newtonian physics. Quantum physicists today speak about a world composed of "strings" of pure energy vibrating in eleven dimensions and generating not one universe, but a "multiverse" of parallel universes. The presiding scientific paradigm now accepted by the world's leading physicists and philosophers would have been considered science fiction only fifty years ago.

If history teaches us nothing else, it clearly teaches that the orthodox view will be repeatedly replaced by what was once the heretical view, and that we should come to expect the unexpected. In the realm of religion, two thousand years ago the "heresy" of Christianity overturned the long-established pagan religions of antiquity and went on to completely reshape western civilization and the lives of half of the world's current population. But a little recognized fact of the Christian revolution is that, in the process of politically conquering the Roman world, Christianity in many ways betrayed its Judaic origins, as well as many of the core teachings of its thoroughly Jewish founder. What was originally the orthodox mainstream of Christianity, comprised of a messianic Jewish community centered on the teachings and leadership of Jesus's immediate family, was, within three hundred years, cast off by the Roman Catholic Church it spawned. Those who continued to hold to Christianity's original Jewish tenets were forced underground, and what was once the mainstream became an underground stream. But, as we shall see, a tiny and seemingly insignificant underground stream, unseen and unnoticed from the surface, can sometimes carry more pure water than a far larger stream that has become stagnant and polluted and is in dire need of an infusion of fresh, pure water.

PART ONE

The Roots of
Jewish Christianity

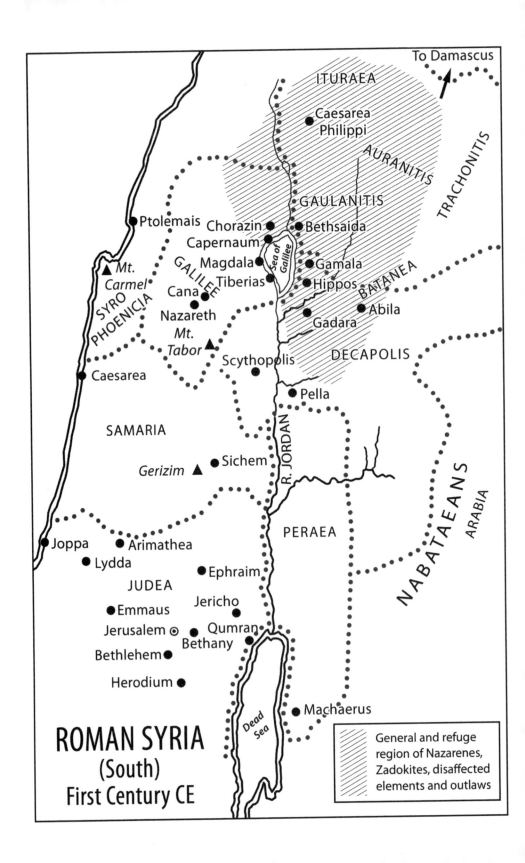

To Damascus

ITURAEA

Caesarea
Philippi

AURANITIS

TRACHONITIS

GAULANITIS

Ptolemais

Chorazin • Bethsaida

Capernaum

Magdala • Gamala

GALILEE

Sea of Galilee

Tiberias • Hippos

Mt. Carmel

SYRO PHOENICIA

Cana

BATANEA

Nazareth

Abila

Mt. Tabor

Gadara

Scythopolis

DECAPOLIS

Caesarea

Pella

SAMARIA

R. JORDAN

Gerizim ▲ Sichem

NABATAEANS

ARABIA

PERAEA

Joppa

Arimathea

Lydda

Ephraim

JUDEA

Jericho

Emmaus

Jerusalem ◉ Qumran

Bethany

Bethlehem

Herodium

Dead Sea

Machaerus

ROMAN SYRIA
(South)
First Century CE

General and refuge region of Nazarenes, Zadokites, disaffected elements and outlaws

JERUSALEM IN JESUS'S TIME

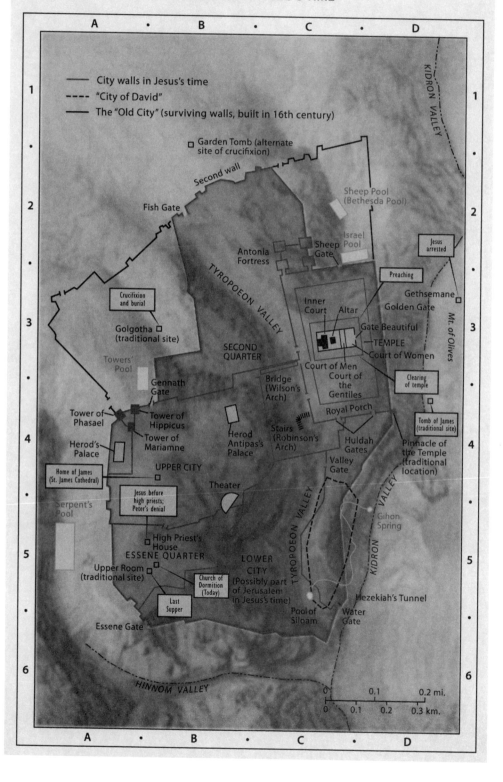

- ——— City walls in Jesus's time
- – – – "City of David"
- ——— The "Old City" (surviving walls, built in 16th century)

KIDRON VALLEY

Garden Tomb (alternate site of crucifixion)

Second wall

Sheep Pool (Bethesda Pool)

Fish Gate

Israel Pool

Antonia Fortress

Sheep Gate

Jesus arrested

Preaching

Gethsemane

Golden Gate

Inner Court

Altar

Gate Beautiful

TEMPLE

Mt. of Olives

TYROPOEON VALLEY

Crucifixion and burial

Golgotha (traditional site)

SECOND QUARTER

Court of Women

Court of Men

Court of the Gentiles

Clearing of temple

Towers' Pool

Gennath Gate

Bridge (Wilson's Arch)

Royal Porch

Tomb of James (traditional site)

Tower of Phasael

Tower of Hippicus

Herod Antipas's Palace

Stairs (Robinson's Arch)

Huldah Gates

Pinnacle of the Temple (traditional location)

Tower of Mariamne

Herod's Palace

Valley Gate

Home of James (St. James Cathedral)

UPPER CITY

Theater

Jesus before high priests; Peter's denial

TYROPOEON VALLEY

KIDRON VALLEY

Serpent's Pool

Gihon Spring

High Priest's House

ESSENE QUARTER

LOWER CITY (Possibly part of Jerusalem in Jesus's time)

Upper Room (traditional site)

Church of Dormition (Today)

Last Supper

Hezekiah's Tunnel

Essene Gate

Pool of Siloam

Water Gate

HINNOM VALLEY

0   0.1   0.2 mi.

0   0.1   0.2   0.3 km.

1

AN UNHERALDED FAMILY
The Bloodline of Jesus

So God created humankind in his image, in the image of
God he created them; male and female he created them.
God blessed them and God said to them, "Be fruitful and
multiply, and fill the earth . . ."

GENESIS 1:27–28

Have you not read that the one who made them at the
beginning "made them male and female," and said, "For
this reason a man shall leave his father and mother and
be joined to his wife, and the two shall become one flesh?"

JESUS (MATTHEW 19:4–5)

Was Jesus married? The intriguing idea of a married Jesus has struck a
harmonious and resonating chord in the souls of many who would otherwise have little interest in theology or the Bible, but who have read *The
Da Vinci Code* in rapt awe at the sheer power of such an idea. But what are
the facts? Simply this: While there is no incontrovertible proof that Jesus
was married, there are enough tantalizing hints in the New Testament
and in early historical writings to say that the idea is highly plausible.

There are, in fact, many groups of people throughout history who have held strongly to this belief, some of whom we shall examine within these pages. And for a rapidly growing number of people, belief in a married Jesus has led to a sacred Grail quest to uncover the hidden and suppressed evidence of what is commonly called the "sacred marriage" or the "divine union" in literature on the subject.[1]

I wish to state up front that I have no personal theological objection to the idea of a married Jesus. Like a growing number of theologians and clergy, I find the idea of a married Jesus highly compelling for theological reasons. A married Jesus would certainly be a more human Jesus, and one of the theological rationales behind the central Christian dogma of the Incarnation is the idea that God became incarnate in Jesus Christ in order to participate fully in the human condition, including suffering and even death.* Indeed, to not fall in love, to not marry and rear children, to not experience sexual fulfillment would be to miss out on some of the key components of being human. If one is to take the idea of the incarnation of God seriously, it would seemingly have to include these core components of humanity. The only possible theological objection that could be raised *against* Jesus being married is the antiquated notion that sex is somehow inherently sinful, as the medieval church taught, based on a tragically mistaken interpretation of the story of the fall of Adam and Eve. While this was a widespread belief at one time—and thanks mainly to the church father, Jerome, gave rise to the requirement of priestly celibacy in the Roman Catholic Church—there is no reputable modern theologian of any ecclesiastical persuasion who holds to this outmoded idea. In fact, in the creation story in Genesis 1, sexual reproduction is blessed, and even commanded, by God.

While it would therefore seem almost theologically necessary for God to experience the intimacy of romantic love and sexual procreation in order to fully experience being human (if we are to take seriously the idea of the Incarnation in all its fullness), historically speaking, the hypothesis

---

*This is fully explicated in *The Crucified God,* the magnum opus of the contemporary German theologian, Jürgen Moltmann.

of a married Jesus is still that—a tantalizing hypothesis. While it is not my purpose in this book to examine evidence for the marital status of Jesus, it *is* my purpose to show that there is indisputable evidence in the New Testament, as well as in the writings of the church fathers and early ecclesiastical historians, that *Jesus's brothers were married,* and this indeed has implications for the marital status of Jesus. We have, for example, the firsthand testimony of St. Paul:

> This is my defense to those who would examine me. Do we not have the right to our food and drink? Do we not have the right to be *accompanied by a wife,* as the other apostles *and the brothers of the Lord* and Cephas? (1 Corinthians 9:3–5, RSV)

Here, Paul is defending himself against critics who are taking him to task for living off the charity of the early Christian communities while engaging in his missionary work. Paul justifies his practice by pointing out that this was the right of the apostles, as well as Jesus's brothers. But what is especially significant to our purposes here is Paul's clear and unequivocal statement that *Jesus's brothers were married,* as was the apostle Peter (Cephas, the name Paul uses, was Peter's name in Aramaic, the Hebrew dialect spoken by Jesus).

This, of course, flies in the face of two key teachings of the Roman Catholic Church: the dogma of the perpetual virginity of Mary, and the requirement of priestly celibacy. These are both the result of the huge influence on Catholic thinking of the church father, Jerome (ca. 342–420). A strict ascetic, Jerome was obsessed with the need for celibacy among Christians, particularly priests. Jerome was the first to formally propose that Jesus's mother remained a lifelong virgin (a doctrine known as the "perpetual virginity" of Mary). The Catholic belief that the brothers and sisters of Jesus mentioned in the New Testament were actually Jesus's *cousins* is called the "Hieronymian Theory," after Jerome (whose original Latin name was Eusebius Hieronymus; a variant of his surname was Hierome, which, in English, is Jerome). Jerome even opposed the idea put forth by the church father Epiphanius (ca. 315–403) that

Jesus's brothers were actually his *step*brothers,* children of Joseph from a prior marriage (an alternate way of upholding Mary's perpetual virginity), because Jerome believed that Joseph also remained a lifelong virgin. The so-called Epiphanian theory, named for Epiphanius, would become the official explanation of the Eastern Orthodox Church as to the identity of those figures the New Testament refers to as "brothers" and "sisters" of Jesus.

In this book we will follow the third main theory on the identity of Jesus's siblings—the Helvidian Theory, named after the fourth-century Roman theologian Helvidius, who strongly opposed Jerome and the growing exaltation of virginity in the church. Helvidius believed that the brothers and sisters of Jesus mentioned in the New Testament were full-blood siblings of Jesus, born to Joseph and Mary following the virgin birth of Jesus. The Helvidian understanding has become the position of almost all Protestant churches.

The main evidence in support of the Helvidian theory is simply a plain reading of the New Testament, as well as taking at face value the writings of many of the church fathers. It cannot be emphasized enough that *whenever siblings of Jesus are mentioned in the New Testament, nowhere does it ever imply that they are anything other than full-blood siblings of Jesus.* The following are some of the main references to Jesus's brothers and sisters found in the New Testament:

Then his mother *and his brothers came;* and standing outside, they sent to him and called him. A crowd was sitting about him; and they said to him, *"Your mother and your brothers and sisters are outside,* asking for you." (Mark 3:31–35, see also the parallel passages in Matt. 12:46–50 and Luke 8:19–21)

Jesus . . . came to his hometown . . . On the Sabbath he began to teach in the synagogue, and many who heard him were astounded.

---

*Whether one considers them stepbrothers or half brothers of Jesus depends on whether one believes that Jesus was literally the Son of God, without human father.

They said, "Where did this man get all this? What is this wisdom that has been given to him? What deeds of power are being done by his hands! Is not this the carpenter, the son of Mary *and the brother of James and Joses and Judas and Simon, and are not his sisters here with us?*" (Mark 6:1–3, see also Matt. 13:54–58)

Now the Jewish festival of booths was near. *So his brothers said to him,* "Leave here and go to Judea so that your disciples also may see the works you are doing; for no one who wants to be widely known acts in secret. If you do these things show yourself to the world." (For not even *his brothers* believed in him.) (John 7:2–5)

[Following the wedding at Cana] After this he went down to Capernaum with his mother, *his brothers,* and his disciples; and they remained there a few days. (John 2:12, note that this passage belies the argument that the brothers are actually Jesus's *disciples* [that is, his "spiritual brothers"], as they are mentioned alongside the disciples here.)

[Following the Ascension] Then they returned to Jerusalem from the mount called Olivet . . . When they had entered the city, they went to the room upstairs where they were staying, Peter, and John, and James, and Andrew, Philip and Thomas, Bartholomew and Matthew, James son of Alphaeus, and Simon the Zealot, and Judas son of James. All these were constantly devoting themselves to prayer, together with certain women, including Mary the mother of Jesus, *as well as his brothers.* (Acts 1:12–14, note that here, too, Jesus's brothers are clearly distinguished from the apostles and they are again, as in the previous passage, *associated with Mary.*)

Then after three years I went up to Jerusalem to visit Peter, and remained with him fifteen days. But I saw none of the other apostles *except James the Lord's brother.* (St. Paul, Galatians 1:18–19)

In addition to these references, there are many other specific references to Jesus's oldest brother, James, who played a huge role in the leadership of the disciples following Jesus's crucifixion.* And, in addition to the New Testament material, there are even more references to Jesus's siblings to be found in the writings of the church fathers and early ecclesiastical historians. Here are just a few of the more representative citations regarding James:

Josephus (first-century Jewish historian)—"The Sanhedrin of judges . . . brought before them *the brother of Jesus,* who was called Christ, whose name was James . . ." (*Antiquities of the Jews* 20.9.1)

Eusebius (Bishop of Caesarea, ca. 265–339)—"*Then there was James, who was called the Lord's brother; for he, too, was named Joseph's son* . . . This James, whom the people of old called 'the Just' because of his outstanding virtue, was the first, as the records tell us, to be elected to the Episcopal throne of the Jerusalem Church." (*The History of the Church* 2.1.2)

Clement of Alexandria (Christian philosopher, ca. 150–215)—"Control of the Church passed together with the apostles, *to the brother of the Lord, James,* whom everyone from the Lord's time till our own has named 'the Just' . . ." (*Hypostases* ["Outlines"], cited in Eusebius, *The History of the Church* 2.23.3]

Once again, in *none* of these citations is it ever implied that James was anything other than a full-blood brother of Jesus.

The Greek word that gets translated as "brother" in the early Christian writings is *adelphos* (which can be seen in the name of the city of Philadelphia, the "city of brotherly love"—*philo-adelphia*). Jerome put forth the argument that adelphos can mean "spiritual brother" or "fellow

---

*Thoroughly explored in my previous book, *The Brother of Jesus and the Lost Teachings of Christianity.*

countryman," which is true, but the term normally means a blood brother unless the context clearly indicates otherwise. But nowhere in *any* of the references to Jesus's brothers and sisters in the New Testament is anything other than a full-blood relationship ever implied. And, in fact, there are also several passages in which the gospel writers clearly indicate that Joseph and Mary had normal conjugal relations following the birth of Jesus:

> And she gave birth to her *firstborn* son and wrapped him in bands of cloth and laid him in a manger, because there was no place for them in the inn. (Luke 2:7)

If Jesus was the *only* son, why does Luke say "firstborn"?

> This is how the birth of Jesus Christ came about: His mother, Mary, was pledged to be married to Joseph, *but before they came together* she was found to be with child through the Holy Spirit. (Matthew 1:18, NIV, "Before they came together" is a classic biblical euphemism along the lines of "Adam *knew* Eve.")

> When Joseph awoke from sleep, he did as the angel of the Lord commanded him; he took her as his wife, *but had no marital relations with her until she had borne a son.* (Matthew 1:24–25; enough said!)

The idea of the perpetual virginity of Mary first arose in the mid-second century due to an apocryphal writing called *The Protevangelium of James*. The Protevangelium (Proto-gospel) portrays Joseph as a widower with children from his previous marriage when he marries the much younger Mary. This apocryphal text is the basis for Bishop Epiphanius's idea that Jesus's brothers and sisters were actually *step*-siblings of Jesus. But in Jerome's eyes, Epiphanius did not go far enough in separating Jesus from his siblings, or in separating Mary and Joseph from the taint of sexual sin. So Jerome deemed these problematic siblings to be *cousins* of Jesus.

Unfortunately for historical truth, it is thanks to Jerome's pushing of the idea of Mary's perpetual virginity that the knowledge of Jesus's siblings became widely lost. When Catholicism became the dominant form of Christianity in the early fourth century, and the perpetual virginity began to be accepted by almost all Christians as dogma, Jesus ipso facto did not have siblings, and any lingering interest in Jesus's brothers and their important role in the leadership of the early church quickly waned. Fortunately, we can still catch a glimpse of James's huge leadership role in the book of Acts* and in Paul's letter to the Galatians. James's role as the successor to Jesus and first bishop of the Church will be discussed in chapter 4.

MARRIED WITH CHILDREN

In 1 Corinthians 9:4–6, where Paul defends himself by referring to "the brothers of the Lord" as examples of outstanding missionaries, he is referring to the three other brothers of Jesus who get far less acclaim than the better-known James. Fortunately, we know their names—Judas (Jude), Symeon (Simon), and Joses (Joseph)—from Mark 6:3 cited above. Paul is most likely not including James in this citation because James was not a traveling missionary but the settled leader of the Christian community based in Jerusalem; however, at a minimum, based on Paul's use of the plural in reference to Jesus's brothers, we can firmly conclude that at least two of Jesus's brothers were married. And beyond any shadow of a doubt they would have had many children, since Jews accepted God's command in Genesis to "be fruitful and multiply" as a binding law. That Jesus had many nephews and nieces has significant implications that will reverberate throughout the rest of this book.

In using this example of Jesus's brothers taking their wives with them

---

*The book of Acts, the full title of which is the Acts of the Apostles, was written by the same author as the Gospel of Luke. It tells how the apostles, primarily Peter and Paul, took the gospel message to the Gentiles and established the Christian Church after Jesus's ascension.

on their missionary journeys, Paul also gives us the invaluable piece of information that Jesus's brothers (as well as their wives) were part of the earliest group of traveling missionaries, and Paul holds them in the same light as Peter and the other apostles. By using Jesus's brothers as an example in a letter written to distant Corinth (near Athens in Greece), Paul gives us solid evidence that it was well known in Christian communities throughout the empire that Jesus's brothers were among the most important and influential leaders in the early church.

While James is mentioned in a number of places in the New Testament, and it is clear that he played a huge role in the leadership of the early church, the other brothers of Jesus are cited in only a handful of verses. They were important enough, though, that in those precious few verses their names have been preserved for posterity. Both Mark and Matthew record the famous story where Jesus returns to preach in the synagogue in his hometown of Nazareth for the first time since beginning his ministry and achieving fame throughout Galilee. The townspeople are rather skeptical of the "homeboy" made good: "Where did this man get all this? What is this wisdom that has been given to him? . . . Is not this the carpenter, the son of Mary and brother of James and Joses and Judas and Simon, and are not his sisters here with us?" (Mark 6:2–3). These pointed questions are from Jesus's former neighbors and friends, people who knew Jesus since he wore "swaddling clothes," and we can almost read their thoughts: "Why, we know his mother, his late father, and all his brothers and sisters quite well. Just who does he think he is? Seems like little Jesus from down the road is getting a bit big for his britches!"

Most scholars understand the names of the brothers in Mark 6:3 to be listed in chronological order, eldest first, since this was standard methodology in writings of the ancient world (and is why scholars have always assumed James to be the eldest). The parallel passage in Matthew 13:55 makes two minor alterations to the list, giving the names as: James, Joseph, Simon, and Judas. Going on the universally accepted theory of "Markan priority" (that Mark's gospel was written first and was used as a blueprint by the authors of Matthew and Luke), Matthew has made two changes to the list in Mark: He has changed the name of the second oldest brother from Joses to Joseph, and he has reversed the order of the two youngest brothers. The first change is understandable, as Matthew's gospel was written for a Jewish Christian community and Mark's for a Gentile Christian community. Writing for Gentiles, Mark uses Joses, which is the Greek form of the Hebrew, Joseph. Writing for a Jewish audience, Matthew changes Joses back to its original Hebrew form.

The second change—the reversing of the latter two names—is less easy to understand. It is likely intentional and not accidental. The most reasonable possibility is that Matthew (the Jewish author) had a more reliable list of the names of the brothers, or simply knew from tradition handed down to him that Simon was older than Judas, and so corrected Mark. Since Matthew was a Jewish Christian, it is plausible that he had more accurate information on such technical details than what was available to the Gentile Mark. Simon is the Greek equivalent of the Hebrew Symeon, which was also Peter's original Hebrew name before Jesus gave him the nickname Petros (Aramaic for "Rock" or "Rocky") following Peter's confession of Jesus as Messiah at Caesarea Philippi,* and this is why Peter is often referred to in the gospels as Simon Peter. Judas is more commonly known in English as Jude, and has traditionally been believed to be the author of the second to last book of the New Testament, the Epistle of Jude.† All four of these names are among the most common Jewish names of the period (as was the name Jesus).

It is interesting to speculate as to why these particular names were chosen by Joseph and Mary for their children. James, which is the English transliteration of Jacob (Hebrew, Ya'akov), was likely named after the

---

*See Matthew 16:16–18. It is interesting that even though Peter's confession at Caesarea Philippi is part of the "triple tradition" (meaning it is in all three of the synoptic gospels), only Matthew tells of Jesus changing Peter's name from Simon to Peter, evidence of the Jewish Christian audience for whom Matthew wrote.

†While the vast majority of scholars today doubt that Jesus's brother was the actual author of this epistle, I accept Richard Bauckham's view that Jude is much earlier than most scholars have thought, and that it is likely written by Jesus's brother. See Bauckham, *2 Peter and Jude,* Word Biblical Commentary #50 (Waco, Texas: Word Books, 1983).

great Hebrew patriarch Jacob, the grandson of Abraham. In light of James's taking over the reins of leadership of the Christian community after Jesus's death, it is interesting that in Hebrew the name Jacob means "he who supplants."* The name Jacob was also perhaps chosen because, according to the genealogy in the first chapter of Matthew, Joseph's father was named Jacob, and James may have been named after his grandfather. The next brother, Joseph, who is obviously named after his father, was also named for another great patriarch, the eleventh and most important son of Jacob, whose famous story takes up the last fourteen chapters of the book of Genesis; this story has become famous in our own day thanks to having been turned into a successful Broadway play, *Joseph and the Amazing Technicolor Dreamcoat*. As for Simon and Judas, these were also the names of patriarchs—the second and fourth sons of Jacob, respectively. A number of scholars have speculated that Simon and Judas may also have been named after two Jewish heroes—the revered freedom fighters of the Hasmonean dynasty, Simon and Judah Maccabeus (The Maccabees).

THE SISTERS OF JESUS

Although sisters are also mentioned in the gospels, the New Testament was very much a product of a patriarchal society, so their names are not given. However, since the plural is used we know that there were at least two sisters. Later tradition assigns a few different names to these sisters, but the two most attested are Mary and Salome. Professor Richard Bauckham, who has done the most in-depth research into Jesus's family of any scholar, believes there is a good probability that the tradition is correct on these two names. Bauckham, who is a conservative scholar both theologically and methodologically, makes an observation about the sisters of Jesus that would be wise to keep in mind as we delve further into the history of the descendants of Jesus's family:

---

*This etymology originally referred to the idea that Jacob supplanted his twin brother Esau, who had been born first and was cheated out of the all-important birthright by Jacob, as told in Genesis 25.

If two sisters of Jesus were remembered by name in at least one branch of early Christian tradition, then the probability is that they played some part in the early Christian movement, though they cannot have been as prominent as those women disciples of Jesus whose names are preserved in the gospel traditions.

By contrast, the preservation of all four names of the brothers of Jesus in Matthew and Mark indicates that all four brothers were well-known figures in the early church.[2]

Bauckham then remarks on his methodology:

I consider it as a good general rule—not without exceptions—that where the early Gospel tradition preserves the names of characters in the Gospel story (other than those of public figures such as Pilate and Caiaphas), these named people were Christians well known in the early church. In circles where they ceased to be known, their names often dropped out of the tradition (for example, the name Bartimaeus, given in Mark 10:46, is dropped in Luke 18:35, doubtless because Luke's readers would not have known the name).[3]

This observation gives us much food for thought, as we tend to think that figures whose names appear only once or twice in the New Testament had little stature or influence; but, as Professor Bauckham points out, the very fact that their names are recorded in the New Testament at all means that these figures must have been of considerable importance in the early Christian community.

OTHER RELATIVES OF JESUS

While the brothers and sisters of Jesus are known at least to the Protestant and Orthodox branches of Christianity, less well known is the existence of reliable information on other relatives of Jesus in the New Testament. We shall not examine here the account of Mary's cousin Elizabeth and her husband Zechariah, the parents of John the Baptist, who, according to the infancy narrative in Luke 1, is Jesus's second cousin. While this account may contain a kernel of historical information, most modern scholars, including some of the best Roman Catholic scholars, discount the infancy narratives as being largely legendary in nature,[4] so any familial relationship between Jesus and Elizabeth, Zechariah, and John we will consider out of bounds (and, in any event, not strictly necessary for our purposes in this book). It should be noted that one scholar who does take seriously John's familial relationship to Jesus and its important implications for Jesus's ministry is Dr. James Tabor, chair of the religion department at the University of North Carolina at Charlotte, who makes a fascinating and compelling case in his recent bestselling book, *The Jesus Dynasty*.[5]

There are other passages in the gospels, however, that provide vital information on relatives of Jesus that is highly pertinent to our purposes in this book. Especially key to our pursuit of descendants of Jesus's family is the name of Clopas (or Cleopas), a character cryptically referred to in the gospels (Luke 24:18; John 19:25), as well as by the earliest church historian, Hegesippus. Tragically, Hegesippus's history of the Church (*Memoirs,* or *Memoranda,* written in the first half of the second century) has been lost, except for a few precious quotes and citations preserved in Bishop Eusebius's *Ecclesiastical History* (also known as *The History of the Church*), the final edition of which appeared ca. 325.* Fortunately for us, Eusebius quotes a fascinating piece of information from Hegesippus's *Memoirs* when he discusses how the disciples chose a successor to lead the Church after the martyrdom of Jesus's brother James:

> After the martyrdom of James and the capture of Jerusalem which instantly followed, there is a firm tradition that those of the Apostles and disciples of the Lord who were still alive assembled from all parts together with those who, humanly speaking, were

---

*Tantalizingly, *Memoirs* was said to have still been in a few libraries as late as the seventeenth century, and there is always the possibility a copy will turn up one day, as did the recently recovered Gospel of Judas.

kinsmen of the Lord—for most of them *were still living.* Then they all discussed together whom they should choose as a fit person to succeed James, and voted unanimously that Symeon, son of the Clopas mentioned in the gospel narrative, was a fit person to occupy the throne of the Jerusalem see. He was, so it is said, a cousin of the Savior, for Hegesippus tells us that Clopas was Joseph's brother.[6] (Italics mine.)

We shall discuss the intriguing character, Symeon, successor to James and second bishop of the Jerusalem Church, in a later chapter. While Symeon is not mentioned in the New Testament, as Hegesippus notes, his father Clopas is. Many scholars assume this is the same Clopas (or Cleopas) to whom Jesus makes a post-resurrection appearance on the Emmaus Road (Luke 24:13). More pertinently, in John 19:25, there is the famous passage about a group of women watching Jesus's crucifixion: "Meanwhile, standing near the cross of Jesus were his mother, and his mother's sister, Mary the wife of Clopas, and Mary Magdalene." Depending on how one interprets the syntax of this sentence, there could be three or four women listed here. Is "Mary the wife of Clopas" meant to be understood as Jesus's mother's sister (making for three women) or as a separate person (making for four women)? Reams have been written about this particular question and, fortunately, the details need not detain us here. But the fact that this Mary's husband, Clopas, is named at all tells us a lot and enables us to make some important connections. Richard Bauckham asserts:

> Clopas, since he is named, must have been a known figure in the early church. There is therefore little room for doubt that he is the Clopas to whom Hegesippus refers as the brother of Joseph and therefore uncle of Jesus, and the father of Symeon or Simon who succeeded James the Lord's brother in the leadership of the Jerusalem Church.[7]

This kind of evidence which indicates that the leadership of the early church stayed within Jesus's family has led a few scholars, notably Adolf von Harnack and Ethelbert Stauffer, and most recently James Tabor, to postulate that there was a dynastic factor at work here, that the first leaders of the Jerusalem Church formed a kind of Christian caliphate.

THE BLOODLINE

There is, in fact, solid testimony from the church fathers and early ecclesiastical historians that descendants of Jesus's family continued to lead the Church for many decades after his death, the evidence for which we will be examining in detail later in this book. For now, it is just important to begin by noting that there is indeed indisputable evidence of a bloodline descended from Jesus's family, although at least as far as we can presently prove, it comes not from Jesus himself, but from his immediate family—his brothers, sisters, nephews, nieces, and cousins. Jesus's intimate relation with his family, as well as their enormous influence in his ministry and in the continuance of his mission and teaching after his death, has gone astoundingly and regrettably unnoticed by the vast majority of theologians and biblical scholars. In fact, until only very recently almost all scholars worked under the assumption that Jesus was at odds with his family and that they played next to no role in his ministry. Thankfully, in recent years a few prescient investigators, most notably Christian scholars John Painter and Richard Bauckham, along with Jewish scholars such as Robert Eisenman, Hyam Maccoby, and the late Hugh Schonfield, have begun to pull back the curtain to reveal that the prevailing paradigm of the past 2,000 years is false; Jesus's family was, in fact, a vital, indispensable part of his ministry and mission, a development I thoroughly explored in *The Brother of Jesus and the Lost Teachings of Christianity*.[8] Coming right on the heels of my book, James Tabor has issued the first thorough assessment of the role of Jesus's family and their Davidic ancestry in Jesus's ministry in *The Jesus Dynasty,* a long overdue and most welcome addition to our knowledge of the historical Jesus, which has, not surprisingly, been widely denigrated by conservative scholars. It is my personal conviction that maligned scholars such as Schonfield, Maccoby, Eisenman, and Tabor will one day be vindicated as prophets. Sad to say, it is likely not mere happenstance that these scholars, more than any others, have emphasized the thorough Jewishness of Jesus and his family.

The evidence very clearly shows that not only was Jesus's family an integral part of his ministry during his lifetime, but, as we shall see within these pages, they were just as significant and even more vital in the continuance of his teaching and mission subsequent to his death. We can be quite certain that Jesus's nephews and nieces and their descendants held their family relationship to the Messiah dear in their hearts and minds, and the knowledge of their distinguished ancestry would have been cherished, preserved, and passed on from generation to generation. For these were descendants of the Messiah and the family of King David! But there were very real dangers to being a Davidide.* We will be examining historical evidence that shows that the Romans kept a very close eye on anyone of Davidic descent as a potential revolutionary. We will look at the fascinating account of two of Jesus's great-nephews—grandsons of Jesus's brother Jude—being hauled before the Emperor Domitian for interrogation because they were Davidides, and therefore considered potential rebels.

So, while being a descendant of Jesus's family would have been a source of great pride, it was not something that could be shouted from the rooftops. At first this knowledge had to be carefully hidden from the Roman authorities, and by the end of the first century, from the rabbinic Jewish authorities as well, since they had by this time expelled the followers of Jesus from their synagogues. By the beginning of the fourth century this knowledge had to be hidden even from Church authorities, for whom descendants of Jesus's family were seen as a threat to ecclesiastical authority. By the time of Constantine in the early fourth century, the belief in the divinity of Jesus was becoming widespread and would become ineffably stamped as Church dogma at the Council of Nicaea in 325. Once the divinity of Jesus became official Christian doctrine, and especially when the perpetual virginity of Mary became dogma, the evidence for Jesus having brothers and sisters was suppressed, since the idea of Jesus having earthly siblings tended to undermine his full divinity.

---

*Scholars use the term "Davidide" to refer to persons of Davidic descent.

Thus it was that theories such as the Hieronymian and Epiphanian theories developed, to explain away these siblings. Jewish Christian groups such as the Ebionites and Elkesaites, who did not accept the belief in Jesus's divinity, revered James as Jesus's successor, and loudly denigrated Paul, were declared heretics and persecuted by the Catholic Church. It is quite tragic that these Jewish Christians who could trace their ancestry back to the original Jerusalem Church, except for a brief period of a few precious decades following the death of Jesus, never again enjoyed a majority position in the Christian movement.

But despite continuing persecution, it is highly unlikely that the knowledge of one's illustrious ancestry would ever be completely lost. Jews in general, and particularly those of Davidic ancestry, kept meticulous genealogies, and certainly Jesus's family would have done so. Knowledge of one's Davidic heritage and relation to Messiah Jesus, while imperative to keep private, would surely have been treasured and carefully passed down from generation to generation.

THE DESPOSYNI

So, what ever happened to the descendants of Jesus's family? Why are the pages of history so silent about them? This is a fascinating question that has never been asked by the Church and is almost completely ignored by the vast majority of theologians and biblical scholars. It is the prime question we will attempt to answer in this book. We will find that despite the need for strict secrecy, some key information has been handed down to us about the descendants of Jesus's family in the historical records. The early historian Julius Africanus used the Greek term *desposynoi* (in Latin, *desposyni,* those who belong to the Lord) to refer to the descendants of Jesus's family. The word "desposyni" is derived from the Greek word *despotes,* which can mean "lord," "master," or "ship owner" and is the origin of the English word "despot." Africanus tells us that the Desposyni took great pride in their ancestry, and it was they who circulated the genealogy that is now found in the beginning of the Gospel of Matthew. Here is some precious testimony from Africanus, as preserved by Bishop Eusebius in his

History of the Church, which tells how the Desposyni carefully preserved their genealogies:

> [T]he Saviour's human relations, either in an ostentatious spirit or simply to give information, but in either case telling the truth, have handed down this tradition . . .
>
> . . . in the archives were still inscribed the Hebrew families . . . So Herod, who had no drop of Israelitish blood in his veins and was stung by the consciousness of his base origin, burnt the registers of their families, thinking that he would appear nobly born if no one else was able by reference to public documents to trace his line back . . . A few careful people had private records of their own, having either remembered the names or recovered them from copies, and took pride in preserving the memory of their aristocratic origin. These included the people mentioned above, known as Desposyni because of their relationship to the Saviour's family. From the Jewish villages of Nazareth and Cochaba they passed through the rest of the country, expounding the genealogy discussed above, quoting from the book of Chronicles as far as they could trace it.[9]

When one stops to think about it, the genealogies of Jesus's ancestors that appear at the beginning of Matthew and Luke's gospels, tracing Jesus's ancestry back to David, would have had little importance or meaning for Gentile Christians, and would have been of significance only to Jewish Christians. So it is quite unlikely that the gospel writers invented these genealogies out of whole cloth. The preservation of these genealogies and their appearance in the gospels attests to their authenticity and vital importance to the Jewish Christians. Some scholars have noted that the genealogy in Matthew (the only gospel written for a Jewish Christian audience) is mnemonic in form—arranged in three groups of fourteen names to aid in memorization, and "answering to the three letters of the name David (DVD) in Hebrew, the numerical value of which is fourteen."[10] This memorization was fortunate, for, as Africanus tells us, Herod ordered the burning of genealogies to cover up the fact that he was not a full Jew. The burning of genealogies, especially legally registered ones, would make proving one's Davidic ancestry, or one's relationship to Jesus's family, impossible. Despite this lack of official documentation, the descendants of Jesus's family continued to be sought for leadership by the early Jewish Christians into the second century and beyond, plainly attesting to their status. Hegesippus also says of the Desposyni, "Consequently they came and presided over every church, as being . . . members of the Lord's family, and since profound peace came to every church they survived till the reign of Trajan Caesar."[11]

It is quite likely that the line of the Desposyni continued on long after the reign of Trajan (98–117). There is a thoroughly fascinating account of Pope Sylvester I interrogating Desposyni some two hundred years later in 318. This account comes from the controversial Roman Catholic priest, Malachi Martin, in his bestselling book, *The Decline and Fall of the Roman Church*:

> . . . A meeting between Sylvester and the Jewish Christian leaders took place in 318. . . . The vital interview was not, as far as we know, recorded, but the issues were very well known, and it is probable Joses, the oldest of the Christian Jews, spoke on behalf of the Desposyni and the rest.
>
> . . . That most hallowed name, desposyni, had been respected by all believers in the first century and a half of Christian history. . . . Every part of the ancient Jewish Christian Church had always been governed by a desposynos, and each one of them carried one of the names traditional in Jesus's family—Zachary, Joseph, John, James, Joses, Simeon, Matthias, and so on. But no one was ever called Jesus. Neither Sylvester nor any of the thirty-two popes before him, nor those succeeding him, ever emphasized that there were at least three well-known and authentic lines of legitimate blood descent from Jesus's own family . . .
>
> . . . The Desposyni demanded that Sylvester, who now had Roman patronage, revoke his confirmation of the authority of the Greek Christian bishops at Jerusalem, in Antioch, in Ephesus,

and in Alexandria, and to name desposynos bishops to take their place. They asked that the practice of sending cash to Jerusalem as the mother church be resumed . . . These blood relatives of Christ demanded the reintroduction of the Law, which included the Sabbath and the Holy Day system of Feasts and New Moons of the Bible. Sylvester dismissed their claims and said that, from now on, the mother church was in Rome and he insisted they accept the Greek bishops to lead them.

. . . This was the last known dialogue with the Sabbath-keeping church in the east led by the disciples who were descended from blood relatives of Jesus the Messiah.[12]

This highly intriguing account is, sadly, impossible to substantiate. As far as I can ascertain, the late Father Martin is the only source for this and, unfortunately, he did not cite the source of this startling information.* Martin was a Jesuit, and at one time, a Vatican insider. It is not outside the realm of possibility that this was privileged information contained in some secret archive and passed on by someone whose identity Father Martin was not able to share, and hence the lack of a source citation. It is actually quite surprising that Father Martin would divulge this information; he was a traditionalist Catholic much opposed to the modernizations of Vatican II, a fact that lends much veracity to his account, which definitely has all the hallmarks of authenticity.

It is, first of all, quite likely that Desposyni bishops of the Ebionite variety were still extant in Palestine and Syria in the time of Sylvester (evidence for which we will examine later). The purported demands that they made of Sylvester comport very well with what we know of the Ebionite Jewish Christians of the third and fourth centuries. Especially interesting is their demand that financial support be sent to the mother church in Jerusalem, something which, according to the New Testament, was standard practice

---

*If anyone can provide any further information on Martin's source, the author would be deeply grateful. I can be contacted through the publisher or through my website: www.thebrotherofjesus.com.

in the first century; and it is well known that Paul took up a collection for the support of Jerusalem on his missionary journeys. And, lastly, we must ask why Father Martin (or his source) would invent such a story. To what purpose? It certainly does not support Roman Catholic claims of apostolic succession!* We'll revisit this in chapter 7 when we discuss the Ebionites, who staunchly maintained that they were descendants of Jesus's family and heirs to the original Jerusalem Church.

THE UNDERGROUND STREAM

Even after we lose track of them in the flesh, the continuing influence of the Desposyni can be seen in later Jewish Christian sects such as the Ebionites and Elkesaites, some of whom survived even into the seventh century, hanging on in remote areas of Syria and northwestern Arabia and playing a surprising role in the life of the prophet Muhammad and the rise of Islam, which we will discuss in chapter 11. And even after the persecution and eventual extinction of these Jewish Christian sects, the underground stream that perpetuated the original teachings of Jesus and James continued to flow and branch off into many theological rivulets. The continuing influence of Jewish Christian belief and piety inspired and informed the rise of medieval Christian sects such as the Paulicians, the Bogomils, and the Cathars, all of whom were hunted down as heretics by the Roman Catholic Church. The Albigensian Crusade, which has the dubious distinction of being the only Crusade waged on European soil against Christian people, was launched specifically to put an end to the Cathar heresy.

The legacy and influence of Jewish Christianity can also be seen in the rise of a Christian monastic group that had one of its its main bases of operations in the heart of Cathar country in southern France—the Knights Templar. The Templars were known to have Cathar sym-

---

*Apostolic succession is the lineage of Catholic bishops dating back to Jesus's apostles, believed to be imbued with the Holy Spirit and thus respositories of the true doctrine of the Catholic Church.

pathies and there is much debate as to their level of support for the Albigensian Crusade. Like the Ebionites, Elkesaites, and Cathars who preceded them, the Knights Templar would be declared to be heretics by the Church and tried, tortured, and burned at the stake. But this was still not the end for Jewish Christianity. The underground stream of Jewish Christian influence can be traced into the fraternal brotherhoods that rose up out of the Templar ashes, such as the Rosicrucians and Freemasons. Though modern Freemasons deny that their fraternity is religious, we shall see that their rituals, ethics, and mission are largely rooted in Jewish Christian theology.

And, as we shall see at the conclusion of our quest to trace the course of Jewish Christianity, the tough and stubborn vine that repeatedly sprouted from the underground stream managed to produce one last fruit in the revolutionary birth of a new nation created in a heady brew of Jewish Christian theology mixed with Enlightenment Era ideals. This new nation—the United States of America—was seen by its Masonic founding fathers as being the "New Jerusalem," the shining beacon on a hill. We shall see in the concluding chapter that the United States was actually founded on Jewish Christian principles that found their way into Freemasonry via the underground stream.

The underground stream of Jewish Christianity is a pure, sparkling stream, one which I have come to firmly believe has been divinely guided and protected in order to purify the stagnant waters of the Gentile Christian Church, which long ago became polluted by ancient heresies and tainted by the desire for political gain. The entire course of this underground stream can be traced back to a maverick Jewish rabbi whose Davidic family believed him to be the Messiah of Israel, and whose parents named him Yeshua, which means "he will save." But the question that is still before us today, a question more compelling than ever, is the question Jesus asked of his disciples long ago: "Who do people say that I am?" In the past two centuries scholars have been on an ever-intensifying quest to find the true historical Jesus; and despite much debate and rancor among the many scholars involved, after two hundred years of questing we are finally reaching some solid, but shocking, conclusions.

2

"WHO DO YOU SAY THAT I AM?"

The Quest for the Historical Jesus

And on the way he asked his disciples, "Who do people say that I am?" And they answered him, "John the Baptist; and others, Elijah; and still others, one of the prophets." He asked them, "But who do you say that I am?" Peter answered him, "You are the Messiah."

THE GOSPEL ACCORDING TO MARK 8:27–29

The venerable Albert Schweitzer (1875–1965) wrote one of the most influential books in modern Christian scholarship, *The Quest of the Historical Jesus,* in 1906, a book as relevant today as when it was first published. Schweitzer himself was an anachronism, perhaps the last true Renaissance man, adept in many areas and making notable contributions in fields as diverse as philosophy, theology, music, and medicine, for which he deservedly received the Nobel Peace Prize. But none of his many notable achievements have been as lastingly influential as *The Quest of the Historical Jesus.* Schweitzer was so disturbed by his own conclusions in this earthshaking work that he renounced society and spent the last fifty years of his life as a medical missionary in Africa, living out Jesus's command to "give up everything you own" (Matt. 19:21) and "take up your cross and follow me" (Matt. 16:24).

The blurb that appeared on the back cover of Macmillan's 1962 paperback edition of *The Quest of the Historical Jesus* is not merely engaging in sales hyperbole when it states:

> When *The Quest of the Historical Jesus* first appeared, it rocked the theological world. . . . written when [Schweitzer] was only 33, [it] has lost none of its power to challenge and inspire a thinking faith. It is still considered one of this century's most important contributions to biblical thought.[1]

Today, at the beginning of the third millennium and a century since its original publication, Macmillan's 1962 assessment still stands. Indeed, at a time when the quest for the historical Jesus seems to once again be moving into high gear, aided and abetted by all manner of new archaeological discoveries and sensational bestsellers purporting iconoclastic new views of Jesus, Schweitzer's century-old work remains vital and indispensable. There are not many books of this vintage for which that can be said. So before we launch into our quest for the family of Jesus, we would do well to look back at Schweitzer's work in order to reacquaint ourselves with the beginnings of the modern quest for the historical Jesus and reassess the vital legacy that Schweitzer has bequeathed to us, lest we fall into some precarious traps. The quest for the historical Jesus, and especially his family's legacy, is strewn with landmines for the unwary.

The Quest of the Historical Jesus is indispensable, first of all, for its thorough overview of the quest for the historical Jesus from its beginnings in the 1700s up to the end of the so-called Old Quest at the turn of the nineteenth century. It was, in fact, Schweitzer's book that closed the door on the Old Quest with a resounding clang—the clang of a cell door closing; a cell in which Schweitzer had piled the rotting corpses of all the eighteenth- and nineteenth-century liberal lives of Jesus to which he had laid waste. Schweitzer's book is also indispensable because, while it closes one door, it opens a wider door to reveal a fresh new way of approaching the historical Jesus. Schweitzer's century-old book also remains indispensable as a kind of field guide for avoiding the many booby traps that can easily ensnare those engaged in the so-called New Quest for the historical Jesus that sprouted in the 1950s and is finally growing to maturity in our own day.

The Quest of the Historical Jesus also remains remarkably fresh in its writing style, still making for a surprisingly pleasant read (something that can be said for few other hundred-year-old books). Part of Schweitzer's genius is the lively, engaging style with which he writes, rather surprising for a nineteenth-century academic (but in light of the author's deep humanism, not unexpected). His style ranges from the sublimely poetic to the crudely rustic, with many colorful metaphors and images interspersed throughout this spectrum. The following is an example of one of his more crude and colorful assessments of the efforts of a German scholar by the name of Wilhelm Weiffenbach, long lost to historical memory:

> In the end Weiffenbach's critical principle proves to be merely a bludgeon with which he goes seal hunting and clubs the defenceless [*sic*] Synoptic [gospel] sayings right and left. When his work is done you see before you a desert island strewn with quivering corpses.[2]

That certainly leaves an indelible mental image! Schweitzer obviously possessed quite a bit of scholarly panache.

The bulk of *The Quest of the Historical Jesus* is Schweitzer's cogent analysis of all the significant purported lives of Jesus (as well as many rather insignificant ones) that had been written up to the end of the nineteenth century. Beginning with the work of Hermann Samuel Reimarus in the first half of the 1700s and ending with William Wrede in 1901 (hence the book's original German title, *From Reimarus to Wrede: The Quest of the Historical Jesus*), Schweitzer pores over the work of more than sixty of the most significant theorizers who comprise what is now called the Old Quest for the historical Jesus. It is Reimarus (1694–1768) who generally gets credit for being the first to challenge the prevailing orthodox understanding of Jesus (at least the first to be widely heard) and could therefore rightly be credited as the founding father of the Quest. One of Reimarus's great new insights was to look at Jesus in the context of first-century Judaism as a Jew, an insight that influenced Schweitzer greatly and is absolutely indispensable today.

It is fascinating and elucidating to read Schweitzer's overviews of the many astoundingly varied "lives" of Jesus that followed Reimarus, simply because of the many surprising, and often shocking, twists and turns they take, some of which are quite twisted indeed. For example, the "lives" produced by Karl Friedrich Bahrdt and Karl Heinrich Venturini are little more than conspiracy theories that would give Dan Brown a run for his money. Both of these now virtually unknown scholars (but highly respected in their day) posited that Jesus was a member of a secret society that plotted out Jesus's every move behind the scenes. In Bahrdt's picture, this secret society was the Essenes (the sect that most contemporary scholars believe collected and preserved the Dead Sea Scrolls) who, with the assistance of the Jewish supreme court—the Sanhedrin—staged Jesus's crucifixion. With the further assistance of ancient drugs and the medical skill of Luke the physician (the author of the Gospel of Luke), Jesus is made to appear dead and then later resuscitated. It would seem that the thesis of the shocking 1960s bestseller, *The Passover Plot,* is not so original.

There are more than a few lives of Jesus that Schweitzer somehow patiently presents that are, frankly, laughable; they serve as a sobering reminder that the sheer nonsense that can sometimes come packaged under the label of "scholarly" has a long pedigree. According to another long-forgotten scholar by the name of Paul de Régla, Jesus effected many of his miraculous cures through hypnotism. Pierre Nahor has Jesus schooled in both Egyptian and Indian philosophy (Jesus's "missing years" were apparently exceedingly busy!). Ernest Bosc presents a Jesus who is a theosophical occultist. If one were so inclined, a Jesus could be custom-built by picking and choosing from the array of templates that Schweitzer presents. Any little pet theory or heresy ever personally entertained is sure to be found somewhere within Schweitzer's catalogue of Jesuses.

What also makes this book fascinating is encountering the anti-quated and disproven critical theories of bygone days. It's illuminating to be able to look back and see how far historical-critical research of the New Testament has come. Many of these lives of Jesus were written at a time when John, not Mark, was considered the earliest and most reliable gospel, and the synoptic gospels were considered to be of dubious value for recovering actual history. Working in 1882, Gustav Volkmar wrote his life of Jesus under the assumption that John predated Mark, and that Matthew and Luke belonged to the second century. Both Volkmar and a scholar named Christian Gottlob Wilke considered Matthew to be a combination of Mark and Luke produced around 110 CE.

But amidst the jungle of bizarre theories and historical curiosities within these pages, two sobering facts lurk beneath the surface. First is the fact that the quest for the historical Jesus began as an anti-Christian, anti-Church movement. The agenda in those heady days of positivism and rationalism was to show that the entire superstructure of Christendom was based on exaggerations, misunderstandings, and outright lies and deceptions. Some of the most important early lives of Jesus were brewed in a cauldron of hate and rebellion. To quote Schweitzer:

> [H]ate as well as love can write a life of Jesus, and the greatest of them are written with hate . . . that of Reimarus . . . that of David Friedrich Strauss. It was not so much hate of the person of Jesus as of the supernatural nimbus with which it was so easy to surround Him . . . They were eager to picture Him as truly and purely human . . . And their hate sharpened their historical insight. They advanced the study of the subject more than all the others put together . . .[3]

The other sobering reminder that *The Quest of the Historical Jesus* leaves us with is that our present knowledge of the historical Jesus was won at a great price. The quest is not without its martyrs. Reimarus knew better than to publish while he was still alive; it was his student, G. E. Lessing, who published Reimarus's *The Aims of Jesus and His Disciples* posthumously. But for David Strauss, who was daring (or foolhardy) enough to go to market during his lifetime, his *Das Leben Jesu* (The life of Jesus), published in 1835, was his ruin. Strauss wrote about how it affected his life in very stark terms: "I might well bear a grudge against my book for it has done me much evil. It has excluded me from public teaching ... it has torn me from natural relationships and driven me to unnatural ones; it has made my life a lonely one."[4] Strauss did not suffer alone. Karl Friedrich Bahrdt and Bruno Bauer also had their careers ruined by publishing their accounts of the life of Jesus. Schweitzer reminds us that intellectual freedom is not without cost: "The world has never seen before, and will never see again, a struggle for truth so full of pain and renunciation as that which the Lives of Jesus of the last hundred years contain the cryptic record."[5]

With the publication of *The Quest of the Historical Jesus,* Schweitzer dealt a resounding deathblow to the entire quest up to that point. Through his thorough analysis of the lives of Jesus to that time, Schweitzer was able to demonstrate that all of these "Jesuses" were, in the end, psychological mirror images of the writers who created them. A famous metaphor Schweitzer used in his rather psychoanalytical evaluation is that it was as if all the historical Jesus writers had looked into a well and merely seen their own reflections peering back at them. Schweitzer summed up his analysis by wryly commenting: "There is no historical task which so reveals a man's true self as the writing of a Life of Jesus."[6]

As to Schweitzer's own take on the life of Jesus, he presents it only in the final chapter and in a mere seventy pages (it is interesting that quite a few of the earliest "lives of Jesus" were well under a hundred pages), and it is perhaps not surprising that Schweitzer's own portrait is the only one in his compendium that remains vital for its seminal portrayal of a thoroughly Jewish Jesus. What Schweitzer presents is essentially a summary of his earlier work, *The Secret of the Messiahship and the Passion: A Sketch of the Life of Jesus,* originally published in 1901. Schweitzer's sketch of Jesus is a surprisingly conservative one, a bit at odds with nineteenth-century liberal scholarship on Jesus. Schweitzer's Jesus is thoroughly Jewish and thoroughly certain that he is the Messiah of Jewish expectation. The most controversial part of Schweitzer's presentation is his assertion that Jesus shared the apocalyptic worldview of the majority of his fellow Jews (as particularly seen in the Essene community) and was convinced that God would use him to bring about the *eschaton,** the final "day of the Lord." According to Schweitzer, Jesus believed with all certainty that God would bring the world to an end through his ministry; but, most surprisingly in Schweitzer's presentation, Jesus is ultimately mistaken in his belief that God's final judgment was at hand. On the final page of his volume, Schweitzer presents a poignant summary of his life of Jesus that is both tragic and sublime, and which has become perhaps the most memorable quote in all of historical Jesus scholarship:

> There is silence all around. The Baptist appears, and cries: "Repent, for the Kingdom of Heaven is at hand." Soon after that comes Jesus, and in the knowledge that He is the coming Son of Man lays hold of the wheel of the world to set it moving on that last revolution which is to bring all ordinary history to a close. It refuses to turn, and he throws Himself upon it. Then it does turn; and it crushes Him. Instead of bringing in the eschatological conditions, He has destroyed them. The wheel rolls onward, and the mangled body of the one immeasurably great Man, who was strong enough to think of Himself as the spiritual ruler of mankind and to bend history to His purpose, is hanging upon it still. That is His victory and His reign.[7]

In Schweitzer's estimation, the greatness of Jesus is that, even though his expectations of the end of world history were not met, he did indeed cause the great wheel of history to turn by taking upon himself the great suffering he believed was about to come down upon Israel and the world. And the world has indeed been changed forever by his example. Jesus became the suffering servant, and now calls us all to follow him in laying down our lives to change the world.

With *The Quest of the Historical Jesus,* Schweitzer threw down a gauntlet that marked a decisive turning point in the quest for the historical Jesus, and all subsequent Jesus scholarship has taken on his ideas in some form. Nineteenth-century scholars had almost completely dis-

---

*Greek for "the end."

tanced Jesus from his Jewish roots and attempted to turn him into a Hellenistic wisdom teacher (something scholars associated with the current Jesus Seminar* are again trying to do). In his iconoclastic presentation of a thoroughly apocalyptic Jesus, Schweitzer followed the lead of another influential scholar, Johannes Weiss, who had earlier reached this same breakthrough conclusion in *Jesus' Proclamation of the Kingdom of God* (1892). According to both Weiss and Schweitzer, Jesus was a Jewish prophet who believed himself to be the long-awaited Messiah and took his mission statement from the "suffering servant" passages of Isaiah. In their view, Jesus believed that through his voluntary death on behalf of all Israel, the day of the Lord would be ushered in and God would commence the final eschatological judgment, and create the new heavens and earth foretold by Isaiah and Malachi. But Schweitzer was also thereby forced to conclude that Jesus saw his ethical teaching as being only an "interim ethic" to be lived out in the brief time before the eschaton, and not a universal teaching for all time. It was Schweitzer's personal conviction of this unanticipated conclusion that caused him to leave society behind and set up shop as a medical missionary in Africa, in order to follow Jesus and spend the rest of his life helping the poorest of the poor.

Due to Schweitzer's tour de force, the quest for the historical Jesus came to a standstill. Schweitzer's presentation was powerful and compellingly influential, except for one sticking point: the idea that Jesus was thoroughly mistaken about the timeline of the final eschatological judgment was something that even the most liberal scholars could not bring themselves to accept. As a result, almost everyone rejected Schweitzer's understanding of Jesus as a Jewish apocalyptic prophet. This rejection of Schweitzer's conclusion was the springboard that gave rise to the hugely influential work of Rudolf Bultmann (1884–1976). It was in part as a reaction to Weiss and Schweitzer that Bultmann came to insist that we could know almost nothing about the historical Jesus, that the words and deeds of Jesus presented in the gospels were almost completely the work of

---

*The Jesus Seminar is a group of scholars who examine the New Testament to determine what Jesus actually said and did, as opposed to what was written in the Bible.

the early church retrojecting *their* needs and *their* beliefs about Jesus. And because almost nothing of any certainty could be known about the actual historical Jesus, Bultmann insisted that Christianity must be based solely in the early church's *kerygma* (proclamation) about Christ. Almost all mainline theologians pretty much fell in step with Bultmann's ideas until the hugely influential Swiss theologian, Karl Barth (1886–1968), ushered in the counterreaction of neo-orthodoxy. But even in neo-orthodoxy, the quest for the historical Jesus was seen as a dead end. For theologians and clergy who were disciples of either Barth or Bultmann (and that was the vast majority), the kerygma was all that mattered. One simply preached and taught what the scriptures said because historical reconstructions of the actual events and the actual words of Jesus were considered futile. Almost all mainline clergy thereafter saw a great danger in attempts at historical reconstruction—if it were left to scholars to determine what actually happened, then the scholars would become the high priests, in that their conclusions would determine Christian proclamation. So, for the vast majority of clergy and theologians, all that mattered for Christian faith was what the early church proclaimed about Jesus (the kerygma); for that represented the vital, lasting impact of Jesus. This was the dominant theological position in Christianity for most of the twentieth century, and it is still the position taken in most mainline Christian seminaries today. Because of the huge influence of these three giants—Schweitzer, Bultmann, and Barth—the quest for the historical Jesus was dead and would not be resurrected until almost a half a century after the appearance of *The Quest of the Historical Jesus*. Ironically, the quest would be renewed by Bultmann's own students, most notably Ernst Käsemann.

A TWO-WAY STREET

Schweitzer forced all subsequent scholars to make a decision on where they stood in their basic understanding of the historical Jesus. The choices are summed up by the title of Schweitzer's last chapter: "Thoroughgoing Scepticism [*sic*] and Thoroughgoing Eschatology." The choice between these two alternatives still faces any researcher of the historical Jesus today.

According to Wrede, who took the approach of thoroughgoing skepticism, all that we could know of Jesus was that he was a teacher or prophet from Galilee who said and did amazing things and was executed; a view that Bultmann would share and champion. In Wrede's view, as well as Bultmann's, Mark's gospel, from which the others were derived, is almost entirely a fictional work of the early church. Many liberal scholars on the far left still hold this position today, especially those associated with the Jesus Seminar, who consider only a small percentage of Jesus's words in the gospels to be genuinely from his mouth. The only really viable alternative to this rather bleak and barren picture is to take Schweitzer's approach of understanding Jesus as a thoroughly eschatological Jewish prophet, which then enables one to accept far more of the synoptic gospels as being historical, steeped as the gospel accounts are in Jesus's apocalyptic preaching of the imminent arrival of the kingdom of God.

These two alternatives—thoroughgoing skepticism or thoroughgoing eschatology—are still the two poles around which historical Jesus researchers today align themselves. The New Quest, represented by the Jesus Seminar, opts for a rather thoroughgoing skepticism, a minimalist approach to what we can know of the historical Jesus. On the other hand, scholars of what is referred to as the "Third Quest" (favored by this author) see Jesus, as Schweitzer did, as a thoroughgoing, apocalyptic, Jewish prophet and generally accept the gospels as basically reliable historical accounts. A leading voice in third quest scholarship is N. T. Wright, an Anglican theologian and clergyman, who has dubbed these two alternatives with appropriate German names: Wredestrasse (Wrede Street) and Schweitzerstrasse (Schweitzer Street), after the two authors. In just the last twenty years or so the traffic on both of these streets has become quite congested. Wright remarks, "As we turn to the current scene in Jesus studies, we discover that these two streets have become broad highways, with a good deal of traffic all trying to use them at once."[8]

The New Quest approach is represented by such well-known scholars as Burton Mack (*The Lost Gospel: The Book of Q and Christian Origins*), Lutheran scholar Marcus Borg (*Meeting Jesus Again for the First Time*), and most notably, the widely admired Catholic scholar John Dominic Crossan

(*The Historical Jesus: The Life of a Mediterranean Jewish Peasant*). New questers generally feel that the apocalyptic sayings of Jesus in the gospels were largely creations of the early church and did not come from the mouth of the historical Jesus. They tend to see Jesus as more of a rogue Hellenistic philosopher, a wandering Jewish peasant Cynic philosopher* whose teachings were more in line with Old Testament wisdom writings than the teachings of any first-century Jewish rabbis. Marcus Borg, however, has taken a position on the apocalyptic sayings in the gospels that provides a bridge between the new questers and the third questers. Borg argues that modern scholars have completely misread these sayings, looking at them through modern eyes as being predictions of the end of the space-time universe. Rather, Borg argues, these apocalyptic sayings need to be understood in their historical context as predictions of the imminent invasion of Rome and the destruction of Jerusalem and the temple. Thus, Borg, while largely accepting the New Quest picture of Jesus as a Cynic philosopher, also allows that Jesus's apocalyptic sayings are genuine, albeit misunderstood.

In the Third Quest school of thought, the main scholar who has run with this idea is N. T. Wright, who expounds upon it most fully in two large tomes: *The New Testament and the People of God* and *Jesus and the Victory of God,* the first two volumes in a trilogy on the historical Jesus collectively called *Christian Origins and the Question of God.* Of the difference in his approach Wright says, "I believe that Crossan, in common . . . with the great majority of New Testament scholars, has misunderstood the nature of apocalyptic. . . . I have argued . . . that 'apocalyptic' writings . . . were read in the first century as describing not 'the darkening scenario of an imminent end to the world' but the radical subversion of the present world order."[9] While entering onto the Schweitzerstrasse, Wright pushes for a refinement of our understanding of Jewish apocalyptic:

---

*The Cynic philosophers, who date back to ancient Greece in the time of Socrates, perceived their self-training to be the most expedient route to a virtuous life. They believed that happiness could best be achieved through living in agreement with nature and rejecting the desire for wealth, power, fame, and possessions.

[T]he attempt to follow Schweitzer has resulted in a major refinement of what precisely Jewish eschatology and apocalyptic really was. One of the things for which Schweitzer has become most famous is now increasingly questioned: "apocalyptic" was, for him and for the ninety years since he wrote, almost synonymous with the end of the space-time universe, but it is now clear that this is a bizarre, literalistic reading . . . Once the necessary adjustments have been made, many elements in Schweitzer's reconstruction can in turn be salvaged. His basic position (Jewish eschatology as the context for Jesus, joining forces with skepticism to confront naive traditionalism, but then defeating skepticism with appropriate historical reconstruction) survives intact . . .[10]

And later, Wright gives a nice summary of where we have arrived on the Schweitzerstrasse:

It has commonly been assumed, at least since Weiss and Schweitzer, that Jesus . . . expected the imminent end of the present space-time order altogether . . . in the post-Bultmannian New Quest it was assumed that talk of the "kingdom of god" [*sic*], or of the "son of man coming on the clouds of heaven," was to be taken as a literal prediction of events, shortly to take place, which would close the space-time order. But not only is it unnecessary to read apocalyptic language in this way; it is actually necessary as historians that we refuse to do so. Apocalyptic language was . . . an elaborate metaphor-system for investing historical events with theological significance. . .

. . . It is time . . . to reject the old idea that Jesus expected the end of the space-time universe—though this does not mean, as the "Jesus Seminar" has imagined, that Jesus did not use apocalyptic language. . . . Jesus's warnings about imminent judgment were intended to be taken as denoting . . . sociopolitical events, *seen as the climactic moment in Israel's history,* and, in consequence, as constituting a summons to *national* repentance. In this light, Jesus appears as a successor to Jeremiah and his like, warning Israel that persistence in her present course will bring political disaster, which in turn should be *understood* as the judgment of Israel's own god [*sic*]. But Jesus is not merely a successor, one in a continuing line of prophets. His warnings include the warning that he is the last in line. This is, I think, what Jesus's eschatology is all about."[11]

I have included this lengthy citation by Wright because it neatly sums up my own position on eschatology and apocalyptic. While not all Third Quest scholars would fully agree with Wright's assessment, they all agree on the absolute necessity of placing Jesus firmly and fully within his Jewish context. Some notable scholars who have taken this position include: S. G. F. Brandon (*Jesus and the Zealots*), Martin Hengel (*The Charismatic Leader and His Followers*), Geza Vermes (*Jesus the Jew*), Bruce Chilton (*Rabbi Jesus*), E. P. Sanders (*Jesus and Judaism*), James Charlesworth (*Jesus Within Judaism*), Ben Witherington (*The Jesus Quest: The Third Search for the Jew of Nazareth*), John Meier (*A Marginal Jew*), and James D. Tabor (*The Jesus Dynasty*). Many more could be added to this list, and while those cited mark quite a theological range—from liberal to conservative, from Jewish to Catholic to Evangelical Protestant—they all share a basic methodological approach that places them squarely in the Third Quest camp. Wright nicely sums up their shared approach:

> There is now a real attempt to do history seriously. Josephus, so long inexplicably ignored, is suddenly happily in vogue. There is a real willingness to be guided by first-century sources, and to see the Judaism of that period in all its complex pluriformity . . . Qumran and the apocalyptic writings are not merely part of the dark backcloth against which the great light of the gospel shines the more brightly . . . The crucifixion, long recognized as an absolute bedrock in history, is now regularly made the center of understanding: What must Jesus have been like if he ended up on a Roman cross?
>
> . . . The "Old Quest" was determined that Jesus should look as little like a first-century Jew as possible. The renewed "New Quest," following this line, has often downplayed the specifically Jewish fea-

tures of Jesus . . . it has also downplayed to a large extent the significance of Jesus's death . . . The present "Third Quest," by and large,
will have none of this. Jesus must be understood as a comprehensible
. . . first-century Jew, whatever . . . the consequences.[12]

The consequences can indeed be startling and disturbing, especially
to traditional Christians who are not at all aware of the modern quest
for the historical Jesus. I largely explored those consequences in my previous volume, *The Brother of Jesus and the Lost Teachings of Christianity*,
but there largely confined myself to the time period of the earliest church
under the leadership of James. In this present volume we will continue to
explore those consequences and focus on their continuing reverberations
down through the centuries.

FULL CIRCLE

One hundred years after Schweitzer, the methodology really hasn't
changed much in the quest for the historical Jesus. In fact, the following
quote from *The Quest of the Historical Jesus* could just as well have been
written today:

> For the last ten years modern historical theology has more and
> more adapted itself to the needs of the man in the street. More
> and more, even in the best class of works, it makes use of attractive
> headlines as a means of presenting its results in a lively form to
> the masses. Intoxicated with its own ingenuity in inventing these,
> it . . . has come to believe that the world's salvation depends . . .
> upon the spreading of its own "assured results" broadcast among
> the people.[13]

In light of this rather eerie parallel with the contemporary scene,
we would be wise to heed one more warning from Schweitzer, which
speaks volumes to our present situation and offers a clarion call to forge
ahead:

As of old Jacob wrestled with the angel, so . . . theology wrestles with Jesus of Nazareth and will not let him go until He bless it—that is, until He will consent to serve it and . . . be drawn . . . into the midst of our time and our civilisation [sic]. But when the day breaks, the wrestler must let Him go . . . Jesus of Nazareth will not suffer himself to be modernised [sic]. As an historic figure he refuses to be detached from His own time. He has no answer for the question, "Tell us thy name in our speech and for our day!" But he does bless those who have wrestled with Him, so that, though they cannot take Him with them, yet, like men who have seen God face to face and received strength in their souls, they go on their way with renewed courage, ready to do battle with the world and its powers.[14]

Indeed, one of the major problems with the practitioners of the Old Quest, as well as with many practitioners of the New Quest, is that they tried, and still try, to draw Jesus "into the midst of our time and our civilization." They have not heeded the warning of Schweitzer that the face they see when peering into the deep "well" of historical Jesus research is their own. And this is where the practitioners of the Third Quest have a distinct advantage: They allow the real, historical Jesus to rise up to us from his *own* time and civilization. As N. T. Wright neatly sums it up:

[Current] scholarship has at least one great advantage over its predecessors. Since Weiss and Schweitzer . . . it has been realized that Jesus *must be understood in his Jewish context.* The only sense in which the old nineteenth-century "Quest" had really attempted this was by producing a sharp contrast. The Jews had the wrong sort of religion; Jesus came to bring the right sort. The game was then to cut off all those bits of the "Jesus" piece that appeared too Jewish, too ethnically restricted, leaving the hero as the founder of a great, universal, "spiritual" religion . . . Weiss and Schweitzer, however, rightly insisted that the historical jigsaw must portray Jesus as a credible and recognizable first-century Jew, relating comprehensibly in speech and action to other first-century Jews. *No solution which claims to be talking about history can ever undo this basic move."*[15] (Italics mine.)

So, what happens when Jesus is restored to his proper Jewish context? The result is the much more accurate historical picture captured by the scholars mentioned above who are currently engaged in the Third Quest. When we look at the earliest Christian Church through this lens, the picture of the earliest Christian community also becomes thoroughly Jewish, as neatly summed up by Third Quest scholar David Catchpole: "We have a picture of a community whose outlook was essentially Jerusalem-centered, whose theology was Torah-centered, whose worship was temple-centered, and which saw . . . no incompatibility between all of that and commitment to Jesus."[16] In the pages that follow we shall take up this basic position for the purpose of using it to gain a clearer historical picture of Jesus's family and their dynastic and spiritual heirs. The resulting picture of Christian history is both surprising and thoroughly refreshing, as a long-suppressed underground stream comes bubbling to the surface, cooling us in its healing waters.

3

IN THE BEGINNING
The Nazarenes and the Jewish Origins of Christianity

Do not think that I have come to abolish the law or the prophets; I have come not to abolish but to fulfill. For truly I tell you, until heaven and earth pass away, not one letter, not one stroke of a letter, will pass from the law until all is accomplished. . . . For truly I tell you, unless your righteousness exceeds that of the scribes and the Pharisees, you will never enter the kingdom of heaven.

JESUS, THE SERMON ON THE
MOUNT (MATTHEW 5:17–20)

Jesus was a Jew. This is a fundamental truth that no modern scholar of Christianity, of whatever theological or scholarly stripe, would dispute. However, there are still an astounding number of Christian laypeople who don't fully grasp this, or simply don't wish to accept it, for the implications of Jesus's Jewishness are staggering for Western religion and for those with long-vested interest in maintaining the status quo. Many conservative Christians will admit that, yes, Jesus grew up practicing Judaism, but will insist that Jesus made a complete break from Judaism, replacing the dysfunctional, outmoded religion of his birth with a new religion based in "salvation by grace through faith" (as Luther put it), rather than adherence to the Torah (the law of Moses). This has been the traditional understanding of the Christian Church for almost the entirety of its existence. But if this traditional understanding is correct, then how does one explain Jesus's words in the quote from the Sermon on the Mount that opens this chapter? These particular words are perhaps the most overlooked and ignored of Jesus's teachings, for they portray a Jesus and a message quite different from what the Christian Church has understood and proclaimed for the past two thousand years. These words starkly reveal a *thoroughly* Jewish Jesus, a Jesus who, in the words of Albert Schweitzer, "comes to us as One unknown," a Jesus completely unfamiliar to the vast majority of Christians who would claim to know Jesus oh so well.

WHEN DID CHRISTIANITY BEGIN?

If we start, then, with this basic presupposition that Jesus was a Jew, then we are forced to ask: When did the Christian religion begin? Is there any event in Jesus's life and ministry that we can point to and say that it marks the official beginning of Christianity? Many Christians naively assume that Christianity began at the moment of Jesus's birth in Bethlehem. Others assume Christianity began with Jesus's baptism by John the Baptist in the Jordan River, which marked the official commencement of Jesus's public ministry. Still other Christians believe that Christianity began at the moment of Jesus's death upon the cross, when Jesus's atoning sacrifice made possible the salvation of humankind. Others are of the opinion that Christianity officially originated with Jesus's disciples proclaiming the "Good News" of his resurrection from the dead.

The fact that there are many differing understandings of when the Christian faith began raises the question of whether there is any single event in Jesus's life of which we can say that it officially marks the transition point from Judaism to Christianity. The Christian Church itself has traditionally identified its birth as occurring *after* Jesus—on the day of Pentecost, fifty days after Easter, the day of his resurrection. On this day, according to the book of Acts, the Holy Spirit descended on the apostles in the form of tongues of flame, empowering them to speak in foreign languages in order to proclaim the gospel of Jesus Christ to Jews from all over the Roman world who were gathered in Jerusalem for the festival of Pentecost. According to Acts, this outpouring of the Holy Spirit resulted in the conversion of three thousand Jews to Christianity (Acts 2:41), so it is easy to see why the Church marks this as its official beginning.

Today, however, many scholars are taking a rather more startling position on the question of Christianity's origins by pushing it forward several decades after Jesus, arguing that the Christian Church was not actually started by Jesus at all, *but by Paul,* who, with the commencement of his missionary activity among the Gentiles, transformed what was originally a Jewish sect into a Gentile religion that rejected its Jewish roots and based salvation on having faith in the atoning sacrifice of Jesus on the cross. And there are a number of scholars who take the even more radical position that Christianity as we know it today really begins *centuries* later, in the year 325, when the Council of Nicaea officially declared what was orthodox Christian doctrine and what wasn't, thus establishing an orthodox standard of belief at a time when many different Christian sects were heatedly arguing over who Jesus really was. These scholars would argue that it is only with the Council of Nicaea's declaration that Jesus was fully divine that Christianity as we know it today truly began.

So, as we can see, the question of when Christianity actually began is a thorny one. Did Christianity begin with Jesus, with his first followers, or with a later historical event or institution? No matter what the conclusion on this question, we are still left with a single undeniable fact with which almost no one (except, perhaps, a few Christian fundamentalists) would disagree: Jesus was a Jew, as were all of his first followers. While this statement may be rather unremarkable today (although this has certainly not always been the case), a more startling fact that emerges from this is that *Jesus's disciples continued to practice Judaism.* As evidence of this, there is a fascinating passage in Acts that describes the very earliest Christian community and its worship practices, a passage that forms the conclusion of the Pentecost story:

Awe came upon everyone, because many wonders and signs were being done by the apostles. All who believed were together and had all things in common; they would sell their possessions and goods and distribute the proceeds to all, as any had need. Day by day, *as they spent much time together in the temple,* they broke bread at home . . . praising God and *having the goodwill of all the people.*" (Acts 2:43–47, emphasis added.)

Here we have irrefutable evidence that the earliest Christian community did not break away from the temple, but continued to worship God there along with their fellow Jews, and in fact enjoyed their "goodwill."

Earlier in Acts we are told that this group that continued to worship at the temple included not only the apostles but, surprisingly, Jesus's family as well:

Peter, and John, and James, and Andrew, Philip and Thomas, Bartholomew and Matthew, James son of Alphaeus, and Simon the Zealot, and Judas son of James. All these were constantly devoting themselves to prayer, together with certain women, *including Mary the mother of Jesus, as well as his brothers.* (Acts 1:13b–14, emphasis added.)

Here we have evidence that there was no animosity between Jesus's family and the apostles, as was often supposed—an idea thoroughly dismantled in *The Brother of Jesus and the Lost Teachings of Christianity.* The very fact that Jesus's disciples and family worshipped in the temple (and thus did not break with the ceremonies and rituals of Judaism) and also enjoyed "the goodwill of all the people" indicates quite clearly that the original followers of Jesus were not perceived as heretical in any way by their fellow Jews. This is all the more remarkable when we consider that Jesus's family and disciples were newcomers to Jerusalem, most being natives of the generally despised Galilee, an area considered to be an embarrassing backwater by the more cosmopolitan Judeans. But while Jesus's disciples may have differed from the Judeans culturally, the only thing that really distinguished them from other Jews *religiously* was their unique belief that Jesus was the Davidic Messiah. And even this would not have been seen as all that unusual, for there is considerable historical evidence that many of the Jews in Jesus's day looked to other charismatic Jewish leaders as the messiah, a major case in point being the disciples of John the Baptist, who believed their master to be the promised Messiah.* In *The Jesus Dynasty,* James Tabor makes an interesting case that Jesus and John were both seen as messiahs, in fact as "co-messiahs," with John, who was of Levitical descent, being the priestly messiah; and Jesus, who was of Davidic descent, the royal messiah.[1] While that claim may sound outrageous to some, it is not without precedent; we know from the Dead Sea Scrolls that the Essenes were expecting two messiahs—one priestly, one royal.

Jewish scholar Hyam Maccoby has pointed out the rather startling implications of the fact that Jesus's disciples continued to worship in the temple, implications that the vast majority of Christians do not usually stop to think about:

> [Jesus's disciples] were not Christians in any sense that would be intelligible to Christians of a later date. They were Jews who subscribed to every item of the Jewish faith. . . . They continued to circumcise their male children, thus inducting them into the Jewish covenant. . . . They kept the Jewish dietary laws, the Jewish Sabbaths and festivals . . . the Jewish purity laws . . . and they used the Jewish liturgy for their daily prayers . . . the first follower of Jesus with whom Paul had friendly contact, Ananias of Damascus, is described as a "devout observer of the Law and well spoken of by all the Jews of that place." (Acts 22:12)[2]

And lest anyone object that Maccoby may simply be looking at things through "Jewish colored glasses," a fairly conservative Christian scholar, the widely respected James D. G. Dunn, shares a similar assessment:

---

*There is a modern sect in Iraq, known as the Mandeans, that still today claims that John the Baptist, and not Jesus, was the Messiah.

[I]t is evident that *the earliest* [Christian] *community in no sense felt themselves to be a new religion, distinct from Judaism* . . . [T]hey saw themselves simply as fulfilled Judaism . . . Indeed we may put the point more strongly . . . the earliest Christians were not simply Jews, but in fact continued to be quite orthodox Jews.

. . . [T]his is the group with whom Christianity proper all began. Only their belief in Jesus as Messiah and risen . . . mark them out as different from the majority of their fellow Jews.[3]

The bottom line is that Christianity as a separate and distinct religion from Judaism had not begun even in the wake of Pentecost. In actual fact, the set of organized beliefs and practices (in academic terminology, the *cultus*) that we know today as Christianity only slowly developed after the death of Jesus, and did not crystallize into Christianity as we recognize it today until the late-third to early fourth century. Prior to the Council of Nicaea (325) there were, in fact, many different and competing "Christianities." Professor Bart D. Ehrman of the University of North Carolina has provided a thorough overview of the many varieties of Christianity that existed in the first few centuries in two invaluable companion volumes that have become surprising bestsellers: *Lost Christianities* and *Lost Scriptures*. These early Christian sects ranged from ultraconservative Jewish Christians who continued to observe every letter of the Torah, to Gnostic Hellenistic Christians who rejected the God of the Old Testament as an evil demigod. These various Christian and semi-Christian groups were known by names such as the Nazoraeans, the Ebionites, the Elkesaites, the Marcionites, the Manichaeans, and the Valentinians, to name just a few. Ehrman makes the fascinating observation that, "All of these groups insisted that they upheld the teachings of Jesus and his apostles, and they all possessed writings that bore out their claims . . ."[4]

Obviously, only one of these groups could be correct in that assertion, and the others all deviated to a greater or lesser extent from Jesus's original teachings. Today, both the Roman Catholic Church and the Eastern Orthodox Church make the claim that they represent the original teaching of Jesus and the apostles. The third major branch of Christianity, the

Protestant Church, while not being able to claim direct descent from the apostles, claims to have brought Christianity back to the original teachings of the apostles, from which the Reformers felt the Roman Church had strayed. But in actual fact, *none* of the modern-day churches can legitimately claim to represent the actual teachings of Jesus; all have deviated to a greater or lesser extent from Jesus's original intent. In this book I shall present evidence to show that the only group able to legitimately claim to have carried on Jesus's original teachings is the earliest group of Jesus's first disciples, referred to in the New Testament as the Nazarenes. Based in Jerusalem, the Nazarenes were able to carry on Jesus's mission in its purest form until the Roman invasion in 70; and then, after the destruction of Jerusalem, carried Jesus's message to Pella and elsewhere in the Transjordanian regions east of Palestine. But as they became geographically distanced from Jerusalem and chronologically distanced from their theological roots, the Nazarenes inevitably began to deviate from Jesus's vision and slowly morphed into variant sects such as the Ebionites, who became increasingly conservative in their Judaism; and the Elkesaites, who became increasingly Gnostic. At the same time, Paul's churches, which rapidly became the majority and were in many ways in competition with the Nazarenes, became increasingly Hellenistic in their beliefs and practice.

RABBI JESUS

No one today would disagree that the ultimate roots of Christianity, in all its variegated forms throughout history, are to be found in the teachings of a Palestinian, Jewish, religious teacher whose name was Yesh'ua (Joshua, later Latinized and Anglicized into Jesus). According to the gospels, Jesus's fundamental identity among the people to whom he ministered was that of *rabbi* (Hebrew for "teacher"). Rabbi, or teacher, is the title used almost exclusively when people address Jesus in the gospels; but very few Christians take this title and its import very seriously. Most Christians today would find it hard to conceive of Jesus as anything at all like a real, first-century Jewish rabbi. Very few Christians are aware of the fact that Jesus wore the traditional Jewish *tallit*—the fringed tassels (*cicith*) stipulated for Jewish men to wear in the book of Numbers.[5]

But the fact that Jesus was a Jewish teacher is one of the very few commonly accepted conclusions in the otherwise cantankerous quest for the historical Jesus. I would also make the claim that this is perhaps *the only thing* upon which all Christians today—of whatever church, sect, or theological persuasion—would agree. Where the disagreement between both Christian and secular scholars begins is with the follow-up question: *What kind* of Jewish teacher was Jesus?

There are two general answers to this question, from which an astounding diversity of theological understandings of Jesus have arisen; but the answers generally fall into one of two categories: Either Jesus was a completely human Jewish teacher wanting to reform Judaism, but with no intent of starting a new religion; or Jesus was God incarnate in human flesh, who came to institute God's New Covenant for the salvation of both Jew and Gentile. In the latter understanding, the goal of Jesus's entire ministry was to do away with Judaism and institute a new universal religion for all people.

One of the most controversial questions in modern scholarship, which marks a kind of dividing line between conservative and liberal scholars, is this question of whether Jesus intended to start a new religion or was merely attempting to reform Judaism. A parallel can be drawn here with the Protestant reformer Martin Luther. Luther did not set out to start a new church. Luther was a loyal Catholic priest who merely called for the reform of the Roman Catholic Church. Unfortunately, Luther's call for reform got him excommunicated from the Church and left no other option open to him. But Jesus was never formally ousted from Judaism, although there are many stories of his being driven out of synagogues by fellow Jews enraged at his call for reform.

The question of whether it was ever Jesus's intent to sow the seeds of a new religion to supersede Judaism has been at the heart of Jewish and Christian dissension from the time that St. Paul began his evangelistic mission among the Gentiles, and it is the major theological issue that underlies almost all of Paul's letters. In order to answer this question, we need to go back to the very beginning and attempt to take a fresh look at just what the immediate legacy of Jesus's teaching and ministry among the Jewish people was. With so many differing interpretations of Jesus and his message, our surest clue to what the original message really was can only be found by closely examining what the immediate aftermath of Jesus's ministry was. What did Jesus's original disciples *do* after his death and resurrection?

AFTERMATH

Following Jesus's one to three year ministry,* and subsequent to his death, what immediate legacy did he leave behind? Jesus left no writings of which we are aware. After his death, all that remained as the fruits of Jesus's ministry were some one hundred and twenty or so Jewish disciples,[6] a significant number of whom were members of his family, and all of whom were convinced—and willing to die a martyr's death for this conviction—that Jesus was the Messiah of Israel foretold by the Hebrew prophets. How were their lives changed as a result of this belief?

One of the most solid pieces of evidence we have concerning these earliest Christians is that except for their unique belief in Jesus as Messiah, their religious practices remained unaltered, as we have already begun to see. For all intents and purposes they remained practicing Jews. Most of them—mainly the members of Jesus's immediate family and apostolic circle—although originally hailing from the northern Palestinian territory of Galilee, relocated to the southern territory of Judea, where they now centered their life around the Jerusalem Temple. They worshipped both in the temple and in the synagogues with their fellow Jews, who, by

---

*The exact length of Jesus's ministry is a subject of much debate. In the Synoptic gospels (Matthew, Mark, and Luke), it would appear there was about a year from the inauguration of his ministry (following his baptism by John) until his crucifixion. John's gospel, however, seems to present a picture of a three-year ministry. The length of Jesus's ministry is one of the fundamental unresolved questions in historical Jesus research. In my mind, the most logical proposal of a three-year ministry, based on the chronology in John, has been provided by James Tabor in *The Jesus Dynasty*.

all accounts, considered them to be especially upstanding in their piety and devotion to the Torah. This is particularly remarkable considering that most Judeans had an ingrained prejudice against Galileans that dated back to the split between Israel and Judah in the days of King Solomon. Yet, Jesus's brother James, who took over the reins of leadership after Jesus's death, was held in such high esteem for his outstanding righteousness under the law that he was nicknamed "the Just One." As evidence of the high esteem in which James was held by those who were scrupulous in upholding the Torah, when James was unjustly executed by the new high priest Ananus in the year 62, high-ranking Pharisees in Jerusalem protested to Rome, resulting in Ananus's abrupt removal from office. It therefore seems quite likely that James and the disciples were closely affiliated with the Pharisees, as evidenced by the fact that many Pharisees became members of the Jerusalem Church (the generally accepted name for the earliest Christian community under James). At the so-called Jerusalem Conference, the first general Church council described in Acts 15, the Pharisees were represented. In the account of Paul's last visit to Jerusalem, when Paul is greeted by James and the elders, they proudly tell him, "You see, brother, how many thousands of believers there are among the Jews, and *they are all zealous for the law*" (Acts 21:20). It is quite plain that for James and the apostles there was no discrepancy at all between believing in Jesus and adhering to the Torah.[7]

Under James's leadership, the original followers of Jesus were not even called Christians. This is a name bestowed upon them only decades later in the Gentile Church at Antioch, as recorded in a famous passage in Acts: ". . . it was in Antioch that the disciples were first called 'Christians'" (Acts 11:26). Prior to this, according to the New Testament itself, Jesus's original Jewish followers were known as Nazarenes. The word *Christian* is used only three times in the New Testament, and these references are from quite late in the first century (Acts 26:28, 1 Peter 4:13, and 4:16). In comparison, the term "Nazarene" is used fourteen times in the gospels and Acts.[8]

It is quite likely that the designation "Jesus of Nazareth" was originally "Jesus the Nazarene," a name describing the messianic "Jesus party," which was just one of many religious parties within Judaism at the time, and included the Sadducees, Pharisees, Essenes, and Zealots. In order to distinguish the earliest Jewish disciples of Jesus from the later Gentile disciples, we will refer to Jesus's original Jewish disciples as Nazarenes throughout this book. While a number of scholars use the term Nazorean or Nasorean, I prefer the more commonly used Nazarene, not only because it is found most often in English Bibles, but because it serves to distinguish the first Christians from a later Jewish Christian sect called the Nazoraeans, which we will discuss later. Likewise, I will use the term "Jewish Christianity" to refer to the type of Judaism that the Nazarenes adhered to, although this term is also not without its problems.

Many scholars now make the argument that the name Jesus of Nazareth was a mistranslation of the original phrase, Jesus the Nazarene, and that it did not refer to the town of Nazareth at all. A few scholars argue that Nazareth may not yet have even been in existence at the time of Jesus (although archaeological evidence seems to indicate it was). While Nazareth is nowhere mentioned in historical writings from the period, this may simply be due to the fact that it was a tiny, inconsequential backwater town. By the second century, when Gentile Christians became the majority, the actual meaning of the term "Nazarene" was soon lost. The words *Nazarene* and *Nazareth* are derived from the Hebrew root N-S-R,* which has two meanings: One is "to watch" or "to observe," which may refer to observing or upholding the Torah. In Hebrew, Jesus and his disciples were called the Notsrim, which can be translated as "keepers," or "preservers." The Hebrew scholar, Dr. Hugh Schonfield, states that the name could be understood as,

> . . . those who maintained the true teaching and tradition, or who cherished certain secrets which they did not divulge to others, as did the Zadokite-Essenes. . . .

---

*Hebrew, like most Middle Eastern languages, did not originally contain vowels. One simply had to know from usage how to make the vowel sounds between the consonants.

. . . In the Gospel parables Jesus refers to secrets (mysteries) of the Kingdom of God made known exclusively to his disciples, but not disclosed to "those outside" . . . that they should see, but not perceive; and hear, but not understand. (Mark 4:10–12; Matthew 13:10–17)[9]

But N-S-R can also mean "shoot" or "branch," as in King David being the offshoot of his father, Jesse. This term may have been applied to Jesus as the "branch of Jesse," a phrase used in many Christmas carols and Advent hymns, such as the beloved "Oh Come, Oh Come, Emmanuel": *Oh come, strong Branch of Jesse, free / Your own from Satan's tyranny.* James Tabor makes the fascinating assertion that the town of Nazareth may have taken its name from the fact that many Davidic descendants lived there, that Nazareth may have meant something along the lines of "Branchtown."[10] The original usage may have invoked both of these meanings.

This all raises a significant question: If Jesus was from Nazareth and his disciples were all from Galilee, why would they have relocated to Jerusalem after Jesus's death? Why would they have been so focused on the temple? One simple and obvious reason for this is that the disciples, as well as Jesus, had *always* centered their life on the temple. From the time of his birth, Jesus's parents regularly took him to services and took part in sacrifices at the temple. Jesus was consecrated in the temple with the required offering stipulated in the Torah of either "a pair of turtledoves or two young pigeons" (Luke 2:22–24). Jesus's family went to the temple at least once a year for the Passover festival (Luke 2:41), and likely the other two major festivals as well,* and Jesus continued to attend the festivals in Jerusalem during his ministry (see John 2:13).

There are a few other important reasons why the Nazarenes centered their religious life around the temple after Jesus's death. First, the temple was not only the center of Jewish worship, but of all of Jewish life. While

---

*The other two major festivals were Shavuot (Pentecost) and Sukkot (Feast of Tabernacles). These are known as the "pilgrim festivals," for according to the Torah, all ablebodied men were required to make the pilgrimage to the temple in Jerusalem at these three times in the year (Exodus 23:14–17).

Jesus and his brother James were critical of the many ethical failings of the Sadducean party that controlled the temple and of the corruption of the Herodian priesthood, and while James (and maybe Jesus as well) may have been a proponent of doing away with animal sacrifices, as we will discuss later, both still held the temple to be the house of God* and the only possible focus of their worship. Secondly, this was the temple envisioned by King David and built by his son, King Solomon; it was the temple of Israel's first messiahs.† The temple was, therefore, the site where Messiah Jesus was expected to return and where he would establish the seat of God's kingdom on earth—the coming kingdom that was the heart and soul of Jesus's (as well as John the Baptist's) proclamation. The imminent Parousia (second coming, in Greek) of Messiah Jesus was at the center of the Nazarene proclamation of the Good News. When Messiah Jesus returned, God's kingdom would commence with the creation of a new heaven and a new earth, as well as a New Jerusalem (see Revelation 21).

It was this sure and certain hope that imbued the small band of Nazarenes with fearless courage in the wake of the execution of their Messiah, Jesus. They were at first in fear of their lives from the Roman authorities, for they were accomplices of one whom the Romans crucified for the crime of high treason against the empire. But the Nazarenes soon became fearless in the face of their enemies, convinced that Messiah Jesus had risen from the dead and would return within their lifetimes§ to reestablish the kingdom of Israel and the reign of God over all the earth. The stirring conclusion to part II of Handel's *Messiah* could have been the Nazarene anthem: "The kingdom of this world is become the king-

---

*As evidenced by Jesus quoting Isaiah during his protest in the temple: "It is written, 'My house shall be called a house of prayer'; but you are making it a den of robbers" (Matthew 21:13).

†The word "messiah" (Hebrew, *mashiah*) literally means "anointed one." The term was applied to all the kings of Israel, who were anointed with holy oil by the high priest at the time of "coronation."

§See Matthew 24:34—"Truly I tell you, this generation will not pass away until all these things have taken place."

dom of the Lord and of his Christ; and he shall reign forever and ever." It was the power of this strong belief that imbued the entire Nazarene community with a boldness of conviction that electrified those who heard them preach and stirred the hearts of those to whom their teacher had ministered—the poor, the disabled, and the outcast—and gave them a hope that neither the corrupt leadership of the Sadducees nor the pagan Roman government could offer.

THE EVANGEL

It was the proclamation of Jesus's resurrection and his imminent Parousia that the Nazarenes called the "Good News" of Jesus Christ. The word "gospel" is the English translation of the Greek word *evangel,* which literally means "good news," and from which the term "evangelist"—literally, "a proclaimer of the good news"—is derived. It was the power of that Good News—of life over death, of good over evil—that caused the Nazarene party to grow by leaps and bounds in Jerusalem, in Judea, in Galilee, and soon in the Gentile world as well. As Hugh Schonfield notes, "... for a great many Jews, among them members of all the eschatological groups, the Nazorean Party must have had convictions with which they could readily identify. It must have incorporated a great deal of their ideology."[11] The book of Acts likely does not exaggerate very much when it describes the result of the outpouring of the Holy Spirit on Pentecost:

> [A]nd that day about three thousand persons were added. They devoted themselves to the apostles' teaching and fellowship, to the breaking of bread and the prayers. Awe came upon everyone . . . (Acts 2:41–43)

Under the leadership of Jesus's brother, James, the Nazarenes carried out an amazingly energetic evangelistic enterprise which rapidly radiated out from its central base in Jerusalem. The Nazarenes proclaimed the evangel in the synagogues, marketplaces, and even in the temple itself. In the eyes of the Jewish leaders (the party of the Sadducees), the

Nazarenes were just another messianic sect, of which there were many offering a cure for the nation's political ills. While Jesus was still alive, it was the political aspects of his message that attracted members of the radical militant party of the Zealots to his circle of followers. The apostle Simon, mistakenly called Simon Zealotes in many English translations of the New Testament, was correctly Simon "the Zealot." It is quite possible that Jesus's message was far more political than the gospel writers (writing mainly for, and trying to appease, a Roman audience) allowed us to know. At the very least, Jesus's message also captured the imagination of those with revolutionary political aims.

There is increasing recognition among scholars today that Jesus's preaching of the imminent arrival of God's kingdom may not have been as purely otherworldly as is commonly supposed. In addition to the presence of a Zealot among the twelve, there is also the curious story of Peter's being armed with a sword in the Garden of Gethsemane, where, at least according to John's gospel, that sword was put to expert use in cutting off the ear of the high priest's servant, Malchus (John 18:10). One of the first scholars to purport that Jesus's mission was political, and even militaristic, in nature was Robert Eisler in the 1920s,* followed later by British scholar S. G. F. Brandon. Hindsight has shown that Eisler went quite a bit overboard in stressing the militancy he believed to be present in Jesus's ministry, but one of his main conclusions remains valid:

> [T]he announcement of the resurrection was originally disseminated among the people by the Jewish Christians in connection with a purely political message and with a distinctly political aim. The resurrection of Jesus was originally preached, not to a circle of mystics . . . The Jewish partisans of Jesus preached to the people the certainty of the impending "liberation from bondage"; nor did they mean, like Paul, liberation from the bondage of sin and wicked spirits, but quite literally liberation from the yoke of their well-known worldly oppressors.

---

*Not to be confused with the modern Dead Sea Scrolls scholar, Robert Eisenman, who has adopted Eisler's approach.

Jesus was to return and liberate Israel from bondage in no other sense than King Arthur was believed by the Welsh of the Middle Ages to return to free his people from their Saxon and Norman oppressors.[12]

That Eisler's main thesis was correct is borne out by the account of Jesus's ascension in the book of Acts, which clearly shows that the apostles did indeed think of Jesus's mission in political terms:

> After his suffering he presented himself alive to them by many convincing proofs, appearing to them during forty days and speaking about the kingdom of God. While staying with them, he ordered them not to leave Jerusalem, but to wait there for the promise of the Father. . . .
>
> So when they had come together, they asked him, "Lord, *is this the time when you will restore the kingdom to Israel?*" He replied, "It is not for you to know the times or periods that the Father has set . . ." (Acts 1:3–9)

While the historical accuracy of Acts has been widely called into question in modern times, it is safe to say that, at the very least, this passage gives an authentic sense of the expectation of the apostles following Jesus's crucifixion, and comports well with Eisler's thesis that their expectation (if not Jesus's expectation) was largely of a political nature.

Eisler's ideas were later taken up by the controversial British Scholar, S. G. F. Brandon, most notably in two major works, *The Fall of Jerusalem and the Christian Church* (1951) and *Jesus and the Zealots* (1967). Brandon convincingly demonstrates that, at the least, Jesus would have had sympathy for the concerns of the Zealot party. While it is well known among scholars that the authors of the gospels and the book of Acts went to great lengths to publicly present the Christian movement as not being at all at odds with Rome, when one reads between the lines it quickly becomes clear that this was an expedient whitewashing of the actual state of affairs. A snippet of Brandon at this point will serve to demonstrate this. Here he speaks of King Herod Agrippa (who was half-Jewish) and his concerns for his homeland at the beginning of his reign in the year 39:

If Agrippa . . . was intent on providing for the future well-being of Israel, any factors within the state that were likely to exacerbate relations with the Romans would be marked for suppression. Now, since there is reason for thinking that the Messianic hopes of the Christians fomented trouble in both Rome and Alexandria during the reign of Claudius, it is understandable that Agrippa should have sought to deal with the source of the movement in his own kingdom. That he should have begun by proceeding against James [the son of Zebedee] and Peter is surely significant [James was the first apostle to be executed, Peter was the first to be imprisoned, see Acts 12]; for both had been members of the inner circle of Jesus's disciples and both were characterized as men disposed to energetic action. The execution of James by the sword suggests the penalty for a political offence, since stoning was the mode of punishment for those guilty on a capital charge against the religious law. . . .

That Agrippa should have singled out the Christians . . . for suppression on the grounds of their being dangerous to the maintenance of good Romano-Jewish relations, is remarkable in view of the fact that no action against the Zealots is recorded. The most probable reason that suggests itself for this distinction could be of considerable significance for our assessment of the relation between the Zealots and the Jewish Christians. . . . [I]t is . . . likely that much had been heard of their Parousia [second coming] hopes . . . and that the knowledge of it led Agrippa to regard those leaders who had been most vociferous as the most politically dangerous in his kingdom. The selection of James, the son of Zebedee, as the first victim would suggest that he had distinguished himself in some form of energetic advocacy of the Messiahship of Jesus, and such action recalls the violent disposition attributed to him in the Gospel tradition, together with his brother John, and their sobriquet of "Sons of thunder."*
That Peter should also have been regarded as politically dangerous is

---

*The Greek term *boanerges* (sons of thunder) may derive from the Aramaic *bene regesh*, which literally means "sons of rage."

not surprising in view of the strong and impetuous nature that finds expression in the gospels and Acts . . .[13]

While most scholars today, especially Christian scholars, doubt that there was any militancy in Jesus's mission, we have the testimony of the gospels themselves that Jesus was not beyond resorting to violent, indeed *terrorist* tactics; he overturned the money changers' tables and wielded a whip in public protest in the temple over the abuses of the temple's sacrificial system, a most serious protest demonstration, and one with huge political import. Yet, one of the few universally accepted findings of current historical Jesus research is that it was this public, violent protest that directly led to Jesus's arrest. Equally clear is that, after his execution, Jesus's message was spread entirely by peaceful means, means which proved to be the most successful religious enterprise ever accomplished in the history of the world. Unfortunately, in the next three- to four hundred years, as the Church gained rapid and unexpected political power—and quickly wielded it—these peaceful beginnings did not last.

Of one thing there is no doubt: It was the belief in Jesus's resurrection from the dead that formed the heart of the Christian proclamation of the evangel. History abounds with stories of self-proclaimed messiahs and saviors whose death was the end of their vision, and whose names are merely a footnote in the historical records. In the case of Jesus, however, his death was not the end, but a new beginning. Within three days of his crucifixion some of Jesus's disciples were making the bold claim that their Messiah had been raised from the dead and had appeared to them. Although the disciples had headed for the hills immediately after Jesus's arrest in fear for their lives, following the resurrection appearances they fearlessly proclaimed the Good News of Christ's resurrection to anyone who would listen, and refused to recant even when severely tortured and threatened with death. As is well known, many early Christians died an unimaginably gruesome martyr's death—eaten alive by wild animals as public sport or burned as human torches to light Nero's palace grounds. What turned the terrified disciples into fearless martyrs? There is little doubt that it can be attributed entirely to their unwavering conviction of Jesus's resurrection from the dead.

To Jesus's thoroughly Jewish followers, his execution as a criminal on a Roman cross was the most shameful death imaginable. The legal prohibition against coming into contact with blood—one of the core elements of the Torah—made Jesus's death an abomination in Jewish eyes; if there had been no resurrection, Jesus's shameful death would have forever marked his claim of being the Messiah as fraudulent. But three days after his blood-soaked death, his disciples became convinced beyond any shadow of a doubt. After Jesus's shocking announcement at Caesarea Philippi that the goal of his mission was to go to Jerusalem at Passover to suffer and die (Mark 8:27), many of his disciples had begun to seriously doubt that Jesus was indeed the long-awaited Messiah—which is likely what spurred Judas to betray Jesus; he and the other disciples were starting to think that Jesus may have gone off the deep end and had a death wish. But immediately after Jesus's bloody death the disciples became filled with such conviction that within their own generation the fervor of their testimony had produced Christian communities in every major city of the Roman Empire, an incredible feat that historically has been greatly underappreciated. It was the depth of their conviction in Jesus's resurrection and his messiahship—which even the most skeptical could clearly see in the faces of the Nazarenes as they faced torture and death—that produced many a convert to the nascent movement.

Equally persuasive was the kind of life the Nazarenes lived. Their everyday lives in the workplace, in the synagogue, and in the community—the way in which their fellow Jews knew them best—displayed an enviable simplicity, peace, and joy that has been a precious and rare commodity throughout human history. The eminent scholar of world religions, Huston Smith, in his classic, *The World's Religions* (originally called *The Religions of Man*), memorably identified "two qualities in which their lives abounded":

The first of these was mutual regard. One of the earliest observations about Christians that we have by an outsider is, "See how these Christians love one another." Integral to this mutual regard was a total absence of social barriers; it was a "discipleship of equals," as one New Testament scholar [Elizabeth Schüssler Fiorenza] puts it. Here were men and women who not only said that everyone was equal in the sight of God, but lived as though they meant it. The conventional barriers of race, gender, and status meant nothing to them, for in Christ there was neither Jew nor Gentile, male nor female, slave nor free.

Smith then identifies the second quality that abounded in their lives— joy:

Jesus once told his followers that his teachings were to the end "that my joy may be in you, and that your joy may be complete" (John 15:11), and to a remarkable degree that object appears to have been realized. Outsiders found this baffling. These scattered Christians were not numerous. They were not wealthy or powerful. If anything, they faced more adversity than the average man or woman. Yet, in the midst of their trials, they had laid hold of an inner peace that found expression in a joy that seemed exuberant. Perhaps radiant would be a better word. Radiance is hardly the word used to characterize the average religious life, but none other fits as well the life of those early Christians.[14]

These two qualities that Smith describes—mutual regard and joy—will become a kind of leitmotif for the story of the Nazarenes and their descendants as it unfolds in the rest of this book.

Under the leadership of Jesus's brother James, the Nazarenes boldly proclaimed the evangel throughout Judea, Samaria, and Galilee; and, after James's death and the fall of Jerusalem, in the Transjordanian regions as well. With the aid of the new convert Paul, this message, in an altered form, would be taken to the farthest reaches of the Roman world. While the story of the Gentile enterprise headed by Paul has been told many times, it is the largely unknown missionary activity of the Nazarenes and their descendants, the Ebionites and the Elkesaites, which will be the focus of the rest of this book.

PART TWO

The History of Jewish Christianity

4

THE CALIPHATE BEGINS
James and the Jerusalem Church

*Observe the greatest caution, that you believe no teacher
unless he brings from Jerusalem the testimonial of James
the Lord's brother, or of whosoever may come after him.*

ST. PETER PREACHING AT TRIPOLIS,
PSEUDO-CLEMENTINE "RECOGNITIONS" (4.35)

There is at least enough truth in the words attributed to St. Peter in the Jewish Christian text known as the *Pseudo-Clementine* "Recognitions," apocryphal though they may be, to show that in its earliest days the Christian community looked to the mother church in Jerusalem and its "bishop,"* James, as the final authority in matters of doctrine and polity. We will soon examine more of this remarkable document associated with the Jewish Christian sect known as the Ebionites. The authenticity of the assertion of James's authority contained in the above citation is confirmed by several key passages in the book of Acts, as well as in Paul's letter to the Galatians.[1]

At first James and the disciples in Jerusalem engaged in an evangelistic mission solely to their fellow Jews, since this was Jesus's directive

---

*Greek *episkopos,* literally "overseer."

to them, as recorded in the Gospel of Matthew: "Go nowhere among the Gentiles, and enter no town of the Samaritans, but go rather to the lost sheep of Israel" (Matt. 10:5–6). There is also a fascinating quote attributed to Jesus, which Clement of Alexandria preserved from an apocryphal text called the *Preaching of Peter:* "If anyone of Israel wishes to repent, and by my name to believe in God, his sins shall be forgiven him. *After twelve years* go forth into the world, that no one may say, 'We have not heard'" (emphasis added).[2] While this apocryphal saying may be falsely attributed to Jesus, it does accurately reflect that there came a point in time when some of the apostles began to take the gospel beyond Judea, as indicated in Jesus's apostolic commission in Acts. The wording here reveals the geographically progressive nature of the Nazarene mission: "You will be my witnesses in Jerusalem, in all of Judea and Samaria, and to the ends of the earth" (Acts 1: 8).

But, in fact, for some time James and the apostles in Jerusalem did not make any concerted effort to reach either Jew or Gentile outside of Palestine. The explosive success of their mission in Judea (as recorded in the second and third chapters of Acts) must have kept them quite busy for a number of years, and soon necessitated a more formal structure and organization for their community. We have evidence of what precipitated that more formal structuring of the community in Acts 6, which also provides evidence that the initial missionary activity was, indeed, largely confined to the environs of Jerusalem:

Now during those days, when the disciples were increasing in number, the Hellenists [foreign-born Jewish Christians] complained against the Hebrews [native Palestinian Jewish Christians] because their widows were being neglected in the daily distribution of food. And the twelve called together the whole community of the disciples and said, "It is not right that we should neglect the word of God in order to wait on tables. Therefore, friends, select from among yourselves seven men of good standing, full of the Spirit and wisdom, whom we may appoint to this task, while we, for our part, will devote ourselves to prayer and to serving the word." What they said pleased the whole community, and they chose Stephen, a man full of faith and the Holy Spirit, together with Philip, Prochorus, Nicanor, Timon, Parmenas, and Niclaus, a proselyte of Antioch. They had these men stand before the apostles, who prayed and laid their hands on them.

The word of God continued to spread; the number of disciples increased greatly in Jerusalem, and a great many of the priests became obedient to the faith. (Acts 6:1–7)

These seven appointed men were the first deacons (from the Greek *diakonos,* one who serves) of the church, whose main role was originally to see to the distribution of alms. This was a custom of the synagogue, where these servers were called *parnasim.* This ordering of roles among the disciples actually marked the establishment of a Nazarene synagogue in Jerusalem, which only much later came to be called the Jerusalem "Church." But the Jerusalem Church was indeed a synagogue. In the Septuagint (the Greek translation of the Hebrew Bible), two synonymous terms are used for the assembled people of God: "synagogue" (*synagoge*) and "assembly" (*ekklesia*). It was the latter term that later Christians came to use for what we today call a "church." Ekklesia came into Latin as *ecclesia* (root of the word "ecclesiastical"), and into Spanish as *iglesia*. Perhaps a more accurate designation for the earliest Christian community, which avoids the anachronistic Christian nomenclature of "church," would be to call it the Nazarene or Jerusalem Yachad. The Hebrew word yachad literally means "root," and is commonly used to refer to a community, or brotherhood. Yachad is actually the term that the Essenes use most often in sectarian writings for their community.

The Nazarene synagogue, or Yachad, was just one of numerous synagogues in Jerusalem established for different nationalities of Jews (much like the modern Orthodox Church is divided into Russian Orthodox, Greek Orthodox, Syrian Orthodox, and so on), and attracted many followers. As Hugh Schonfield notes:

From its inception the [Nazarene] party embraced many foreign-born Jews. They had enclaves in Jerusalem where those from different areas of the Empire could find themselves at home among fellow countrymen, and where they had their own synagogues in which they could meet. There was one for the North Africans—those from Libya, Cyrenaica, and Alexandria; and another for the Asiatics—those from Lydia, Pamphylia, and Cilicia (Acts 6:9); and similarly those from other regions. They were lumped together as Hellenists by the native-born Jews because they largely spoke Greek, and in the [Nazarene] party, which a number of them had joined, there began to show itself a disposition to discriminate against them in daily distribution of food. Native Jews should first be served, and the foreigners should have what was left over.[3]

Synagogues were also established for those who worked at particular trades, as well as for those who followed particular "ways," or varieties of worship and belief. We know from Acts that another designation for the earliest Jewish Christian community was "the Way of Jesus" (Acts 9:2, 19:23, 22:4). It is well known that any group of Jews who comprised ten *batlanim*, or "men of leisure," could form a synagogue; no official building was required. Since the discovery of an important, early Jewish Christian document called the *Didache* (The Teaching, short for The Teaching of the Twelve Apostles), a manual for proper ethical conduct and worship practice dating from the early second century, we know that many elements of the earliest Christian liturgy were derived from the form of worship used in first-century synagogues.

The Nazarene synagogue in Jerusalem was likely located near other synagogues devoted to particular ways, based on the subsequent passage in Acts 6:

Stephen, full of grace and power, did great wonders and signs among the people. Then some of those who belonged to the synagogue of the Freedmen (as it was called), Cyrenians, Alexandrians, and others of those from Cilicia and Asia stood up and argued with Stephen. But they could not withstand the wisdom and Spirit with which he spoke. (Acts 6:8–10)

The apostle Paul was likely a member of the synagogue of the Cilicians, as his original name prior to his conversion to the Way of Jesus was Saul of Tarsus. Tarsus was located in the Roman province of Cilicia in Asia Minor (modern-day Turkey). Stephen's fierce debate with these other Jews would end up with his being hauled before the Sanhedrin and stoned for blasphemy, an execution that Paul (still Saul at this time, prior to his conversion) aided and abetted: "Then they dragged him out of the city and began to stone him; and the witnesses laid their coats at the feet of a young man named Saul" (Acts 7:58). Thus Stephen became the first Christian martyr.

It was the outspokenness of disciples like James the son of Zebedee, Peter, and Stephen that would result in the persecution of followers of the Way of Jesus, a persecution that was greatly inflamed by Paul. Acts goes on to tell us:

> And Saul approved of their killing him. That day a severe persecution began against the church in Jerusalem, and all except the apostles were scattered throughout the countryside of Judea and Samaria. . . . Saul was ravaging the church by entering house after house; dragging off both men and women, he committed them to prison. (Acts 8:1–3)

And in the next chapter we are told:

> Meanwhile, Saul, still breathing threats and murder against the disciples of the Lord, went to the high priest and asked him for letters to the synagogues at Damascus, so that if he found any that belonged to the Way, men or women, he might bring them, bound, to Jerusalem. (Acts 9:1–2)

It is, of course, while on the road to Damascus that Paul encounters the risen Christ and has his famous conversion experience, resulting in his becoming a follower of the Way of Jesus. While Luke, the author of Acts, is quite candid in his account of Paul's persecution of the Nazarenes, we need to keep in mind that it is now widely recognized by scholars that

Luke goes to great lengths to harmonize the very real friction that existed between Paul and the Jerusalem Church, and there is likely much more that we are not told. The document known as the *Pseudo-Clementine* "Recognitions," associated with the Ebionites, which some scholars have called the "Nazarene Acts," tells us far more about Paul's violence against the Nazarenes than what Luke is willing to tell.

THE *PSEUDO-CLEMENTINES*

The term "pseudo" was applied to this collection of writings because of their purportedly false attribution to the church father, Clement of Rome (not to be confused with the better-known Clement of Alexandria). This Clement was bishop of Rome at the end of the first century and the *Pseudo-Clementines* purport to tell his story. The majority of scholars today consider the *Pseudo-Clementines,* at least in their final form, to be no earlier than the fourth century; but a number of scholars believe that underlying traditions contained within them are much older, and parts of it may go back to the late second century.[4] This is supported by the fact that the collection is an anthology of smaller works. There are two main components of the *Pseudo-Clementines:* the "Homilies" and the "Recognitions." These are both comprised of even smaller works that scholars have come to call the "Ascents of James," the "Kerygmata Petrou" (The Proclamation of Peter), and the "Epistula Petri" (The Epistle of Peter).

The "Ascents of James," which is part of the "Recognitions," takes its name from a startling incident in which James ascends the steps of the temple to engage in a public debate about whether or not Jesus is the Messiah. The debate that James enters into is more of a dispute, started by Peter and Clement with the high priest Caiaphas and other opponents of Jesus outside the temple. With great rhetoric James is on the verge of persuading the crowd of Jews to be baptized when someone mysteriously referred to only as "a certain hostile man" and an "enemy" enters the temple, creates an uproar, and physically accosts James, throwing him down from the top of the steps. One of the most shocking things about the "Ascents of James" is that it is quite obvious that this unnamed persecutor is none other than Saul (Paul, prior to his conversion) engaging in one of his well-known acts of violence against those who proclaimed Jesus to be the Messiah. The "Ascents of James" gives us a chilling insight into the level of Saul's hatred for the Nazarenes:

> When the matter was at the point that they would come and be baptized, a certain hostile man, entering the temple at that time with a few men, began to shout and say, "What are you doing, O men of Israel? Why are you so easily led away? Why are you led headlong by men who are most miserable and deceived by a magician?" While he was saying these things and adding more to them, and as he was overcome by James the bishop, he began to incite the people and raise dissensions, so that the people could not hear those things which were being said. Therefore he began to disturb everything by shouts, and to undo those things, which had been arranged with much labor. At the same time he accused the priests and enflamed them by revilings and reproaches, and like a madman incited everyone to murder, saying, "What are you doing? Why are you stopping? Oh sluggish and idle ones, why do we not lay our hands on them and dismember them all?" And when he had said these things, seizing a brand from the altar he began to murder. Others also, when they saw him, were carried away by a similar madness. There was loud shouting by all, the murderers and the murdered alike. Much blood flowed. There was a confused flight, during which that hostile man attacked James, and threw him down headlong from the top of the steps. As he believed him to be dead, he was not concerned to beat him further. (*Pseudo-Clementine* "Recognitions," 1.70) [5]

James does not die, however, but recovers from his wounds and subsequently sends Peter to spy on Paul and send back regular reports on his activities! Paul then attempts to arrest Peter, pursuing him as far as Damascus, and it may even have been while in pursuit of Peter that he had his dramatic encounter with the risen Christ, resulting in his sudden conversion.

Those scholars who believe the "Ascents" to be a late writing see the above passage as a legendary embellishment of the accounts of Paul's violent persecutions in Acts. It is certainly not impossible, however, that the "Ascents" records actual history, and while most scholars see the accounts in the *Pseudo-Clementine* "Recognitions" as being dependent on the gospels and Acts, the gospels and Acts may have gotten some of their information from the earliest versions of "Recognitions," particularly the "Ascents of James." Dr. Robert E. Van Voorst, who has done the most in-depth recent research into the "Ascents of James," concurs with a majority of scholars that the work "was written in Pella between 150–200 in a Jewish Christian community that saw itself as the heir of the earliest church in Jerusalem."[6] This Jewish Christian community is the one known as the Ebionites, who will be discussed in detail in a later chapter. Pella was a town in Transjordan (modern-day Jordan) to which, according to a number of ancient sources, the Nazarenes fled prior to the Jewish War with Rome, and it is probable that the *Pseudo-Clementines* are their memoirs. It was during their sojourn in Pella that the Nazarenes' beliefs and practices changed enough to make it preferable to then call them Ebionites, to distinguish them from their Judean ancestors, the Nazarenes.

The intriguing story of Paul's attack on James is but one of many examples of a virulent anti-Paulinism that pervades the *Pseudo-Clementines*. In light of Paul's track record, such an attitude on the part of the Jewish Christian community is certainly understandable. We know from Paul's own letters that he had indeed been a violent persecutor of the Christian community prior to his conversion. In light of Luke's well-known tendency to put everything in the best possible light in Acts, and considering Paul's well-known temper and hatred for the early Christians, it is certainly not improbable that Paul did more than just hold the cloaks of the perpetrators at the stoning of Stephen. Is it possible that the "Ascents of James" contains an actual historical account of a violent attack that Paul made on James? In view of the way Paul is portrayed in Acts, this is not at all unlikely; in fact, it is quite plausible. And why would the early Jewish Christians completely make up such a story? Acts shows just how wary the apostles were of Paul after his conversion, when he returns to Jerusalem and attempts to join the Yachad: "When he had come to

Jerusalem, he attempted to join the disciples; and they were afraid of him . . ." (Acts 9:26).

There are even a few scholars, most notably Dr. Robert Eisenman, who believe that the account of the stoning of Stephen in Acts is an intentional whitewashing of the account of Paul's attack upon James. While Eisenman's controversial theories have not won over many scholars, it should be noted that the eminent historian of Jewish Christianity, Hans-Joachim Schoeps, came to the same conclusion long before Eisenman did. Schoeps notes that the speech James makes prior to being attacked by Paul is remarkably similar to the speech made by Stephen prior to his stoning:

> [T]he . . . speech parallels remarkably Stephen's speech in Acts 7. . . . [The] central section of Stephen's speech, which is doctrinally unique both in the New Testament and in the literature of the ancient church, has, as far as I know, only a single parallel in terms of content, viz., this passage of the *Recognitions* which we have attributed to the Ebionite Acts. This gives pause for thought! . . .
>
> As is well known, the Lucan Acts makes the narrative of Stephen's martyrdom the occasion for the entrance of Saul . . . While 7:58 ascribes to Saul a significant part in the stoning of Stephen and 8:1 (see also 22:20) passes over the details of his role with the statement, "Saul consented to his death," the Ebionite Acts explicitly make Paul responsible for the fall of [James] from the temple step. . . .
>
> According to the Ebionite Acts, the event proved much more incriminating for Paul than Luke allows us to see, inasmuch as Paul both originated and executed a plot to murder the head of the Church, James the Brother of Jesus. In both accounts, however, it is through Paul that a persecution is loosed against the primitive Church.[7]

While this conjecture on the part of Schoeps and Eisenman may seem shocking to many Christians who think of Paul as a great saint, we need to recognize that Paul's violent acts are starkly attested to by the author of the book of Acts (who was Paul's staunch ally). The early Jewish Christian sect known as the Ebionites may have had their own unique (and perhaps even earlier) book of Acts that presented their early apostolic history from the perspective of Jewish Christianity, as opposed to the canonical book of Acts that represents the viewpoint of Gentile Christianity. Many scholars believe that the "Ebionite Acts," as Schoeps calls it, is preserved in various sections of the *Pseudo-Clementines*. The fourth-century church father, Bishop Epiphanius of Salamis, railed against the Jewish Christian sect of the Ebionites for their use of this heretical writing:

> They say that there are other Acts of apostles; and these contain much utterly impious material, with which they deliberately arm themselves against the truth. They prescribe certain degrees and directions in the "Degrees of James," if you please, as though he discoursed against the temple and sacrifices, and the fire on the altar— and much else that is full of nonsense. Nor are they ashamed to accuse Paul here with certain false inventions of their false apostles' villainy and imposture.[8]

The part of the *Pseudo-Clementines* known as the "Epistula Petri" (Epistle of Peter, or Epistle of Peter to James) serves as an introduction to the "Kerygmata Petrou" (Proclamation of Peter). Here, veiled references are again made to Paul, who is referred to as the "hostile man" who "teaches lawless doctrine." It is quite obvious to all scholars that the role played in this writing by a character called "Simon Magus" is a veiled allusion to Paul (Simon Magus appears in Acts 8:9–24 as a sorcerer who tries to buy the power of the Holy Spirit from Peter and John). Also striking in the "Epistula Petri" is that Peter addresses this letter to: "James, *the lord and bishop* of the holy Church." In this fascinating missive (written at a time when Paul, at least according to the accounts in Acts and Galatians, had been accepted by the Nazarenes and had commenced his mission to the Gentiles), Peter expresses reservations to James about Paul's distortion of their teaching:

> For some from among the Gentiles have rejected my lawful preaching and have preferred a lawless and absurd doctrine of the man

who is my enemy. And indeed some have attempted, whilst I am still alive, to distort my words by interpretations of many sorts, as if I taught the dissolution of the law . . . But that may God forbid! For to do such a thing means to act contrary to the law of God, which was made known by Moses and was confirmed by our Lord in its everlasting continuance. For he said, "The heaven and the earth will pass away, but one jot or one tittle shall not pass away from the law." (Letter of Peter to James, 2.3–5)[9]

If the animosity between Peter and Paul portrayed in this apocryphal letter is historically true, it is interesting to speculate who the author of the canonical 2 Peter* may be accusing, as the words of 2 Peter certainly echo the "Epistula Petri":

But false prophets arose among the people . . . many will follow their licentious ways, and because of these teachers the way of truth will be maligned. (2 Peter 2:1–2)

For they speak bombastic nonsense, and with licentious desires of the flesh they entice people who have just escaped from those who live in error [the Gentiles]. They promise them freedom, but they themselves are slaves of corruption . . . For if, after they have escaped the defilements of the world through the knowledge of the Lord and Savior Jesus Christ, they are again entangled in them and overpowered . . . it would have been better for them never to have known the way of righteousness than, after knowing it, to *turn back from the holy commandment that was passed on to them.* (2 Peter 2:18–21)

These last words may be a reference to Paul's conversion ("it would have been better for them never to have known the Way"), and the fact that the Nazarenes and Ebionites saw Paul as turning "back from the holy

---

*2 Peter is thought by most scholars to be one of the latest writings in the New Testament and thus could not have been written by Peter, but by a later disciple of Peter.

commandment" (the law). The accusation of "enticing people who have just escaped from those who live in error" could very well refer to Paul's teaching of a law-free gospel to the Gentile converts. These words certainly seem to echo the sentiments expressed against Paul in the "Epistula Petri," and, as most scholars believe 2 Peter is one of the very latest of the New Testament writings (some putting it as late as 130–150 CE), it would not be far removed in time from the "Epistula Petri," which could well be as early as mid-second century.

The section of the *Pseudo-Clementines* known as the "Recognitions" goes even further in its attack on Paul. The argument is made that Paul could not have received a revelation from Jesus because his teaching does not agree with that of James and Peter; and it is further argued that Paul cannot be considered an apostle because he is not one of the twelve (4.35). Peter is upheld as the *true* apostle to the Gentiles, who gives them the genuine (law-based) gospel. Books 4–6 of "Recognitions" tell of a missionary journey to Tripolis undertaken by Peter. Preaching at Tripolis, Peter warns his audience to beware of false apostles who might come after him: ". . . believe no teacher, unless he brings from Jerusalem the testimonial of James, the Lord's brother . . ." (4.35). Peter refers to James as "our James" and "James the bishop" (1.66). He is also called the "chief of the bishops" and "archbishop" (1.68). Clement even addresses James as "my lord James" (3.74). It is quite obvious that the Jewish Christian community that produced the *Pseudo-Clementines* revered James and Peter for their upholding of the Torah, and despised Paul for his attempts to do away with the Torah. While much in these apocryphal writings may be exaggerated, at the very least the *Pseudo-Clementines* give us a startling and valuable insight into how one group of second-century Jewish Christians, a group that could, in fact, claim legitimate descent from the Jerusalem Church, looked back upon their history.

DISPERSAL AND GROWTH

The increasingly violent attacks on the Nazarenes, incited by Paul, resulted in the temporary dispersal of the community. If the stoning of

Stephen and the attack upon James are not, in fact, variations of the same event, as Schoeps and Eisenman have theorized, it is likely that Paul's attack on James on the steps of the Temple followed very soon after the stoning of Stephen. Whatever the actual history, it is quite certain, as the aforementioned Acts 8 tells us, that a severe persecution led by Paul immediately ensued: "That day a severe persecution began against the church in Jerusalem, and all *except the apostles* were scattered throughout the countryside of Judea and Samaria. . . . Saul was ravaging the Church by entering house after house; dragging off both men and women, he committed them to prison." If Eisenman and Schoeps are correct in correlating the attacks on Stephen and James, perhaps "that day" was the day of Paul's attack on James. In any event, Acts is correct that many of the Nazarenes were either imprisoned or fled, with a striking exception: "all except the apostles." This statement has long puzzled scholars, and many have seen it as simply a reverential literary turn, perhaps implying God's divine protection of the apostles. But there is another, more logical explanation if we look at what Acts says about the dissension between the Hebrews and the Hellenists. Stephen was a Hellenist, and in light of his speech it would seem that the Hellenist Nazarenes were more outspoken against the Torah and Jewish tradition than were the Hebrew Nazarenes, as might be expected. As we have seen, the Hebrew Nazarenes were held in high esteem by their fellow Jews, while Hellenistic Jews were always looked at with some suspicion by native Judeans. So it is not unlikely that the earliest persecution of the Nazarenes was focused on the more maverick Hellenistic foreigners who had joined the Way, while the more loyal, native Hebrews were spared. Hugh Schonfield gives the following well-reasoned summary:[*]

> The sequence of events appears to have begun with argument in the Hellenist synagogues, where Hellenist Nazoreans like Stephen were active propagandists. These Nazoreans favored Essene views, and in

---

[*]Schonfield also notes that it was during this persecution that a sect known today as the Mandaeans, who still exist in Iraq, also were exiled. We shall say more about the Mandaeans later.

the heat of debate used intemperate and inflammatory language about the hierarchy and Temple cult. Congregants, among them Saul of Tarsus, hailed Stephen before the Sanhedrin, where his hostile outspokenness assured his condemnation. Following this, Saul and his associates went on the rampage. They did not attack the Nazorean Pharisees or the loyalist apostles of Jesus, but those on the sectarian fringe who appeared to be lending themselves to disruptive propaganda.[10]

The Hellenists certainly did not remain silent, even after their persecution and dispersal: "Now those who were scattered went from place to place, proclaiming the word" (Acts 8:4). As Acts goes on to relate, many new converts were made among the provincial Jews in Samaria, Galilee, and in the Judean countryside. Philip made many converts among the Samaritans, and soon Peter and John were also sent to Samaria, most likely to check up on how well the teaching of the Hellenists conformed to Jewish doctrine; this is a pattern that would be repeated many times as Paul's Gentile enterprise took off. It is certainly not surprising that after the persecution's ringleader joined the persecuted, Acts relates that ". . . the church throughout Judea, Galilee, and Samaria had peace and was built up" (Acts 9:31).

Some of the Hellenist Nazarenes even began to venture farther than the Palestinian provinces: "Now those who were scattered because of the persecution . . . traveled as far as Phoenicia, Cyprus, and Antioch, *and they spoke the word to no one except the Jews*" (Acts 11:19, emphasis mine). It is interesting that Acts affirms that the first evangelists to go outside of Palestine were indeed restricting their mission to the Jews. But we are also told that some converts from Cyprus and Cyrene now began evangelizing Gentiles at Antioch, and Antioch would become the first mixed Jewish-Gentile Nazarene community. And as Acts famously tells us, ". . . it was in Antioch that the disciples were first called 'Christians'" (Acts 11:26). Since the word *christos* is the Greek translation of the Hebrew Messiah, the word "Christian" literally means a "Messianist," and this is what the Nazarenes were: followers of one particular Jewish "Way" that held that their rabbi was the Messiah of Israel.

Word soon reached Jerusalem of the rapid growth in the number of Gentile Christians, and James and the Jerusalem Yachad sent one of the Hellenists, a Levite by the name of Joseph, to investigate the situation. In keeping with what would seem to be a tradition among the Nazarenes of changing one's name when joining the Way, the apostles gave Joseph the name Barnabas (Acts 4:36). For reasons unexplained, Barnabas recruited their former persecutor, Paul, to aid in the mission at Antioch, perhaps because of Paul's affinity with Gentiles, and perhaps also because of his great erudition. Few of the Nazarenes were highly educated, and Paul may have been seen by Hellenist Nazarenes as a natural spokesperson. The recruitment of Paul is, however, the key development that eventually leads to a parting of the ways between the Hebrew Nazarenes and Paul's Gentile Christians.

PERSECUTION AND CONSOLIDATION

The Nazarene Way had become so successful that soon the Roman civil authorities joined forces with the Jewish religious authorities to tame and subdue the more vocal of the Nazarene ringleaders, who continued to be seen by some as presenting an ongoing threat to Roman authority. The crucifixion of their rabbi had not resulted in the demise of this particular Way as expected; instead the movement surprisingly grew with the claims that their Messiah had risen from the dead and would soon return as the apocalyptic "Son of Man," as the prophet Daniel called the coming Messiah. In a further attempt to squelch the movement, King Herod Agrippa ordered that James, son of Zebedee, be put to the sword; and Peter was imprisoned but would miraculously escape, as recounted in Acts 12. The Church historian, Bishop Eusebius, relays a moving account of James's end, which he took from Clement of Alexandria:

> Referring to this James, Clement in *Outlines* Book VII tells an interesting story, on the strength of an authentic tradition. It appears that the man who brought him into court was so moved when he saw him testify that he confessed that he, too, was a Christian: So they

were both taken away together, and on the way he asked James to forgive him. James thought for a moment; then he said, "I wish you peace," and kissed him. So both were beheaded at the same time. (*Ecclesiastical History* 2.9)[11]

If it was not clear before, following the death of James it became even more imperative to have a more regimented structuring of the community in order to provide cohesiveness and authority for the followers of the increasingly scattered Nazarenes. Although more and more Gentiles were being added, the Nazarene Way, with its headquarters in Jerusalem, continued to be a thoroughly Jewish movement, and its more formal structuring continued to follow the synagogue model. This involved the establishment of satellite Nazarene synagogues, such as the famous one at Antioch that later drifted from its Jewish roots to become a more recognizable Christian Church.

There is no reason to doubt that the organization and polity of the Nazarene synagogues followed established precedent and included the appointment of officials for each synagogue, including a president (*nasi*), deacons, precentor (choir director), and teachers. In the case of the Nazarene synagogue at Jerusalem, James the Brother of Jesus was elected nasi (and would anachronistically be called "bishop" in later Church histories, such as those of Hegesippus and Eusebius). "The Epistle of Clement to James" in the *Pseudo-Clementine* "Recognitions" bears testimony to James's role as nasi and to the organizational structure in its opening salutation:

Clement to James, the lord and bishop of bishops, who governs the holy church of the Hebrews at Jerusalem and those, which, by the providence of God, have been well founded everywhere, together with the presbyters and deacons and all other brethren. Peace be with you always. (*Epistle of Clement to James* 1.1)[12]

Three officials in each synagogue formed a tribunal for judging any problems or conflicts over such things as finances, internal ethics, and the admission of proselytes. This tribunal reported to Jerusalem, where more serious cases were referred. The supreme tribunal consisted of James, Peter, and John, the son of Zebedee. The twelve apostles (and their eventual replacements) were likely set up like the circle of twelve who, according to the the Dead Sea Scrolls, administered the Essene community at Qumran, each of the twelve representing one of the twelve tribes.

First-century synagogues also saw to the dispersal of itinerant teachers and to the collection of dues for maintaining the synagogue. This is firmly evidenced by Paul in Galatians 2, where he recounts his visit to Jerusalem to gain the approval of the Nazarene tribunal for his Gentile mission: ". . . and when James and Cephas and John, who were acknowledged pillars, recognized the grace that had been given to me, they gave to Barnabas and me the right hand of fellowship, agreeing that we should go to the Gentiles and they to the circumcised. They asked only one thing, that we remember the poor . . ." (Gal. 2:9–10). This marked the launch of an officially recognized mission to the Gentiles run by Paul under the supervision of the Jerusalem tribunal.

Albert Schweitzer pointed out the correlation between the structuring of the early church and the synagogue system a hundred years ago in his wonderful treatise, *The Mysticism of Paul the Apostle:*

> For the Christians of the churches in Asia Minor and Greece, the church at Jerusalem was an authority, in the same sense and to the same extent as the Sanhedrin was for the Synagogues of the Diaspora. The collection, which they made for it, was not so much a gift sent to the poor as a levy comparable with the Temple tax of the Jewish proselytes, which they paid to it.[13]

That the collection for the "poor" that Paul took up throughout his missionary journeys was indeed akin to the temple tax has been realized by a number of scholars today.[14] But it was the much underappreciated Jewish scholar, Dr. Hugh Schonfield, who, more than any Christian scholar, had a remarkable insight into the working of the

Jerusalem Church. He notes that the governing body of the Jerusalem Church was not just akin to the Sanhedrin, but was, in fact, an "opposition Sanhedrin." Schonfield was able to bring such insights because he was looking at the historical records through Jewish eyes, and it is well worth hearing an extensive quote at this point from what may be his magnum opus, *Those Incredible Christians:*

> Prior to the war it is clear from the Christian records that the Nazoreans had established in Jerusalem a Council for the government of all the followers of Jesus, which was in fact an opposition Sanhedrin . . . The Nazoreans saw themselves as loyal Israel which gave allegiance to Jesus as the rightful Jewish king. They were therefore justified, pending the return of Jesus to the throne, to create a government exercising supreme authority and jurisdiction over all believers at home and abroad. Thus the Council had a political as well as spiritual significance, being set up in express rejection of the governmental body which had taken action against Jesus . . . The appointment of James to the presidency had been in no small measure a political appointment, since he was of the blood royal and brother next in age of the absent monarch. This explains why he rather than Peter was chosen.[15]

Schonfield then goes on to explain the rationale behind the internal structuring:

> The ruling body consisted of seventy Elders. It is said that Jesus appointed these after the twelve Apostles; but in the actual Council it would seem that the twelve were part of the seventy, or at any rate also ranked as Elders, though they formed the inner cabinet. In the same way as the president of the Sanhedrin was the high priest, so James, according to tradition, was invested with the high priestly office, and had Peter and John as his deputies, the three constituting "the pillars" referred to by Paul in Galatians.[16]

That James served as the Nazarene high priest makes sense of a puzzling statement made about James by the fourth-century Bishop Epiphanius in his anti-heresy handbook, *The Panarion:*

> James, called the brother and apostle of the Lord, was made the first bishop immediately . . . I find further that he also functioned as a priest in the ancient priesthood. For this reason he was permitted to enter the Holy of Holies once a year, as scripture says the Law commanded the high priest. For many before me—Eusebius, Clement, and others—have reported this of him. He was allowed to wear the priestly mitre besides, as the trustworthy persons mentioned have testified in the same historical writings.[17]

Scholars have long puzzled over these statements by Epiphanius and other early historians, and generally disregard this as "Ebionite fantasy," but if Schonfield's reconstruction is correct, it is plausible that James would have worn priestly vestments. This also makes sense of a statement that Eusebius makes regarding a literal throne of James: "The throne of James—who was the first to receive from the Savior and His apostles the episcopacy of the Jerusalem Church . . . has been preserved to this day."[18] While this also seems incredible, Eusebius seems to be making a factual assertion of its existence in his day, and, in fact, the Armenian patriarchate in modern day Jerusalem still displays a symbolic representation of this ancient relic (see plate 31).[19] Schonfield gives this summary of the Nazarene administration:

> In the Acts we find the Nazorean Council acting exactly like the Sanhedrin. They send out officers to supervise new communities of believers, Peter and John to Samaria, Barnabas to Antioch. They dispatch, with the president's commission, a delegation to Antioch to investigate the terms of admission of Gentile converts, and when there is a dispute on this matter the case is referred back to Jerusalem for final decision, and James the president gives the judgment. The verdict is conveyed by letter by envoys of the Council, and is binding on all

Christian communities [Acts 15]. The interference with his work and teaching, which Paul so much resented, was action mandated to its official representatives by the Christian Sanhedrin in accordance with its supreme authority and in due performance of its obligations.[20]

In his letters Paul rails constantly against "false apostles" who try to undermine his work among the Gentiles, who call them back to obeying the Torah. Christian scholars have often derogatorily referred to these adversaries of Paul as "Judaizers." The best-known example of their running interference with Paul is the so-called Antioch incident described by Paul in Galatians 2, wherein James sends emissaries to investigate reports that Jewish Christians in Antioch are not eating kosher; it is a fascinating account that we will examine in the next chapter. As Schonfield bluntly comments on their activity: "This was no unauthorized action by Judaizers."[21]

It would seem that everything was in place both structurally and spiritually for a most successful evangelistic enterprise to Jews in Palestine and throughout the Roman Empire. But then things hit a snag.

THE GENTILE MISSION

A signal event soon happened that would have significant implications for the future of the Nazarene Way and for a new religion that would develop out of it, called "Christianity." The Nazarene synagogue at Antioch sent out missionaries with the purpose of reaching not only Hellenistic Jews, *but Gentiles as well.* Acts 10 records the well-known story of Peter converting the Gentile Cornelius, according Peter the honor of converting the first Gentile to the Way (that is, a Gentile who was not already a convert to Judaism). But it cannot be emphasized enough that it was the expectation of everyone to that point, including Peter, that Gentile converts to the Nazarene Way were becoming *Jews.* The synagogue at Antioch was, however, now bringing in many converts to the Nazarene Way who had not first been converts to Judaism.

There had always been Gentiles who were greatly attracted to Jewish teaching and wished to participate in Jewish religious life without taking the full step of becoming circumcised, and thus becoming full converts. These semi-converts, or Noahides were generally referred to as "God-fearers," and they were expected to adhere to a bare minimum of the Torah known as the "Noahide Laws" (named after Noah), which mainly stipulated adherence to Jewish dietary and sexual immorality laws. At every Jewish synagogue in the Roman world there were significant numbers of such God-fearers. Acts 13 tells how Paul and Barnabas were set apart at Antioch to lead an evangelistic mission starting in Seleucia, Antioch's seaport, then setting sail for the island of Cyprus, and from there journeying to various cities in Asia Minor. Repeatedly, Paul addresses the synagogues they visit in the following way: "You Israelites, *and others who fear God* . . ." (Acts 13:16, see also 13:26). To the God-fearers who heard Paul preach, following Jesus and becoming part of the Nazarene Way seemed to offer personal salvation and *full* admittance into the Jewish faith *without the need for circumcision,* a grueling procedure that obviously few men would wish to undertake. Paul thus made the Nazarene Way very attractive to Gentiles. Acts tells us that when Paul and Barnabas returned to Antioch, "They called the church together and related all that God had done with them, and how he had opened a door of faith for the Gentiles" (Acts 14:27).

The rapidly increasing numbers of Gentiles coming into the Way of Jesus presented a problem, however. What exactly was their status? Until that point, Gentile converts to Judaism, unless they underwent circumcision, were not fully Jews and could not, for example, take part in the Passover Seder meal. It was becoming increasingly clear to the Nazarene leaders at Jerusalem that Paul was giving the Gentiles false expectations of what their conversion to the Way meant. According to Acts, a delegation was sent from Jerusalem to Antioch to correct any misunderstandings: "Then certain individuals came down from Judea and were teaching the brothers, 'Unless you are circumcised according to the custom of Moses, you cannot be saved'" (Acts 15:1). Luke, the author of Acts, being a Gentile himself and lacking insight into the precepts of Judaism, is likely overstating the case here. The *salvation* of Gentile converts was likely not the issue. The God-fearers, for example, knew that they were not full Jews; and the vast majority of Jews (excepting perhaps the most conservative) would not have said the God-fearers could not be saved. The issue before the Jerusalem Council in Acts 15 was Paul giving converts the false expectation of becoming full members of the Jewish community without being circumcised.

The entrance of larger and larger numbers of Gentiles into the Way began to present a major problem as to their status in the Nazarene Yachad. Would they be full proselytes (also called "proselytes of righteousness"), subject to all the laws of the Torah, including circumcision; or would they continue in their status of half-proselytes (God-fearers, or proselytes of the gate) and be subject to only the Noahide Laws? This was a question that simply had to be resolved, and so Paul, Barnabas, and a few other representatives from Antioch were dispatched to Jerusalem to present the matter to the tribunal.

THE JERUSALEM CONFERENCE

At this point it would be good to review the full account of the Jerusalem Conference as described in Acts 15:

> When they [Paul and the delegation from Antioch] came to Jerusalem, they were welcomed by the church and the apostles and the elders, and they reported all that God had done with them. But some believers who belonged to the sect of the Pharisees stood up and said, "It is necessary for them [the Gentiles] to be circumcised and ordered to keep the law of Moses."
>
> The apostles and the elders met together to consider this matter. After there had been much debate, Peter stood up and said to them, "My brothers, you know that in the early days God made a choice among you, that I should be the one through whom the Gentiles would hear the message of the good news and become believers. And God, who knows the human heart, testified to them by giving them the Holy Spirit, just as he did to us; and in cleansing their hearts by

faith he has made no distinction between them and us. Now therefore why are you putting God to the test by placing on the neck of the disciples a yoke that neither our ancestors nor we have been able to bear? On the contrary, we believe that we will be saved through the grace of the Lord Jesus, just as they will."

The whole assembly kept silence, and listened to Barnabas and Paul as they told all the signs and wonders that God had worked through them among the Gentiles. (Acts 15:4–12)

Here we see that certain Nazarenes in Jerusalem, who were members of the Pharisaic party (the conservative "right wing" of the time), believed strongly that circumcision and full adherence to the law was a necessary requirement for Gentile converts. Once again, it cannot be stressed enough that *Jesus and his earliest followers were thoroughly Jewish in their beliefs and practices.* The *only* thing that distinguished the Nazarenes at all from their fellow Jews was their firm belief that Jesus was the Messiah of Israel. Therefore, it was only natural for those first Jewish believers to expect anyone wishing to follow Jesus to become a Jew. They were, in fact, becoming part of the nation of Israel, of which Jesus was the Messiah.

At the opening of this crucial meeting between the delegates from Antioch and the Nazarene Sanhedrin, Peter, Paul, and Barnabas all give testimony as to how God has been at work though the Holy Spirit among the Gentiles, although Acts is confused on another point here: Peter was most certainly not "the one through whom the Gentiles would hear the message." As evidence of this, we have Paul's own firsthand account of this meeting in Galatians 2, where he says. "I had been entrusted with the gospel for the uncircumcised, just as *Peter had been entrusted with the gospel for the circumcised*" (Galatians 2:7). Here is just one of frequent hints of Gentile bias from the author of Acts (Luke); and we need to keep in mind that Luke did not have firsthand information, but as a historian was working from the records and memories of others (see Luke 1:1–4). So, as biblical scholars have long noted, when there are discrepancies like this between Acts and Paul's letters, Paul, as a primary witness, is to be preferred.

In any case, the conversion of so many Gentile believers was seen by many—and Paul most of all—as fulfilling the biblical prophecies that at the end of the age the Gentile nations would come streaming into Jerusalem acknowledging the God of Abraham, Isaac, and Jacob as God of the whole world, culminating in the establishment of God's kingdom on earth with Jesus enthroned as the eternal Davidic king. And at the conference it was Paul who pushed the question that was most painfully at the forefront of the Gentile mind: Was circumcision really a necessary requirement for Gentiles to become part of Jesus's new kingdom?

After all the testimony of all parties was heard, it was not Peter, but *James* who made the final call on this crucial issue, which speaks volumes about James's leadership of the Jerusalem Church:

After they [Paul and Barnabas] finished speaking, James replied, "My brothers listen to me. Simeon [Peter] has related how God first looked favorably on the Gentiles, to take from among them a people for his name. This agrees with the words of the prophets, as it is written,

> After this I will return,
> And I will rebuild the dwelling of David,
> which has fallen;
> from its ruins I will rebuild it,
> and I will set it up,
> so that all other peoples may seek the Lord—
> even all the Gentiles over whom my name has been called.
> Thus says the Lord, who has been making these things
> known from long ago.

Therefore I have reached the decision that we should not trouble those Gentiles who are turning to God, but we should write to them to abstain only from things polluted by idols and from fornication and from whatever has been strangled and from blood. For in every city, for generations past, Moses has had those who proclaim him, for he has been read aloud every Sabbath in the synagogues." (Acts 15:13–21)

Thus ends the speech of James, which comprises, except for the Epistle of James, the only words in the New Testament attributed directly to him. While many scholars have doubted the historicity of this account in Acts, there are solid reasons to believe that there is indeed a substantial historical basis to what is expressed here. First and foremost, James's leadership is plainly demonstrated, which speaks volumes for the passage's authenticity since Luke, himself a Gentile and solidly Pauline in orientation, would have had no reason to invent a situation where James had the final say and where his arguments carried the day. And James does indeed issue the final word on the matter in the so-called Apostolic Decree.

THE APOSTOLIC DECREE

Immediately following upon James's speech, we are told that an official letter regarding the matter was composed and sent back to Antioch with Paul and Barnabas:

> Then the apostles and the elders, with the consent of the whole church, decided to choose men from among their members and to send them to Antioch with Paul and Barnabas. They sent Judas, called Barsabbas, and Silas, leaders among the brothers, with the following letter: "The brothers, both the apostles and the elders, to the believers of Gentile origin in Antioch and Syria and Cilicia, greetings. Since we have heard that certain persons who have gone out from us, though with no instructions from us, have said things to disturb you and have unsettled your minds, we have decided unanimously to choose representatives and send them to you, along with our beloved Barnabas and Paul, who have risked their lives for the sake of our Lord Jesus Christ. We have therefore sent Judas and Silas who will themselves tell you the same things by word of mouth. For it has seemed good to the Holy Spirit and to us to impose on you no further burden than these essentials: that you abstain from what has been sacrificed to idols and from blood and from what is strangled

and from fornication. If you keep yourselves from these, you will do well. Farewell." (Acts 15:22–29)

The four requirements of this Apostolic Decree—abstaining from food offered to idols, from fornication, from eating animals that have been strangled, and from eating rare meat ("from blood")—are ancient regulations found in the law of Moses. In the section of the law given in Leviticus 17–26, known as the "Holiness Code," these same requirements are listed in the same exact order. These were the Noahide Laws, the minimum requirements for Gentiles who wished to follow Judaism without taking the step of being circumcised. That these requirements are correctly listed in the Apostolic Decree certainly lends the document authenticity, belying the notion that Luke, a Gentile, freely composed this section. Logically, it would only be natural for James and the Torah-observant apostles and elders to look to the Torah for guidance on the question of Gentile converts. Adding support to this line of reasoning is the fact that James quotes the Hebrew Scriptures in support of his argument. The quote which James uses is from the book of the prophet Amos (9:11–12), and presents the idea, also expressed by Isaiah, that on the eschatological Day of the Lord, the Gentiles would come streaming into the temple in Jerusalem proclaiming Yahweh as the God of all the earth.

And thus, through the Apostolic Decree, the first major theological crisis in the life of the Nazarene Way was happily resolved to the satisfaction of everyone except the strictest right wing members of the party. The decree was sent to Antioch with Paul and Barnabas, along with representatives from Jerusalem: "When they gathered the congregation together, they delivered the letter. When its members read it, they rejoiced at the exhortation" (Acts 15:30–31).

The Decree inspired Paul to further his efforts, and almost immediately upon their return to Antioch, Paul set out on his second missionary journey. But, as we shall see, this is when further problems developed, and Paul and Jerusalem came into a heated conflict, which was not so easily resolved.

5

JAMES VERSUS PAUL
A Parting of the Ways

*But when Peter came to Antioch, I opposed him to
his face . . .*

ST. PAUL, GALATIANS 2:11–12

After winning official approval for his mission to the Gentiles from
the Jerusalem Council, Paul set out on his second missionary journey
with even greater confidence and vigor. As Paul would later proudly
recall, "They gave to Barnabas and me the right hand of fellowship,
agreeing that we should go to the Gentiles and they to the circumcised"
(Gal. 2:9). But after some time had gone by, rumors started coming back
to Jerusalem that Paul was not abiding by the terms of the Apostolic
Decree and had begun to exalt himself above the apostles in Jerusalem.
That Paul is beginning to feel his oats is clearly evidenced by the
quote that opens this chapter. Here we have Paul's own words that he
directly "opposed . . . to his face" Jesus's right hand man, Peter, presag-
ing a tragic parting of the ways between Paul's mission to the Gentiles,
and Peter and James's mission to the Jews.

Paul's hubris is also evidenced by the rather condescending tone he
uses in Galatians toward the apostolic leadership; for example, he says of
his meeting with the tribunal: "And from those who were supposed to

be acknowledged leaders (what they actually were makes no difference to me; God shows no partiality)—those leaders contributed nothing to me" (Galatians 2:6). In another letter, Paul's sarcasm is even more stinging toward the Jerusalem leadership: "I think I am not in the least inferior to these super-apostles" (2 Corinthians 11:5). To say the least, the arrogance of the "old Saul" was coming out in spades.

When Paul made what would be his final visit to Jerusalem several years later, James immediately confronted him about the problem he was creating: "You teach all the Jews living among the Gentiles to forsake Moses, and you tell them not to circumcise their children or observe the customs" (Acts 21:21). That Paul's mission to the Gentiles presented a heretofore different slant on Jesus's thoroughly Jewish message presented an embarrassing problem for James, Peter, and the apostolic leadership in Jerusalem. They had put their stamp of approval on Paul's mission to the Gentiles, and now Paul seemed to be stabbing them in the back.

It must be emphasized that while the Apostolic Decree loosened the strictures of the Torah *for Gentiles,* there was no such lessening of the Torah demands *for Jews.* But the accusation made by James and the Jerusalem Sanhedrin in Acts 21, above, plainly shows that Paul was not only loosening the strictures of the Torah for Gentiles (as permitted by the Apostolic Decree), but for Hellenistic Jewish converts as well (which was *not* part of the decree). Here we have evidence that the history presented in Acts is not fabricated out of whole cloth, as many liberal scholars have assumed. That Luke, the thoroughly Gentile author of Acts and staunch supporter of Paul, would present such an accusation by the Jerusalem leadership against Paul speaks volumes to this passage's authenticity.

Paul was now moving headlong on a theological path in which he envisioned the gospel of Jesus doing away completely with the need for the Torah for *all* followers of Jesus. Paul was beginning to teach not only Gentiles, but also Diaspora Jews living outside of Israel, that "no human being will be justified . . . by deeds prescribed by the law . . . now, apart from the law, the righteousness of God has been disclosed" (Romans 3:20). In another letter to Gentiles he bluntly states, "If you let yourselves be circumcised, Christ will be of no benefit to you. . . . You who want to be justified by the law have cut yourselves off from Christ; you have fallen away from grace" (Galatians 5:2–4). It gets no plainer than that. Those followers of Jesus who wished to continue following Jewish customs such as circumcision "have cut [themselves] off from Christ," they "have fallen away from grace." Such teaching must have seemed like a slap in the face to the apostles and Jewish Christians who still followed all of the Torah.

Another major problem that resulted from Paul's speaking so boldly against the need to follow the law was that many of his Gentile converts were beginning to take his teaching all too literally. A wanton licentiousness broke out among many of the congregations that Paul had established in the Roman world, which shocked not only the apostles in Jerusalem as they got word of it, but greatly shocked Paul as well; this was not something he had foreseen. Many of Paul's letters show him grappling with unintended ethical scandals that seemed to be sweeping his Gentile congregations. For example, in his first letter to the Christians at Corinth, Paul admonished them for their rumored behavior: "It is actually reported that there is sexual immorality among you, and of a kind that is not even found among the pagans . . ." And to the Church at Galatia, he issued this warning about proper use of their freedom from the law: "For you were called to freedom . . . only do not use your freedom as an opportunity for self-indulgence . . . Live by the Spirit, I say, and do not gratify the desires of the flesh" (Galatians 5:13–16). In Romans, Paul tellingly admits that his message has been grossly misunderstood: ". . . some people slander us by saying that we say . . . 'Let us do evil that good may come . . .'" (Romans 3:8). It is quite probable that the circular letter known as 2 Peter, quoted previously, was issued by later Jewish Christian leaders who continued to grapple with this problem among Gentile Christians:

> These people . . . are like irrational animals . . . reveling in their dissipation . . . they have left the straight road and gone astray . . . with licentious desires of the flesh they entice people who have just escaped from those who live in error [the Gentiles]. *They promise them freedom,* but they themselves are slaves of corruption. . . . it would have been better for them never to have known the way of righteousness

than, after knowing it, *to turn back from the holy commandment . . .
remember the words spoken in the past by the holy prophets, and the
commandment of the Lord and Savior spoken through your apostles.* (2
Peter 2:12–3:2, emphasis added.)

It would surely seem that the author of 2 Peter is calling the Gentile
Christians to return to the law *as taught by Jesus!*

That Paul was beginning to enter into direct conflict with James and
the apostles is clearly seen in what is perhaps the most shocking event
recorded in the New Testament, to which we now turn.

THE INCIDENT AT ANTIOCH

The so-called Antioch incident, when Peter and Paul almost came to
blows over a directive sent from Jerusalem by James, is so shocking that
if we did not have Paul's own firsthand account of it, it would be difficult to believe. The surface incident between Paul and Peter reveals a
much deeper ideological rift between Paul *and James*—a foreshadowing
of the growing chasm between emerging Gentile Christianity and Jewish
Christianity. The Incident at Antioch starkly shows that the apostolic
period was not a time of sweetness and light with the earliest followers
of Jesus all living as one big happy family, as assumed by most Christians
today; on the contrary, it was a time of bitter rivalries as various parties
and factions began to vie for supremacy.

It is not accidental that the growing rift between Paul and Jerusalem
came to a head at Antioch. Antioch was a unique communal experiment,
(which, sadly, ultimately failed), where Jews and Gentiles were in communion and even shared common meals. For Jews, sharing meals with
Gentiles was strictly prohibited. Peter apparently engaged in this new and
controversial practice when he was at Antioch until James got wind of it
back in Jerusalem and sent emissaries to investigate. It should be considered, however, that Peter was eating with converts to the Nazarene Way,
many of whom were already God-fearers. It is doubtful that Peter would
have eaten with "just any" Gentiles. In any case, as a result of the visit by

the Jerusalem investigative team, Peter withdrew from sharing meals with Gentiles. What is of great import is that Paul's close friend and missionary companion, Barnabas, also withdrew from eating with Gentiles. This caused Paul to become passionately angry and accuse Peter of hypocrisy and more. Here are Paul's own words:

> But when Cephas came to Antioch, I opposed him to his face, because he stood self-condemned; for until certain people came from James, he used to eat with the Gentiles. But after they came, he drew back for fear of the circumcision faction. And the other Jews joined him in this hypocrisy, so that even Barnabas was led astray by their hypocrisy. But when I saw that they were not acting consistently with the truth of the gospel, I said to Cephas before them all, "If you, though a Jew, live like a Gentile and not a Jew, how can you compel the Gentiles to live like Jews?" (Galatians 2:11–14)

Paul's audaciousness here is really quite remarkable. The new convert, the former persecutor who aided and abetted in the killing of Nazarenes and who, according to one source, threw James from the temple steps, dares to say that he knows "the truth of the gospel" better than Peter and James! What is most revealing here is that *Peter bowed to James's wishes,* another piece of evidence that James, rather than Peter, was the highest authority in the Jerusalem Church. The other thing that is clearly revealed in this telling incident is that James was a fairly conservative Jew who strictly held to the Torah, and upheld the law as continuing to apply to the Jewish Nazarenes. James was not envisioning any relaxation of the Torah requirements for *Jews,* as Paul plainly was. This is what brought James and Paul into conflict. It was one thing for James to say in the Apostolic Decree that Gentiles could become part of the Christian community without being circumcised, and were required to adhere to only a very limited part of the Torah; it was quite another to figure out how Jews and Gentiles could share in table fellowship without going against the Torah, which forbids such mixing. That James threw his support behind Paul's mission to the Gentiles at the Jerusalem Conference by requiring only minimal observance of the Torah for *Gentile* Christians does not mean that James believed the law was any less in effect for *Jewish Christians*. And in James's eyes, that meant no table fellowship.

Here James would seem to be more conservative than his brother, who, according to the gospel accounts, had no problem eating and drinking with Gentiles and sinners. This was obviously scandalous to any good Jew, and it is one of the main things for which Jesus received heavy criticism. It is likely that this scandalized even Jesus's family. This may be the source of the gospel stories that depict Jesus's family in opposition to his mission (see Mark 3:20–35 and John 7:5). It is likely that Jesus's family, as evidenced by what we know of James, was a conservative, Torah observant family. Jesus, however, was much more liberal in his attitudes and practice. None of this means, however, that Jesus's family opposed his mission, or thought he had "gone out of his mind" (Mark 3:21), a notion I thoroughly refuted in *The Brother of Jesus and the Lost Teachings of Christianity*.[1] In the eyes of his family, Jesus was the Messiah. But after Jesus's crucifixion, with James succeeding to the leadership of the community, Jesus's more radical, liberal practices were no doubt abandoned, and James's more conservative practices became dominant.

Now none of this means that James was opposed to having any fellowship at all with Gentiles. Clearly that is not the case, as it was James who laid down the Apostolic Decree paving the way for Gentiles to become part of the Nazarene community. And, as we saw, there were large numbers of Hellenistic members of the Nazarene synagogue at Jerusalem, but they were either Jews or God-fearers. At Antioch, not all the new Gentile converts were God-fearers; they were coming straight out of paganism into Nazarene Judaism, and adherence to even the bare bones of the Apostolic Decree had apparently been lax at Antioch, likely due to Paul's influence. The late Michael Goulder, a British New Testament scholar, set down in memorably earthy form what the exact problem was at Antioch in his wonderful book, *St. Paul versus St. Peter*:

> [Peter] had come to Antioch because James and he were not too sure of what was going on there, and felt they had better see for themselves.

At first Peter enjoyed the friendly atmosphere and the devotion of the church, and he joined in eating the meat at the church supper, without asking any questions about where it had been bought or how it had been cooked . . . But James in Jerusalem suspected that Peter's kindly heart meant that he would not put his foot down; so he sent a further deputation . . . and they found, just as James feared, that he was not insisting on eating kosher meat, purity laws, and so on. . . . So they said to him quietly, "Look here, which side are you on?"

The following Saturday night there was a scene. Peter said, "Before we go any further, I have to ask: Is this meat kosher? Was it bought at the Jewish butcher's?" Well, the meat actually came from the Antioch market; so Peter said, "Then I'm afraid that all God's people will have to go next door for the Eucharist . . . and leave this meat for those who have not yet put themselves under God's Law." It was a moment of crisis: everyone there had to decide whether Peter or Paul was right. Paul naturally hoped that his church would stand solidly with him, but . . . all the Jewish members had been feeling guilty of breaking the Law, [so] they sided with Peter; even Paul's closest ally Barnabas felt that was right . . .[2]

What is most astounding here is that even Barnabas, Paul's friend and longtime missionary partner, sided with Peter on this crucial issue. In fact, it was immediately after this run-in that Paul and Barnabas, after many missionary journeys together, went their separate ways. This has significant implications. When the incident at Antioch is looked at objectively, we are driven to a clear conclusion that lies far from the traditional Christian understanding that Paul was in the right and Peter stood corrected. As the wisely respected scholar James Dunn explains:

We naturally tend to assume that Paul made his point and won the day—Peter admitting his mistake, and the previous practice being resumed. But Paul does not actually say so . . . if Paul had won, and if Peter had acknowledged the force of his argument, Paul would surely have noted this, just as he strengthened his earlier position by noting the approval of the "pillar apostles" in 2.7–10. In the circumstances then, *it is quite likely that Paul was defeated at Antioch* . . .

Whatever the precise facts of the matter, . . . it is evident that there was a much deeper divide between Paul and the Jewish Christianity emanating from Jerusalem than at first appears . . . the fierceness of his response to Peter at Antioch . . . may well have been a contributing factor of some significance in fueling the antagonism of Jewish Christianity toward Paul.[3] (Dunn's italics.)

Thus, the Church at Antioch, with its increasingly large number of Gentiles, was the harbinger of Christianity eventually breaking away from parent Judaism, tragically foreshadowed in the breaking off of table fellowship in the first mixed Jewish and Gentile community. As might be expected, the rift that emerged at Antioch led to growing animosity between Paul and the Nazarene community in Jerusalem. After this Paul began to be looked upon warily by the Jewish Christians once again, as an apostate from the law, and by the time Paul was wrapping up his third missionary journey and bringing an ever-increasing number of Gentiles into the fold, things were reaching a crisis point. When Paul made his last visit to Jerusalem, his very presence sparked rioting in the streets, and the apostle to the Gentiles had to be taken into protective custody by a Roman tribune to save his life.

REJECTION AT JERUSALEM

Following Paul's rejection by the Jewish Christians at Antioch, he would set out on two other major missionary journeys around the Mediterranean (sans Barnabas) and establish quite a number of Gentile churches that now looked to Paul, and not James, as the supreme authority. All the while, tensions between Paul and Jerusalem festered and grew. Eventually the time came for Paul to return to Jerusalem for the purpose of presenting the "collection for the poor," which Paul had always been intent on fulfilling, and which by this time provided one of the last remaining, tenuous links between Paul's Gentile churches and the Nazarene Yachad. As eager as Paul originally had been to present the collection to James and the apostles, he now went to Jerusalem with great trepidation. After leaving the Christian community in Ephesus, Paul set sail for Palestine and landed in Tyre. According to Acts, the disciples at Tyre, "through the Spirit . . . told Paul not to go on to Jerusalem" (Acts 21:4). But Paul pressed on and went from Tyre to Caesarea, where he stayed with Philip, one of the seven Hellenists who had been appointed as the original deacons in Jerusalem. There Paul received an even more urgent warning not to go to Jerusalem:

> While we were staying there for several days, a prophet names Agabus came down from Judea. He came to us and took Paul's belt, bound his own feet and hands with it, and said, "Thus says the Holy Spirit, 'This is the way the Jews in Jerusalem will bind the man who owns this belt and will hand him over to the Gentiles.'" When we heard this, we and the people there urged him not to go up to Jerusalem. Then Paul answered, "What are you doing, weeping and breaking my heart? For I am ready not only to be bound but even to die in Jerusalem for the name of the Lord Jesus." Since he would not be persuaded, we remained silent except to say, "The Lord's will be done."
>
> After these days we got ready and started to go up to Jerusalem. (Acts 21:10–15)

This is one of the so-called we-sections of Acts—apparently a firsthand account, traditionally thought to be written by Luke himself, although it is also possible that Luke worked into his account a firsthand testimony from an eyewitness. In any event, when Paul arrived, things seemed to begin handsomely:

> When we arrived in Jerusalem, the brothers welcomed us warmly. The next day Paul went with us to visit James; and all the elders were present. After greeting them, he related one by one the things that God had done among the Gentiles through his ministry. (Acts 21:17–19)

After hearing of his successful ministry among the Gentiles, what the elders related to Paul began to throw a foreboding shadow over his visit:

When they heard it, they praised God. Then they said to him, "You see, brother, how many thousands of believers there are among the Jews, and they are all zealous for the law. They have been told about you that you teach all the Jews living among the Gentiles to forsake Moses, and that you tell them not to circumcise their children or observe the customs. What then is to be done? They will certainly hear that you have come. (Acts 21:20–22)

It is plain that James and the elders were quite proud of the zeal for the law that the Jewish believers possessed, something quite lacking among Paul's Gentile converts. It is almost as if the Nazarene elders were trying to "one up" Paul after he detailed his great success among the Gentiles, as if to say: "Oh, really? Well, wait till you hear how many thousands of *Jews* we've converted! *And they obey the law!*"

The elders obviously had quite a bit of concern about the reputation that Paul was garnering among Jewish believers in Jerusalem, due to many rumors that he was turning Jews living outside of Palestine away from the law. There seemed to be concern not only for Paul's reputation, but also for his safety: "What then is to be done? They will certainly hear that you have come." The misgivings of Paul's friends in Tyre and Caesarea would soon be borne out. Fearing for his safety, the elders prescribed a course of action for Paul that would publicly demonstrate to all his loyalty to the law of Moses:

So do what we tell you. We have four men who are under a vow. Join these men, go through the rite of purification with them, and pay for the shaving of their heads. Thus all will know that there is nothing in what they have been told about you, but that you yourself observe and guard the law. (Acts 21:23–24)

More interesting developments: Paul was advised, as a public demonstration of his orthodoxy, to financially sponsor some men who were taking what was known as a "Nazirite vow." The Nazirites were a strict Jewish religious order that observed ascetic practices such as abstaining from alcohol, strict fasting, not cutting their hair, and rigorously upholding the law.

The great biblical hero and Israelite judge, Samson, despite his well-known lust for women, was a Nazirite, as was the prophet Samuel, the last of the Israelite judges. In urging Paul to make a public demonstration of his loyalty by publicly sponsoring these Nazirite novices, James and the elders appeared to be doing everything they could to give Paul the benefit of the doubt, and seemed to realize, or at least hope, that the charges against him were untrue. Indeed, while Paul fought for a minimum adherence to the law for *Gentiles,* it is unlikely that Paul would have taught Jews to abandon the law. And Paul was not being a hypocrite in sponsoring the Nazirites and going through the rite of purification (something that would have been required anyway upon his entering the temple after his many contacts with Gentiles), for though he had fought hard for Gentile liberty from the law, Paul himself remained an observant Jew. In some of his last recorded words in Acts, after being placed under house arrest in Rome, Paul called together local Nazarene leaders to explain his predicament and told them, "I had done nothing against our people or the customs of our ancestors" (Acts 28:17). As further evidence of Paul's personal adherence to the law, we know that on a number of occasions, whenever practical, Paul left the mission field to return to Jerusalem for major festivals.

So Paul did as the elders urged, sponsored the men, and went into the temple with them to undergo the rite of purification. Toward the end of this seven-day ritual, the fears of all were realized when some "Jews from Asia" (Asia Minor, modern-day Turkey) saw Paul in the temple and a riot ensued:

> When the seven days were almost completed, the Jews from Asia, who had seen him in the temple, stirred up the whole crowd. They seized him, shouting, "Fellow Israelites, help! This is the man who is teaching everyone everywhere against our people, against our law, and this place . . ." Then all the city was aroused, and the people rushed together. They seized Paul and dragged him out of the temple, and immediately the doors were shut. While they were trying to kill him, word came to the tribune of the cohort that all Jerusalem was in an uproar. Immediately he took soldiers and centurions and ran down to them. When they saw the tribune and the soldiers, they

stopped beating Paul. Then the tribune came, arrested him, and ordered him to be bound . . . (Acts 21:27–33)

Paul likely owed his life to the quick intervention of the Roman tribune and his cohort. He was taken into protective custody and a series of trials ensued in the Roman courts. Because Paul was a Roman citizen, he managed to have his case taken all the way to the imperial court of the Roman governor Festus, as Acts goes on to relate.

In all of this, Luke seems quite candid in his depiction of the very real friction between Paul and the Jewish Christians; but then, this *is* an eyewitness account written in the first person. Still, we have to wonder how much is left unsaid because of Luke's well-known tendency to whitewash many of the antagonisms that existed between Paul and Jerusalem. The way Luke depicts things, James and the elders were solidly on Paul's side, and the trouble that erupted was all due to a simple misunderstanding among those "zealous for the law." But if Paul had been representing the attitude of James and the elders accurately, one has to wonder why they couldn't have simply explained the truth about Paul's orthodoxy to their more zealous brethren. Would they not have listened to James and their elders?

Intriguing questions have been raised around these issues by James Dunn, who makes some startling suggestions as to what Luke does *not* say in Acts:

> [W]hen Paul was arrested and put on trial we hear nothing of any Jewish Christians standing by him, speaking in his defence [*sic*]—and this despite James's apparent high standing among orthodox Jews . . . Where were the Jerusalem Christians? It looks very much as though they had washed their hands of Paul, left him to stew in his own juice. If so it implies *a fundamental antipathy on the part of the Jewish Christians to Paul himself and what he stood for.*[4] (Dunn's italics.)

As shocking as this may sound, there are some scholars who go so far as to claim that James and the elders purposely lured Paul into a trap.[5] If this idea seems far-fetched, note well the end of verse 30: "They seized

Paul and dragged him out of the temple, *and immediately the doors were shut.*" But such speculations are little more than conjecture. Still, Dunn's assertion, while it goes against the rosy picture of harmonious relations among Paul, Peter, and James that the Church has held throughout the centuries, is congruous with all the other evidence we have seen. That Paul was rather despised by the Jewish Christians should be quite obvious to any objective researcher.

What is also quite curious about chapter 21 of Acts is that the stated reason for Paul's visit to Jerusalem—to deliver the monetary collection that he had gone to such great lengths throughout his journeys to take up on behalf of the poor in Jerusalem—is never mentioned! This is a highly unusual omission of what would have been quite a momentous event in the history of the Church. Why would Luke not discuss this? The silence about the collection being delivered has caused more than a few scholars to conclude that the collection was actually rejected by the elders, for the official acceptance of a collection gathered from Paul's Gentile congregations would be seen as approval of Paul's teachings. The rejection of the offering that Paul went to such great lengths to collect, and to deliver personally against the advice of his friends, would certainly have been a bitter pill for Paul to swallow. If, indeed, the collection was rejected, it is reasonable to suppose that Luke, who was at pains to put a good spin on things, would have covered up this embarrassing faux pas for relations between Paul and Jerusalem. Luke's silence on the collection speaks loudly. If the collection was rejected, as seems likely, then relations between Paul and Jerusalem had indeed reached the breaking point. Even the conservative evangelical scholar, Ralph P. Martin, admits that by the time of Paul's final visit to Jerusalem, his "ministry was decisively rejected by James and the Jerusalem leadership."[6]

THE END OF AN AGE

It had always been Paul's intent to take the evangel to Rome as the capstone of his mission to the Gentiles, and ironically it was his arrest in Jerusalem that ultimately would take him there. While little is known of this period, other than what is related in the final chapter of Acts, there is a strong tradition that Peter arrived there at about the same time as Paul, perhaps even to check up on Paul's activities in the Roman capital, if *The Ascents of James* is to be believed. In 1936 the late Dr. Hugh Schonfield wrote a moving account about Peter and Paul, who had frequently been in conflict, finding their lives providentially intertwined in the end:

> About the same time that Paul arrived in Rome, it would appear that Peter in the course of his pastoral visitations had come there also. Tradition, at any rate, brings these two great Jewish Christians together before the curtain falls on their eventful lives. Each had contributed his share toward setting up the kingdom of God among men, and though often opposed to one another in policy, both were united in an undying devotion to the one whom they believed to be God's Messiah. The Acts of Peter and Paul [an apocryphal book] touchingly records their last meeting: "And seeing each other, they bedewed each other with tears." In the same document the Roman Christians declare: "We have believed, and do believe, that as God does not separate the two great lights which He made, so He is not to part you from each other, neither Peter from Paul, nor Paul from Peter."
>
> The two apostles are believed to have suffered martyrdom about the same time; Peter by crucifixion head downwards, and Paul by beheading. They had fought a good fight, they had finished the course, they had kept the faith: henceforth there was laid up for them a crown of righteousness, which the Lord, the righteous Judge, shall give them at that day.[7]

Tragically, while Peter and Paul were united in death, their respective communities—Jewish Christian and Gentile Christian—would increasingly part ways; and back in Jerusalem the martyrdom of their bishop, James, would occur around the same time as their own. Following the Jewish revolt against Rome that began in 66 and the Roman invasion and sack of Jerusalm in 70, the Jerusalem Church would go into a rapid tailspin, while Paul's Gentile churches would make a meteoric rise to unbelievable heights of power.

6

STORM SIGNALS
The Nazarenes and the War with Rome

*Do you see these great buildings? Not one stone will be left
here upon another; all will be thrown down.*

JESUS, THE GOSPEL ACCORDING TO MARK 13:2

Not only were matters volatile between James and Paul, and between
Jewish and Gentile Christians, but ominous storm clouds were gathering in the bigger picture as relations between Jerusalem and Rome grew
increasingly tense. Under Roman rule the Sadducean leadership and
Jewish elite enjoyed a lavish lifestyle they did not wish to see disturbed,
while the vast majority of Jews were straining ever harder at the bonds
that shackled them. Their harsh life under tyrannical overlords ever
impelled them to thoughts of revolution, just as it had their Maccabean
forebears. Their hopes and dreams for a better life and better world were
stirred by new apocalyptic writings, such as the book of Daniel, and by a
messianic fervor that grew stronger by the day. Potential messiahs seemed
to appear daily, and certainly it was messianic expectation that fueled the
rapid growth of the Nazarene movement.

In the year 46, during the reign of the Emperor Claudius, a great
famine struck Palestine and brought the Jewish peasantry to the brink of
starvation. Paul and delegates from Antioch made a famine relief visit to

Jerusalem, which is recorded in the eleventh chapter of Acts. Resentment of the ruling elite—who enjoyed their lavish lifestyle through the heavy taxation of the peasantry—grew even greater and caused the Jewish Zealots, Essenes, and Nazarenes to unite in common cause, although their solutions varied.

Hugh Schonfield believed that James's influence during this period actually extended beyond the circle of the Nazarenes:

> There is some evidence to show that James the brother of Jesus was made unofficial leader of a united people's party. The title given him, *Oblias* [bulwark], which Eusebius renders "Protection of the People" . . . the tenor of his Epistle, the fact that his influence was so feared by the high priestly party that they illegally put him to death, and that this caused such a popular outcry that the responsible priest was deposed and the revolt accelerated, all point to this conclusion.[1]

Robert Eisler made the suggestion that James was viewed as an "opposition high priest," symbolically and spiritually opposed to the official high priest, Ananus.[2] While this is speculative, Eisler based this idea on a statement from Epiphanius that James wore the diadem—the ornamental priestly headband—of the high priest's office:

> Moreover we have found that he officiated after the manner of the ancient priesthood. Wherefore also he was permitted once a year to enter the Holy of Holies, as the Law commanded of the high priests, according to that which is written; for so many before us have told of him, both Eusebius and Clement and others. Furthermore, he was empowered to wear the high priestly diadem upon his head, as the aforementioned trustworthy men have attested in their memoirs.[3]

While this may sound outrageous at first, Epiphanius claims that many other "trustworthy men" before him had made that same claim, and there is, in fact, testimony that James fulfilled this role from the very early church historian Hegesippus. In his account of James he says, "He alone was permitted to enter the Holy Place [the Holy of Holies], for his garments were not of wool but of linen."[4] Linen was the material of the priest's robes, and only the high priest was allowed to enter the Holy of Holies. While this may all ultimately be legendary, the claim is still rooted in something historical, as Schonfield notes:

> The legend that [James] had officiated as high priest owed something . . . to the position he came to occupy for the Nazoreans as the spiritual and political head of loyalist Israel, which made him *in effect* the high priest's counterpart and rival. This status may well have contributed to his death at the instigation of the high priest Ananus.[5] (Emphasis added.)

While James's serving in an official capacity as high priest may be legendary, it is indisputable that the official high priest, Ananus the Younger (son of Ananus the Elder, called Annas in the gospel), was a ruthless and despised tyrant, as attested by Josephus:

> [H]e was a great hoarder . . . of money. . . . [H]e also had servants who were very wicked, who joined themselves to the boldest sort of the people, and went to the thrashing floors, and took away the tithes that belonged to the priests by violence, and did not refrain from beating such as would not give these tithes to them. So the other chief priests acted in the like manner . . . without anyone being able to prohibit them; so that some of the priests, that of old were wont to be supported with those tithes, died for want of food.[6]

It is likely that it is these kinds of injustices that are being spoken of in the Epistle of James:

> Come now, you rich people, weep and wail for the miseries that are coming to you. Your riches have rotted, and your clothes are moth-eaten. Your gold and silver have rusted, and their rust will be evi-

dence against you, and it will eat your flesh like fire. You have laid up treasure for the last days. Listen! The wages of the laborers who mowed your fields, which you kept back by fraud, cry out, and the cries of the harvesters have reached the ears of the Lord of hosts. You have lived on earth in luxury and in pleasure; you have fattened your hearts in a day of slaughter. You have condemned and murdered the righteous one, who does not resist you. (James 5:1–6)

The statement, "you have murdered the righteous one," is interesting. If it refers to Jesus, which has been the standard Christian interpretation, James's own title—the "just one"—may reflect a title originally applied to his brother. On the other hand, if the letter of James was not written by the brother of Jesus but by a later disciple, as most scholars believe, then this statement could be referring to the martyrdom of James.

As the people's suffering increased, messianic and apocalyptic expectations increased almost exponentially. Messiahs were seen around every corner, signs of the end in every political and astronomical event, and the words of the prophets, especially Daniel, were scoured for clues as to the time of the end. The majority of Essenes had renounced society and retreated to the desert outpost at Qumran, believing that by fully upholding the Torah on behalf of all Israel they might move the hand of God to intervene, just as Jesus thought that he could, in the words of Schweitzer, turn "the wheel of the world to set it moving on that last revolution which is to bring all ordinary history to a close."

While the majority of Nazarenes preferred to await the end peacefully, leaving political events in God's hands as Jesus had taught, there was an increasingly vocal minority with Zealot leanings who would not wait so patiently. It was at this time (ca. 55) that the notorious and much feared guerilla group known as the Sicarii, or daggermen, arose. We know of them from Josephus, who, in *The Jewish War*, calls them "a new form of bandits" (Greek *lestai*, also commonly translated as "brigands"). They conspired to do away with pro-Roman Jews, or those who in any other way were considered an impediment to the Zealot cause. The Sicarii were adept at clandestine assassination. For maximum effect they preferred to carry out their deadly deeds during religious festivals, when they would brazenly approach a priest or aristocrat within the temple precinct, quickly drive a dagger into his heart, and just as quickly disappear into the crowd. Attempting to put the best possible spin on these brutal assassinations for the benefit of his Roman patrons, Josephus remarked:

> Now, as for the affairs of the Jews, they grew worse and worse continually; for the country was again filled with robbers [*lestai*] and imposters who deluded the multitude. . . . Certain of these robbers went up to the city, as if they were going to worship God, while they had daggers under their garments . . . the robbers went up with the greatest security at the festivals . . . and mingling themselves among the multitude, they slew certain of their own enemies, and were subservient to other men for money; and slew others not only in remote parts of the city, but in the temple itself . . . And this seems to me to have been the reason why God, out of his hatred to these men's wickedness, rejected our city; and as for the temple, he no longer esteemed it sufficiently pure for him to inhabit therein, but brought the Romans upon us, and threw a fire upon the city to purge it . . .[7]

With Jesus long gone from the scene, it must have been very difficult for many of the Nazarenes, especially those who had not known Jesus or personally heard his teaching, not to fall in with the siren call of the revolution-minded Zealots, especially since there were many among them. This is evidenced in the Apocalypse of Baruch, written shortly after the fall of Jerusalem:

> For that time will arise which will bring affliction . . . and it will be turbulent coming in the heat of indignation. And it will come to pass in those days that all the inhabitants of the earth will be moved one against another, because they know not that my judgment has drawn nigh. For there will not be found many wise at that time, and the intelligent will be but few: moreover, even those who know will most of all be silent. And there will be many rumors,

and tidings not a few, and the works of portents will be shown . . . And whilst they are meditating these things, then zeal will arise in those of whom they thought not, and passion will seize him who is peaceful, and many will be roused in anger to injure many, and they will rouse up armies in order to shed blood, and in the end they will perish together with them. (Apocalypse of Baruch 47:31–39)

The letter of James advises caution and patience in these turbulent times, evidence that James fell in line with his brother's pacifistic teachings and shared his belief that God would directly intervene: "Be patient, therefore, beloved, until the coming of the Lord. The farmer waits for the precious crop from the earth, being patient with it until it receives the early and the late rains. You also must be patient. Strengthen your hearts for the coming of the Lord is near" (James 5:7–8).

THE DEATH OF JAMES

Sadly, even though James counseled patience and moderation, his visible position as head of the Nazarenes (increasingly associated by Rome with the right wing Zealots) led to James's execution by the newly installed high priest, Ananus. The very fact that this was Ananus's first official act supports the possibility that James did indeed function as an opposition high priest, as some have speculated. If it is true that James served as an opposition high priest and wore the priestly vestments, this no doubt would have incensed the newly appointed Ananus to take action against him, perhaps thinking that he would make a big impression on his superiors with his first official act. If so, his ruse severely backfired.

Thankfully, this informative incident is recorded in some detail for us by Josephus, and the fact that he discusses the execution of James at length is evidence of James's high standing, as well as of the influence the Nazarenes had on the political playing field. The incident took place during a time of political transition when the Judean procurator, Festus, had died and the emperor had sent a replacement. At the same time, King Herod Agrippa replaced the high priest with Ananus:

And now Caesar, upon hearing the death of Festus, sent Albinus into Judea, as procurator; but the king deprived Joseph of the high priest-hood, and bestowed the succession . . . on the son of Ananus, who was also himself called Ananus. . . . but this younger Ananus . . . was a bold man in his temper, and very insolent; he was also of the sect of the Sadducees, who are very rigid in judging offenders . . . therefore, Ananus was of this disposition, he thought he had now a proper oppor-tunity. Festus was now dead, and Albinus was but upon the road; so he assembled the Sanhedrin of judges, and brought before them the brother of Jesus, who was called Christ, whose name was James, and some others . . . and when he had formed an accusation against them as breakers of the law, he delivered them to be stoned; but as for those who seemed the most equitable of the citizens, and such as were the most uneasy at the breach of the laws, they disliked what was done . . . they also sent to the king [Agrippa], desiring him to send to Ananus that he should act so no more, for what he had already done was not to be justified . . . on which king Agrippa took the high priesthood from him, when he had ruled but three months . . . [8]

This account gives us invaluable information regarding James's influence. It has been summed up with great insight by the brilliant New Testament scholar, John Dominic Crossan:

Josephus tells us that Ananus was a Sadducee, but he was much more than that. His father, Ananus the Elder, was high priest from 6 to 15 CE, and is known to us from the gospels as Annas. The elder Ananus was father-in-law of Joseph Caiaphas, High Priest from 18 to 36 CE, a figure also known to us from the gospels [the High Priest who tried Jesus]. He was, furthermore, the father of five other High Priests . . . The immediate family of Ananus the Elder had domi-nated the high priesthood for most of the preceding decades, with eight High Priests in sixty years, *yet the execution of James resulted in the deposition of Ananus the Younger after only three months in office. . . . James must have had powerful, important, and even politically organized friends in Jerusalem. . . .* [W]e need to think much more about James and how he reached such status among Jewish circles that . . . his death could cause a High priest to be deposed after only three months in office.[9] (Italics mine.)

With James's execution causing such repercussions in high places, it is not surprising that among the masses his death fanned the flames of revolt even more, and may well have brought to an end any lingering pleas for patience and moderation. James's unlawful execution by Ananus most certainly did away with any respect that was still held for the chief priests simply by reason of their holy office. Thus the storm clouds hovering low over Jerusalem gathered ever thicker, and the atmosphere became charged with electricity. The unjust execution of the Just One may have indeed provided the initial spark that ignited the conflagration that would eventually devour Jerusalem. Eusebius, quoting Hegesippus, gives a fuller account of James's execution, saying that James was thrown to his death from the pinnacle of the temple (see plates 4, 6, 7).[10] At the end of that account, Eusebius makes an interesting observation: "So remarkable a person must James have been, so universally esteemed for righteousness, that even the more intelligent Jews felt that this was why his martyrdom was immediately followed by the siege of Jerusalem, which happened to them for no other reason than the wicked crime of which he had been the victim."[11] While Eusebius is certainly mistaken when he attributes the fall of Jerusalem (which happened in 70 CE) directly to the death of James (which happened in 62), his statement does reflect the fact that James's death led to ever increasing calls for revolt and turned almost everyone against the Sadducean priesthood.

It can legitimately be said that James's death was speedily avenged. In the earliest days of the Jewish revolt, many of the chief priests were among the first slain by mercenaries whom the Zealots hired and brought to Jerusalem. Their dead bodies were ignominiously cast out of the city without burial. In contrast, according to Hegesippus (writing mid-second century), James was given an honorable burial and "his headstone is still there by the sanctuary."[12]

THE SUCCESSION OF BISHOP SYMEON

As briefly mentioned in chapter 1, following the death of James, a successor to his "throne" was elected—Jesus's cousin Symeon, son of Joseph's brother Clopas, according to most accounts (Clopas is mentioned in the gospels in Luke 24:13 ff and John 19:25). We know of Symeon thanks once again to Eusebius's preserving quotes from Hegesippus, who wrote five books of commentary on the history of the Church in the mid-second century. It is time now to revisit the highly fascinating quote from Hegesippus that we briefly looked at in chapter 1, which is preserved in the third chapter of Eusebius's *History of the Church:*

> After the martyrdom of James and the capture of Jerusalem which instantly followed, there is a firm tradition that those of the Apostles and disciples of the Lord who were still alive assembled from all parts together with those who, humanly speaking, were kinsmen of the Lord—for most of them were still living. Then they all discussed together whom they should choose as a fit person to succeed James, and voted unanimously that Symeon, son of the Clopas mentioned in the gospel narrative, was a fit person to occupy the throne of the Jerusalem see. He was, so it is said, a cousin of the Savior, for Hegesippus tells us that Clopas was Joseph's brother.[13]

And later, Eusebius again quotes Hegesippus:

> When James the Righteous had suffered martyrdom like the Lord and for the same reason, Symeon the son of his uncle Clopas was appointed bishop. He being a cousin of the Lord, it was the universal demand that he should be second.[14]

Of note in these citations is that Hegesippus uses the more Hebraic name Symeon, as opposed to the Greek form, Simon. There are a couple of places where Eusebius quotes Hegesippus using Simon (3.32.3, 6), but Eusebius himself, when not quoting Hegesippus, consistently uses Symeon. This variation between the Hebraic and Greek forms is also seen in Peter's original name, which comes down to us in the two forms Symeon/Simon, as well as in the name of Jesus's brother, Symeon/Simon.

And this brings us to a most interesting question: Was Symeon really Jesus's *cousin,* or is it possible that Symeon was really Jesus's brother? Recall that, according to Mark (6:13) and Matthew (13:55), one of Jesus's *brothers,* likely the second youngest, was also named Simon. Is it possible that the designation of "cousin" in Hegesippus reflects the emerging belief in the perpetual virginity of Mary? It would certainly make sense, if indeed a dynastic succession was in effect, that after the death of James another brother of Jesus would be next in line for the throne. What gives one pause here is that the *Protevangelium of James* (in which the perpetual virginity is espoused) was written at about the same time that Hegesippus was writing. That Hegesippus fell under its influence is perhaps evidenced by his qualification of Jesus's brothers—"according to the flesh." Making Symeon a cousin would solve an embarrassing problem for belief in the perpetual virginity of Mary, and may have contributed to Jerome's later putting his stamp of authority on the idea. To this day in Roman Catholic tradition, Symeon, the second bishop of Jerusalem, is considered to be the same as the Simeon who is called the "brother of the Lord" in the gospels (considering the "brothers" to be "cousins").

What also is curious is that Symeon is called "the son of Clopas." As Richard Bauckham notes, Clopas is an alternate form of the name Alphaeus, and both are alternative Greek forms of the Semitic name Halphai.[15] James Tabor notes the curious fact that the other James who was one of the twelve, commonly known as James the Less, is called James, "son of Alphaeus," in Luke 6:15. Further, Tabor notes, the disciple Matthew, also known as Levi, is called "Levi son of Alphaeus" in Mark 2:14. Tabor believes, based on historic precedent, that Matthew was also known as *Joseph.* This would gives us three disciples who are called "sons of Alphaeus" and whose names match three of Jesus's brothers—James, Symeon/Simon, and Joseph/Matthew. Further, Tabor notes that the apostle Jude is called "Jude of James," which could mean *brother* of James, as well as son of James. Based on these curious coincidences, Tabor comes to the astounding conclusion that all four of Jesus's brothers were part of the twelve. Tabor states that, "This is perhaps the best-kept secret in the New Testament. *Jesus's own brothers were among the so-called Twelve Apostles.*" (Italics Tabor's.)[16]

While such an unorthodox conclusion will seem far too speculative for most scholars, Tabor is not the first to reach it. Robert Eisenman reached the same conclusion in his controversial *James the Brother of Jesus,* and strikingly, a Roman Catholic scholar who has extensively investigated Jesus's family, John McHugh, reached the same conclusion in 1975; McHugh, however, proposes that James, Joseph, Simon, and Jude were Jesus's *foster brothers.* In McHugh's scenario these four brothers were sons of Mary's sister, the wife of Clopas (John 19:25), and were raised in the same household with Jesus after the death of Clopas.[17] Tabor presents a more convincing scenario: "James is called the 'son of Alphaeus' (Luke 6:15), and . . . 'Alphaeus' is another form of the name 'Clophas,' the brother of Joseph and *likely second husband of Mary.*" (Italics mine.)[18] While shocking, this actually makes a good deal of sense. Most scholars have concluded that because Joseph is never heard of again after the Nativity stories in the gospels, that he probably died when Jesus was young. If that is indeed the case, it would be expected, according to Jewish law, that Joseph's brother would take Mary as his wife to prevent her from becoming a destitute widow, and bear children with her (Deuteronomy 25:5–6). It would have been considered a grave sin for Clopas (alternate spelling, Clophas) not to do so. The four brothers of Jesus may well have been the sons of Clopas and Mary.

Whatever the actual state of these familial relations was, it is beyond question that the succession to the leadership of the Nazarene community stayed within Jesus's family, perhaps even into the mid-second century, as we shall discuss in the next chapter. Of course, many scholars will object that Hegesippus's account is legendary or exaggerated. Richard Bauckham soundly refutes such objections and upholds the historicity of Hegesippus's account, and it would be good at this point to lay out Bauckham's argument in full as it provides a solid foundation for all that I am proposing in this book:

[T]here is nothing historically improbable about Hegesippus' account of Symeon's appointment, and a number of considerations are in its favor:

(1) The role of the relatives of Jesus . . . is unlikely to be Hegesippus' creation. It is true that it serves his apologetic purpose: the relatives of Jesus . . . by virtue of their relationship to Jesus [are] guarantors of true Christian teaching. Though he stresses that they presided over the church in conjunction with the apostles (2:23:4; 3:11), they emerge as in fact more important than the apostles, principally because in their case he can establish a succession, which continues to the reign of Trajan. But *Hegesippus would not have been able to give this role to the relatives of Jesus unless the Jewish Christian tradition on which he depends had already focused on their leadership role . . . So it is likely that the role of these relatives in the appointment of Symeon derives from that tradition. . . .*

(2) All the evidence shows that by the time of his death James had attained a position of considerable preeminence in the Jerusalem Church . . . his unique position was already a formally constituted one. It would be natural for such a position not to lapse at his death but to be filled by the election of a successor. The notion of succession in such an office certainly does not need to be regarded as an early Catholic one, but is deeply rooted in Jewish tradition, as [Ethelbert] Stauffer has shown in detail.

(3) . . . Symeon was not one of the elders of the Jerusalem Church. So James's position was not filled by the elders themselves from among their own number. . . .

(4) . . . The status of Jerusalem as the mother church of the whole Christian community had given James an authoritative position not only throughout the Palestinian Church but even further afield . . . The succession to the leadership of the Jerusalem Church would be a matter of concern wherever this authority was acknowledged. So a gathering like the Jerusalem council of Acts 15 is quite possible . . .[19] (Emphasis added.)

With the reliability of Hegesippus on these matters established, let us now examine a major turning point in the history of the Jewish Christian community that some scholars have dismissed as legendary, but is solidly historical.

THE FLIGHT TO PELLA

Conditions in Judea became even worse under the next two Roman procurators, Albinus (62–64 CE) and Gessius Florus (64–66 CE), not because they were more oppressive than their predecessors, but ironically, because they clandestinely joined ranks with the Jewish rebels. This was certainly done more for mercenary than patriotic reasons, since they received bribes for turning a blind eye to rebel activities. Josephus tells of the miserable conditions at this time:

> [T]here were no bounds set to the nation's miseries; but the unhappy Jews, when they were not able to bear the devastations which the robbers made among them, were all under a necessity of leaving their own inhabitations, and of flying away, as hoping to dwell more easily anywhere else in the world among foreigners. And what need I say more . . . since it was this Florus who necessitated us to take up arms against the Romans, while we thought it better to be destroyed at once, than by little and little.[20]

It was at this time that, heeding a prophecy, the majority of the Nazarenes, under the leadership of Symeon, fled Judea and relocated in Pella in the Decapolis region of Transjordan (Peraea), as Eusebius relates:

> [T]he members of the Jerusalem Church, by means of an oracle given by revelation to acceptable persons there, were ordered to leave the City before the war began and settled in a town in Peraea called Pella. To Pella those who believed in Christ migrated from Jerusalem; and as if holy men had utterly abandoned the royal metropolis of the Jews and the entire Jewish land, the judgment

of God at last overtook them for their abominable crimes against Christ and his Apostles, completely blotting out that wicked generation from among men.[21]

While there is distasteful anti-Semitic bias oozing forth from Eusebius's comments, it is an invaluable piece of history that he preserves for us. One other writer also preserves this history, the fourth-century heresy hunter Epiphanius, whose account betrays a bias against the Nazarenes themselves. In the *Panarion* (The Medicine Chest, so called because it was a compendium of remedies against heresies), Epiphanius attacks the heresy of the "Nazoraeans" that was rooted in Pella:

> Today this sect of the Nazoraeans is found in Beroea near Coelesyria, in the Decapolis near Pella, and in Bashanitis at the place called Cocabe—Khokhabe in Hebrew. For that was its place of origin, since all the disciples had settled in Pella after they left Jerusalem—Christ told them to abandon Jerusalem and withdraw from it because of its coming siege. And they settled in Perea for this reason and, as I said, spent their lives there. That was where the Nazoraean sect began.[22]

Unlike Eusebius, Epiphanius considered the Nazarenes that still existed in his time to be heretics, because of their Jewish Christian beliefs and practices. Of great import is the fact that when Epiphanius was writing in the late fourth century, descendants of the Nazarenes were still living in Pella, as well as in other areas of Transjordan. He references this again in a later passage, and there adds another interesting piece of information about these "heretics":

> For since practically all who had come to faith in Christ had settled in Peraea then, in Pella, a town in the "Decapolis" the Gospel mentions, which is near Batanaea and Bashanitis—as they had moved there then and were living there, this provided an occasion for Ebion. . . . There he began his bad teaching—the same place, if you please, as the Nazoraeans whom I have mentioned already. For since Ebion

was connected with them and they with him, each party shared its own wickedness with the other.[23]

Here Epiphanius has to cover his tracks a bit when he notes that "all of those who believed in Christ" came to Pella. Since he cannot very well claim that they are all heretics, he notes that the heresy of the Nazoraeans was rooted in the teaching of Ebion, whom Epiphanius considers the founder of a related Jewish Christian heresy he rails against: the notorious Ebionites. We shall discuss the Ebionites in the next chapter, but we should note here that there was no person named Ebion, and Epiphanius is simply mistaken or distorting information when he claims that the Ebionites were named after their founder. In fact, the Ebionites and the Nazarenes are one and the same.

THE BEAST IS ROUSED

We shall have to temporarily leave the fascinating topic of the descendants of the original Nazarenes living in the Transjordan (to which we shall return in the next chapter) in order to examine conditions in the city they left behind. All too soon the prophecies of doom were fulfilled. War was declared on Rome, and after an initial, brief period of success for the Jewish rebels, the forces of the Emperor Vespasian came sweeping into Palestine like some great devouring beast. Galilee succumbed first, then Samaria, and finally, northern Judea. The predictions of Jesus were being fulfilled before the terrified eyes of the Nazarenes:

> When you see Jerusalem surrounded by armies, then know that its desolation has come near. Then those in Judea must flee to the mountains, and those inside the city must leave it, and those out in the country must not enter it; for these are days of vengeance, as a fulfillment of all that is written . . . Jerusalem will be trampled on by the Gentiles, until the times of the Gentiles are fulfilled. (Luke 21:20–24)

While most liberal scholars believe that apocalyptic words such as these were put into Jesus's mouth by the gospel writers after the event, I believe, in company with the Third Quest school of thought, that Jesus's teaching was steeped in apocalypticism, and that he quite likely spoke words very close to what Luke records. It did not require supernatural knowledge, but simply astute foresight to see the immediate future for Israel if she foolishly attempted to wage war against Rome. Jesus surely saw this, and while he counseled against such foolhardiness, he was also well aware that the growing Zealot faction was setting Israel on an inevitable collision course that would inevitably bring Jerusalem to its last days.

It is a regrettably unrecognized fact that the grossly misinterpreted book of Revelation is actually a Jewish Christian work, one that looks at this period and its aftermath through Nazarene eyes. Once this is realized, it can give us remarkable and much needed new insight into the true nature and meaning of the book of Revelation. This was recognized as far back as the 1930s by a remarkable Jewish scholar who was himself a prophet—the much maligned Hugh Schonfield, whose deep insight into the book of Revelation puts to shame the thousands and thousands of commentaries written by Christian scholars. In just a few brief words, written on the eve of the great apocalypse of World War II, Schonfield brilliantly sums up the book of Revelation:

> The Book of Revelation, the interpretation of which is so much disputed owing to the general ignorance of Jewish Christianity, is a message from one of the Nazarene leaders, deported like many other Jews after the war, to the Christian communities in Asia Minor, explaining to them, necessarily in cryptic language because of the Roman authorities, the state of affairs in Judaea, and bidding them hold fast to their faith, as these calamities were signs of the Lord's speedy return.[24]

That the author of Revelation was a Jewish Christian is evidenced by his knowledge of the Jerusalem Temple and the rites performed in it, his depth of knowledge of the Hebrew Bible (approximately 275 of the

404 verses on Revelation allude to passages in the Hebrew Bible), and his usage of a literary genre (apocalyptic) that was increasingly popular in Palestinian Judaism. The fantastic imagery of beasts and dragons contained in Revelation was a fairly new literary genre of the time, called "apocalyptic" by scholars, and provided a perfect vehicle for concealing the true meaning of things from Roman officials while enabling its Nazarene audience to get the point; to wit, John repeatedly reminds them: "Let anyone who has an ear listen to what the Spirit is saying to the churches" (Revelation 1:7). John likely took these words from Jesus, who also told cryptic parables meant to be understood only by insiders. Jesus regularly concluded his parables with these words: "Let anyone with ears listen."

Even just a brief survey of Revelation reveals its Jewish Christian nature. John opens by explaining that while he was in exile on the island of Patmos, he received a vision in which he was commanded to write of events past, present, and future, a vision meant to buoy the hopes and dreams of his fellow Jewish Christians, also in exile following the war: "I, John, your brother who share with you in Jesus the persecution and the kingdom and the patient endurance, was on the island called Patmos because of the word of God and the testimony of Jesus" (Revelation 1:9). Note well that John mentions the "patient endurance" that is also counseled in the epistle of James.

A little-known fact is that the seven churches to which John writes—Ephesus, Smyrna, Pergamum, Thyatira, Sardis, Philadelphia, and Laodicea—are all predominantly Jewish Christian, and the influx of refugees from the war contributed even further to their numbers. It is no accident that these churches (with the exception of Ephesus) are unknown to the general reader. There are no epistles addressed to these churches by Paul in the New Testament, and most scholars conclude that "Paul's" letter to the Ephesians was not written by Paul, but by a later disciple at the end of the first century when the church at Ephesus had become a predominantly Gentile church. None of the seven churches of Revelation were established or influenced by Paul; they are the churches of James and Peter. We are indeed quite fortunate to have the Jewish Christian book of Revelation in the New Testament, for it almost didn't make the final cut of the Catholic canon, and many attempts were made to have it removed, even as late as Martin Luther who famously remarked that he would have gladly thrown Revelation, along with the few other Jewish Christian books—James, Jude, and Hebrews—into the Elbe River!

Following the exhortations to the seven churches, the next chapters of Revelation give a cursory overview of the events that preceded the war. References are made to the early triumphs of the Nazarene Yachad, the unrest that followed under the tightening Roman yoke, the famine during the reign of Claudius, and the ravages of the Sicarii and the bandits ("the wild animals of the earth"—6:8). None of this is comprehensible, however, without the teaching of the Messiah, who alone can open the heavenly scroll and understand its meaning:

> Then I saw in the right hand of the one seated on the throne a scroll written on the inside and on the back, sealed with seven seals; and I saw a mighty angel proclaiming with a loud voice, "Who is worthy to open the scroll and break its seals? And no one in heaven or on earth or under the earth was able to open the scroll or to look into it. And I began to weep bitterly because no one was found worthy to open the scroll or to look into it. Then one of the elders said to me, "Do not weep. See, the Lion of the tribe of Judah, the root of David, has conquered, so that he can open the scroll and its seven seals."
>
> Then I saw between the throne and the four living creatures and among the elders a Lamb standing as if it had been slaughtered . . . He went and took the scroll from the right hand of the one who was seated on the throne. . . . (Revelation 5:1–7)

The Jewish Christian nature of Revelation is plainly evidenced here in its depiction of Jesus (the Lamb) taking the scroll from God (the one who was seated on the throne). Jesus and God are not one and the same here, as they soon would be in the emerging Catholic Church. Next comes a description of the persecution the Nazarenes suffered at the hands of both Jewish and Roman authorities: "A quart of wheat for a day's pay, and three quarts of barley for a day's pay . . ." (6:6, reminiscent of James

5:4–6), and a reference to the terror endured under Gessius Florus: "... they were given authority over a fourth of the earth, to kill with sword, famine, and pestilence, and by the wild animals of the earth" (6:8), and a reference to the cry of the martyrs: "... they cried out with a loud voice, 'Sovereign Lord, holy and true, how long will it be before you judge and avenge our blood on the inhabitants of the earth?' They were each given a white robe and told to rest a little longer ..." (6:10–11, reminiscent of James 6:7–8).

In chapter 7, the Jewish Christian nature of Revelation is again clearly seen as it discusses the "sealing" of twelve thousand from each of the twelve tribes of Israel (7:4–8), and only then, with the salvation of the Jewish faithful assured, do the Gentiles gather around God's throne to pay homage to Messiah Jesus:

> After this I looked, and there was a great multitude that no one could count, from every nation, from all tribes and peoples and languages, standing before the throne and before the Lamb, robed in white, with palm branches in their hands. They cried out in a loud voice, saying, "Salvation belongs to our God who is seated on the throne, and to the Lamb!" (Revelation 7:9–10)

Then a person who is described only as "one of the elders" (certainly a Nazarene elder) explains to John who this great multitude is: "These are they who have come out of the great ordeal; they have washed their robes and made them white in the blood of the Lamb" (7:14). Then follows some of the most moving, hope-filled words in the Bible, words that are often read at Christian funerals, as the elder tenderly tells John:

> For this reason they are before the throne of God,
> and worship him day and night within his temple,
> and the one seated on the throne will shelter them.
> They will hunger no more, and thirst no more;
> the sun will not strike them, nor any scorching heat;
> for the Lamb at the center of the throne will be their shepherd,

and he will guide them to springs of the waters of life,
and God will wipe away every tear from their eyes. (Revelation 7:15–17)

Then follows a great dramatic pause: "When the Lamb opened the seventh seal, there was silence in heaven for about half an hour" (8:1). Then the seven trumpets of judgment are blown and a storm of fire and hail and blood rains down on the earth (chapter 8). The Roman armies invade (chapters 9–11) and Jerusalem is leveled: ". . . and they will trample over the holy city for forty-two months" (11:2), which happens to be the exact length of the war. But even the complete devastation of Jerusalem does not mean defeat for God's elect. The choir of angels sings a song of triumph, which has reverberated through the ages down to our own time:

The kingdom of the world has become the kingdom of our Lord
and of his Messiah,
and he will reign forever and ever. (Revelation 11:15)

Then follows what is perhaps the most fascinating section—chapters 12 and 13. Chapter 12 begins with a cryptic note that the Nazarenes are safe, having fled to their desert hideaway (Pella): "And the woman fled into the wilderness, where she has a place prepared by God, so that there she can be nourished . . ." (12:6) At least this is how this passage has been interpreted by scholars such as Schonfield, who are cognizant of Revelation's Jewish Christian nature. But there is another intriguing possibility, as we shall see momentarily.

The shock caused by the devastation of Jerusalem reverberated around the world:

Then the dragon [Satan] took his stand on the sand of the seashore. And I saw a beast rising out of the sea . . . In amazement the whole earth followed the beast, and they worshipped the beast saying, "Who is like the beast, and who can fight against it." . . . The beast was allowed to exercise authority for forty-two months [the length of the war]. . . . It was allowed to make war on the saints and to conquer them. It was given authority over every tribe and people and language and nation . . . (Revelation 12:17–13:7)

And again patience is counseled for the Nazarenes:

> Let anyone who has an ear listen:
>   If you are to be taken captive, into captivity you go; if you kill with the sword, with the sword you must be killed.
>   Here is a call for the endurance and faith of the saints. (Revelation 13:9–10)

THE WOMAN CLOTHED WITH THE SUN

Before continuing our survey of events, we should pause for a moment to more closely examine the highly intriguing chapter 12, considered by scholars to be perhaps the most puzzling chapter in Revelation in terms of its enigmatic symbolism; symbolism quite relevant to the current "Magdalene mania" that has so captured the public's attention in recent years. The chapter begins with a description of "a woman clothed with the sun, with the moon under her feet, and on her head a crown of twelve stars" (12:1). The identity of this woman has been interpreted in various ways. For Roman Catholics, this is Mary, mother of Jesus, the "Queen of Heaven." Interpreters looking at this through the lens of Jewish Christianity see this as a symbol of the Jerusalem Church. The Christian Church is often referred to as the "bride of Christ" in both the New Testament and in Church tradition. The basis for interpreting this as a symbol specifically for the Jerusalem Church is verse 6: "and the woman fled into the wilderness, where she has a place prepared by God," often interpreted as a reference to the flight to Pella.

But certain statements make me wonder if this could, in fact, be a veiled reference to Mary Magdalene. If the Magdalene was indeed as significant in the life of Jesus and in the life of the early church as serious alternative historians such as Margaret Starbird claim, we should expect some reference to her in Revelation's overview of Nazarene history. Even James Tabor, who until recently was certain that there was no scriptural or historical evidence of Jesus being married, has done a 180-degree turn in light of his conviction that the woman named Mariamne buried in the controversial Talpiot tomb is Mary Magdalene, the wife of Jesus. If this is true, then Jesus's and Mary's son, Judah, is apparently also buried there, and brings a whole new light to Revelation 12.[25]

We are told of the woman clothed with the sun: "She was pregnant and was crying out in birthpangs, in the agony of giving birth" (12:2). Especially compelling are verses 5 and 6: "And she gave birth to a son, a male child, who is to rule all the nations with a rod of iron. But her child was snatched away and taken to God and to his throne; and the woman fled into the wilderness . . ." In traditional interpretation, this child is Jesus, and his being "snatched away" is a reference to his crucifixion. But if we take the passage at face value, it certainly sounds as if this child was killed in childbirth or shortly after. And if he was the son of Jesus and Mary Magdalene, it would make perfect sense that, as the messianic heir, this child would be the one to "rule all the nations." If the child was Jesus, we would expect some symbolic reference that it was "the beast" of Rome that killed him, some reference to his crucifixion and resurrection; but this child is simply "snatched away" to heaven.

Margaret Starbird and other Magdalene researchers believe that the Magdalene fled to the south of France to protect her child, based on strong and persistent local legends to that effect; the best known of these are found in the medieval "Golden Legend" of Jacobus de Voragine.[26] This also may be alluded to in Revelation:

[T]he dragon . . . pursued the woman who had given birth to the male child. But the woman was given the two wings of the great eagle, so that she could fly from the serpent into the wilderness, to her place where she is nourished for a time, and times, and half a time. Then from his mouth the serpent poured water like a river after the woman, to sweep her away with the flood. But the earth came to the help of the woman . . . (Revelation 12:13–16)

The Roman persecution of any children of Jesus and Mary Magdalene would make sense if Jesus was of Davidic descent. We have the famous account in Matthew 2 of King Herod attempting to kill Jesus after his birth because of his royal blood. If Jesus was crucified by Rome because he was a Davidic pretender, it would make perfect sense that his heirs would also be in danger. We have solid historical evidence, which will be examined in the next chapter, that other relatives of Jesus were watched closely by Rome, some even being hauled in for interrogation; and, as we shall see, James's successor, Symeon, would be executed by Rome.

THE FUTURE OF THE NAZARENES

Up through chapter 13 of Revelation, John presents a summary of the history of the Nazarenes. Commencing with chapter 14 he looks to the future, a future that is ensured by God. The empire is about to feel God's wrath, but as it was the teaching of Moses that "the Lord is slow to anger and abounding in steadfast love" (Numbers 14:18), before the vials are tipped there will be one last chance for repentance:

> Then I saw another angel flying in midheaven, with an eternal gospel to proclaim to those who live on the earth—to every nation and tribe and language and people. He said in a loud voice, "Fear God and give him glory, for the hour of judgment has come . . ." (Revelation 14:6–7)

In the succeeding chapters, the imagery parallels the preceding judgments on Jerusalem, but the horror is turned up another notch for the unrepentant: "Then I saw another portent in heaven, great and amazing: seven angels with seven plagues, which are the last. For with them the wrath of God is ended" (Revelation 15:1). For the Nazarenes, victory is assured: "And I saw what appeared to be a sea of glass mixed with fire, and those who had conquered the beast . . . standing beside the sea with harps of God in their hands" (15:2). For the persecuted Nazarenes, this would bring to mind the victory of their ancestors who looked back at the drowned bodies of their Egyptian pursuers. This passage evokes a "Red Sea of fire" which consumes the neo-Egyptians (the Romans). And as their ancestors sang the victory song of Miriam after their oppressors' defeat (Exodus 15), the faithful descendants of Moses likewise sing a song of victory:

And they sing the song of Moses, the servant, of God, and the song of the Lamb:
"Great and amazing are your deeds, Lord God the Almighty!
Just and true are your ways, King of the nations!
Lord, who will not fear and glorify your name?
For you alone are holy,
All nations will come and worship before you,
For your judgments have been revealed." (Revelation 15:3–4)

Chapter 16 then describes in gruesome detail the judgments that are soon to fall upon Rome. "Then I heard a loud voice from the temple telling the seven angels, 'Go and pour out on the earth the seven bowls of the wrath of God'" (16:1). All the plagues that fell upon Egypt will not compare to the horrors that will be poured out upon the unrepentant worshippers of the beast of Rome. As the waters of the Nile were turned to blood, the waters of the entire earth will turn crimson with the blood of the dead as the apocalyptic battle of Armageddon begins. The plagues that accompany the pouring of each bowl are described in gruesome horror-show detail, and what is perhaps the most graphically horrid chapter in the religious literature of the world reaches its climax:

And there came flashes of lightning, rumblings, peals of thunder, and a violent earthquake, such as had not occurred since people were upon the earth, so violent was the earthquake. The great city was split into three parts, and the cities of the nations fell. God remembered great Babylon and gave her the wine cup of the fury of his wrath. And every island fled away, and no mountains were to be found; and huge hailstones, each weighing about a hundred pounds, dropped from heaven on people . . . (Revelation 16:18–21)

Josephus, in his account of the Jewish Wars, recorded the actual events that likely inspired John's cryptic imagery when he describes the siege of the city of Jotapata by Vespasian: "Vespasian then set the engines for throwing stones . . . round about the city; the number of engines were in all a hundred and sixty . . . and stones of the weight of a talent [a hundred pounds] were thrown by the engines . . . together with fire . . ."[27] In the original Greek, Revelation says that the hailstones from heaven weighed "about a talent."

Chapter 17 makes plain that the fall of Rome is symbolized by the figure of "Babylon the great mother of whores and of earth's abominations," who is "drunk with the blood of the saints and the blood of the witnesses of Jesus" (17:5–6), and her defeat is celebrated with hallelujahs:

> After this I heard what seemed to be the loud voice of a great multitude in heaven saying,
>   "Hallelujah! Salvation and glory and power to our God,
>   for his judgments are true and just;
>   he has judged the great whore who corrupted the earth with her fornication,
>   and he has avenged on her the blood of his servants."
> Once more they said,
>   "Hallejuah! The smoke goes up from her forever and ever."
> (Revelation 19:1–3)

And in the majestic final two chapters (21–22), the New Jerusalem is lowered down from heaven to be God's home among mortals from where Messiah Jesus will reign forever and ever:

> Then I saw a new heaven and a new earth; for the first heaven and the first earth had passed away, and the sea was no more. And I saw the holy city, the new Jerusalem, coming down out of heaven from God, prepared as a bride adorned for her husband. And I heard a loud voice from the throne saying,
>   "See, the home of God is among mortals.

He will dwell with them as their God;
They will be his peoples,
And God himself will be with them;
He will wipe every tear from their eyes.
Death will be no more;
Mourning and crying and pain will be no more,
For the first things have passed away." (Revelation 21:1–4)

These are, in my mind, the most stirring and moving words in the Christian Bible. To understand the true context and meaning of these words, as they were understood by the first- and second-century Nazarenes to whom they were written (as opposed to the many reprehensible modern Christian distortions of these prophecies), makes them even more poignant. The words of Revelation provided great hope and comfort to Jesus's familial and spiritual descendants in their time of greatest tribulation. And perhaps these words still have a message of hope for us today, though certainly not in the distorted sense of Christian fundamentalist interpretation. In the concluding section, the ultimate author of the prophecy is revealed:

"It is I, Jesus, who sent my angel to you with this testimony for the churches. I am the root and descendant of David, the bright morning star."
    The Spirit and the bride say, "Come."
    And let everyone who hears say, "Come."
    And let everyone who is thirsty come.
    Let anyone who wishes take the water of life as a gift. (Revelation 22:16–17)

Here we see the universal message of hope that was held out to all people by Jesus and the Nazarenes. It was remarkably inclusive, especially for the time, of all peoples and nations. *Everyone* who is thirsty can come. *Anyone* who wishes can receive the water of life. It is also pertinent that, in identifying himself, Jesus's primary means of identification is to say

that he is the "root and descendant of David, the bright morning star."
In the following chapters we will see that this continued to be the primary means of identification of the Desposyni—the familial descendants
of Jesus. They would continue to hold out this universal message of hope
rooted in David in succeeding centuries. Their message would reverberate
out into the world like ripples from a stone tossed in a pond, touching
and influencing many other peoples, even unto modern times. We turn
now to examine those still expanding ripples, ripples in a stream that has
been forced to flow underground.

7

AFTERMATH
From Nazarenes to Ebionites

*As long as they seek to be both Jews and Christians, they
are neither Jews nor Christians.*

JEROME, EPISTLE TO AUGUSTINE

Following the devastation of the Jewish War, the Nazarenes took refuge in
Pella, a community in exile, where they lay in anxious wait with their fellow
Jews. From this point on it is preferable to call them the Ebionites. There
was no clear demarcation or formal transition from Nazarene to Ebionite;
there was no sudden change of theology or Christology. But the critical year
of 70 CE is as good a marker as any to indicate the transition from Nazarene
to Ebionite, especially since many scholars refer to the difference between
pre- and post-70 Judaism as Hebrew (or Israelite) religion, and Rabbinical
Judaism. Another indication of a transition from Nazarenes to Ebionites is
the change in leadership from James to Symeon, who was elected second
bishop of Jerusalem after the death of James. While the writings of later
church fathers speak of the Nazarenes and Ebionites as if they were two different Jewish Christian groups, they are mistaken in that assessment. The
Nazarenes and the Ebionites were one and the same group, but for clarity
we will refer to the pre-70 group in Jerusalem as Nazarenes, and the post-70
group in Pella and elsewhere as Ebionites.

We first encounter the term "Ebionite" in Irenaeus, who, late in the second century, uses the term to refer to all Jewish Christians; however, it was apparently a term that the Jerusalem Yachad took as their own self-appellation. It is derived from the Hebrew word *evyonim,* which literally means "the poor." The term may be a technical one, not necessarily indicating peasants living in poverty (though their conditions were indeed relatively poor), but rather a proud self-designation on the part of the Nazarenes, who called themselves the poor because of their chosen asceticism and renunciation of personal possessions (see Acts 2:44–45). The choosing of this name may have been inspired by Jesus himself, who said in the Sermon on the Mount, "Blessed are the poor . . . for theirs is the kingdom of heaven" (Matt. 5:3). Jesus's brother certainly carried on this teaching. In the Epistle of James we read: "Has not God chosen the poor in the world to be rich in faith and to be heirs of the kingdom that he has promised to those who love him?" (James 2:5). It is also interesting that Paul uses the term in association with the Jewish Christians in Jerusalem (Romans 15:26, Galatians 2:10).

THE DIVERGING STREAMS

As a result of the audacious and doomed Jewish rebellion against Rome, the many new Gentile churches that sprang up as a result of Paul's missionary efforts were cold and aloof to the heirs of Jesus's family and the Jerusalem Church. For Paul's Gentile Christians, the destruction of Jerusalem seemed to confirm Paul's teaching that the Torah was a relic of the past, a cursed thing rejected by God now that the New Covenant had been revealed through the death and resurrection of Jesus. As Paul bluntly put it, "For all who rely on the works of the law are under a curse . . ." (Galatians 3:10). The new Christians certainly could not find any sympathy for the nationalistic aspirations of the Ebionites. It seemed to the Christians that the destruction of Jerusalem and the temple was God's judgment on the people of Israel for not accepting Jesus as their Messiah. For the Ebionites, as for all Jews, the end of the temple meant the cessation of temple rites and the end of animal sacrifice. For the

Gentile Christians, this seemed to be the death knell of the law, and Jesus's death on a Roman cross was increasingly understood by them as the sacrifice to end all sacrifices. The Ebionites would later contend in their writings that Jesus and the disciples had spoken against animal sacrifices in the temple. This aspect of Ebionite belief will be discussed further in chapter 9.

The parting of the ways between Ebionites and Christians was fully cemented after the second Jewish revolt under the messianic pretender Bar Kokhba in 135 CE. After this second failed rebellion, the separation was complete and permanent. For the Christians it was a welcome release from the need to adhere to any lingering vestiges of Jewish teachings and practices. They were now free to develop a theology, Christology, and liturgy all their own, inspired and informed by their Hellenistic interpretation of Paul's epistles, a process that would eventually culminate in the dogma set down at the Council of Nicaea in 325 and refined at the Council of Chalcedon in 451. Dr. Hugh Schonfield, in his seminal work *The History of Jewish Christianity* (1936), insightfully and evenhandedly summed up the situation this way:

> Thus by the pressure of political circumstances and racial antipathies Jewish and Gentile Christianity drew apart, each following the path of its inherited tendencies, and developing its beliefs along the lines of its own racial genius. Paul's great ideal of Jew and Gentile, both one in Christ, could not then be realized, because neither would acknowledge the right of the other to regard God's revelation from the standpoint of his own psychology.[1]

To his dying day, Schonfield (1901–1988), who was a true humanist, held out hope that Paul's "great ideal" for the unity of Jew and Gentile might one day be realized through a new appreciation of original Jewish Christianity. We still wait, and as we shall see in the latter chapters of this book, various groups throughout history have worked clandestinely to further this cause. As surprising as it might seem, this ideal of unity is actually rooted more in the beliefs of the Ebionites than it is in Paul.

One of the primary goals of the Ebionites was the reunification of the heirs of the two covenants—the Mosaic Covenant established at Sinai, and the New Covenant established at Golgotha—which will be discussed in chapter 9 when we go into the specifics of Ebionite theology. In our own day there are heartening signs of a potential reconciliation in the rediscovery and reassessment of original Jewish Christianity by both Jewish and Christian scholars. Thanks to the seminal works of Hugh Schonfield and Hyam Maccoby, and recent works by Robert Eisenman, James Tabor, and Barrie Wilson,[2] these findings are finally beginning to become more broadly available.

But in the aftermath of the year 70, tensions between Jewish and Gentile Christians only heightened. The Ebionites accused Paul's Christians of apostasy for having abandoned the original Torah-based teachings of Jesus and James. They took pride in calling themselves the Ebionim, voluntarily poor in worldly possessions, but rich in true faith. They thus contrasted themselves with the relatively wealthy but unfaithful Christians, who, at Paul's insistence, would not even submit to the basic law of circumcision. Later Christians, such as the church father Origen, retorted that it was most fitting for the Jewish Christians to call themselves "the poor," since they had such a "poor" understanding of the divinity of Jesus.[3]

The Church historian Hegesippus, whose work was a major source for Eusebius's later *Church History,* looked back longingly from the second century to apostolic times when unity still existed among the followers of Jesus. Eusebius relates Hegesippus's account as follows:

> In describing the situation at that time, Hegesippus goes on to say that until then the Church had remained a virgin, pure and uncorrupted, since those who were trying to corrupt the wholesome standard of the saving message . . . lurked somewhere under cover of darkness. But when the sacred band of the apostles had in various ways reached the end of their life, and the generation of those privileged to listen with their own ears to the divine wisdom had passed on, then godless error began to take shape through the deceit

of false teachers, who, now that none of the apostles were left, threw off the mask and attempted to counter the preaching of the truth by preaching the knowledge falsely so called.[4]

This is a famous passage that has often been quoted by Christian scholars throughout the ages to rail against the "heretics" (both Gnostic and Jewish Christian) who infested the sub-apostolic church. But what has been little recognized is that Hegesippus was himself a Jewish Christian, and this passage is actually a rant against Hellenistic heresies (mainly Gnosticism) that had infested Jewish Christianity. This is evidenced in a passage preserved by Eusebius wherein Hegesippus discusses his visits to various churches on a journey he made from Palestine to Corinth to Rome. He was satisfied as to their orthodoxy because "in each city all is according to the *ordinances of the law and the Prophets* and the Lord."[5] It is probably not accidental that no copies of Hegesippus's Church history (*Memoirs*) have survived, for it likely told a story that was not at all congenial to the emerging Catholic Church. If a copy of Hegesippus's history is ever recovered, we will have a much more accurate picture of the actual development of the Church.

The Ebionites are formally denounced for the first time in the writings of the church father Irenaeus, Bishop of Lyons (ca. 130–200 CE), the first great heresy hunter. His chief work, *Adversus Haereses* (Against Heresies) was written primarily to refute the rapidly growing Gnostic sects of his day, some of whom would influence an offshoot of the Ebionites that came to be known as the Elkesaites. But Irenaeus also singles out the Ebionites for their "heretical" beliefs and practices. He condescendingly remarks of their Judaic practices: "They practice circumcision, persevere in the observance of those customs which are enjoined by the law, and are so Judaic in their mode of life that they even adore Jerusalem as if it were the house of God."[6] Irenaeus also notes that they pray facing Jerusalem and celebrate the Eucharist using water instead of wine. This latter practice is a unique clue providing evidence that links the Ebionites to later Jewish Christian groups, such as the Elkesaites, and to medieval sects such as the Bogomils and Cathars.

SYMEON AND THE FLIGHT TO PELLA

Unfortunately, we know little about the Ebionites after the year 70, only what we are told by the heresy hunters of the second and third centuries, who, in addition to Irenaeus, include Hippolytus, Epiphanius, and Jerome, and their viewpoint is highly prejudicial. S. G. F. Brandon argued that the reason we hear nothing directly of the Ebionites after 70 is because the Nazarenes perished along with their fellow Jews during the war. Brandon believed that the story of the flight to Pella was a legend promulgated by a later Jewish Christian group called the Ebionites in order to bolster their *false* claim that they were the descendants of the original Nazarenes.[7] The contemporary German scholar of Jewish Christianity, Gerd Lüdemann, agrees with Brandon that the flight to Pella is a fictitious legend.[8] This position is untenable, however. The great German scholar of Jewish Christianity, Hans-Joachim Schoeps, tersely dismissed this notion by saying, "The attempt . . . made by S. G. F. Brandon and Georg Strecker to treat the flight to Pella as unhistorical is so absurd that I will not discuss it."[9] Would Brandon and Lüdemann really have us believe that *none* of the Jewish Christians escaped the siege? Josephus himself attests that "the unhappy Jews, when they were not able to bear the devastations which the robbers [brigands] made among them, were all under a necessity of leaving their own habitations, and of flying away, as hoping to dwell more easily anywhere else in the world among foreigners [than in their own country]."[10] We have already seen evidence that the Nazarenes, as a matter of theological belief, did not take part in the Zealot rebellion.

The actual reason we have no direct records of the Ebionites after the year 70 is that their writings were suppressed and burned by the heresy hunters, including their most precious gospel, commonly called the Gospel of the Hebrews. Also, the first few years of the post-70 period were spent in hiding in Pella, and secrecy was paramount. Fortunately, we do have a few quotes and references from the Ebionite gospel preserved by Epiphanius, which we will examine in the next chapter, as well as at least some authentic recollections of the Ebionite Acts in the *Pseudo-Clementine* "Recognitions."

A major piece of evidence attesting to the continuing existence of the Ebionites is a recorded list of bishops who succeeded James as leaders of the Jerusalem Church, which we will examine momentarily. The flight to Pella may account for the tradition in two of the gospels (Matthew and John) that the disciples returned to Galilee after the crucifixion, since the northern region of Transjordan, where Pella was located, was considered part of the Galilee (see map, p. 8). James Tabor makes a very convincing case that the rugged cliffs and caves around the Wadi Cherith (the brook of Cherith), just south of Pella, had served as a "hideout" for Jesus and his disciples during the winter months prior to his arrest and crucifixion. Thus, the reason the Nazarenes fled there is because Symeon was already familiar with it; it had served Jesus's disciples in the past as a reliable and familiar place of refuge.[11] Hans-Joachim Schoeps had noted this fifty years ago in his groundbreaking work on Jewish Christianity: "Eastern Palestine was . . . the safest place the Jewish Christians could choose in this troubled period. . . . According to . . . topographical studies, Pella is a typical example of a hiding place, lying hidden in a valley on the edge of the Transjordanian high plateau."[12]

Scholars debate exactly when James's successor Symeon took over the reins of leadership, but the time of the flight to Pella gives us a clue. Hegesippus writes that the election of Symeon happened "after the martyrdom of James and the capture of Jerusalem, which instantly followed" (see chapter 6), thus suggesting that the election of Symeon happened following the Jewish War. But it is quite unlikely that following the devastation of the war it would have been possible, as Hegesippus also attests, for "the apostles and disciples of the Lord" to have "assembled from all parts together with . . . kinsmen of the Lord" for an election. The election must have happened prior to the outbreak of the war. Early patristic writers were eager to attribute the fall of Jerusalem to the death of James, and thus telescoped the time frame. It is most logical that the election of Symeon would have happened immediately after James's death in 62, and several years before the flight to Pella, which happens about the year 66.

This scenario is actually attested to in an independent Jewish source, the notorious *Toledoth Yeshu** (Generations of Jesus), which says that it was Symeon who organized and led the exodus to Pella.[13] The *Toledoth Yeshu* also makes another startling assertion—that Symeon wrote books! Epiphanius reports that Jewish scholars in Tiberias in the latter half of the fourth century had collected versions of the gospels of Matthew and John and the book of Acts, all written in Hebrew.[14] According to Hugh Schonfield, these three writings were actually the Ebionite gospel, commonly known as the Gospel of the Hebrews, as well as an underlying source for the book of Revelation known as the Book of John, and the part of the *Pseudo-Clementines* known as the "Ascents of James" (sometimes called the "Ebionite Acts" by scholars).[15] The *Toledoth Yeshu* asserts that all three of these works were composed by Simeon ben Calpus, an honorable old man who was the uncle of Jesus. This is certainly a confused reference to our Symeon, whose father was Cleophas the brother of Joseph. And, as we shall see, Symeon was renowned for the ripe old age to which he lived. While it is highly unlikely that Symeon authored these books, he may well have been associated with them in some way.

The *Toledoth Yeshu* goes on to say that about thirty years after the death of Jesus (which would be about the time Symeon succeeded James), the Jewish Sanhedrin, disturbed by the constant calls for revolt against Rome, sought someone who could remove the Nazarenes from Judea. They called upon "a certain aged man from among the Elders . . . who frequented the Holy of Holies," a man named "Simeon Cepha."[16] This, too, is certainly a garbled reference to our Symeon, and is an independent confirmation of the report in Epiphanius that James served as an "opposition high priest" who was permitted to enter the Holy of Holies once a year. The Ebionites fled to Pella under the direction of Bishop Symeon sometime around 66, set up (or reconstituted) their auxiliary base at the Wadi Cherith for about eight years, and then at least a contingent led by Bishop Symeon returned to reestablish a permanent base on Mt. Zion, likely around the fourth year of the emperor Vespasian in either 73 or 74 CE.

---

*The *Toledoth Yeshu* is the source of the notorious Pandera legend that says Jesus was the bastard son of the rape of Mary by a Roman soldier named Pandera.

RETRENCHMENT ON MT. ZION

There are two ancient authorities who tell us that the Ebionites established a church on Mt. Zion upon their return. Bishop Epiphanius (315–403), who was a native of Palestine, tells us that when the Emperor Hadrian visited Jerusalem about 130–131, he saw on Mt. Zion, "a small church of God. It marked the site of the Hypero-on [upper room] to which the disciples returned from the Mount of Olives after the Lord had been taken up. It had been built on that part of Sion."[17] Apparently, the upper room that some wealthy benefactor provided for Jesus to use for the Passover meal with his disciples (Mark 14:15, Luke 22:12) became a permanent base of operations. This is attested in Acts, which tells us that immediately after the disciples witnessed Jesus's ascension, "they returned to Jerusalem from the mount called Olivet . . . When they had entered the city, they went to the room upstairs where they were staying . . ." (Acts 1:12–13). That this became a permanent headquarters and place of worship is further confirmed by Eusebius, who says, "And the history also contains the remark that there also was a very big Church of Christ in Jerusalem, made up of Jews, until the time of Hadrian."[18] There is obviously some confusion between the reports of Epiphanius and Eusebius as to whether this church was "small" or "very big." One writer may be referring to the size of the physical building, while another may be referring to the size of the congregation.

In any event, while many people assume that the Jews were completely removed from Jerusalem after the year 70, this is certainly not the case. It was only after the second Jewish revolt under Bar Kokhba (132–135) that the Jews were completely forbidden entry to Jerusalem. While their numbers were significantly reduced after the year 70, many stalwarts simply refused to abandon the Holy City. Indeed, if the Jews had been completely removed from Jerusalem after the first revolt, then the statements we have from many of the church fathers that the Jews were expelled from Jerusalem after the Bar Kokbha revolt would make no sense.

Logically, the "church" that was seen by Hadrian on Mt. Zion must have been a Jewish Christian synagogue, since no overtly Christian churches could have been built and remained standing until after the year 313, when Constantine's Edict of Milan made Christianity a legally recognized religion in the Roman Empire. The tenth-century Patriarch of Alexandria, Euthychius (896–940), wrote a history of the Church in which he tells us that shortly after the first war with Rome, the Jewish Christians who had fled to Pella "returned to Jerusalem in the fourth year of the emperor Vespasian (73 CE), and built there their church."[19] This was not a new building they erected, however, but was the reconstruction of an older one that had been destroyed during the Roman siege, a fact that has been established by two archaeologists, Jacob Pinkerfield and Bargil Pixner.[20]

It is known to only a few scholars, and not at all to the general public, that the exact site of this Jerusalem "church" can still be seen and visited on Mt. Zion. Pilgrims and tourists have for centuries visited a building that contains on its second floor what is known as the Cenacle (from the Latin *coenaculum,* or "upper room"), where Jesus and the apostles ate the Last Supper (see plates 11–14). Thanks to the archaeological work of the remarkable late Benedictine priest, Father Bargil Pixner, it has now been established that this building that houses the upper room was originally the headquarters of the Nazarenes, rebuilt after the war by those who returned from Pella. In other words, the building that tourists today visit as the site of the Cenacle was also the first-century headquarters of the Jerusalem Church, which was commonly known in ancient times as the Church of the Apostles, but is more accurately the Synagogue of the Apostles.

Father Pixner was both a biblical scholar and an archaeologist, and was very aware of the Church's roots in Jewish Christianity. No doubt this is because he lived for many years in Jerusalem; in fact, he took his final vows and served as a Benedictine prior at the Hagia Maria Sion Abbey on Mt. Zion, which is not only adjacent to the Cenacle, but was at one time physically connected to it. Pixner took note of the significance of this building when he became aware of archaeological excavations done there in 1951 by the Israeli archaeologist Jacob Pinkerfield. Pinkerfield was enlisted by the Israeli government to restore the building, which had been damaged by a bomb during the Israeli War of Independence in 1948. The Israelis were greatly interested in preserving the site because the first floor, beneath the upper room, houses the purported tomb of King David. So this unique and remarkable building is venerated by both Jews and Christians, and, as we shall see, by Muslims as well, who have had a hand in shaping its history. It is quite possible that the reason the Nazarenes originally used the building was because of its messianic associations with King David.

When Pinkerfield conducted his excavations, he found three earlier floor levels below the present ground level floor, which was built by Muslims. He found, in descending order, floors built by the Crusaders, Byzantines, and then the original floor, which Pinkerfield believed was that of a Roman-period synagogue. Pinkerfield assumed it was a standard Jewish synagogue based on the fact that a niche for housing a Torah scroll was found six feet above the floor (the standard height for such niches), and the niche was oriented in the direction of the temple. But a standard Jewish synagogue it was not. Two pieces of evidence attest that it was, in fact, a Nazarene synagogue. First, this synagogue's niche is not oriented exactly toward the northeast where the temple was located. Instead, it is oriented slightly off north, *exactly toward the present location of the Church of the Holy Sepulchre,* which was built to mark the site where Jesus was crucified, buried, and resurrected. Secondly, in the lowest layer of the excavation, Pinkerfield found pieces of plaster from the original synagogue wall with two telling inscriptions. One inscription has the initials of the Greek words for "conquer, savior, mercy." Another inscription translates as, "O Jesus, that I may live, O Lord of the autocrat." Pinkerfield died before these translations were completed, which is why he never realized that this was no ordinary Jewish synagogue.

When the Ebionites returned from Pella following the final siege of Masada in 73 that ended the war, they found Jerusalem and their synagogue in ruins. Since the return of Messiah Jesus had not happened when the Jews rose up against the Romans, and since God had shockingly allowed the Holy City to be destroyed, it confirmed the Ebionites' conviction that violent resistance was not God's will. And since it was also now clear that their expectation of the imminent Parousia would have to be revised, they set about rebuilding their synagogue. The Ebionites were permitted by the Romans to rebuild because they were still viewed by the Romans as Jews, and not as Christians. Pixner noted that a solid piece of evidence attesting to their thorough Jewishness was their use of large *ashlars* (rectangular stones) taken from the ruins of the temple in their rebuilding project. In fact, the Ebionites now began to refer to the area around their synagogue as Nea Sion (New Zion).* As Father Pixner summed things up, "Very few places in Jerusalem can point to such an enduring tradition as Zion's claim to be the seat of the primitive church. No other place has raised a serious rival claim."[21]

In the year 312, Eusebius, writing a dozen or so years prior to the Council of Nicaea and before Jerusalem became a Christian city, gives solid evidence to support Pixner's claim:

> This is the word of the Gospel, which through our Lord Jesus Christ and through the Apostles *went out from Sion* and was spread to every nation. It is a fact that it poured forth from Jerusalem and *Mt. Sion adjacent to it, on which our Savior and Lord had stayed many times and where he had taught much doctrine.*[22] (Italics mine.)

There are also eyewitness testimonials to the continuing existence of the Synagogue of the Apostles on Mt. Zion. In the year 333, a Christian pilgrim visiting Jerusalem, known to history only as the "Bordeaux Pilgrim," did not visit the Holy Sepulchre first, as all Christian pilgrims customarily did when arriving in the Holy City; according to his travel itinerary, he went to the temple and then ascended Mt. Zion, where he reported that a synagogue was still standing. The Bordeaux Pilgrim's unique itinerary has made many scholars conclude that he was a Jewish Christian. Further supporting evidence that this synagogue was the Synagogue of the Apostles comes from Eucherius, the Archbishop of Lyons, who gave this description of Mt. Zion in about the year 440:

---

*The Hebrew word *Zion* is spelled Sion in Greek and Latin.

The plain upper part is occupied by monks' cells, which surround a church. Its foundations, it is said, have been laid by the Apostles in reverence to the place of the resurrection of the Lord [toward the Church of the Holy Sepulchre]. It was there that they were filled with the Spirit of the Paraclete [the Holy Spirit] as promised by the Lord.[23]

Eucherius is here referring to the fact that the descent of the Holy Spirit on Pentecost is also believed to have taken place in the upper room, or Cenacle (see Acts 2).

In the year 348, St. Cyril, who would later become bishop of Jerusalem, delivered a sermon at the Church of the Holy Sepulchre in which he remarked that it would have been more appropriate for him to preach about the work of the Holy Spirit "in the upper church of the apostles," where the Spirit had first descended upon the apostles.[24] It is interesting that at this date Cyril could not preach in what he called the "Church of the Apostles" because it was still a working synagogue in the hands of the Ebionites, as attested by the Bordeaux Pilgrim. At this time the Ebionites were being denounced as heretics. This is further attested by church father Gregory of Nyssa, who visited Jerusalem in the year 381 and reported that the place where the Holy Spirit had first descended was in turmoil, and that a "counter altar" had been erected there.[25] This could only be referring to the fact that the Ebionites refused to acknowledge the teachings of the "Great Church" that emerged after Nicaea. Father Pixner notes that this is confirmed by Epiphanius, who "declared that Mt. Zion, which was once a privileged height, had now been 'cut off' (as heretical) from the rest of the church."[26]

It is also attested that the Ebionites built a wall around their synagogue to keep out Gentile influence; the Bordeux Pilgrim states that he entered and exited "the wall of Sion." This wall resulted in the Ebionite community living in a kind of Jewish Christian ghetto on Mt. Zion, a situation that would not last very long. A large Byzantine church was erected on Mt. Zion by order of Theodosius I (reigned 379–395), and the Synagogue of the Apostles was soon an annex of the Byzantine Church of Hagia Sion (Holy Zion). The Ebionites of Mt. Zion were integrated into the Byzantine Church through the efforts of St. Porphyrius, a monk of the new Church of Hagia Sion, who is believed to have been of Jewish descent and is remembered as a remarkable preacher who apparently won the affections of the Ebionites on Mt. Zion. It seems likely that the Ebionites of Mt. Zion, surrounded as they were by Roman, Byzantine, and other Gentile Christians who largely accepted the Council of Nicaea, began to slowly conform to, and accept, some of the doctrines and practices of Catholic Christianity. As we shall see in chapter 10, this may account for the fact that the church fathers speak of certain Jewish Christians, whom they call Nazoreans, who were distinguished from the Ebionites by the fact that they accepted the virgin birth and Paul's letters. In any case, the Ebionites of Mt. Zion and their synagogue were absorbed into the Roman Catholic Church. The Synagogue of the Apostles officially became the Church of the Apostles when John II, Bishop of Jerusalem, blessed the altar on the feast of Yom Kippur in or about the year 394, and gave a sermon in which he praised the efforts of an Israelite named Porphyrius.

THE RELICS OF JAMES ON MT. ZION

It is also quite intriguing that not far from the Synagogue of the Apostles on Mt. Zion is the twelfth-century Armenian Orthodox Cathedral of St. James, site of the patriarchate of the Armenian Church. While the James after whom the cathedral is named is the apostle James, son of Zebedee and brother of John (James "the Greater," or St. James "Major"), there are actually more relics of James the Brother of Jesus (whom the Armenians call St. James "Minor" or James "the Less") in the cathedral than there are of James the Greater. One of those relics is a representation of the throne of James (see plate 31). While this ornate chair dates to only the eighteenth century, it is claimed to be a replacement for an older throne, which Eusebius attests belonged to the brother of Jesus:

> The chair of James, who first received the episcopate of the church
> at Jerusalem from the Savior himself and the apostles, and who, as
> the divine records show, was called a brother of Christ, has been

preserved until now, the brethren who have followed him in succession there exhibiting clearly to all the reverence which both those of old times and those of our own day maintained and do maintain for holy men on account of their piety.[27]

When Eusebius refers to "the brethren who have followed him in succession there," he is referring to the bishops of the Jerusalem Church.

Beginning in the eleventh century, the Armenians, who had already established a presence on Zion as early as the third century, began buying up large chunks of property on the top of Mt. Zion, to the point where today the southwestern corner of Jerusalem is known as the Armenian Quarter. The Armenians claim that the bones of James are buried under their main altar and that the cathedral is built over James's home in Jerusalem. I was privileged, on a recent trip to Jerusalem, to be shown the foundations of the home upon which the cathedral was built and to be allowed to photograph the throne of James (see plates 28–32). I was also startled to see over their baptistery a symbol that is very familiar to all Freemasons (see plate 34). The "all-seeing eye" of God is the main symbol of the Armenian Church and figures prominently on the Armenian patriarch's coat of arms (see plate 33). This symbol provides a potential link to the Knights Templar, who had a major hand in the reconstruction of the Synagogue of the Apostles, and also links Jewish Christianity to modern day Freemasonry, all of which will be discussed in later chapters of this book.

I think it is far from coincidence that the Synagogue of the Apostles, the Armenian Cathedral of St. James, and the Roman Catholic Dormitian Abbey (marking the place where Catholics believe Mary, mother of Jesus, died), are all in close proximity to each other on Mt. Zion. While there are three places that have been purported to be the burial place of Mary (the others are Ephesus and the Eastern Orthodox shrine on the Mt. of Olives), it seems that the Roman Catholic Dormition Abbey has the best claim to authenticity, since the upper room where the disciples gathered with Mary and Jesus's brothers following the Ascension (Acts 1), and which became their headquarters, is right next door (see plates 24–27). The Armenians claim that the home of James was right around the corner (see map, p. 9). And if, as James Tabor claims, James is the "beloved disciple" of the fourth gospel to whom Jesus entrusted the care of their mother (a conjecture that makes perfect sense since James was the next of kin),[28] Mary would have lived out her days with James on Mt. Zion. It is likely that the Knights Templar, who established their first headquarters in the Holy Land on the Temple Mount just south of Mt. Zion, and who later rebuilt the Synagogue of the Apostles, became privy to all this information regarding the Holy Family's presence on Mt. Zion. But this is a story that must await a later chapter. Let us now go further afield to trace the records of the Desposyni outside of Jerusalem.

THE DESPOSYNI IN THE DIASPORA

While Symeon continued to provide overall leadership of the Ebionite Yachad from Jerusalem, both Hegesippus and Julius Africanus confirm that the Desposyni presided over the Ebionite communities in the Diaspora. Hegesippus reports of the Desposyni: "Consequently they came and presided over every church, as being martyrs and members of the Lord's family, and since profound peace came to every church they survived till the reign of Trajan [ruled 98–117] . . ."[29] As we discussed in the first chapter, the Desposyni were extremely proud of their heritage, not only because their ancestry was rooted in Jesus's family but also because of their ultimate ancestry in King David; and it is because of that ancestry, even more than their relationship to Jesus, that they became victims of Roman persecution. It is thanks to the Desposyni that the genealogy found in the opening of Matthew's gospel has been preserved; indeed this Jewish genealogy marks the very beginning of the New Testament canon, which is remarkable since the canon and its ordering was produced by the Gentile Christian Church, and such a genealogy would have been of little importance to Gentiles. Julius Africanus attests that the preservation of this genealogy is thanks to the Desposyni:

> A few . . . having private records of their own, either by remembering the names or by getting at them in some other way from the archives,

pride themselves in preserving the memory of their noble descent; and among these happen to be those already mentioned, called desposyni, on account of their connection with the family of the Savior. And these coming from Nazara and Cochaba, Judean villages, to other parts of the country, set forth the above-named genealogy as accurately as possible from the Book of Days [i.e., Chronicles].[30]

It would at first seem logical to assume that the aforementioned "Nazara" refers to Nazareth, but that may not be the case. Hugh Schonfield believes that Nazara and Cochaba were villages in the Transjordan, north of Pella in a region called the Hauran (see map 1). In fact, Schonfield believes that it is from here, not Nazareth in western Galilee, that Jesus and his family hailed. He bases this on what Epiphanius says in the *Panarion* about the dwelling places of the Jewish Christian sects in his day (late fourth century). Because this is an idea that goes against scholarly consensus, it would be good to examine Schonfield's own words stating his quite plausible case:

> The Nazoreans of all kinds, including Ebionites were to be found, says Epiphanius, in Beroea (Aleppo), in Coele-Syria, also on the Decapolis in the proximity of Pella, and generally in Transjordan, in Batanea (Bashan) at a place called Cochaba (Hebrew, Cochabe) . . . see Panarion xviii.1, xxix.7, xxx.2.
>
> The point about this information . . . is that it largely directs us to the eastern side of the Jordan. . . . Western Galilee, upper and lower, does not appear in this picture as an area of concentration . . .
>
> This gives rise to the much debated Nazareth problem . . . It remains in doubt whether the Nazareth to which millions of Christians have directed their steps was in fact the place where the family to which Jesus belonged were settled. . . . Apart from a doubtful reference which may go back to the third century AD no mention of this Nazareth is made in any previous description of western Galilee. . . .
>
> The territory, then, to which we have been chiefly directed is . . .

the northern Transjordan country which in the [first century AD] was the home of Jewish militants and messianists. . . .[31]

Later, citing Julius Africanus's statement about the family of Jesus coming from Nazara and Cochaba, Schonfield continues:

> Here toward the end of the first century AD we have members of the family of Jesus residing at places significantly called Nazara (Sproutville) and Cochaba (Starville). They are called Jewish villages because they were in an area where there were many non-Jews and not far from the Greek cities of the Decapolis. It was to Pella in the Decapolis that the Christian Nazoreans had removed from Judea and Jerusalem shortly before the war with the Romans. If we accept the statement of Epiphanius . . . that Cochaba was in Batanea, then we should look for Nazara in the same district. . . .
>
> The question then arises, when had these messianically-named villages come into existence? . . . [W]hen the relations of Jesus are found in these villages after the war, were they returning to their ancestral homes?[32]

This hypothesis also explains another vexing problem found in the gospels:

> The initial activities of Jesus were all to the north of the Sea of Galilee, a considerable distance from the traditional Nazareth. It is not explained why from somewhere in western Lower Galilee Jesus and his family (John 2:12) should move to Capernaum at the head of a lake. But if they were coming from Batanea this would be quite natural. . . .[33]

Adding further evidence to support this hypothesis is the fact that other maverick figures in Jewish history were located in the same area:

> Judas, one of the prime movers of the . . . Zealot [movement] had come

from Gamala, east of the Sea of Galilee. The movements of John the Baptist at around the same time had Galilean adherents . . .

We have pointers, therefore, to an original breeding ground of prophetic . . . movements in the area to the northeast and east of the Sea of Galilee, the activity fed upon elements, which were a legacy from the ancient Northern Kingdom of Israel, which had retained a certain hostility to Judah and regarded its religion as corrupt.[34]

Pulling all of these strands of evidence together, Schonfield hypothesizes the area of eastern Galilee and western Transjordan as a Nazarene tetrarchy that he calls "Nazarene country":

We encounter a reference in Pliny to a Nazarene tetrarchy (*Natural History* v. 81). This was adjacent to Coele-Syria. . . . how he picked up the name is a mystery. The only tetrarchy in the vicinity was that allocated by Augustus to Philip, son of Herod the Great, which embraced Batanea (Bashan), Auranitis, Trachonitis, and part of Iturea. . . . Auranitis (the Hauran) had a reputation for being the haunt of rebels and malcontents.

. . . as a working hypothesis it may be suggested that the region was natively known as Nasarene or Nazarene Country . . . Some scholars have proposed that the eastern zone of Galilee of the Nations was called Nasara of Galilee. The broader area seems to be indicated in the prophecy of Isaiah that in the Last Times "God will make glorious the way of the sea, beyond Jordan, Galilee of the Gentiles" (Isaiah 9:1–2) . . .

Was, then, the native land of Jesus the eastern zone of Galilee? And did its reputation create the Judean proverb, "Can anything good come out of Nazareth?" (John 1:46).[35]

Unfortunately, it is likely because of Schonfield's reputation as a bit of a maverick himself that his hypothesis has not won over many scholars. But it is rather obvious that this hypothesis ties together a number of loose ends and answers many puzzling questions. We shall find further evidence in support of this when we turn to the Jewish Christian sects that inhabited the area in later centuries, some of which have even survived to the present day. But to balance things out, let us also take a look at what Richard Bauckham has to say on this question of Nazarene and Ebionite origins and geography, since he upholds the more traditional view:

> The name Kokhaba, given by Julius Africanus as one of the two villages from which the *desposynoi* traveled throughout Palestine, has sometimes been identified with Kokhaba in Batanea, to the east of Jordan, which was a center of Jewish Christianity at a later date. To associate the desposynoi of the first Christian generation with this Kokhaba would be most improbable. But the matter requires more careful consideration.
>
> A place called Kokhaba . . . occurs in Epiphanius as one of the main centers of both Nazarene and Ebionite Christianity. It is located in Basanitis or Batanea, and should be identified with the modern Kaukab, just north of the northern border of modern Jordan. Eusebius (*Onomasticon* 172) refers to another place with the similar name of Khoba as an Ebionite village. Eusebius located it fairly precisely: "Khoba, which is to the left of Damascus. There is also a village of Khoba in the same district in which there are Hebrews who believe in Christ, called Ebionites." This appears to distinguish two places called Khoba in the area of Damascus. . . .
>
> Julius Africanus, however, associates Kokhaba with Nazareth, and there are two places of this name not far from Nazareth. One, to the southwest, is modern Kokhav Hayarden or Kaukab el-Hawa, site of the Crusader fortress of Belvoir;* but closer to Nazareth, in the hills north of Sepphoris, sixteen kilometers from Nazareth, is the modern village of Kaukab, which should surely be identified as the Kokhaba of Julius Africanus. . . . That this, rather than the transjordanian Kokhaba, must be the home of the *desposynoi,* along with Nazareth,

---

*It is fascinating that a crusader fortress was built here, and we shall see that this may not be a coincidence when we discuss the Knights Templar in the Holy Land.

would never have been disputed, had it not seemed too much of a coincidence for both Kokhabas to be Jewish Christian centers. . . . but there is a further consideration which may make us wonder whether in fact the apparent coincidence does not reflect a deliberate choice by Jewish Christian émigrés who established their center at Kokhaba in Batanea.[36]

And here Bauckham goes into a revealing explanation of the roots of the names of Nazareth and Kokhaba, which is well worth citing:

The Semitic name [Kokhaba], of course, means "star," a word fraught with messianic significance in the period. . . . It would have suggested Balaam's prophecy of the star (*kokab*) of Jacob in Numbers 24:17. But we also know that Nazareth was probably related, by means of the pesherlike pun, to the prophecy of the messianic branch (*neser*) from the root of Jesse (Isaiah 11:1). . . . Probably also the term Nazarenes as a designation for the Jewish Christians (Acts 24:5) was accepted because it was associated with the messianic pun . . . It seems a remarkable coincidence that the two bases of the mission of the *desposynoi* should have names which would be connected with the two titles—Star and Branch—that these two prophecies gave to the Davidic Messiah. Perhaps some of the family did happen to live in Kokhaba, but it was this name, which led the *desposynoi* to give this village the status, along with Nazareth, of a center for their mission. Then, given the significance they would have seen in the name Kokhaba, we can readily suppose that the Kokhaba of Batanea became a center for Jewish Christians who moved east of the Jordan precisely because of its name. The same can be said for the Khoba/Khokaba, which Eusebius locates near Damascus, if this is in fact a third Jewish Christian Kokhaba.[37]

It seems rather far-fetched to suppose that the Desposyni would have intentionally located in towns that just happened to have messianic names. It seems far more likely that these towns were given their names because of the fact that the Desposyni lived there, and perhaps were even named by them. This would lend credence to Schonfield's hypothesis that these towns in Transjordan were bases for the Desposyni from the beginning, and not later places of immigration, as Bauckham asserts. One major scholar of Jewish Christianity who does agree with Schonfield's theory is Hans-Joachim Schoeps, who presents another line of reasoning to affirm Transjordan as a center of both the original Nazarenes, including Jesus, and later the Ebionites:

> At the very beginning of his ministry Jesus directed his attention to Galilee in order to fulfill the prophecy of Isaiah 9:1 that a great light would dawn upon the territory of the tribes of Zebulun and Naphtali and upon the way to the sea, upon Peraea [in Transjordan] and Galilee of the Gentiles. The citation of this Isaianic prophecy in Matthew 4:15 can be interpreted to mean that the Evangelist understood the land of promise, the territory of Zebulun and Naphatali, to be situated *beyond* the Jordan . . . In this case the primitive community would have moved precisely into that region which Matthew regarded as Isaiah's land of promise, and to which Jesus, when in Capernaum, preached his sermon on the kingdom of heaven. . . . The area "beyond the Jordan" belongs to the land of promise. Clearly this enlarged Galilee was regarded by the Evangelists, as it had been by the prophets, as the land of eschatological fulfillment. . . .
>
>   . . . And if Jesus's preaching, originating in Capernaum, caused this great light to dawn upon the land "beyond the Jordan," how much more obvious the fulfillment when his congregation settled down in that land! It is probable that they also expected his Parousia to occur precisely in this region.[38]

Pella may, in fact, have become a new focus for the hope of Jesus's Parousia after the destruction of Jerusalem in the year 70. But since we know that a contingent of the Ebionites returned and reestablished the Jerusalem Yachad, it seems likely that they hedged their bets and, in any case, now had two main bases of operations.

Finally, Schoeps also concurs with Schonfield's assessment of the cultural geography of the region: "In the first century the eastern border of Galilee was by no means firmly established. Places east of the Sea of Gennesareth [Galilee], such as Gadara—which was actually somewhat farther east than Pella—were regarded by Josephus as lying in Galilee."[39] But now, bearing in mind these geographic considerations, let us return to the plight of the family of Jesus after the flight to Pella and the destruction of Jerusalem.

PERSECUTION OF THE DESPOSYNI

In his *Church History,* Eusebius discusses a number of persecutions of the Jews under the emperors Vespasian, Domitian, and Trajan, and mentions that three of these persecutions were instigated for the sole purpose of rounding up Davidic pretenders who potentially could lead insurrections against Rome. Again citing Hegesippus as his source, Eusebius records a fascinating and invaluable account of how, in the second persecution, Domitian arrested two grandsons of Jesus's brother Jude and brought them in for interrogation:

> Of the family of the Lord there were still living the grandchildren of Jude, who is said to have been the Lord's brother according to the flesh. Information was given that they belonged to the family of David, and they were brought to the Emperor Domitian by the Evocatus [a veteran soldier]. For Domitian feared the coming of Christ as Herod also had feared it. And he asked them if they were descendants of David, and they confessed that they were. Then he asked them how much property they had, or how much money they owned. And both of them answered that they had only nine thousand denarii, half of which belonged to each of them; and this property did not consist of silver, but of a piece of land which contained only thirty-nine acres, and from which they raised their taxes and supported themselves by their own labor. Then they showed their hands, exhibiting the hardness of their bodies and the callousness

produced upon their hands by continuous toil as evidence of their own labor. And when they were asked concerning Christ and his kingdom, of what sort it was and where and when it was to appear, they answered that it was not a temporal nor an earthly kingdom, but a heavenly and angelic one, which would appear at the end of the world, when he should come in glory to judge the quick and the dead, and to give unto every one according to his works. Upon hearing this, Domitian did not pass judgment against them, but, despising them as of no account, he let them go, and by a decree put a stop to the persecution of the Church. But when they were released they ruled the churches because they were witnesses and were also relatives of the Lord. And peace being established, they lived until the time of Trajan. These things are related by Hegesippus.[40]

Unfortunately, Hegesippus does not state where this family farm was located, which would have given us more evidence to weigh in making a decision as to the location of their original base of operations. However, quite remarkably, another early anonymous account does provide the names of the two grandsons of Jude:

When Domitian spoke with the [grand]sons of Jude, the brother of the Lord, and learned of the virtues of the men, he brought to an end the persecution against us. Hegesippus also reports their names, and says that one was called Zoker and the other James.[41]

As might be expected, scholars debate the authenticity of these accounts, many contending that they are legendary. Richard Bauckham has scrupulously studied all the alternatives and arrived at a measured conclusion that would be valuable to read in full:

Allowing for the apologetic and hagiographic concerns of the [story], we may accept as reliable that the two grandsons of Jude were prominent leaders in the Jewish Christian churches and that they came under suspicion by the Roman authorities because they were known to be (and their status in the churches was no doubt partly connected with the fact that they were) relatives of Jesus . . . Their appearance before Domitian and the connection of their arrest with a Domitianic persecution of Christians must be considered rather doubtful.

That Zoker and James were poor farmers is no doubt also accurately remembered, and the size of their smallholding . . . is so precisely stated that perhaps this too is accurate tradition. . . . Their farm was no doubt the inherited family property, which may have remained in the possession of the family and its size have been well known in . . . second-century Palestinian Jewish Christian circles . . . Though not located by Hegesippus, we can safely assume that the farm was in Galilee. It should also be borne in mind . . . the rural, agricultural context of the letter of James (5:4, 7) and its denunciation of wealthy landowners (5:1–6).

Hegesippus' statement that Zoker and James [ruled the churches] . . . may be an exaggeration (and presumably, since according to Hegesippus this leadership of the churches was contemporary with the leadership of the Jerusalem Church by Simon, the son of Clopas, he means only that they participated in the leadership of the churches throughout Palestine). . . . He may therefore have exaggerated the authority of Zoker and James. But their prominence in the Jewish Christian tradition he reports can assure us that they were at least important leaders in the churches of Galilee.[42]

Bauckham's reasoned conclusions seem sound. All the evidence we have seen points to the fact that the relatives of Jesus played key leadership roles both during Jesus's ministry and in the years after his death. What exact role Zoker and James played we do not know, and it would seem clear that their main occupation was as farmers, not traveling missionaries. They likely provided jurisdictional leadership of local house churches in Galilee and in the Hauran in Transjordan, under the ultimate supervision of Symeon in Jerusalem.

THE MARTYRDOM OF SYMEON

According to Eusebius, the third persecution, under Trajan, resulted in the martyrdom of Bishop Symeon, who was accused of being both a Christian and a Davidide:

> It is reported that after the age of Nero and Domitian, under the emperor whose times we are now recording [Trajan], a persecution was stirred up against us in certain cities in consequence of a popular uprising. In this persecution we have understood that Symeon, the son of Clopas, who, as we have shown, was the second bishop of the church of Jerusalem, suffered martyrdom. Hegesippus, whose words we have already quoted in various places, is a witness to this fact also. Speaking of certain heretics he adds that Symeon was accused by them at this time; and since it was clear that he was a Christian, he was tortured in various ways for many days, and astonished even the judge himself and his attendants in the highest degree, and finally he suffered a death similar to that of our Lord. But there is nothing like hearing [Hegesippus] himself, who writes as follows: "Certain of these heretics brought accusation against Symeon, the son of Clopas, on the ground that he was a descendant of David and a Christian; and thus he suffered martyrdom, at the age of one hundred and twenty years, while Trajan was emperor and Atticus governor." . . . And it might be reasonably assumed that Symeon was one of those that saw and heard the Lord, judging from the length of his life, and from the fact that the Gospel makes mention of Mary, the wife of Clopas, who was the father of Symeon, as has been already shown. The same historian says that there were also others, descended from one of the so-called brothers of the Savior, whose name was Judas, who, after they had borne testimony before Domitian, as has been already recorded, in behalf of faith in Christ, lived until the same reign. . . . And after being tortured for many days he suffered martyrdom, and all, including even the proconsul, marveled that, at the age of one

hundred and twenty years, he could endure so much. And orders were given that he should be crucified."[43]

Symeon was martyred sometime around the year 106 or 107. It is certainly not the case that he lived to the age of 120. This is surely artistic license taken to demonstrate the righteousness of Symeon. Subsequent to the great flood in the book of Genesis, God says that the longest that any human shall live is 120 years (Gen. 6:3), and only the most righteous, such as Moses, live to that age. It is definitely possible that Symeon lived to quite a ripe old age, perhaps near 100, and his great longevity led to his legendary status of living to 120. It is quite fascinating to consider, as Eusebius notes, that he was likely the last living person to have personally seen and heard Jesus speak.

SUCCESSORS TO SYMEON

Eusebius also provides an invaluable list of the leaders of the Ebionites subsequent to Symeon (commonly referred to by scholars as the "Jerusalem bishop's list") up to the time of the second Jewish revolt under Bar Kochba in 132 CE:

The chronology of the bishops of Jerusalem I have nowhere found preserved in writing; for tradition says that they were all short lived. But I have learned this much from writings, that until the siege of the Jews, which took place under Adrian [*sic*], there were fifteen bishops in succession there, all of whom are said to be of Hebrew descent, and to have received the knowledge of Christ in purity, so that they were approved by those who were able to judge of such matters, and were deemed worthy of the episcopate. For their whole church consisted then of believing Hebrews who continued from the days of the apostles until the siege, which took place at this time; in which siege the Jews, having again rebelled against the Romans, were conquered after severe battles. But since the bishops of the circumcision ceased at this time, it is proper to give here a list of their names from the beginning. The first, then, was James, the so-called brother of the Lord; the second, Symeon; the third, Justus; the fourth, Zacchaeus; the fifth, Tobias; the sixth, Benjamin; the seventh, John; the eighth, Matthias; the ninth, Philip; the tenth, Seneca; the eleventh, Justus; the twelfth, Levi; the thirteenth, Ephres; the fourteenth, Joseph; and finally, the fifteenth, Judas. These are the bishops of Jerusalem that lived between the age of the apostles and the time referred to, all of them belonging to the circumcision.[44]

While we have no statement from Eusebius that any of these subsequent leaders were of the Desposyni, such an assertion could logically be made. It is interesting that the third leader is Justus; it would seem likely he was named after James. The eleventh leader is likewise named Justus, and the last two are Joseph and Judas, who share names with two of Jesus's brothers, and quite possibly were named after Jesus's brothers.

The length of Eusebius's list of bishops has caused some scholars to doubt its veracity, as all of these would have had to serve in a brief, twenty-five-year period between the death of Symeon (ca. 106–107) and the end of the Bar Kochba revolt in 135, and Eusebius himself notes that their reigns "were all short lived." Schonfield speculated that perhaps they served under an annual appointment.[45] James Tabor thinks that because twelve are listed after Justus, perhaps this is not a list of successive bishops, but a council of twelve.[46] Richard Bauckham concurs and makes this interesting and logical observation:

> If we suppose the third name in Eusebius' list (Justus) to be the last Jewish Christian leader of the church in Jerusalem, who occupied the position between Symeon's martyrdom and the Bar Kochba revolt, we are left with *twelve* names. These can readily be understood as a college of twelve elders who presided over the Jerusalem Church along with James. A list of these will have been subsequently misunderstood in the tradition as successors to James.[47]

We have already seen that a cabinet of twelve was a feature of the government of the Essene community at Qumran. It is possible that these twelve (following Justus) were the successors to the twelve apostles. Also fascinating is that Epiphanius records the same list, but with some minor variations that show his list was probably independent of Eusebius's list, thus adding to the list's credibility. The most intriguing difference in Epiphanius's list is that rather than "Justus" as the third name, he lists "Judas."[48] And this raises the question of whether this might be Jesus's brother, Jude. Bauckham thinks it probable that the last named Judas and the Joseph who preceded him were Jesus's brothers.[49] James Tabor believes that not only Jesus's brothers, but a few of the original twelve apostles were still holding office and their names appear on the list:

> It is entirely possible that the next to last name might be Jesus's remaining brother Joseph . . . it is also possible that John, Matthew, and Philip are the aged but original members of the Twelve whom Jesus had chosen. We do have reliable tradition that John, in particular, lived on well past age one hundred.
>
> The *Apostolic Constitutions* . . . in the fourth century AD, says that the third person in line, the Jude who succeeded Simon, was a third brother of Jesus. The possibility is quite significant in that it would trace the Jesus dynasty through *four* successive brothers: Jesus, James, Simon, and Judas![50]

While Tabor admits to the uncertainty of this, he sums up nicely what is firm fact regarding Jesus's dynastic family:

> [W]hat we can know, with some certainty, is that the royal family of Jesus, including the children and grandchildren of his brothers and sisters, were honored by the early Christians well into the second century AD, while at the same time they were watched and hunted down by the highest levels of the Roman government in Palestine.[51]

THE SECOND JEWISH WAR

In the year 132, a second revolt of the Jews against the Romans broke out, instigated by a messianic pretender, Simon Bar Kochba. This second foolhardy rebellion took place because the emperor Hadrian (ruled 117–138) changed his formerly pacifistic policy toward the Jews to a much less tolerant one. Bar Kochba was an able but ruthless leader who managed to train an elite fighting force, as did his Maccabean predecessors; and Hadrian had to bring his most skilled general, Julius Severus, all the way from Britain to squelch the revolt. The stories that have been handed down about Bar Kochba tell us that he was as ruthless toward the Ebionites—many of whom were tortured for their refusal to follow him—as he was toward his own soldiers.[52] It is said that he ordered all his soldiers to cut off a finger to prove their courage and loyalty to him. It was at this time that the Ebionites came to be persecuted on all sides— from both Jews and Christians—even though the Ebionites suffered the same Roman retribution as both of those groups. Despite the fact that they often shared the same hiding places in caves and mountain hideaways in the hinterlands of Galilee and Transjordan, the Ebionites were increasingly despised by both Jews and Christians.

Finally, after the latest rebellion was put down, Jerusalem was literally buried by the ancient equivalent of bulldozers—horse-drawn plows— and a completely new Roman city, Aelia Capitolina, was built over the ruins. On the former temple site a pagan Roman temple was built and dedicated to Jupiter. A statue of Hadrian was erected in the exact spot where the temple altar had been. And a new Gentile Christian church established itself in what was now a pagan city under the first Gentile bishop of Jerusalem, a man with the Roman name of Marcus. Whenever Ebionites or Jews tried to approach the smoldering ruins of their former capital, they were forced back by the spears of the Roman guards. And not only were the Ebionites kept at bay from their homeland by Roman spears, they were also kept at arm's length by Christians, who sensed danger by association. Hans-Joachim Schoeps notes that at this time, "the settlement at Pella must have received a new wave of immigrants. The

Jewish Christians apparently expanded from Pella into the rest of Perea, i.e., the whole territory east of the upper Jordan."[53]

Although the Ebionites expand the boundaries of their territory, after the year 135 they were on a slow road to eventual extinction; they were considered heretics by the emergent Christian Church, now based in Rome. The Ebionites essentially lived in backwater ghettoes in Transjordan, in the environs of Syria, in the northwestern deserts of Arabia, and even, as we have seen, in a self-imposed ghetto on Mt. Zion, to which they would eventually return once again, though their numbers were greatly reduced. But their influence would still be felt in surprisingly strong ways, even as they were driven to the brink of extinction by Catholic heresy hunters.

Not only were the Ebionites disenfranchised from emerging Christianity, but after the year 90 they were also barred from the new Jewish synagogue system that replaced the temple. This is attested in a parenthetical note in the Gospel of John: ". . . for the Jews had already agreed that anyone who confessed Jesus to be the Messiah would be put out of the synagogue" (John 9:22). As a very forceful sign of their unwelcome status in the synagogue, at the conclusion of every Sabbath service a curse was invoked against the Ebionites and other apostates—the *Birkath ha-Minim* (Malediction Against Heretics), part of the *Shemonah Esrei* (Eighteen Benedictions): "May the apostates have no hope, may the dominion of wickedness be speedily uprooted in our days, may the *nozrim* [Nazarenes] and *minim* [heretics] quickly perish and not be inscribed together with the righteous. Blessed art thou, the Eternal, our God, who crushes the wicked."[54] As Jerome, centuries later, would appraise the no-man's land the Ebionites inhabited: "While they will be both Jews and Christians, they are neither Jews nor Christians."[55]

8

THE EBIONITE EVANGEL
The Mission of Jewish Christianity

There are two ways: one of life and one of death! And there is a great difference between the two ways.

THE *DIDACHE*

Following the devastation of the Bar Kokhba revolt, and with little remaining influence among Palestinian Jews, the Ebionites took up a new mission that is reflected in the closing words of the Jewish Christian Gospel of Matthew: "Go, therefore, and make disciples of all nations . . ." (Matthew 28:19). Sadly, the Ebionites could not fulfill that lofty mission, for better and for worse that would be the task of the Gentile Christian Church. But the Ebionites, now mainly centered in Pella, would have some modest success in the next century or so. As the great nineteenth-century scholar Johannes Weiss asserted: "That the church here [in Pella] subsisted not merely as an intimidated flock in hiding, but continued its communal living and its propaganda, is undoubtedly probable."[1] Now the mission of the Ebionites was on a parallel but colliding path with Paul's mission, some authentic remembrances of which have been preserved in the "Ebionite Acts"—the *Pseudo-Clementine* literature.

According to Eusebius and Epiphanius, the second most important city for the Ebionites was Cochaba (or Kochaba). As we saw, there is confusion about which Cochaba is being referred to—the one near Nazareth, or the one in Transjordan. Julius Africanus noted that Cochaba was one of the centers of the Desposyni. Hans-Joachim Schoeps theorized: "If this second Cochaba was founded from Pella, we may assume that this new settlement was named after the home city of earlier generations."[2] It seems almost certain that Eusebius and Epiphanius are referring to the Cochaba in Transjordan, for Epiphanius says of the Ebionites, in his usual disgusted way: "[T]he roots of these thorny weeds come mostly from Nabataea and Banias, Moabitis, and Cocabe in Bashanitis beyond Adrai—in Cyprus as well."[3] Schoeps elucidates:

> [T]hey had settled practically the entire border zone separating Syria from Arabia—admittedly a rather narrow strip of land—extending from Damascus to the southern tip of the Dead Sea in a north-south strip. Under these circumstances they must also have expanded into Arabian Nabataea . . .*
>
> . . . the Ebionite communities of the second, third, and probably also the fourth centuries inhabited the territory east of the Jordan. . . . In Transjordan, the Ebionites found Essenes (Ossaioi) . . . and other Jewish baptismal sects, who had preceded them in migratory flight . . . Catholic Christianity did not penetrate this area for a long time; its establishment in eastern Palestine cannot be affirmed before the middle of the third century. . . . Catholic bishops in Pella are mentioned for the first time in the fifth century.[4]

The Ebionites carried with them their own gospel written in Hebrew, sometimes called the "Gospel of the Hebrews," but also known as the "Gospel of the Ebionites" or the "Gospel of the Nazoraeans." According to Eusebius, a late second-century Christian missionary by the name of Pantaenus, upon visiting India "reported that among persons there who knew of Christ, he found the Gospel according to Matthew, which had anticipated his own arrival. For Bartholomew, one of the apostles,

---

*See map on page 8.

had preached to them, and left with them the writing of Matthew in the Hebrew language, which they had preserved till that time."[5] Based on the eyewitness testimony of Pantaenus, the Ebionites were definitely not limited to Palestine, but carried their evangel sometimes surprisingly far afield—as far as India in the east and Cyprus in the west. The Ebionites also established a presence in Mesopotamia, where they came under the influence of Gnosticism, leading to the development of a later Gnostic branch of Ebionitism known as the Elkesaites, to be discussed in chapter 10. But, aside from such distant missions, the Ebionites mainly established synagogues in Galilee, Transjordan, Syria, and northwestern Arabia. A manual for the instruction of new converts—the first Christian catechism—was also written. While the full title of this remarkable document translates as "The Teaching of the Lord through the Twelve Apostles to the Gentiles," it is today most commonly referred to simply as the *Didache* (The Teaching).

THE *DIDACHE*

Although quotes from the *Didache* had been known from other ancient literature, it was only discovered in its entirety in a monastery in Istanbul in 1873, and translated into English in 1884. As with most noncanonical writings, a wide range of dates have been proposed for the *Didache*. It should come as no surprise that the dates that scholars propose for any disputed text often reflect the theological leanings of the scholars proposing them. A remarkable exception is the anticonsensus date that Dr. Aaron Milavec persuasively proposes for the *Didache*. While most scholars have dated the text to the first half of the second century, with some advocating a date as late as the third century, Milavec convincingly dates it between 50 and 70 CE, which would make it as old as Paul's letters and a little older than the Gospel of Mark. The *Didache* is clearly not, as some scholars contend, dependent on, or derivative of, any of the canonical gospels. As Milavec notes, "My extensive study of this issue demonstrates that the internal logic, theological orientation, and pastoral practice of the *Didache* run decisively counter to what one finds within the received gospels."[6]

As we shall see, the *Didache* is clearly Jewish Christian in its orientation. Milavec also notes these quite remarkable features of the *Didache:*

> This *Didache* reveals more about how Christians saw themselves
> and how they lived their everyday lives than any book in the
> Christian Scriptures. It is not a gospel and, accordingly, it does
> not attempt to offer guidance by narrating a life of Jesus. In fact,
> it is older than the canonical gospels and was written in the gen-
> eration following the death of Jesus . . . the *Didache* was created
> at the time of Paul's mission to the Gentiles, but it shows not the
> slightest awareness of that mission or of the theology that under-
> girded it.[7]

The *Didache* was a catechism for Gentiles that was used by the Nazarenes even before Paul's mission to the Gentiles had begun. It contains three main sections: a training program for Gentile catechumens, rules for properly administering Baptism and conducting the Eucharist, and guidelines for communal organization. That it was a handbook for Jewish Christians ministering among Gentiles is acknowledged by the *Catholic Encyclopedia* of 1913, which states as follows:

> [The *Didache*] . . . is in origin a Jewish work, intended for the
> instruction of proselytes . . . the agreement of ch. 2 with the Talmud
> may be certain . . . the rest of the work . . . though wholly Christian
> in its subject matter, has an equally remarkable agreement with the
> Talmud . . . Beyond doubt we must look upon the writer as living
> at a very early period when Jewish influence was still important in
> the Church.[8]

The first section, which comprises about half of the document, is commonly referred to as the "Two Ways," for it begins: "There are two ways: one of life and one of death! And there is a great difference between the two ways."[9] The "way of life" is then expounded upon in words that Jesus once said were the heart and summation of the Torah:

> On the one hand, then, the way of life is this:
>> first: you will love the God who made you;
>> second: you will love your neighbor as yourself.
> On the other hand, the way of life is this:
>> As many things as you might wish not to happen to you,
>> Likewise do not do to another. (1:1–2)

The latter is, of course, the converse of Jesus's "golden rule." It is quite fascinating that the *Didache* opens with words that are thoroughly rooted in the heart of Jewish teaching. It is also interesting that the closest parallel to this "Two Ways" doctrine is found in the teaching of the Essenes, as seen in the Dead Sea Scrolls. The Nazarenes, and later the Ebionites, who used this material for catechetical purposes believed that Jesus's message was intended for both Jews and Gentiles.

But what is perhaps most striking about the *Didache* is that it never once tries to prove that Jesus was the Son of God or the Messiah, or to bring people to have faith *in Jesus,* which, of course, is the core purpose of the gospels. Ironically, though, the *Didache* does show in a remarkable way *why* people were so attracted to the Way of Jesus, as Aaron Milavec explains:

> The *Didache* holds the secret of how and why Jesus of Nazareth, a seemingly insignificant Galilean Jew executed as a Roman criminal, went on to attract and convert the world. Sure enough, the members of the Jesus movement regarded him as both "Son of God" and "Son of David" . . . however, such exalted claims were a commonplace within the religious flux of the Roman Empire . . . and, at first glance, barely caused a ripple in the day-to-day business of deciding which of the many religious systems was worthy of personal adherence. In truth, potential members assessed the movement not so much on the basis of claims made on behalf of Jesus, who was absent, but on the basis of their experience of the way of life of members who were very much present to them. It is no surprise, therefore, that the entire system of the *Didache* displays little taste for negotiating, defin-

ing, and defending the exalted titles and functions of Jesus. Rather, the *Didache* is taken up with the business of passing on the Way of Life revealed to its authors by the Father through his servant Jesus.[10]

We mentioned this same quality—the way of life demonstrated by the Nazarenes—at the conclusion of chapter 3, where Huston Smith noted that the Nazarenes' love for one another and joy for living were their foremost qualities for attracting new converts. We will encounter this again when we discuss the medieval Cathars.

While much more could be said about the *Didache* for the light it sheds on the day-to-day life of the Nazarenes and Ebionites, space permits us to comment on only one other significant aspect of this remarkable document: the surprising (perhaps, to some, disturbing) way in which the *Didache* describes the earliest practice of the Lord's supper:

> Now concerning the Eucharist, give thanks this way. First, concerning the cup: We thank thee, our Father, for the holy vine of David Thy servant, which you have made known to us through Jesus Thy Servant; to Thee be the glory for ever.
>
> And concerning the broken bread: We thank Thee, our Father, for the life and knowledge which You madest known to us through Jesus thy Servant; to Thee be the glory for ever. (9:1–3)

The first item of note is that the order of bread and cup is reversed, with the blessing of the cup first.* Most significantly, no mention is made of this meal being a remembrance of the Last Supper. Even in the thanksgiving prayer, which is prescribed for use after the meal, no mention is ever made of the atoning death of Christ! The prayers give thanks only "for the life and knowledge" that God has made known through Jesus, and for "the holy vine of David."

What is clearly most important for the community that produced the *Didache* is the new way of life made known to them, a way of life that was

---

*Also reflected in the Gospel of Luke.

a foretaste of the coming Kingdom of God, which was the heart of Jesus's message. Milavec sums up what the Eucharist meant for the Nazarenes:

> [T]he Eucharist of the *Didache* perpetuated the proleptic foretaste of the Kingdom that marked the table fellowship of Jesus. Fed on the Eucharist, therefore, those who shared the Way of Life of the Father were nourished in their altered social reality. They were not of this world . . . they thought and acted in anticipation of the world to come. As brothers and sisters bound together . . . they shared their resources, their Way of Life, and their dreams. Each new Eucharist, consequently, celebrated the group identity, the standards . . . and the habits . . . the community needed to champion in the name of the Lord.[11]

The Nazarenes took two differing approaches in their efforts to bring others into the way of life that was a foretaste of the coming messianic kingdom. When reaching out to Gentiles, they took an oral approach through preaching; but, when propagating the Good News among Jews their approach was mainly literary, following the model of rabbinical debate over the interpretation of scripture. The Hebrew scriptures were pored over for proof-texts demonstrating that Jesus fulfilled the messianic prophecies, an approach that is strikingly seen in the New Testament in the Gospel of Matthew. An example of their evangelistic method can be seen in the book of Acts: "That very night the believers . . . went to the Jewish synagogue. These Jews were more receptive than those in Thessalonica, for they welcomed the message very eagerly and examined the scriptures every day to see whether these things were so" (Acts 17:10–11). Since native Palestinian Jews were quite opposed to translating their scriptures into any language other than Hebrew,* this supports the likelihood that the Nazarene gospel—most commonly known as the Gospel of the Hebrews—is the original version of Matthew before it was amended and translated into Greek.

---

*In the minds of the rabbis, the translation of the Hebrew Bible into Greek of the Septuagint was an abomination.

THE GOSPEL OF THE HEBREWS

The most popular Jewish books around the time of the Jewish wars were, as we have seen, the many new apocalypses such as the book of Daniel, and works that never made it into the canon but were very popular at the time, such as the *Testaments of the Twelve Patriarchs* and the *Apocalypse of Ezra,* works that provided hope for the restoration of the Jewish people and the promise of destruction of their enemies. These writings were the mother lode for the Ebionites in their mining for prophecies of the coming messianic kingdom of Jesus. But it was their very popularity and usage in evangelism by the Ebionites that would lead to a rabbinical ban on these books.

That the Gospel of the Hebrews was the most precious book of all to the Nazarenes and Ebionites is attested by Eusebius when he discusses books that were disputed in his day: "And among these some have placed also the gospel according to the Hebrews, with which those of the Hebrews that have accepted Christ are especially delighted."[12] He later adds: "These men [the Ebionites], moreover, thought that it was necessary to reject all the epistles of the apostle [Paul], whom they called an apostate from the law; and they used only the so-called gospel according to the Hebrews and made small account of the rest."[13]

This gospel, so beloved of the Ebionites, is sadly lost except for a few references and quotes in patristic literature, especially in the *Panarion* of Epiphanius and the writings of Jerome. Jerome apparently found this work important enough that he translated the Gospel of the Hebrews into both Greek and Latin. There are also fascinating references in Jewish literature indicating that this gospel was well known among Jews early in the second century. The Talmud* preserves words of Jesus taken from the Gospel of the Hebrews: "I am not come to take away from the law of Moses, and I am not come to add to the law of Moses."[14] This may well sum up this gospel's understanding of Jesus.

Church father Justin Martyr provides us with evidence that Jewish

*Rabbinical commentary on the Torah, which, for Jews, is a second Bible.

intellectuals were quite familiar with the Gospel of the Hebrews. In Justin's *Dialogue with Trypho the Jew,* the Jewish philosopher Trypho tells Justin, "I am aware that your [Christian] precepts in the so-called Evangelion [gospel] are so wonderful and so great, that I suspect no one can keep them; for I have carefully read them."[15] This was not mere hyperbole. As Hugh Schonfield remarks, "Trypho's words might have been echoed by many a Jew of his time."[16] Apparently there was nothing in the Gospel of the Hebrews overtly offensive to Jews, and much they admired.

Unfortunately, there is much confusion among scholars about the Gospel of the Hebrews due to the fact that there are other Jewish Christian gospels mentioned in the patristic literature, such as the Gospel of the Ebionites and the Gospel of the Nazoraeans. The question of whether these were distinct writings or simply one gospel known by different names has been called "the most enigmatic and irritating problem in the New Testament Apocrypha."[17] Adding to the confusion is the fact that if specific titles were attached to these works, the patristic writers who cite these gospels intentionally withheld them since, in their minds, this might have given them validity. It seems apparent that the reason these writings have come to be known under variant names such as the Gospel of the Ebionites and the Gospel of the Nazoraeans is that the church fathers discussed them according to which groups used them, and this has likely given the false impression that there was more than one Jewish Christian gospel. It would seem most logical that there was just one Hebrew gospel (written in the Aramaic dialect) and that this was the original version of Matthew before it was translated into Greek. This is the conclusion of Hans-Joachim Schoeps: "As far as the few extant fragments permit conjecture, one may assume that it is a matter of different editions of the same work, that is, of various stages in the literary history of the Matthew tradition."[18] Jerome himself attests that this was the accepted view in his day: ". . . the Gospel that the Nazareans and Ebionites use, which I recently translated from Hebrew into Greek . . . *most people consider the authentic version of Matthew . . .*"[19] The title "Gospel of the Hebrews" is as descriptive a title as any by which to recognize this Jewish Christian Gospel, and the one we will adopt here.

Plate 1. Eastern wall of the Temple Mount from the Mount of Olives. The golden Dome of the Rock is on the right and the dome of the Al Aqsa Mosque is on the left—the holiest sites in Jerusalem for Muslims. (All photographs by the author unless otherwise noted.)

Plate 2. Southwestern corner of the Temple Mount. The Wailing Wall, all that is left of Herod's Temple, is to the left in front of the Dome of the Rock.

Plate 4. The Kidron Valley runs between the Mount of Olives and the Temple Mount. At top right is the Pinnacle of the Temple Mount, from which James the brother of Jesus was thrown to his death.

Plate 3. Southern wall of the Temple Mount. The Al Aqsa Mosque on the left, the Pinnacle on the right. The Templars' headquarters was directly adjacent to the place of James's martyrdom. The Mount of Olives is in the background.

Plate 5. Three tombs in the Kidron Valley. L to R: the tomb of Absalom, the tomb of the Bnei Hezir ("sons of Hezir," a priestly family), which some Christians believe to be the tomb of James, the brother of Jesus, and the tomb of Zechariah.

Plate 6 (above left). The Pinnacle from the tomb of James. Even if his burial here is legendary, one can see why this tomb became associated with James. The pillars are claimed by some Masonic authors to represent the pillars of Jachin and Boaz at the entrance to Solomon's Temple.

Plate 7 (above right). The Pinnacle. According to the Church Fathers Hegesippus and Clement of Alexandria, James was thrown into the Kidron Valley for proclaiming that Jesus was the Messiah. Hegesippus reports that James was buried nearby.

Plate 8. Tomb of the Bnei Hezir. The Armenian Christians in Jerusalem believe this is where James was buried after his martyrdom. They claim his body was later reinterred beneath the main altar in the Cathedral of St. James on Mount Zion.

Plate 9. The Al Aqsa Mosque. Believed to have been built over King Solomon's stables, this became the headquarters of the Knights Templar. Much of the present building, including the arched entranceway, was built by the Templars.

Plate 10 (left). Dome of the Rock with Dome of the Chain in foreground. The Dome of the Rock is believed to have been built directly over the Holy of Holies of the temple. The Knights Hospitaller converted the Dome of the Chain into a chapel dedicated to James.

Plate 11. Northern wall of the Synagogue of the Apostles. The niche near the top of the arch is where the Torah scroll was kept. This is the only synagogue where the niche does not face the temple, but faces the Church of the Holy Sepulchre, conclusively showing this was a Nazarene synagogue.

Plate 12. Southern wall of the Cenacle (upper room). The first floor contains what many Jews believe to be the tomb of King David. The second floor, where Jesus ate the Last Supper, later became the Synagogue of the Apostles (also known as the Jerusalem Church).

Plate 13. Southern wall of the upper room. This Muslim *mihrab* marks the direction of Mecca. That the Muslims converted the upper room into a mosque shows that they also considered this site holy to the memory of the prophet Isa (Jesus).

Plate 14. The Cenacle, or upper room. The original was destroyed and what is seen here is the reconstruction by the Knights Templar.

Plate 15. Crusader graffito on the northern entrance pillar of the upper room. This may be the heraldic shield of the last Templar grand master, Jacques De Molay, who was burned at the stake.

Plate 16. Another Crusader graffito. Crossed battle axes. These mysterious carvings merit serious attention from scholars.

Plate 17. Ceiling medallion in the upper room. The victorious Lamb of God was one of the main symbols of the Knights Templar.

Plate 18. Another ceiling medallion. The Lion of Judah was a symbol of Jesus's messiahship and another important symbol of the Knights Templar.

Plate 19. Mysterious mason's mark on outer southern wall of the Cenacle. The controversial Talpiot Tomb, which lies due south, has a similar triangle over the entranceway.

Plate 20. Master Mason's apron showing the *tau* symbol that is prominent in the Royal Arch branch of Freemasonry. (Photograph courtesy of "Masonic for Masons")

Plate 21 (above). Carvings of pelicans on top of a pillar in the upper room. The pelican is an ancient symbol of sacrifice that came to be associated with Jesus in Christian art.

Plate 22 (at right). Other pillar carvings. Those familiar with Rosslyn Chapel may wish to make comparisons.

Plate 23. Monument marking the site of the headquarters of the Knights Hospitaller in Jerusalem, not far from the Church of the Holy Sepulchre. There is no such monument in memory of the Knights Templar.

Plate 24. Benedictine Church of the Dormition from the roof of the Cenacle. The English word "dormant" (asleep) is derived from the Latin *dormire* (to sleep). The church marks the place where Mary the mother of Jesus "fell asleep."

Plate 25. Effigy of Mary in the Church of the Dormition, marking the spot where Roman Catholics believe Mary fell asleep. That this site is so close to the Synagogue of the Apostles lends to its veracity. According to Acts, Mary spent much time in this area after the crucifixion.

Plate 26 (above). Jewish *mikvah,* or ritual bathhouse, just south of the Cenacle and Tomb of David. Located at the highest point on Mt. Zion, this is one of the largest mikvahs ever found. Church of the Dormition in background.

Plate 27 (top right). Steps leading down to the ritual bath. This mikvah was certainly used by the Nazarenes before attending their synagogue.

Plate 28. Entrance to the Armenian Cathedral of St. James on Mt. Zion. The Cenacle and Church of the Dormition are located not far to the south.

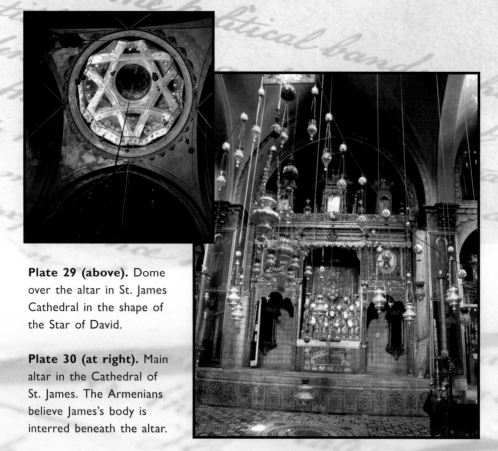

Plate 29 (above). Dome over the altar in St. James Cathedral in the shape of the Star of David.

Plate 30 (at right). Main altar in the Cathedral of St. James. The Armenians believe James's body is interred beneath the altar.

Plate 32. Opening in the floor of the sacristy revealing what the Armenians claim is the foundation of the house in which James lived. This is quite possible, for James did become a permanent resident of Jerusalem and the site is just north of the Synagogue of the Apostles where James presided over the Nazarene community.

Plate 31 (above). A replica of the Throne of James faces the altar in the Cathedral of St. James. A painting depicting James seated on the throne is to the upper right.

Plate 33 (at right). The Coat of Arms of the patriarch of the Armenian Church prominently displays the All Seeing Eye within a triangle.

Plate 34 (below). The All Seeing Eye of God is prominently displayed over the baptistery in the Cathedral of St. James. It is one of the main symbols of the Armenian Church, as well as a main symbol of Freemasonry.

Herod's Temple

Royal Porch

Court of Priests

Gentile's Court

Most Holy Place

Holy Place

Main Temple

Altar

Court of Israel

Court of Women

Temple Courtyard

© ElBibleTeacher.com

Approx 1000 cubits (1500 ft)

Approx 670 cubits (1000 ft)

Plate 35. Plan of Herod's Temple shows that the temple was in the shape of a tau.

Plate 36. The author taking part in the Mt. Zion archaeological expedition, June 2008. Directed by Dr. Shimon Gibson and Dr. James Tabor, we were uncovering intact homes from the wealthiest neighborhood in first-century Jerusalem. To the upper right, behind the buses, lies the Cenacle and Church of the Dormition. (Photograph courtesy of Doug Allen.) For more on the dig go to: digmountzion.com.

A complete collection of all the extant quotes from the Gospel of the Hebrews can be found in Bart Ehrman's invaluable compendium, *Lost Scriptures: Books that Did Not Make It into the New Testament*. Following are a few representative quotes that illustrate the unique Jewish Christology of the Ebionites. First, Jerome, writing against the Pelagians, sees fit to quote from this gospel to support a point (and here we can see his own confusion over nomenclature):

> In the Gospel according to the Hebrews, which is written . . . in Hebrew characters, and is used by the Nazarenes to this day (I mean the Gospel according to the Apostles, or, as is generally maintained, the Gospel according to Matthew, a copy of which is in the library at Caesarea), we find, "Behold, the mother of our Lord and His brethren said to Him, John the Baptist baptizes for the remission of sins; let us go and be baptized by him. But He said to them, what sin have I committed that I should go and be baptized by him?[20]

Here we see that the Ebionites believed in a sinless Jesus. Muslims also hold that Jesus (along with all of the prophets) was sinless, a connection between Ebionites and Muslims that will be explored further in chapter 11.

The Gospel of the Hebrews also gives this interesting and unique description of John the Baptist:

> John came baptizing, and there went out unto him Pharisees and were baptized, and all Jerusalem. And John had a garment of camel's hair, and a girdle of skin about his loins. And his meat was wild honey, whose taste was the taste of manna, as a cake in oil.[21]

According to the Gospel of the Hebrews, John is a vegetarian. As opposed to the canonical gospels, John does not even eat locusts. Vegetarianism is a unique emphasis of the Ebionites, as we will discuss in detail in the next chapter when we examine Ebionite theology and practice.

Jesus's baptism is also described in a unique way in the Gospel of the Hebrews:

> When the people had been baptized Jesus came also and was baptized of John. And as he came up out of the water the heavens were opened, and he saw the Holy Spirit in the form of a dove, which descended and entered into him. And there came a voice from heaven saying, Thou art my beloved Son, in thee I am well pleased, and again, This day have I begotten thee.[22]

Note the emphasis here, which is found nowhere in the canonical gospels: "*This day* have I begotten thee." The Ebionites believed that Jesus was *adopted* as God's son at his baptism, a belief scholars refer to as "adoptionism," another of the hallmarks of Ebionite Christology.

Another unique emphasis of Ebionite Christology is that Jesus is the last in the line of prophets that God had long been awaiting:

> And it came to pass when the Lord was come up out of the water, the whole fount of the Holy Spirit descended and rested upon him, and said unto him: My son, in all the prophets was I waiting for thee that thou shouldst come, and I might rest in thee.[23]

Here we see that the Ebionites did not consider Jesus to be eternally pre-existent, but simply a prophet like others. As we will see in the next chapter, Jesus is considered to be the prophet most like Moses, calling people back to the law, as we see here:

> The second of the rich men said unto him: Master, what good thing can I do and live? He said unto him: O man, perform the law and the prophets.[24]

Jesus's emphasis that salvation comes through following the law and the prophets is also seen in the canonical Gospel of Matthew, and is emphasized at the very beginning of the Gospel of the Hebrews when Jesus first calls the twelve:

> There was a certain man named Jesus, and he was about thirty years

old, who chose us. And coming into Capernaum he entered into the house of Simon who was surnamed Peter, and opened his mouth and said: As I passed by the Lake of Tiberias, I chose John and James, the sons of Zebedee, and Simon and Andrew and . . . Thaddaeus and Simon the Zealot and Judas Iscariot; and thee, Matthew, as thou satest at the receipt of custom I called, and thou followedst me. You, therefore, I will to be twelve apostles for a testimony unto Israel.[25]

Here we see that the Gospel of the Hebrews was uniquely written in the first person, and claims to be written by Matthew himself, which would make it the only gospel directly written by one of the twelve.* Also of note is that the calling of the twelve is explicitly stated to be for "a testimony *unto Israel*." This is also emphasized in the canonical Gospel of Matthew, and according to all of the gospels it was actually quite unusual for Jesus to reach out to Gentiles during his ministry.[26]

This brief survey covers almost all of the extant quotes we have from the Gospel of the Hebrews. But there is one more that is of particular significance because of the unique emphasis it places on James. Here is the citation by Jerome:

The Gospel also which is called the Gospel according to the Hebrews, and which I have recently translated into Greek and Latin, and which also Origen† often makes use of, after the account of the resurrection of the Savior says, "But the Lord, after he had given his grave clothes to the servant of the priest, appeared to James (for James had sworn that he would not eat bread from that hour in which he drank the cup of the Lord until he should see him rising again from among those that sleep)" and again, a little later, it says, "'Bring a table and bread,' said the Lord." And immediately it is added, "He brought bread and blessed and brake and gave to

---

*Though the Gospel of John may be largely based on the reminiscences of the "beloved disciple," who traditionally has been identified as John (see John 21:24).

†Origen (ca. 185–254) was a teacher and theologian who is considered the greatest Bible scholar of the early church.

James the Just and said to him, 'My brother eat thy bread, for the son of man is risen from among those that sleep.'" And so he ruled the church of Jerusalem thirty years, that is until the seventh year of Nero, and was buried near the temple from which he had been cast down. His tombstone with its inscription was well known until the siege of Titus and the end of Hadrian's reign. Some of our writers think he was buried in Mount Olivet, but they are mistaken.[27]

This is an astounding passage for a number of reasons. First, it makes the remarkable claim that James was present at the Last Supper! This would mean that James was one of the twelve, and not a later convert who did not believe in Jesus during his lifetime, as is traditionally claimed by the Church. It further claims that James was the first to whom Jesus appeared after his resurrection. I have dealt with these issues at length in *The Brother of Jesus and the Lost Teachings of Christianity,* and we need not dwell on them here; but, what is also of note is Jerome's remark that the burial place of James was well known in the early second century, and that his tomb was close by the temple. Jerome also remarks that in his own day there was a tradition that James had been buried on the Mount of Olives. It is very interesting that there is a prominent tomb that still exists in the Kidron Valley (at the foot of the Mount of Olives), which some early Christians considered to be the tomb of James (see plates 5 and 8). This tomb has been shown to actually be the tomb of a Maccabean family, the Bene Hezir, but a visit to this tomb makes it readily apparent why it became associated with James: This tomb looks out directly upon the southeast corner of the Temple Mount, from which it was said that James was thrown to his death.[28] A photograph of this remarkable juxtaposition can be seen in the photo insert section (see plate 6).

JEWISH CHRISTIANITY IN THE TALMUD

In addition to the knowledge we can gain of the Ebionites through these few and precious morsels from the Gospel of the Hebrews, we are again indebted to the Jewish rabbis for preserving in the Talmud some invaluable historical recollections of their disputes with the Ebionites. Let us begin with a passage that Hugh Schonfield calls, "of the utmost importance to Christian antiquities."[29] In this passage, Rabbi Eliezer, the brother-in-law of Rabbi Gamaliel (whom we know from Acts had sympathy for the Nazarenes) is accused of heresy and taken to a Roman tribunal for judgment, where he is declared innocent. In reflecting on why he could possibly have been associated with heresy, Eliezer recalls that, "I was once walking in the upper-market of Sepphoris when I came across one of the disciples of Yesu han-nosri [Jesus the Nazarene], Jacob of Kephar Sikhnaya by name . . ."[30] Rabbi Eliezer goes on to say that Jacob quoted to him a teaching of Jesus, the truth of which he found pleasing, and it is to this that he attributes having become infected with heresy. This Jacob of the village of Kephar Sikhnaya (more commonly known as Sikhnin) is mentioned in other places in the Talmud, and was apparently a well-known Jewish Christian of the first century, whom we will discuss further in a moment.

But first, there is another passage in the Talmud about Rabbi Eliezer's contacts with Ebionites in Galilee. Eliezer's wife goes to a certain "philosopher" for advice on a legal matter concerning her inheritance from her father. The philosopher tells her, "From the day you were exiled from your land the law of Moses is invalid and the law of the gospel has been substituted . . ." These words clearly indicate that this philosopher is a Christian, and he apparently refers to Jesus's teaching in the Gospel of the Hebrews in advising this Jewish woman on the matter of inheritance. He quotes a passage from the Gospel of the Hebrews that we have already examined: "I have looked further to the end of the book, and in it is written, 'I am not come to take away from the law of Moses, and I am not come to add to the law of Moses.'"[31] So, here again, the unfortunate Rabbi Eliezer came into contact with the heresy of the Notsrim.

Another intriguing passage from the Talmud discusses the case of a nephew of Rabbi Ishmael, Rabbi Eleazar ben Dama, who is bitten by a serpent and seeks healing from the aforementioned Jacob of Sikhnin, who apparently also had the reputation of a healer (interesting, since according to the gospels and Acts, the Nazarenes continued the healing ministry of Jesus). Ben Dama's uncle counsels him not to go, and while Ben Dama is attempting to show his uncle that seeking such healing is permitted in the Torah, he dies.[32]

Another example in the Talmud of the Nazarenes' reputation for healing is the case of a grandson of Rabbi Joshua ben Levi, who gets something stuck in his throat. A healer whispers something in the grandson's ear in the name of Jesus, and he recovers. But his grandfather is not at all pleased, remarking to the healer that it would have been better if his grandson had died rather than be healed in the name of Jesus.[33]

Similar to these accounts in the Talmud, Bishop Epiphanius (a native of Palestine) relays a firsthand account of his conversation with a converted Jew by the name of Josephus, who testifies that before he became a follower of Jesus, he had once been extremely sick and a Jewish elder (obviously a Jewish Christian) tried to heal him by whispering in his ear, "Believe in Jesus, crucified under Pontius Pilate the governor, Son of God first, yet later born of Mary; the Christ of God and risen from the dead. And believe that he will come to judge the quick and the dead."[34] Epiphanius also tells of another Jew on the verge of death who heard whispered in his ear, "Jesus Christ, the crucified Son of God, will judge you."[35] Epiphanius says that such accounts of healings in the name of Jesus by the Ebionites were common. It is because of these healings being done in the name of the "heretic" Jesus that they were, thankfully for posterity, recorded in the Talmud. They give us invaluable independent evidence of the continuing healing ministry of the Ebionites. But of these Ebionites, the only two mentioned by name in the Talmud are the aforementioned Jacob of Sikhnin, and a man known to history as Conon the Martyr, both of whom, interestingly, are of the Desposyni.

THE LAST DESPOSYNI

Scholars have attempted to identify Jacob (James) of Sikhnin with one of the other Jameses in the New Testament, on the reasoning that for his name to appear in the Talmud he must have been a prominent figure, well known to the Jewish rabbis. Some scholars have theorized that he was one of the disciples of Jesus named James, or even Jesus's brother himself, on the supposition that Rabbi Eliezer could well have encountered one of them at some point.[36] Of all these very speculative hypotheses, one that seems to have some validity is put forth by Richard Bauckham, who proposes that Jacob of Sikhnin was actually James the grandson of Jude, who, as we have seen, was a prominent leader in the Galilean churches. As evidence, Bauckham points out that the modern town now known as Sakhnin lies only six kilometers from the town of Cochaba, which, as we have seen, was one of the two main centers of the Desposyni.[37] Bauckham also notes that the archaeologist Bellarmino Bagatti claimed to have found Jacob of Sikhnin's tomb, which, provocatively, locals claim to be that of James the Just, but which would much more logically be that of Jacob of Sikhnin.

If Jacob of Sikhnin was not of the Desposyni, then Bishop Symeon and the grandsons of Jude—James and Zoker—are the last leaders of the Ebionites known to us by name that we can definitely say were of the family of Jesus. Of course, it is possible, even likely, that one or more of the people named in the Jerusalem bishop's list is of the Desposyni, but we cannot say this with any real confidence. There is, however, one other person we do know by name who was of the Desposyni, and he lived more than a century after the time of Symeon, James, and Zoker, a man with the interesting Greek name of Conon.

The case of Conon is fascinating, for he is remembered on the Roman Catholic calendar as a martyr.[38] From what little we know, he was martyred during a Christian persecution under the emperor Decius, which took place in 250–251. According to historical records he was a gardener who worked on the emperor's estate. He was martyred in Pamphylia, a city in Asia Minor where he was put on trial. When Conon was questioned in court as to his identity, he made the following intriguing reply: "I am of the city of Nazareth in Galilee, I am of the family of Christ, whose worship I have inherited from my ancestors, and whom I recognize as God over all things."[39] While some may say that Conon's claim to be of the family of Jesus is spurious or legendary due to the late date of the event, Richard Bauckham asserts its authenticity on exactly that basis:

[T]he sheer unexpectedness of a record of a member of the family of Jesus in Pamphylia at a time when, to judge by extant Christian literature of the period, the church at large had lost all interest in living members of that family, argues for [its] authenticity . . . Conon's employment as a gardener is consistent with what we know of the socioeconomic status of the *depsosynoi*.[40]

In addition, Bellarmino Bagatti has found archaeological evidence to support the authenticity of Conon's claim at the fifth-century Byzantine Church of the Annunciation in Nazareth. Beneath this church Bagatti found the remains of a third-century synagogue, apparently Jewish Christian, built over two small caves that were used for Christian worship, and containing a cross and prayers inscribed to Jesus.[41] While the architecture of the synagogue is Jewish, what marks it as Jewish Christian is an equal-armed cross on its mosaic floor. There is also a mosaic inscription at the foot of the steps that lead down from the synagogue to the caves that reads: "Gift of Conon, Deacon of Jerusalem." While this cannot be the same Conon, it would seem that Deacon Conon's gift was inspired by the fact that he shared the same name as Conon the Martyr, and so made a donation to the place that commemorated his namesake's martyrdom.

What all of this tells us is that at least a few Desposyni were still alive in Nazareth in the first half of the third century, but were finding it increasingly difficult to survive. Let us hear a final word from Richard Bauckham as to the state of affairs of the Jewish Christians in Galilee at this time, which will set the stage for the next leg of our journey tracing the underground stream of Jewish Christianity:

That Conon was revered as a martyr in the Catholic Church of the fourth century . . . suggest[s] that the *desposynoi* had not thrown in their lot with those Jewish Christian groups, such as the Ebionites, who were regarded as sectarian and heretical by Catholic writers. They can most plausibly be placed among those "Nazarene" Jewish Christians whose distinctness from Gentile Catholic Christianity was cultural rather than doctrinal, even to the extent of remembering Paul and the Pauline mission with full approval. Such groups, however, were slowly dwindling, under the impact of the consolidation of rabbinic Judaism in Galilee, the success of Ebionite, Elkasite, and Gnostic influences in Jewish Christianity east of the Jordan, and cultural isolation from the Gentile Church. We might have expected descendants of the family of Jesus to have retained the memory of such illustrious ancestry for many centuries. That they disappear so rapidly and completely from history can only be attributed to the marginalized status of the groups to which they belonged. Had the literature of those groups survived in more than the few fragments we have, we might know much more about the *desposynoi*. Meanwhile, while the Catholic Church delighted in elaborating legends about the family background of Jesus, those who might have been able to seek out the surviving members of the family and record some really valuable traditions—Eusebius, Epiphanius, Jerome—seem to have had not the slightest interest in doing so.[42]

The reason why these church fathers had no interest in seeking out any remaining Desposyni is obvious. The Desposyni retained memories (dangerous memories for the leaders of the newly emerging Catholic Church) that the origins of Christianity were quite different from what the Church was proclaiming. The Desposyni were an embarrassing reminder that Jesus had a family that included brothers, sisters, nieces, and nephews, and this was quite contrary to the new dogma of the perpetual virginity of Mary. Not only that, but these relatives of Jesus were among the first and most important leaders of the Jerusalem Church. Their existence belied the claim of the Church of Rome that Peter was the first pope. The Desposyni were skeletons in the closet of the Roman Church that could never be let out. The new breed of heresy hunters, including Irenaeus, Hippolytus, and Epiphanius, did their utmost to ensure that the key to that closet door would be thrown away forever. But what the case of Conon the Martyr also shows us is that in the third century there were now Jewish Christians who were more amenable to the doctrine of the emerging Gentile Catholic Church. Jewish Christianity was becoming a much more complex entity.

9

EBIONITE THEOLOGY
A Third Religion
Between Church and Synagogue

Our Lord neither asserted that there were gods except the
Creator of all, nor did He proclaim Himself to be God.
THE *PSEUDO-CLEMENTINE* "HOMILIES" 16:15

By the end of the second century and the beginning of the third, a century or so before the Gentile Church would consolidate its variegated doctrines at the Council of Nicaea, Jewish Christianity was spreading, but not consolidating, and becoming more variegated. In order to better understand the Jewish Christian "enemy," the Catholic heresy hunters were now categorizing the "heretical" Jewish Christians into various groups. In addition to the Ebionites, seven other heretical groups that are named in the patristic writings are the Elkesaites, Symmachians, Cerinthians, Ossaeans, Sampsaeans, Nazoraeans, and Nasaraeans. These were not all distinct groups into which the Ebionites had splintered, however, but confused names for the same basic group as it evolved over time and at different locales. This is especially evident in the confused spellings of Nazoraean and Nasaraean; and some of these named groups, such as the Symmachians and Cerinthians, were not actually Jewish Christian sects at all. In this chapter and the next we shall examine each of these groups to see how this false taxonomy evolved.[1]

AN EBIONITE BY ANY OTHER NAME

The first of the heresy hunters, Irenaeus, author of *Adversus Haereses* (Against Heresies), described three distinguishing characteristics of the Ebionites: they venerated Jerusalem, used only the Gospel of Matthew, and regarded Jesus's birth as a natural one. They believed that Jesus was the naturally born son of Joseph and Mary, chosen by God to be the Messiah because of his Davidic descent and his holy life, and anointed as Messiah by John at his baptism when God declared: "You are my Son, the Beloved; with you I am well pleased" (Mark 1:11). The Ebionite belief that Jesus was "adopted" as God's son at his baptism is referred to as "adoptionism" by scholars.

The title "Son of God" that the Nazarenes had used, and which, according to the gospels, was first confessed by Peter (Matt. 16:16), was not unique. In fact all the kings of Israel were called "sons of God" and all were "messiahs," a Hebrew term that literally means "anointed one," referring to the ancient and widespread practice whereby a new king had holy oil poured over his head. Gentile Christians were unfamiliar with the Jewish understanding of the term "Son of God" and understood it in the Hellenistic sense of a king literally born of a god. It is fascinating to look at how the early church father Justin Martyr, in his *First Apology to the Greeks,* attempted to defend the Gentile Christian understanding of Jesus as the literal "Son of God":

And when we say also that the Logos,* who is the firstborn of God, was produced without sexual union, and that he, Jesus Christ, our Teacher, was crucified and died, and rose again, and ascended into Heaven, we propound nothing different from what you believe

---

*Greek for "word" (or "reason" or "logic"), the symbolic designation used for Jesus in the first chapter of the Gospel of John.

regarding those whom you esteem sons of Jupiter. . . . And if we assert that the Word of God was born of God in a peculiar manner, different from ordinary generation, let this, as said above, be no extraordinary thing to you, who say that Mercury is the angelic Word of God. But if anyone objects that he was crucified, in this also he is comparable to those reputed sons of Jupiter of yours, who suffered . . . And if we even affirm that he was born of a virgin, accept this in common with what you accept of Perseus. And in that we say that he made whole the lame, the paralytic, and those born blind, we seem to say what is very similar to the deeds said to have been done by Aesculapius.[2]

This is a succinct summary of how the Gentile Christians thought of Jesus as the Son of God. It is an understanding that became, ironically, an embarrassment to later Christians who went out of their way to emphasize the uniqueness of Jesus, rather than similarities to the Greek gods, a trend that continues in Christian apologetics to the present day. While Gentile Christians considered the more naturalistic Ebionite view of Jesus to be heresy, the Jewish Christians considered the Hellenistic understanding of Jesus to be the real heresy.

The next church father to write about the Ebionites is Tertullian (ca. 160–220), who repeats the earlier complaints of Irenaeus and adds that the founder of the Ebionites was a man named Ebion. This is complete fantasy and is likely based in Tertullian's belief that all heresies had to have a founding figure. Epiphanius would later pick up on and repeat this mistaken notion, as noted earlier in chapter 6. The next major heresy hunter, Hippolytus (ca. 170–236), author of the *Refutatio Omnium Haeresium* (Refutation of All Heresies),* asserted that the Ebionites

---

*There is considerable confusion in the scholarly literature as to the exact titles of the works of the patristic heresy hunters, and the original titles are not always known. While the work of Hippolytus is most commonly referred to as Refutation of All Heresies, it is a popularized title that was given to it much later. It has also been known as "Philosophumena." Epiphanius's *Panarion* is also sometimes called the "Refutation of All Heresies." Both Irenaeus and Tertullian have antiheretical works that are variously called *Adversus*

believed Jesus became the Christ as a result of his exceeding righteousness and strict observance of the law. Origen (ca. 185–254) was the first to state that the etymology of the name "Ebionites," meaning "the poor," was quite appropriate due to their being "poor in understanding" as to Jesus's actual divine nature. By the fourth century, Eusebius, Epiphanius, and Jerome, reliant as they were on the early heresy hunters for their knowledge of the Ebionites, would all parrot these by now familiar criticisms; but these later church fathers did have some new knowledge based on direct encounters with the descendants of the Ebionites in their day, though by that time Ebionitism had evolved and changed.

In sum, the church fathers all understood Ebionitism to be a heresy that developed among Jewish followers of Jesus after the year 70, and were oblivious to the fact that the Ebionites actually carried on the faith of Jesus's family and first disciples. As we saw, the famous phrase of the Jewish Christian historian Hegesippus—"They used to call the Church a virgin"—which originally was a denunciation of the new Hellenistic understanding of Jesus, was now turned against the Ebionites, as if they were the heretical innovators. Blinded by their Hellenistic understanding of Jesus, the church fathers simply could not fathom that the Ebionites might actually trace their roots back to the first disciples and have the correct understanding of Jesus, something the Ebionites themselves always resolutely maintained. The great authority on Jewish Christianity, Hans-Joachim Schoeps, summarized the situation this way:

> [A]s a group with a separate destiny and distinctive doctrinal views, Jewish Christianity first appeared at the moment of its organizational separation from the rest of primitive Christianity. To this extent Epiphanius is quite correct when he dates the origin of the Ebionites and Nazoreans at the time of the capture of Jerusalem

---

Haereses (Against Heresies) and *Adversus Omnes Haereses* (Against All Heresies). Even the best scholars confuse the titles. Here we shall go by what seems to be a consensus: Hippolytus's work shall be called "Refutation of All Heresies," Tertullian's work shall be called "Against All Heresies," Irenaeus's work shall be called "Against Heresies," and Epiphanius's work shall be called by its known Greek title, *Panarion* (The Medicine Chest).

(*Panarion* 30.2.7; 29.5.4). And yet it is not a contradiction when he
. . . [dates] the beginnings of the Nazoreans to the earliest period of
the primitive church in Jerusalem, directly after the death of Jesus
(29.7). Both dates are correct, depending upon whether one is speaking of the beginnings of Ebionitism as an institution, or of its spiritual beginnings.[3]

The most prolific of the heresy hunters, Epiphanius (ca. 315–403),
author of the *Panarion,* had direct knowledge of a Jewish Christian group
called "Nazoreans," who were still extant in his time, spoke Hebrew or
Aramaic, and were closely related in their doctrine and practice to the
Ebionites. But he is also aware from the gospels and the book of Acts that
the earliest Christians were called by a very similar name (Nazarenes),
which led to a great deal of confusion about these Jewish Christian
groups among the church fathers, and continues to do so today. As Hugh
Schonfield put it,

> Bishop Epiphanius, who devoted himself to dealing with numerous
> sects in his massive *Panarion,* wrestled manfully with the problems
> of identification arising from a similarity of names—Osseans and
> Jesseans, Nasarenes and Nazoreans—and what relationship these
> had to the Christians who were also called Nazoreans. There was
> the added complication of the Jewish devotees called Nazirites. The
> tangle is certainly a difficult one to sort out, since all these groups
> were to be found roughly in the same region.[4]

HACKING THROUGH THE FOREST

To simplify what can be a most complex and confusing topic, we can
classify all of the many later Jewish Christian sects into three distinct
groups. While we hear the church fathers speak of eight different Jewish
Christian groups, it is not too difficult to separate a lot of chaff from the
wheat. We can immediately rule out the Symmachians and Cerinthians
as being Jewish Christian sects. First, the Cerinthians: According to

Irenaeus, the Cerinthians were led by a man named Cerinthus, who expounded Gnostic views about Jesus in Asia Minor.[5] Hippolytus, who writes about the same group, is clearly borrowing from Irenaeus. What is clearly Jewish Christian in the teachings of Cerinthus is that he espoused circumcision, taught that Jesus was not born of a virgin, and said that Paul and his disciples were deceitful.[6] Tertullian and Eusebius also speak of this man named Cerinthus, but it is Epiphanius who first calls his followers Cerinthians.[7] This is a misnomer, however. The Cerinthians were not a distinct group, but Ebionites with a touch of Gnosticism thrown in, a trend which reached full bloom in the Gnostic Elkesaites.* The so-called Cerinthians were actually a later group of Ebionites in Asia Minor led by a bishop named Cerinthus, and not a separate group.[8]

Likewise, Eusebius writes of a Jewish Christian named Symmachus, whose writings were still extant in his day.[9] Symmachus was well known. Schonfield notes that he was a pagan convert who undertook the huge task of doing a new translation of the Old Testament into Greek, a translation that was quite influential:

> Symmachus appears to have been, like Clement,[†] a convert to Jewish Christianity, and may have been of Samaritan origin. He flourished toward the end of the second century. His object in undertaking a new translation of the Old Testament is believed to have been to provide a rendering in idiomatic Greek, free from Semitisms. . . . And its influence still remains, as it was largely . . . [used] by Jerome in his revision of the Latin Bible. Eusebius mentions that in his own day (fourth century) there were *Commentaries* of Symmachus still extant, in which it would seem that he criticized the Greek version of Matthew's Gospel, which had lately been accepted by the Gentile Church.[10]

---

*Chapters 10 and 12, where we will discuss the Elkesaites, also include a discussion of the nature of Gnosticism and its closely related theology of dualism.

†Schonfield is referring to Clement of Rome, who lived in the late first century, and not the later Clement of Alexandria, who lived in the third century.

The latter point—the criticism of the Greek version of Matthew—would seem to clearly demarcate Symmachus as a Jewish Christian. A writer named Ambrosiaster also speaks of a Jewish Christian group called Symmachians who, he says, are descendants of the Pharisees who follow the law but claim to be Christians.[11] But here again, we are rather obviously not looking at a separate and distinct group from the Ebionites.

This is just about all we know of both Cerinthus and Symmachus, but as a result of these few references in the church fathers, many modern writers have erroneously understood the Cerinthians and Symmachians to be distinct Jewish Christian sects. Klijn and Reinink, after thoroughly considering all the evidence, conclude that no case can be made for either the Cerinthians or Symmachians being distinct groups from the Ebionites. The patristic writers made a false assumption based on the fact that they had seen writings by and about two Jewish Christians named Cerinthus and Symmachus. Klijn and Reinink bluntly conclude that Cerinthians and Symmachians are merely "a product of the imagination of early Christian authors."[12] This clears the tangled undergrowth a bit, and leaves us with six groups to consider. It is fortunate that, for simplicity's sake, we can likewise eliminate the so-called Ossaeans and Sampsaeans.

Of all the patristic writers, it is only Epiphanius in his *Panarion* who mentions Ossaeans and Sampsaeans. He says that the Ossaeans are led by a man named Elxai. As we shall see, Elxai was indeed the founder of a distinct Jewish Christian group known as the Elkesaites, whom we shall discuss in some depth in the next chapter. Based on this fact alone, we can rule out the Ossaeans as being a separate and distinct group. Reinforcing this is the fact that Epiphanius further says that the Sampsaeans are the Elkesaites under a different name.[13] The name "Ossaean" may derive from Jessaean, which was likely an alternate name for the original Nazarenes, since Jesus was known as the "Son of Jesse" (Jesse being King David's father). Ossaean may also have been a variant spelling of Essene, and, as is well known, the Essenes and Nazarenes shared a number of similarities.

Whatever the actual case may be, we are now left with four groups of Jewish Christians discussed by the heresy hunters—the Ebionites, Elkesaites, Nazoraeans, and Nasoraeans—and we can quickly whittle this down to three as it is quite apparent that "Nazoraean" and "Nasoraean" are simply variant spellings for the same group. This group is not to be confused with the original Nazarenes, however, though they are descended from them and the close similarity in their names has led to confusion among the patristic writers. Thus we are finally left with three legitimate, distinct Jewish Christian sects. Although we have already dealt with the Ebionites rather extensively, we have mainly focused on their history and it is to the specifics of their theology that we shall turn next. Then we'll turn the spotlight on the Nazoraeans, once we have a fuller basis for comparison of their beliefs vis-à-vis the Ebionites, and explore their evolution toward, and ultimate merger with, the Roman Catholic Church. The Elkesaites will be more thoroughly discussed in the next chapter, as the waters of this branch of the underground stream of Jewish Christianity provide us with a fascinating and crucial linkage to later European heretical sects such as the Paulicians, the Bogomils, and the Cathars.

SOURCES FOR EBIONITE THEOLOGY

Much of our knowledge of Ebionite theology comes from the heresy hunters—primarily Irenaeus (second century), Hippolytus (third century), and Epiphanius (fourth century). While other patristic writers talk about the Ebionites, a comparative analysis of their writings reveals that they were all getting their information from one of the "big three." Even though Epiphanius is the latest writer, and we might therefore expect him to be less accurate, this is not the case. Epiphanius says much more than Irenaeus and Hippolytus combined, and goes into much greater detail. Epiphanius states that he is quoting directly from Ebionite writings and has had personal interaction with Ebionites. While this would prima facie seem to make him better informed, we also need to keep in mind that the theology of the Ebionites had evolved by his day, generally in a more conservatively Jewish direction; the Elkesaites had evolved in a more Gnostic direction, and the Nazoraeans in a Hellenistic direction more amenable to the emerging Catholic Church with which they would ultimately merge. While Irenaeus and Hippolytus are writing a century to two centuries earlier than Epiphanius, they do not claim to have any direct knowledge of the Ebionites as Epiphanius has. It is fortuitous, therefore, that nothing that either Irenaeus or Hippolytus says contradicts anything Epiphanius says, and we thus have multiple attestation that what they all say is essentially accurate.

Our other source for knowledge of Ebionite theology is the *Pseudo-Clementines,* or so-called Ebionite Acts, the background to which we have already discussed at length, so here we can focus on what they reveal of Ebionite theology. When comparing what Epiphanius says to what the *Pseudo-Clementines* say, another serendipitous fact emerges. As Keith Akers, who has made an in-depth comparison, puts it: ". . . virtually everything that Epiphanius says about the Ebionites is duplicated in either the [*Pseudo-Clementine*] 'Recognitions,' the [*Pseudo-Clementine*] 'Homilies,' or both."[14] Of course, this correspondence could be due to Epiphanius's having at least parts of the *Pseudo-Clementine* literature in front of him. Epiphanius says that he has, in fact, seen the Ebionite gospel, the Ebionite "Acts of the Apostles," and two documents tantalizingly titled the "Degrees of James" and the "Travels of Peter." It would seem logical to conclude that the "Degrees of James" is the writing known to us as the "Ascents of James," one of the writings incorporated into the *Pseudo-Clementines.* We also know of another writing called the "Circuits of Peter," which is likely the same as Epiphanius's "Travels of Peter." It would seem that this document also was incorporated into the *Pseudo-Clementines,* since they tell the story of Clement following Peter in his travels.

The bottom line is that between the *Pseudo-Clementines* and Epiphanius's *Panarion* we have a solid basis for compiling an accurate list of Ebionite beliefs. As Keith Akers puts it, "This 'multiple attestation' validates much of what Epiphanius says; it means that anything mentioned by Epiphanius, that is also found in the 'Recognitions' or 'Homilies,' is almost certainly an Ebionite idea."[15] Akers has compiled an inventory of beliefs that we can almost conclusively say formed the core of Ebionite theology and practice. Before we examine this list, it is important to note that while many of these beliefs clearly go back to the original Nazarenes, there are some that do not, that are unique ideas that evolved along with the Ebionites, and which the Ebionites later wrongly claimed went back to the Nazarenes.

EBIONITE THEOLOGY 101

The following is a "top ten" list of the core Ebionite doctrines as culled from Epiphanius and the *Pseudo-Clementines*:

1. Jesus is the "true prophet" predicted by Moses.

In the *Panarion* Epiphanius states that the Ebionites "say that the Christ is the True Prophet" (30.18.5). While the "Suffering Servant" passages in Isaiah[16] were beloved by the Gentile Church as foretelling Jesus as a suffering Messiah, the Ebionites favored Deuteronomy 18:15–22 as showing that God had foretold through Moses the coming of a mighty prophet like Jesus: "I will raise up for them a prophet like you from among their own people; I will put my words in the mouth of the prophet, who shall speak to them everything I command" (Deut. 18:18). Hans-Joachim Schoeps noted that this emphasis in Ebionite theology on Jesus as the true prophet "led to significant conclusions with respect to religious toleration . . ."[17] Unlike the Gentile Christians, who denounced and persecuted the Jews, the Ebionites remained supportive of their Jewish brethren who did not accept Jesus as the true prophet, since the Ebionites believed that God had instituted two different covenants for salvation through Moses and Jesus. Schoeps underscores the implications of this:

> Both [Moses and Jesus] were sent by God to establish covenants with mankind. Just as Moses was the teacher of the Jews, so Jesus was the teacher of the Gentiles (*Hom.* 2.52). Since the two kinds of teaching are identical, God accepts everyone who believes in either of them (*Hom.* 8.6). Conversion to Jesus, therefore, is for them precisely the same thing as conversion to God and to the Jewish law.[18]

Schoeps also notes that the Ebionites' inclusive stance may have been partly in opposition to Paul's teaching of the gospel of Jesus as a complete replacement for the old law established at Sinai.

As we noted at the beginning of chapter 7, the Ebionites, in a more fruitful way than Paul, worked hard for the unification of Jews and Gentiles. Schoeps agrees with Schonfield that, "At an early date they evidently conducted a mission seeking converts to the Covenant at Sinai as it had been reformed by Christ, regarded as the basis for the salvation of the whole world. They must have propagated this religion, which existed independently of the religions of the church and the synagogue, before the middle of the second century . . ."[19] Schoeps refers to Ebionitism as a third religion, midway between church and synagogue, and notes that while this third religion was not successful, it still retained great potential:

> The belief of the primitive church in Palestine [the Nazarenes] and of the Ebionites in Transjordan that Jesus Christ is the new Moses has been condemned to remain unproductive by the Church throughout her history; yet the economy of salvation presupposed in this belief, namely that, expressed in modern terms, *God established two covenants with mankind through the revelations on Sinai and Golgotha, which in the last resort are nevertheless one*—this striking interpretation of the coexistence of Judaism and Christianity in world history represents a conviction of Ebionite Jewish Christianity which remains worthy of note even today.[20]

If Ebionitism had prevailed over early Catholicism, the world could well be a far different and better place today. It is reasonable to suppose that many of the greatest atrocities in human history, which can be laid squarely at the feet of Gentile anti-Semitism, might have been avoided. Schoeps dourly notes of the actual outcome: "This expectation of ancient Jewish Christianity that the two great religions from which it derived would be brought together in a morality of good works was not realized . . ."[21] As we shall see in the concluding chapter, Schoeps is not quite correct here. This unity of Judaism and Christianity expressed through a "morality of good works" would become the hallmark of Freemasonry, a fraternity which, while it officially denies being a religion, comes as close as possible to being a third religion between church and synagogue.

2. Jesus is not God.

In the *Pseudo-Clementine* "Homilies" we read, "Our Lord neither asserted that there were gods except the Creator of all, nor did He proclaim Himself to be God" (16.15). According to Ebionite theology, it was theoretically possible for anyone to have become the Christ. As Hippolytus reports of their Christology: "Had another likewise fulfilled the precepts of the law, he too would have become Christ, for by like deeds other Christs could occur."[22] Jesus *became* the "Righteous One," the only one who ever perfectly fulfilled the law of Moses, and thus God elected him to be the Christ. God therefore "adopted" Jesus as his Son at his baptism in fulfillment of the royal coronation Psalm: "He said to me, 'You are my son; today I have begotten you'" (Psalm 2:7). According to Ebionite belief, Jesus was not a preexistent being as in Catholic theology, but was made the Christ through the power of the Holy Spirit in the baptismal waters. According to the *Pseudo-Clementine* "Recognitions," Jesus is the one "who in the waters of baptism was called Son of God" (1.48).

3. The Christ came into Jesus.

While Jesus was not preexistent, the Christ was, and entered into Jesus. In Ebionite theology the Christ was an angelic being who entered into Jesus at his baptism. According to Schoeps, the Ebionites "believed that Jesus had actually been transformed by his exaltation to heavenly Messiah into a kind of supernatural angelic being, and their millenarian expectation looked for him to return to bring a supernatural angelic kingdom at the time of his return."[23] This understanding can be seen in the book of Revelation, where Jesus, in the form of the heavenly lamb, is seated on the throne of God surrounded by the court of angels. According to the Ebionites, this angelic being (actually an archangel) had also been present in Adam and in other figures in Jewish history.

While this may all seem rather ludicrous at first, it is an idea solidly rooted in Jewish tradition. In Jewish theology there were said to be seven righteous men in whom the divine Spirit had dwelled. The Jewish mystical tradition, as represented in the Kabbalah, viewed these seven righteous men as reincarnations of the original man, Adam Kadmon. The Spirit of God present in these righteous men was referred to as the wandering Shekinah, the "glory of God." This idea can be seen in the "Recognitions," which speaks of "the true Prophet, from the beginning of the world hastening through the age" (2.22). "Homilies" 17.4 and "Recognitions" 2.47 name the members of this succession as being Adam, Enoch, Noah, Abraham, Isaac, Jacob, and Moses. In Ebionite thought, Jesus is the eighth righteous man. This idea is also seen in Paul, who speaks of Christ as the "new Adam." The Ebionites believed that the Shekinah came to rest finally and forever in the Messiah, Jesus. As we shall see, this idea would continue to reverberate in the teachings of the Elkesaites and in the Muslim Qur'an. This teaching was actually anti-Gnostic in that, "Precisely in opposition to Marcion's sundering of the two Testaments, Ebionitism insists on the full identity and unity of true Judaism and true Christianity by means of the Spirit of the True Prophet."[24] So, in this rather (to our ears) strange teaching, the Ebionites were ultimately upholding the unity of the heirs of the two covenants forged at Sinai and Golgotha.

4. This world has been given over to Satan.

In "Homilies" 20.2 we read, "God appointed two kingdoms, and established two ages, determining that the present world should be given to the evil one . . . but He promised to preserve for the good one the age to come . . ." Here, Ebionitism takes a somewhat Gnostic and dualistic turn, but it is a turn that is also reflected in the New Testament where Satan is called the lord of this world.[25] While not overly emphasized by the Ebionites (or by the Gentile Christians), this belief would come much more to the fore in the later Elkesaites and their theological heirs, the Cathars, whom we shall discuss shortly.

5. The value of poverty.

The Ebionite rejection of possessions is summed up quite succinctly in "Homilies" 15.9: "Possessions are sins." We have already commented on this Ebionite value to a great extent and not much more needs to be said here. We can just add that the Nazarene "love-communism" (as Schoeps called it)[26] is attested to in the famous passage in Acts that describes how the believers lived "together and had all things in common; they would sell their possessions and goods and distribute the proceeds to all, as any had need" (Acts 2:44–45). The very name Ebionim, as we have seen, means "the poor." But we also must be aware that this ideal may not have been seen as an ethic for all people for all time, but merely as an "interim ethic" between this age and the impending new age. As Schoeps points out: "Apparently, the view that the end of history was imminent made any kind of earthly possession seem unimportant and unnecessary."[27] While the eschaton did not arrive as the Nazarenes and Ebionites expected, their belief in the value of poverty and rejection of possessions hardened into a permanent ethic. As Schoeps notes, "Apparently, the social conditions of the later Ebionites were extremely impoverished and wretched . . . Nevertheless, the *Clementines* allow us to see that for the Ebionites it was not so much the possession of goods itself that was sinful, but rather the greed for new possessions and for becoming rich."[28] And here the Ebionites were surely reflecting the teachings of Jesus on this subject, just as we see in Jesus's "intensification" of the law in the Sermon on the Mount—anger leads to murder, and lust to adultery. Envy and covetousness lead to greed and stealing. Schoeps notes that the ethical ideal of poverty was so ingrained that "the later Ebionites on Cyprus about the year 377 still appealed to the position taken by their ancestors in Jerusalem . . ."[29]

6. The practice of vegetarianism and rejection of animal sacrifice.

This is a topic about which we have not yet commented. It is stated succinctly in the *Pseudo-Clementines:* "And the things that are well-pleasing to God are . . . not to taste dead flesh, not touch blood" (*Homilies* 7.4). Epiphanius attests that in the Ebionite gospel Jesus speaks against eating meat at the Last Supper: "I have no desire to eat the meat of this Passover lamb with you;" and against the temple sacrifices: "And if you do not stop making sacrifice, God's wrath will not stop afflicting you."[30] The degree to which the Ebionite rejection of meat and the temple sacrifices reflect the practice of the original Nazarenes and the teaching of Jesus is not at all clear. Certainly Jesus does not outrightly advocate vegetarianism or criticize vegetarianism in the canonical gospels, though it has been argued that his temple protest may have been a protest against sacrifice.

Keith Akers (who is a noted vegetarian) is the main proponent of the theory that the Ebionite rejection of meat and sacrifice was an accurate reflection of the teachings and practice of Jesus.[31] But it is difficult to believe that the Nazarenes would have continued to worship in the temple, as we have seen they unquestionably did, if Jesus had rejected sacrifice, for animal sacrifice was a core practice in the temple. Especially on Yom Kippur, the Jews reveled in the expiation of sin that came through the blood of the sacrifice, and the sacrifice of the Passover Lamb was such an integral part of Jewish history and practice that it is exceedingly difficult to believe that Jesus, in all other respects a good Jew, would have rejected it. If Jesus had rejected sacrifice, this criticism surely would have been included in the list of grievances against him in the gospels.

That being said, it is indeed quite clear that one of the key doctrines of the Ebionites was the rejection of animal sacrifice and the concomitant practice of vegetarianism. So how, then, are we to account for the development of vegetarianism among the Ebionites if it did not exist in Jesus or the Nazarenes? Schoeps explains as follows:

> This dogmatic vegetarianism undoubtedly represents an intensification of the Mosaic food laws. It is well known that these laws permit the eating of the meat of an animal only after its blood has been drained. In many passages the Torah prohibited the eating of blood . . . The practice of bleeding slaughtered animals must have seemed inadequate to the Ebionites. They based their vegetarianism on the commandment of Genesis 9:4, "the flesh with its soul, its blood, you shall not eat" . . . they achieved a more rigorous practice than that prescribed for the Jews by the Mosaic food laws. Since the ritual incision does not completely drain the blood of the slaughtered animal, they

preferred the radical solution of complete abstinence in order to conform completely to the biblical commandment. In their rigorism they probably extended the prohibition to the use of fish of any kind . . .[32]

Schoeps goes on to explain that the firm emphasis of the Ebionites on vegetarianism caused them to "correct" the New Testament accounts of the practice of Jesus and the disciples:

> They portrayed Peter as a vegetarian who lived only on bread and olives (*Hom.* 12.6; *Rec.* 7.5). . . . They alleged that the patriarchs of the Old Testament and Moses abstained from "animal things," so they also claimed that Jesus himself became a vegetarian when, according to the Ebionite "Acts," he declined the suggestion that he eat meat at the Passover. In all these "corrections," which in part are clearly contradicted by the biblical accounts, we see the Ebionites' tendency toward radicalism; they wanted to manifest their "better righteousness" (Matt. 5:20) by the intensification of the Pharasaic practice of the law.[33]

Here we see that the Ebionites may have taken Jesus's injunction in the Sermon on the Mount—"Unless your righteousness exceeds that of the scribes and Pharisees, you will never enter the kingdom of heaven" (Matt. 5:20)—to an extreme that would have alarmed Jesus, for Jesus (unlike his brother James, from whom the Ebionites inherited their ethic) was clearly not an ascetic. It is difficult to believe that the gospels would include the charges that Jesus was a glutton and wine bibber if it were not indeed the case that Jesus enjoyed a good party. While the gospels do not overtly portray Jesus as eating meat, he does eat fish, and one of his greatest miracles is the multiplication of the loaves and fish to feed the five thousand. And it is exceedingly difficult to believe that Jesus, good Jew that he was, would have rejected lamb at the Passover meal. It is, on the other hand, possible, perhaps likely, that the Ebionites garnered their practice of vegetarianism from Jesus's more ascetic brother James, or from Essene influence.

7. There are "false texts" in the scripture.

Though the Ebionites were known for their dedication to the Torah and their upholding of the law in daily life, they had a quite surprising understanding of what comprised the genuine Torah. The Ebionites had a kind of premodern understanding of the Bible in that they believed that not everything in it came from God, that there were erroneous parts of purely human origin that needed to be rejected. Epiphanius reports that the Ebionites accepted only certain parts of the Pentateuch and blasphemed the Torah.[34] This likely tied in with their rejection of animal sacrifice. Obviously, if one takes an antisacrificial stance, one must explain why so much of the Torah is devoted to precise details on the way in which sacrifice is to be properly performed. The Ebionites thus rejected large portions of the Pentateuch as not being of divine origin. "Homilies" 2.38–44 contains a long list of passages that the Ebionites considered false. It could be said that they were carrying out in detail a program of correcting the Torah that had begun with Jesus, in the Sermon on the Mount, where over and over he said, "You have heard that it was said to those of ancient times . . . But I say to you . . ." As Schoeps says of their efforts, "On the one hand they . . . abbreviated and enlightened [the Torah]; on the other hand, they wanted to augment it and make it more difficult by intensifying that which was essential."[35]

Is this not in fact what we see Jesus doing? On one hand, Jesus says that all of the law can be summed up in two commandments—to love God and to love your neighbor as yourself. But on the other hand, in the Sermon on the Mount Jesus intensifies the meaning of the Torah by saying things like: "You have heard that it was said to those of ancient times, 'You shall not murder. . . .' But I say to you that if you are angry with a brother or sister, you will be liable to judgment" (Matt. 5:21–22). In many of these "intensification" passages Jesus seems almost dismissive of the Torah, and it may be from this aspect of Jesus's teaching that the Ebionites came to reject passages from the Torah wholesale. Schoeps explains their view of the Torah:

> This ambivalent treatment of the law was based on the assumption that some passages in the Torah were not as original as others and were,

in fact, later falsifications. The True Prophet [Jesus] had instructed his own concerning these passages. False pericopes are contained in the genuine "tradition of Moses" because God's will was consigned to oblivion by means of evil instruction, erroneous interpretation, and many other causes (*Hom.* 1.18; *Rec.* 1.15). Thus, it was charged, the forefathers were responsible for the fact that the revelation had not been transmitted without falsification; because the law had been lost (*Hom.* 3.47), the revelation had become burdened in later editions with additions which were contrary to God's will.[36]

As startling as some of this may sound, we know that the Torah had been lost for quite some time, and was only rediscovered during Josiah's renovation of the temple (2 Kings 22). 2 Kings bluntly tells us that as a result of the Torah having been lost, even such a central observance as Passover had not been observed for a shockingly long time: "No such Passover had been kept since the days of the judges who judged Israel, or during all the days of the kings of Israel or the kings of Judah" (2 Kings 23:22). The corruption of the kings of Israel and Judah (including David and especially his son, Solomon) caused the Ebionites to reject the monarchy. "Homilies" 3.52 tells us specifically what they rejected from the Old Testament: "The sacrifices, the monarchies, the female prophecies, and other such things came in that were not instituted by God. For this reason he [Jesus] said: 'Every plant which the heavenly Father has not planted will be rooted up'" (Matt. 15:13). The Ebionites interpreted this as applying to false passages of scripture that had been added by misguided men. Here they appealed also to Jesus's reference to Isaiah 29:13: "In vain do they worship me, teaching human precepts as doctrines" (Matthew 15:9). Another passage the Ebionites appealed to was Jeremiah 8:8: "How can you say, 'We are wise, and the law of the Lord is with us,' when, in fact, the false pen of the scribes has made it into a lie?" And Ezekiel 20:25 has God himself declaring that the laws regarding sacrifice were "not good." In summation, Schoeps notes that the passages we have "from the Ebionite gospel . . . make it clear that this theory is as old as their gospel and that Jesus must therefore have been regarded by Jewish

Christian circles in the primitive church as the one who originated this doctrine."[37]

If one takes such a stance on the nature of scripture, it raises a question that fundamentalist Christians today ask of liberal Christians who accept modern methods of biblical criticism: "In view of the fact that each man can now find in the Bible whatever he wants as a result of the falsifications (*Hom.* 3.9), how is order to be restored where there is chaos?"[38] Here, too, the Ebionites gave a surprisingly modern answer:

> The Ebionite answer . . . is: Jesus, who was the True Prophet, *did* restore order and transmitted the knowledge of this ("the mystery of the Scriptures," *Hom.* 2.40; 3.4, 28; 17.10; 19.20) as secret instruction to Peter and through him to the Ebionite congregations. By this time the apostles were regarded as the legitimate interpreters of those things in Scripture which are not clear . . .[39]

Of course, this has always been the basis of the Roman Catholic doctrine of the Church as the rightly guided interpreter of scripture. Obviously, though, the Ebionite interpretation and the Catholic interpretation differ drastically. Here, the Ebionites would see themselves as the "watchers" or "keepers" of the true tradition, and, as we have seen, these are possible meanings of the name Nazarene. As Schoeps observes:

> Here again we come upon the esoteric character of the Ebionite teaching, a *secret tradition,* for the well-disposed, regarded as originally Mosaic and subsequently Petrine [or Jamesian]. . . . The scribes and Pharisees were originally the legitimate incumbents of the seat of Moses, the true experts in the law, the initiated who possessed the knowledge (gnosis) with which to distinguish between the true and the false in the Scriptures. They betrayed their calling . . . For this reason Jesus arose from the "seat of Moses" and restored "that which was hidden from times immemorial to the worthy" through his proclamation. They [the Ebionites] are now the experts with respect to "the good basis of the Scriptures."[40] (Italics mine.)

In this idea of a "secret tradition" that carried the true "knowledge," we see the Ebionites beginning to go in a more Gnostic direction, which will come to full fruit in the later Elkesaites and will, we shall see, become the seedbed for Freemasonry. Schoeps summarizes the trajectory of the true knowledge given by God in the beginning:

> The eternal law was inscribed by God's hand on the world at the Creation . . . It was known to Adam (*Hom.* 3.48) and revealed anew to Moses, but it became increasingly obscured through errors until finally, through Jesus, it was elevated to eternal validity. The standard for the proclamation of Jesus is the distinction between what is genuine and what is false in the law. For the Ebionites, therefore, to believe in Jesus means to be instructed by him concerning the law and to obtain the "knowledge of the secrets" . . .[41]

As we will see later, this Ebionite idea of false passages in scripture will also inform the Islamic understanding of the Old and New Testaments.

8. Baptism is necessary.

While the Ebionites rejected the central Jewish ritual of sacrifice, they replaced it with a new central ritual: baptism and the associated practice of daily repentance and cleansing through ritual bathing. As Schoeps explains:

> According to "Recognitions" 1.35 ff., the real point of Jesus's mission is the annulling of the sacrificial law combined with complete loyalty to and affirmation of the rest of the Mosaic law. Animal sacrifice . . . was permitted on a temporary basis by Moses only because of the people's hardness of heart; Jesus abolished it and replaced the blood sacrifice of animals with the water of baptism.[42]

More than just a one-time baptism as initiation into the new life in Christ, regular daily immersion in water was necessary because contamination through contact with unclean things—as decreed by the Torah—

was practically unavoidable in normal day-to-day living. This idea of daily cleansing was also a much more practical replacement for sacrifice, and after the year 70, with the destruction of the temple, became a necessity. This was not a new innovation of the Ebionites, for ritual immersion as a substitute for sacrifice was already practiced by the Essenes even before 70. Schoeps summarizes:

> [T]he complex of . . . commandments in Leviticus 15 concerning ritual cleanness and uncleanness played a special role among the Ebionites. The failure to distinguish between the clean and the unclean was for them the mark of a life alienated from God, according to "Homilies" 15.10. Epiphanius (*Pan.* 30.2) reports that the Ebionites handled nothing that belonged to foreigners; this was apparently due to the fact that they constantly feared defilement or demonic pollution, which they attempted to counter by means of minute rites of purification. . . .
>
> The Peter of the Clementine novel fastidiously observes the . . . washing of hands. He washes his hands after contact with foreigners, before and after eating, before prayers, and on other occasions. According to Epiphanius, the Ebionites appealed to the example of the apostles in support of their daily lustration.[43]

It is clear in this instance, as in others, that in the *Pseudo-Clementines* the Ebionites are retrojecting their own beliefs and practices onto the apostles. The canonical gospels make it quite clear that one thing Jesus's disciples came under criticism for was *not* ritually washing their hands before eating (see Mark 7:1–5). It is difficult to believe this criticism would have been invented out of thin air by the gospel writers. To what end? This is why we have to be very careful about using the *Pseudo-Clementines* as evidence of earlier Nazarene practice. Just because the Ebionites practiced certain things does not mean the original Nazarenes did; there was an evolution of doctrine and practice from the Nazarenes to the Ebionites. But what is indisputable is that for the Ebionites baptism was seen as an extinguishing of the sacrificial fires. The *Pseudo-Clementines* say that it was Jesus, "who by the grace of baptism, extinguished that fire which the high priest used to kindle for sins" ("Recognitions" 1.48). For the Ebionites, as for the emerging Catholic Church, baptism was an unrepeatable initiation rite. The daily lustration was not related to baptism and was only for cleansing from ritual defilement, whereas the later Elkesaites, whom we shall discuss shortly, engaged in repeated baptism as a healing rite.

9. The Jewish law is still in force; and 10. Paul is a false apostle.

These last two go hand in hand and have already been extensively commented on, so we need not say much more here. Both Christians and Jews regarded the strict Ebionite adherence to the law as their chief characteristic. The church father, Ambrosiaster, considered the Ebionites to be Pharisees.[44] On the other side, a leading rabbi, Resh Laqish, writing around the year 250, praised the Ebionites for their adherence to the law and for their many good works, saying that the fires of hell had no power over them.[45] The *Pseudo-Clementine* writings clearly uphold the eternal validity of the law (but in a purified form): "The only good God . . . appointed a perpetual law to all, which can neither be abrogated by enemies, nor is vitiated by any impious one, nor is concealed in any place, but which can be read by all" ("Homilies" 8.10). Notable is the Ebionite belief that the law is for all people ("a perpetual law to all") and not just the Jews. This is simply a reiteration of what was declared when God made the original covenant with Abraham: "I will make of you a great nation, and I will bless you . . . so that you will be a blessing. . . . In you all the families of the earth shall be blessed" (Genesis 12:2–3). Paul is considered a false apostle because he preaches the abrogation of the law and teaches that the gospel is a replacement for the law.

To wrap up this survey of the main Ebionite doctrines, let us close with a telling quote from Schoeps, which nicely sums things up. Here Schoeps argues against the prevailing idea put forward by orthodox Christian theologians that the beliefs and practices of the Ebionites were either innovations or perversions of the teaching of Jesus:

It is contrary to all historical sense to assume that the Ebionites combined alien conceptions with Christianity . . . since these allegedly alien conceptions were so central in the Ebionite religious system. . . . It is more probable that in second- and third-century Ebionitism we have a conservative, early form of primitive Christianity which was excluded from the tradition of the Great Church. . . . *The following conception must have had its origin among the twelve apostles and the first disciples of Jesus* [italics mine]: Jesus came as the messianic prophet to teach us the deeper meaning of the messianic law . . . This means that they must have believed that the law contained falsifications, that the bloody sacrificial cult derived from these, and that baths for purification are recommended. In the century following Jesus's death the religious system of the "Kerygmata Petrou" [the opening section of the *Pseudo-Clementines*] developed from these rudiments and moved toward a new way of life for Jewish Christianity, *a third religion between the church and synagogue*. . . .

The Ebionite treatment of the Mosaic law . . . is undoubtedly the most interesting and the most original part of this religious system. It altered and narrowed the original teaching of Jesus concerning the law in a different way than Paul did . . . but not the way the early Catholic Church did. . . . We have only meager fragments of the debates and struggles, which occurred before consolidation produced the Mishnah* on the one side and the dogma of the Church on the other. The victorious parties—the Catholics and the Pharisees—had no interest in preserving the arguments of their opponents. Neither side was interested in recording or even remembering the debates with the Ebionites, the group that confronted both of the victorious parties without merely being on the defensive.[46]

---

*The Mishnah is the earliest codification of the oral law and makes up the first part of the Talmud.

THE BATTLE LINES ARE DRAWN

Of course, the main battle the Catholic Church fought was not against the Jewish Christians, but against the Jews themselves. They plumbed the Jewish scriptures, which they now called the "Old Testament," for proof-texts to support their contention that the Church was the "new Israel," and anyone who denied that Jesus was the Messiah of Israel was declared to be damned to the fires of Gehenna for eternity. The Ebionites were only attacked secondarily because of the "poverty" of their beliefs about Jesus. Both Jews and Jewish Christians responded to the Gentile attacks with their own broadsides. The Jews were making the claim, as we have already noted in our discussion of the *Toldoth Jeshu,* that not only was Jesus not the Son of God, but that he was not even the son of Joseph; that Jesus was the product of Mary's rape by a Roman soldier named Pandera. The Ebionites, in their turn, railed against the apostasy of the new Catholic Christians, especially vilifying their hero Paul, saying that he was not a Jew but a Greek who converted to Judaism only because he wanted to marry the high priest's daughter, and when he was spurned turned his anger against the Jewish people.[47]

There are two later Christian groups now left for our consideration—the Nazoraeans and the Elkesaites. The former adopted many of the doctrines of emerging Catholicism and were soon absorbed into the Catholic Church, while the latter group took Jewish Christianity in a more Gnostic direction that would influence the rise of later Christian sects, such as the medieval Bogomils and Cathars. The Ebionites themselves would persevere in Transjordan, Syria, and Arabia, where they would undergo a slow extinction. However, Ebionite theology could not be so easily extinguished. In one of the great ironies of western history, the Ebionites in Arabia would greatly influence the rise of a new Abrahamic religion— Islam. We turn now to Part III, where we will trace the course of all these fascinating developments, as the underground stream of Jewish Christianity continues to flow and sometimes rise unexpectedly to the surface in many new and surprising ways.

PART THREE

The Legacy of Jewish Christianity

10

FROM EBIONITES
TO ELKESAITES
The Evolution of Jewish Christianity

*For there went forth a stream and became a river great
and broad; for it flooded and broke up everything and
it brought water to the temple; and the restrainers of
the children of men were not able to restrain it, nor
the arts of those whose business it is to restrain waters;
for it spread over the face of the whole earth, and filled
everything . . .*

ODES OF SOLOMON 6

We know frustratingly little about developments in Jewish Christianity
directly from the Jewish Christians themselves after the Bar Kokhba
revolt in 135 CE. But from the writings of the heresy hunters, especially
Epiphanius, we can say with certainty that they had numerous synagogues scattered throughout the regions of Syria, the Hauran, Batanea,
the Decapolis, northwestern Arabia, and as far east as Mesopotamia (see
map 1). Epiphanius informs us that their worship rituals remained quite
close to those conducted in the Jewish synagogues,[1] and the Talmud refers
to their places of worship as Beth Nizraphi (Houses of ?) a term that cannot

be translated, but clearly has connections with the N-Z-R Hebrew root.[2] Schonfield sums up what little we can know with certainty:

> There is evidence that their performance of circumcision and the weekly fasts were on different days from those customary among the rabbinists. This was a result of the growing religious antagonism which ousted them from the Synagogue and brought them in the end to repudiate even the name of Jew. Their communities subsisted frugally by agricultural labor, and they lived in daily expectation of the return of the Messiah to restore the kingdom to Israel, in which, for their constancy, they would have a ruling part.[3]

No doubt the Desposyni envisioned a royal status for themselves in the new messianic kingdom despite having to forge a daily living through agriculture, a livelihood that is not unexpected from what we have seen of the agricultural lifestyle of Judas's grandsons, James and Zoker.

We also know that by the end of the second century there was a split in the Ebionite community. In the mid-second century, Justin Martyr distinguished two Jewish Christian groups: a moderate group that was part of the Christian Church but exerted a Jewish influence on Christian doctrine; and a more "extremist" group that refused to have any interaction with Gentile Christians.[4] Writing several decades later, Origen likewise remarks that there are two varieties of Jewish Christians in his day:

> Let it be admitted, moreover, there are some who accept Jesus, and who boast on that account of being Christians, and yet would regulate their lives, like the Jewish multitude, in accordance with the Jewish law—and these are the twofold sect of Ebionites, who either acknowledge with us that Jesus was born of a virgin, or deny this, and maintain that He was begotten like other human beings.[5]

Finally, Eusebius, in his *History of the Church* written in the early fourth century, also talks about a split in doctrine within the Ebionite community. First, he gives the typical description of the standard Ebionites (along with

the prerequisite invective!), but nevertheless points out their strong devotion
to Christ:

> There were others whom the evil demon, unable to shake their devo-
> tion to the Christ of God, caught in a different trap and made his
> own. Ebionites they were appropriately named . . . in view of the
> poor and mean opinions they held about Christ. They regarded Him
> as plain and ordinary, a man esteemed as righteous through growth
> of character and nothing more, the child of a natural union between
> a man and Mary; and they held that they must observe every detail
> of the Law . . .[6]

And then Eusebius goes on to describe a different kind of Ebionite, more
to his liking:

> A second group went by the same name, but escaped the outrageous
> absurdity of the first. They did not deny that the Lord was born of
> a virgin and the Holy Spirit, but nevertheless shared their refusal to
> acknowledge his preexistence as God . . .[7]

From all of this it is apparent that there was indeed a splintering in
some sections of the Ebionite community, with some Ebionite synagogues
(logically, those situated near Christian churches) beginning to accept
some Christian dogma. Dr. Ray Pritz, who has written an influential
book on Jewish Christianity—*Nazarene Jewish Christianity*—gives a nice
summary of what was happening:

> [W]e may say that Justin knows of two divisions of Jewish Christians,
> one of whom held an orthodox Christology with regard to the vir-
> gin birth and preexistence of Jesus. Origen, who also knows of two
> groups, identifies the unorthodox group of Justin as Ebionites.
> While he calls his more orthodox Jewish Christians Ebionites [also],
> he is inconsistent in this, and we may be justified in concluding that
> *the two groups did not carry the same name.* Eusebius, in his turn,

cannot avoid seeing—in his sources, if not also from hearsay—two distinguishable Jewish Christian groups, but . . . for him there is only one name, Ebionite.

This establishes the continued existence, into the third century at least, if not later, of a Jewish Christian entity whose doctrines tend to distinguish it—in the direction of "orthodoxy"—from the Ebionites. *These are the Nazarenes.*[8] (Italics mine.)

While Pritz calls this group Nazarenes, I feel it preferable to call them Nazoraeans, as most scholars do, in order to distinguish them from the original Nazarenes. Pritz's research is invaluable for providing one of the only in-depth studies done of the Nazoraeans, but, in my mind, a major failing is that he conflates the later Nazoraeans with the original Nazarenes, attributing to the first Nazarenes later Catholic ideas about Jesus that were not subscribed to by the original group. Basically, Pritz appears to be a conservative scholar who wishes not to believe that the original Nazarenes were in any way theologically unorthodox.

THE NAZORAEANS

Epiphanius is, as far as we know from historical records that have been preserved, the first writer to mention a distinct Jewish Christian sect of Nazoraeans, in chapter 29 of his *Panarion*. According to the *Panarion*, the Nazoraeans began when Jewish followers of the apostles who practiced circumcision and lived by the Torah left the "church" after the ascension.[9] To put Epiphanius's view in modern terms, he understands the Nazoraeans to be Jewish Christians who backslid and reverted to Judaism. Epiphanius is confused by the fact that he knows of a Jewish Christian sect called Nazoraeans existing in his own day, but he also knows from the book of Acts that the earliest Christians were called by a similar name (Nazarenes): "For this group did not name themselves after Christ or with Jesus's own name, but 'Nazoraeans.' However, at that time all Christians were called Nazoraeans in the same way."[10]

Epiphanius contradicts himself, however, when he goes on to say that the beginnings of the Nazoraeans can be traced to a group of Christians in Transjordan who had fled Jerusalem before its capture in 70 CE.[11] When he later says that the Ebionites originated from the sect of the Nazoraeans,[12] it becomes obvious that he is confusing the later sect of the Nazoraeans with the first Christians who were called Nazarenes, due to the similarity of nomenclature.

Epiphanius confirms what we know from other sources that these Nazoraeans lived in Pella and Kokhaba, and also adds the name of the village of Beroea, near Syria. Beroea, which is some distance from Pella and Kokhaba, is not mentioned in any other source as a dwelling for Jewish Christians, except for Jerome, who independently confirms this. Epiphanius considers the Nazoraeans to be somewhat orthodox because they believe in the resurrection of the dead and believe that Jesus is the Son of God.[13] These are, however, things the Ebionites also accepted, though they understood the title "Son of God" in its original Jewish sense, as we have discussed. Epiphanius does not consider the Nazoraeans to be sufficiently orthodox, however:

> They are different from Jews, and different from Christians, only in
> the following. They disagree with Jews because they have come to faith
> in Christ; but since they are still fettered by the Law—circumcision,
> the Sabbath, and the rest—they are not in accord with Christians.[14]

But the fact that Epiphanius considers the Nazoraeans more orthodox than the Ebionites is likely why he mistakenly says that the Ebionites grew out of the Nazoraeans, for he considers the Nazoraeans to be earlier, and hence more orthodox.

It is Jerome who further tells us that the Nazoraeans accepted Paul as the apostle to the Gentiles.[15] Klijn and Reinink sum up the evidence we can glean from Epiphanius and Jerome as follows:

> The remarks on the Nazoraeans in Epiphanius and Jerome can
> be taken together to form a picture of this Jewish Christian sect.
> We are speaking of a Syriac- or Aramaic-speaking group of Jewish

descent. They lived according to the Jewish Law but accepted the virgin birth and Paul. They used an Aramaic or Syriac Gospel . . . we may conclude that these Nazoraeans originated among Christians living in Palestine at a very early date.[16]

While this latter statement is true, what we can conclude from all of the available evidence is that the Nazoraeans did not directly originate from the earliest followers of Jesus, but were an offshoot of the Ebionites who began to accept doctrines of the emerging Catholic Church. We saw in chapter 7 how this happened to the Ebionites of the Jerusalem Church on Mt. Zion, and how they were absorbed into the Byzantine Church in the late fourth century. In that the Ebionites on Mt. Zion came to accept Catholic doctrine, we can say they evolved into Nazoraeans, though they were likely not known by that name in Jersualem. The Nazoraeans living in Transjordan, who were known by that name, were slowly absorbed into the Christian churches of neighboring Syria, leaving their Ebionite forebears, who refused to accept the Catholic dogma, to slow extinction. Schonfield remarks that the willingness of the Nazoraeans to merge with the Christian Church was a new development: "Certain individual Jewish Christians had already associated themselves with the dominant church, but group action was a new move. The phase was a most important one, for its genesis produced at Antioch the Gospel of Matthew as we now have it."[17]

THE NAZORAEAN GOSPEL OF MATTHEW

The Gospel of Matthew is perhaps the most puzzling of the four gospels as to its origin and audience. As we have noted, it is clearly the most Jewish of the four gospels, containing Jesus's ringing endorsement of the eternal validity of the Torah, as well as his support for the authority of the Pharisees. On the other hand, it also contains, along with the Gospel of John, some of the most anti-Semitic vitriol found in the gospels. How can these two features exist side by side? This has been a mystery that no scholar, to my knowledge, has ever adequately addressed until the recent publication of *How Jesus Became Christian,* by Canadian scholar Barrie

Wilson. As Wilson succinctly puts it, "Matthew is simultaneously the most 'pro-Jewish' gospel we have, as well as the most 'anti-Jewish' one."[18] It is, after all, Matthew who includes what may be the most anti-Semitic comment in any gospel when, at Jesus's trial, Pilate washes his hands of Jesus's blood and Matthew has the Jews respond, "His blood be on us and our children!" (Matt. 27:25).

Wilson roots his answer to this seemingly irreconcilable dichotomy in the pioneering work of Judaism scholar Anthony J. Saldarini, who points out that what we see in the Gospel of Matthew is an internal debate within Judaism.[19] Matthew's gospel rips into the Pharisees because Matthew's Jewish Christian community was "ripe from the rejection by the Pharisaic leaders of the local congregation. Matthew addressed his gospel to *them,* to these local leaders as well as the Pharisaic community at large."[20] Matthew's community was rejected because it was more Nazoraean than Ebionite, leaning more toward the divinity of Jesus than the Ebionites, something the Pharisees could not tolerate. But as we have seen, Matthew, unlike the other gospels, still upholds the validity of the Torah and recognizes the authority of the Pharisees. As Wilson explains, ". . . there still remained substantial common ground. Both groups agreed on the necessity for keeping the law, and in this they were closer than Matthew would have been to Paul's Christ movement."[21]

That Matthew's Jewish Christian community was Nazoraean, rather than Ebionite, is seen above all in Matthew's version of the Nativity story, which clearly understands Jesus to be born of a virgin, more so than Luke's version, which is a bit vague on the topic. It was the Matthean community's acceptance of the virgin birth and the divinity of Christ that was the sticking point that caused emerging rabbinic Judaism to reject the Nazoraeans, while it was their willingness to accept those doctrines that ingratiated them with the Gentile Church. It is my belief that this group intentionally rejected the name Ebionite, which had become pejorative, for the name Nazoraean, a name in which they could take pride of ancestry and uphold their connection to the original Jerusalem Yachad and the Desposyni. Schonfield notes that in places where Jewish Christians were in close contact with Gentile Christians, their rejection was difficult to handle:

[P]articularly in Syria, where there was a closer contact with the Catholic Church, which had made outcasts of the descendants of the founders of the great Churches of Antioch and Damascus, the position was intolerable. In consideration of fraternal relations extended to them, they were prepared to accept some of the dogmas of the new orthodoxy.[22]

That they were able to trace their roots back to the first apostles and Desposyni garnered respect from the Gentile Christians: "The native Syrian Christians were willing to allow the antiquity of the [Nazoraeans], and to accept the fact that they possessed genuine independent traditions concerning the life of Christ, which they were avid to learn and utilize."[23] But the Nazoraeans' willingness to fall in with the Gentile Christians created a backlash from their fellow Ebionites.

EBIONITE RETRENCHMENT

It is to be expected that the Nazoraeans' lapse from Jewish orthodoxy would cause a counterreaction among the Ebionite communities from which they had strayed. This unforeseen development caused the Ebionites to become even more entrenched in rigidly upholding Jewish doctrines and practices, and it is this that would lead to their ultimate demise as Catholicism slowly began to predominate in the Roman Empire. It was this period of defensive counterreaction that gave rise to the production of the *Pseudo-Clementine* literature, and is the reason for much of its anti-Pauline vitriol. In the many discussions, dialogues, and debates that pervade the narrative of the *Pseudo-Clementine* "Recognitions" and "Homilies," the original Jewish Christian orthodoxy is staunchly defended against the new Hellenistic heresies that had infected the Gentile Christian churches and were now drawing away members of the Ebionite communities.

Another little-known literary production of the Ebionites that was produced at this time is the *Odes of Solomon,* a collection of forty-two hymns. There has been a lot of scholarly debate over the authorship of this unique and enigmatic work, but in the 1930s Hugh Schonfield put forth a theory that could solve the riddle of the origins of this work, but which has received almost no attention:

> [T]here is conclusive evidence that the collection represents at least part of the Nazarene hymnbook. As such the work is of enormous importance, first because it reveals the elevated character of Jewish-Christian theology, and makes plain many obscurities relating to their beliefs and traditions; and second, because a Church with a hymnary is a living Church, and not a moribund institution, as many would suppose Nazarenism in the third century to have been.[24]

As one example, the following is a fascinating passage from Ode 36, which has long puzzled theologians. Here it is purported to be the Messiah Jesus speaking (italics mine):

> I rested in the Spirit of the Lord: *and the Spirit raised me on high: and made me stand on my feet in the height of the Lord, before His perfection and His glory,* while I was praising Him by the composition of His songs. The Spirit brought me forth before the face of the Lord: and, *although a son of man, I was named the Illuminate, the Son of God: While I praised amongst the praising ones, and great was I amongst the mighty ones.* For according to the greatness of the Most High, *so He made me:* and like His own newness He renewed me; and He anointed me from His own perfection: And I became one of His neighbors; and my mouth was opened like a cloud of dew; and my heart poured out as if it were a gushing stream of righteousness, and my access to Him was in peace; and I was established by the Spirit of His government. Hallelujah.

As Schonfield points out, this enigmatic ode makes perfect sense from the Ebionite understanding of Jesus: ". . . the Nazarene belief of the acquired divine attributes of the Messiah, who was born a man amongst men, is clearly seen."[25] The Ode states, "He made me." Jesus is not coeternal with God. "Although a son of man," Jesus was "named" the Son of God. Jesus stands before God's "perfection and glory;" he is not equal to God.

And here is a beautiful passage from Ode 6, which is a defense of the Ebionite orthodoxy and nicely sets the theme for the rest of this book:

> As the hand moves over the harp, and the strings speak, so speaks in my members the Spirit of the Lord, and I speak by His love. For it destroys what is foreign and everything that is bitter: For thus it was from the beginning and will be to the end, that nothing should be His adversary, and nothing should stand up against Him. The Lord has multiplied the knowledge of Himself, and is zealous that these things should be known, which by His grace have been given to us. And the praise of His name He gave us: our spirits praise His holy Spirit. For there went forth a stream and became a river great and broad; For it flooded and broke up everything and it brought water to the temple; And the restrainers of the children of men were not able to restrain it, nor the arts of those whose business it is to restrain waters; For it spread over the face of the whole earth, and filled everything: and all the thirsty upon earth were given to drink of it; And thirst was relieved and quenched: for from the Most High the draught was given. Blessed then are the ministers of that draught who are entrusted with that water of His: They have assuaged the dry lips, and the will that had fainted they have raised up; And souls that were near departing they have caught back from death: And limbs that had fallen they straightened and set up: They gave strength for their feebleness and light to their eyes: For everyone knew them in the Lord, and they lived by the water of life forever. Hallelujah.

This beautiful Ebionite hymn expressing their hope that the stream of the waters of life that went forth from the teaching of Messiah Jesus would refresh the world is a classic example of Ebionite universalism. At the time this was composed, it was not foreseen that this stream of pure life-giving water would be forced to flow underground for almost two millennia. But the stream of sparkling water that flowed from the mouth of the Messiah through the Ebionite evangel was all too quickly going to be diverted underground.

THE DIVERTED STREAM

The beginning of the fourth century was like a bright and glorious new morning for the Gentile Christian Church. Eusebius wrote at this time, "From that time on a day bright and radiant, with no cloud overshadowing it, shone down with shafts of heavenly light on the churches of Christ throughout the world . . ."[26] The Emperor Constantine had issued the Edict of Milan in the year 313, making Christianity a legally recognized religion in the Roman Empire. But this bright new day for Gentile Christians was for Ebionites and Jews, "one of darkness and gloom. The era of persecution by pagan Romans was passing away, only to be succeeded by the more terrible and prolonged persecutions by Christian Romans . . . massacres became frequent, and burning synagogues a Christian recreation."[27] Palestine soon lost almost all of its Jewish population, which took refuge in the eastern locales to where Jews had fled in former times of diaspora—Persia and Mesopotamia. "The name of Nazarene, formerly honored by every follower of the man of Nazareth, was now wholly discarded by the Catholic Church, and reserved exclusively for the 'heresy' of the faith which he had founded."[28]

Ironically, it was through Jewish Christians heading eastward to Mesopotamia that Jewish Christianity would ultimately go west, but in a much altered Gnostic form acquired in Mesopotamia that gave rise to a new Jewish Christian sect. As Schonfield poetically explains of the great transformation that would now overtake the Ebionite remnants:

It has been said that what is hated enough will in the end become hateful, and this aphorism is so far exemplified in the history of the Nazarenes that having been continually treated as heretics they did eventually become heretical. Cut off from communion with one another with their brethren by race on one side and faith on the other, their resistance of Gnostic influences was steadily worn down, and their doctrines became more and more divergent from the tradition which had supported them for nearly five hundred years.[29]

In the early decades of the fourth century, the split between the Nazoraeans living in the regions of Syria and the Ebionites in Transjordan was complete, the Nazoraeans becoming wholly absorbed into the Christian Church and the remaining Ebionites dying of slow dehydration in the northwestern regions of Arabia (but not without the Ebionite stream first watering the desert sands and making the desert bloom, as we shall see in the next chapter). Before examining the influence of the Ebionites on the rise of the third revealed religion based upon the Bible, we must chronologically examine a sect closely related to the Ebionites that arose in southern Mesopotamia in the second century.

THE ELKESAITES

The first problem in examining this unique Jewish Christian group is discerning its correct name from among the multitude of variations that have appeared. In addition to the spelling we prefer here, just some of the other variations are Elkasites, Elcesaites, Elchasaites, and Helkesaites. We prefer Elkesaites simply because this variant has been used by some of the best modern scholars of Jewish Christianity (Schoeps, Klijn and Reinink, Pritz). Our earliest and most extensive information about this group comes from Hippolytus.[30] Epiphanius, interestingly, does not have a separate chapter on the Elkesaites in his massive *Panarion,* but interjects information about them into chapters dealing with other Jewish and Jewish Christian groups. This could mean one of two things: Either Epiphanius did not consider them to be a major threat, or he considered them to be so religiously different as to not be a Christian heresy at all.

From Hippolytus we gain some very specific historical information as to how the group began. He tells us that during the time of Pope Callixtus I (217–222 CE), a Syrian native named Alcibiades brought a book to Rome that he claimed contained a revelation given to a man named

Elkesai* by an angel who stood ninety-six miles tall, measured twenty-four miles across the shoulders, and had footprints fourteen miles long, four miles wide, and two miles deep! This angel was the Son of God and was accompanied by his sister, the Holy Spirit, who was of equal dimensions. Alcibiades said that in the third year of the emperor Trajan's reign (100 CE) the angel had proclaimed to Elkesai a new remission of sins through the process of water baptism. Hippolytus reports that Alcibiades taught circumcision, that Christ was a man like other men, and that Christ had been born many times on earth of a virgin. Alcibiades also taught that a second baptism was necessary for the remission of sins "in the name of the great and most high God and in the name of His Son the great King," and that the baptism had to be accompanied by the invocation of seven witnesses: sky, water, the holy spirits, the angels of prayer, oil, salt, and earth. Keith Akers notes that some of these elements are mentioned in the *Pseudo-Clementine* literature: "Bread and water are elements of the Ebionite Eucharist, and water is the means of baptism. Salt is used by Peter twice; at *Homilies* 14.1 it is part of the Eucharist, and as part of the meal at *Homilies* 19.25. Olives are part of Peter's sparse vegetarian diet (*Recognitions* 7.6, *Homilies* 12.6)."[31]

Hippolytus further reports that two of Elkesai's descendants were sisters named Marthus and Marthana, and Epiphanius reports that they were alive in his day and were reverenced as goddesses; the dust of their feet and their spittle was used to cure diseases.[32] All of this detail would seem to suggest that Elkesai was an actual person, a leader of an early Ebionite community to whom Alcibiades ascribed the book he brought with him to Rome. While many scholars accept that there was a living person by the name of Elkesai, others believe that there was only a book attributed to a fictional person of that name. Although its title is unknown, the existence of the book, commonly referred to as the "Book of Elkesai," is not in doubt and was almost certainly written within the first two decades of the first century.[33] The book is believed to have originally been written in Aramaic, which is significant for connecting it to Jewish Christianity. Supporting the actual existence of a man named Elkesai is Epiphanius, who tells us

---

*Sometimes spelled Elxai.

that Elkesai joined the Ebionites during the reign of the emperor Trajan.[34] He also reports that, "They appear to call Elxai a power revealed . . . since *el* means 'power,' but xai is 'hidden.'"[35] Schonfield points out that the name may have been taken from the ancient Jewish high priest Hilkia, following the manner of the Jewish sect of the Zadokites.[36]

Epiphanius also tells us that the Book of Elkesai condemned virginity and abstinence and made marriage obligatory.[37] This is further evidence of the Jewish nature of this book, since this was always the Jewish view on marriage. Celibacy was virtually condemned in Jewish tradition as disobedience to God, and the emphasis on this among the Elkesaites may have been a counter-reaction to the newly emerging emphasis on celibacy in Gentile Christianity. Epiphanius also reports that Elkesai was greatly honored as a prophet by both the Ebionites and Nazoraeans, who held his book in great esteem.[38] It is interesting, therefore, that, like the Ebionites, the book of Elkesai directs that prayer be done facing Jerusalem, which provides evidence that the Elkesaites were an offshoot of the Ebionites, and not an independent Gnostic sect as some scholars have contended. Additionally, the Book of Elkesai, like the *Pseudo-Clementines,* vehemently rejects animal sacrifice and denies that the Jewish patriarchs ever engaged in the practice. And, of course, as among the Ebionites, Paul and his writings are rejected.

But Epiphanius concludes that the Elkesaites are neither Jews nor Christians, nor pagans, but keep to "the middle way."[39] One unique aspect of their teaching, which is not encountered in other Jewish Christian groups, and which attests to the fact that they were a persecuted group, is that they held that forgiveness would be given by God if they denied their faith in order to save their lives.[40] This is a unique belief that will provide us with a tie-in to later medieval European heretical groups. Their worship of Marthus and Marthana as goddesses, a unique feminine aspect of Elkesaism, also may have influenced the Cathars. Keith Akers notes another link to the Ebionites: "Marthus and Marthana were 'worshipped as goddesses' because they were descended from Elxai himself. Here we have some sort of religious dynasty being founded . . . This is similar to the Ebionite reliance on the family of Jesus."[41]

One other unique aspect of their teaching is given by Hippolytus, who reports that Elkesai asserted "that Christ was not for the first time on earth when born of a virgin, but that both previously and that frequently again He had been born and would be born. Christ would thus appear and exist among us from time to time, undergoing alterations of birth, and having his soul transferred from body to body."[42] While this clear belief in reincarnation may sound startling, there is evidence even within the New Testament that first-century Jews had some kind of belief in reincarnation.[43] This would all indicate that the Elkesaites were Ebionites who had evolved in a more Gnostic direction. For some time, Gnosticism had been making inroads among the Jewish people, a trend that would reach its culmination in the medieval mystical branch of Judaism that would produce the Kabbalah. As far as the Elkesaite influence on the Ebionites, Schonfield summarizes as follows:

> The Jewish-Christian refugees from the overthrow of Jerusalem were thrown into close proximity with . . . offshoots of Judaism [Zadokites, Essenes, Hemerobaptists, Masbotheans, Elkesaites], and only the strength of their convictions prevented an early amalgamation with the Jewish sectaries with whom they had so much in common. The Elkesaean propaganda shows clear traces of infiltration of Nazarene ideas, and Epiphanius tells us the founder of this heresy was greatly honored by the Nazarenes and Ebionites who highly esteemed his book. To many of the rabbinical Jews, the tenets of the Eastern Gnostics made a strong appeal. They caught them on the reaction of their political hopes.[44]

Because Gnosticism had such an influence on the Elkesaites, as well as other Jewish Christian groups we will be discussing, it would be good at this point to provide an overview of Gnosticism.

GNOSTICISM 101

The root of the word "Gnosticism" is the Greek word *gnosis,* which basically means spiritual "knowledge." In Gnosticism salvation comes through the obtaining of certain esoteric knowledge of the true nature of reality and the human condition. In this sense it resembles the Buddhist religion with its goal of attaining enlightenment about the nature of ultimate reality. As we shall see, Buddhism actually had an influence on the form of Gnosticism that existed in the Persian empire. Like Buddhism, Gnosticism is an incredibly diverse philosophy because it is syncretistic in nature, meaning it has borrowed elements from many other religions and philosophies. What unites all of these diverse strands is Gnosticism's basic underlying belief that (as in Hinduism) a human is a divine soul trapped in a material body. What is distinct about Western Gnosticism is the belief that this physical world in which we live was created by an imperfect god, technically called the Demiurge, who is frequently identified with the God of the Old Testament. The Demiurge is sometimes depicted as an embodiment of evil, but at others, merely imperfect and as benevolent as its inadequacy permits. The Demiurge exists alongside the remote and unknowable supreme God that embodies good. In order to free oneself from the inferior material world, one needs to gain gnosis—knowledge—of this cosmic state of affairs. Jesus is identified by some Gnostic sects as an embodiment of the supreme being who became incarnate to bring gnosis to the earth.

At one time scholars considered Gnosticism to mostly be a heretical corruption of Christianity, but it is now clear that Gnosticism predates the Christian Era and pervaded the Mediterranean and the Middle East until its suppression by Christianity beginning in the third century of the Common Era. As we discussed, Gnosticism would greatly influence the development of the mystical branch of Judaism known as Kabbalism in the early Middle Ages. The few remaining strongholds of Christian Gnosticism in the Middles Ages included the Languedoc region of southern France, where it took the form of Catharism; and the Balkan region of southeastern Europe with its large numbers of Paulicians and Bogomils, to be discussed in chapter 12. While all of these groups would be persecuted to the brink of extinction, a few isolated communities continue to exist in these areas to the present day. Gnostic ideas reemerged and became influential in the philosophies of various esoteric mystical movements of the late-nineteenth and twentieth centuries in Europe and North America, including some that explicitly identify themselves as revivals or even continuations of earlier Gnostic groups. In the last fifty years the study of Gnosticism has become a hot topic in academia due to the discovery of the Gnostic writings buried in the sands of Nag Hammadi in Egypt, now commonly known as the Nag Hammadi library. These writings were popularized in the 1970s with the publication of Elaine Pagels's groundbreaking work, *The Gnostic Gospels*. And, of course, in just the past few years popular interest in these writings was given an unprecedented boost by the book and film version of *The Da Vinci Code,* in which they feature.

Early Christianity was especially influenced by Gnosticism in Egypt, and it was seen as such as threat by the early church fathers that "it took all the thunder of eminent divines like Irenaeus, Hippolytus, and Tertullian to vanquish the intruder."[45] That Gnosticism was seen as a threat in the early church is evidenced in the first epistle to Timothy (generally accepted as being written sometime between 110 and 130), the final words of which warn: "Avoid the profane chatter and contradictions of what is falsely called knowledge [gnosis]; by professing it, some have missed the mark as regards the faith" (1 Timothy 6:20–21).

Another key doctrine of Gnosticism is the belief that there are "emanations" of God, called *aeons* in some Gnostic systems, *archons* in others. God, the first being, is also an aeon and has an inner being within itself, known variously as Ennoia (thought), Charis (grace), or Sige (silence). The perfect being conceives the second aeon, Caen (power), within itself. Along with the male Caen comes the female aeon Akhana (truth, love). The aeons usually come in male/female pairs called *syzygies,* which are variously numbered from seven pairs to thirty. Two of the most commonly listed aeons were Jesus and Sophia. The aeons together constitute the *pleroma,* or region of light. The lowest regions of the pleroma are closest to the darkness; that is, the physical world. When the aeon named Sophia emanated without her partner aeon, the result was the Demiurge, a creature that never should have come into existence. Some Gnostic groups, such as the Cathars, equate the Demiurge with Satan. This creature does not belong to the pleroma, and God emanates two savior aeons, Christ and the Holy Spirit, to save humankind from the Demiurge. Christ took the form of the man, Jesus, in order to be able to teach humankind how to achieve gnosis and return to the pleroma.

These examples are only a sample of the various Gnostic interpretations. The roles of familiar beings such as Jesus Christ, Sophia, and the Demiurge usually share the same general themes among different Gnostic systems, but may have somewhat different functions or identities ascribed to them. In late antiquity some variants of Gnosticism used the term *archon* to refer to several servants of the Demiurge, the "creator god" who stood between spiritual humanity and the transcendent God, who could be reached only through gnosis. In this context they may be seen as having the roles of angels and demons. In sum, human beings have within them a divine "spark" trapped in the evil physical world of matter, which was created by the Demiurge. This world is not our true home and our goal here is to attain the gnosis—divine knowledge—of the truth that will set us free.

Later Jewish Christianity is clearly affected by these doctrines as evidenced in the following passage from the *Pseudo-Clementine* "Homilies." Here, the words that are put into the mouth of Peter, which make him sound like a Hellenistic Jewish philosopher on a par with Paul, offer a classic example of Gnostic teaching:

> Now that he might bring men to the true knowledge of all things, God, who himself is a single person, made a clear separation by way of pairs of opposites, in that he, who from the beginning was the one and only God, made heaven and earth, day and night, life and death. Among these he has gifted free will to men alone so that they may be just or unjust. For them he has also permitted the appearing of the pairs of opposites, in that he has set before their eyes first the small and then the great, first the world and then eternity, this world being transitory, but the one to come eternal; so also ignorance precedes knowledge [gnosis]. In the same way he has ordered the bearers of the prophetic spirit. For since the present is womanly and like a mother gives birth to children, but the future, manly time,

on the other hand takes up its children in the manner of a father, therefore there come first the prophets of this world . . . those who have the knowledge of eternal things follow them because they are the sons of the coming age. Had the God-fearing known this secret, then they would never have been able to go wrong . . .[46]

The statement about a succession of prophets "of this world" and those who follow "who have the knowledge of the eternal things" is a great example of what, in Jewish Christian theology, separates a false prophet from a true prophet such as Jesus. In Peter's statement we also learn that this present world is feminine in character, and therefore evil. In the Gnostic gospel known as the Gospel of the Egyptians, Jesus says, "I have come to destroy the works of the woman," meaning the works of this evil world.[47] One thing that unites all the various Gnostic schools is that this world is evil, matter is evil, and flesh is evil. Only the spirit is good.

This core Gnostic belief that matter and the flesh are evil would give rise to a strict asceticism in some groups, and could include celibacy and vegetarianism. In a great irony, it was this aspect of Gnosticism that would actually inspire the rise of monasticism in the Church, mainly through the teaching of Clement of Alexandria and Origen (who was considered somewhat heretical himself by the later church fathers), and give birth to the Desert Fathers in Egypt and Arabia, who would influence the rise of Islam: "It was these ideas which people the deserts . . . with myriads of monks wrestling with their bodies, those prison-houses of the soul, struggling to die to the world of matter, that their ethereal souls might shake themselves free."[48] While celibacy never became important to the Jewish Christians (in fact, as we have seen, just the opposite was stressed), vegetarianism did become an essential part of Ebionite practice, so that they even altered the teachings of the gospels to suit. Epiphanius attests that in the Ebionite gospel John the Baptist does not eat locusts, and Jesus speaks against eating meat at the Last Supper: "I have no desire to eat the meat of this Passover lamb with you."[49]

We have gone into this overview of Gnosticism at such length because all of these characteristics came to the fore in the Elkesaites and in the later medieval sect of the Cathars, the heirs of a gnosticized form of Jewish Christianity who became such a threat that the Catholic Church ultimately launched a crusade against their own people in an effort to eradicate their heresy.

GNOSTIC INFLUENCES ON JEWISH CHRISTIANITY

Hippolytus tells us that the Book of Elkesai was written in Parthia, an expansion of the Persian Empire that, at the time of its writing, included Mesopotamia.[50] This information provides us with invaluable evidence that ties the Elkesaite system to Gnosticism. The most infamous and influential branch of Gnosticism, which was without doubt the most powerful of all Christian heresies and a contending rival to emerging Catholic Christianity, was Manichaeism, named after its founder, the infamous Mani. We know quite a bit about Mani. He was a Persian born April 14, 216 in Babylon, a city reputed for its religious eclecticism and tolerance. Mani was the scion of a noble line of the Arsacid dynasty that had ruled Iran since 250 BCE, although Christian polemicists would later claim he was the freed slave of a widow.[51] This little detail will become significant as we discuss Jewish Christian influences on Freemasonry in the concluding chapter. Mani's father had joined a Jewish baptizing sect in Babylonia called Mughtasilah (washers, or practitioners of ablution), or Katharoi (pure ones), recently and conclusively shown to be a branch of the Elkesaites.[52] We shall say more about Mani, the Mughtasilah, and other baptizing sects in Mesopotamia in chapter 12.

In conclusion, we have clear evidence of Jewish Christian influence in the easternmost regions of the Middle East. This Eastern stream of gnosticized Jewish Christianity would eventually return west to influence another major threat to Catholicism in the High Middle Ages—the Cathars. But first, we must detour to the south, to examine a most unexpected terrain that was also fed by the underground stream of Jewish Christianity—the religion of Islam.

11

JEWISH CHRISTIANITY
IN ARABIA
Muhammad and the Rise of Islam

*We sent forth Jesus son of Mary, confirming the Torah
already revealed, and gave him the Gospel, in which there
is guidance and light, corroborating what was revealed
before it in the Torah: a guide and an admonition to the
righteous.*

THE QUR'AN 5:46

Now that we have traced the Desposyni and the remnants of the Jewish
Christian sects as far as the historical records allow, we can engage in
some fascinating speculation as to how Jewish Christianity continued to
inform and shape subsequent religious history in often surprising ways.
While much of what we discuss in these final chapters will be speculative, it will be informed speculation that is not without basis in history.
We will constantly be revisiting the beliefs and practices of the Nazarenes,
Ebionites, and Elkesaites to show how Jewish Christian theology and
practice continued to be a surprisingly strong and influential force on
later religious movements, even into modern times.

There is both tragedy and irony in the demise of the Synagogue of the Apostles (also known as the Jerusalem Church) that started it all, and the rise of the Jewish Christian sects it spawned. A sudden and merciful extinction due to either internal implosion or imposed extermination, which is often the fate of new religious movements, was not the fate of Jewish Christianity. Awaiting the Ebionites was a slow fragmentation of their once proud and vibrant community into diffuse groups that barely remembered their regal origins. In their scattered isolation they became subject to various outside influences, such as Gnosticism and Catholicism, as we have seen. It would be illuminating to know the full story behind each particular expiration, but the successive waves of Persian and Arab invaders that swept through Syria and Palestine resulted in the complete loss of any recorded history of these communities, and even the fate of the Gentile Christian communities in these areas is largely unknown.

JEWISH CHRISTIAN SURVIVAL

How long did the Ebionites and other Jewish Christian communities manage to survive? If we give credence to Jerome (342–420), the Ebionites were still extant at the end of his days in the early fifth century. This is reinforced by Augustine (354–430), and, as Ray Pritz notes, "While Epiphanius was the first to brand them clearly as heretical, it was the authority of Augustine's acceptance of this judgment that seems to have fixed their fate and led to their final rejection by the Church."[1] With these references to lingering Jewish Christian groups in the early fifth century, we historically lose contact with Jewish Christianity. The general assumption of scholars has been that any lingering Jewish Christian sects—Ebionite, Elkesaite, or Nazoraean—slowly faded out of existence in the late-fifth to early-sixth century. As we saw, the Elkesaite communities in Syria were absorbed into the Syrian Orthodox Church, but managed to hold on longer to the east in Persia, as we will see in the next chapter. The last holdout of the Ebionites seems to have been northwestern Arabia, where they were absorbed into Islam. But the Jewish Christians in northwestern Arabia were not only absorbed into Islam, but actually informed and inspired its rise in the late-sixth to early-seventh century.

The last Ebionite holdouts were seemingly pushed into Arabia by the growing Christian communities. Hans-Joachim Schoeps notes that when the Ebionites originally fled Jerusalem for the Transjordanian regions, "they had settled practically the entire border zone separating Syria from Arabia—admittedly a rather narrow strip of land—extending from Damascus to the southern tip of the Dead Sea in a north-south strip. Under these circumstances they must also have expanded into Arabian Nabataea."[2] The church fathers considered Nabataea to be part of Arabia (see map 1). In fact, to clarify a common misunderstanding, "the Roman imperial province called 'Arabia' was confined to a fairly small territory lying, roughly speaking, between the Jordan Valley and the desert to the east. When St. Paul referred to his sojourn 'in Arabia' (Galatians 1:17), he did not mean what we call Saudi Arabia."[3]

One possible historical reference to surviving Ebionite communities in this part of Arabia as late as the eleventh century can be in found the *Sefer Ha'masaot* (Book of Travels) written by a Spanish Rabbi, Benjamin of Tudela, who was a kind of Jewish Marco Polo who visited many Jewish communities in his travels, and who mentions encountering groups in the Arabian cities of Tayma and Tilmas that closely resemble the Ebionites.[4] Likewise, the twelfth-century Muslim historian, Muhammad al-Shahrastani, speaks of Jews living in Medina and Hejaz who accepted Jesus as a prophet, but otherwise followed traditional Judaism.[5]

THE RELIGIOUS TOLERANCE OF ISLAM

It is very likely that most of the Ebionites in Arabia later converted to Islam, with which they had much in common. It is well known that both Jews and Christians, sometimes in surprisingly large numbers, converted to Islam when the Muslims conquered all of the Middle East and large parts of the Byzantine Empire. Indeed, minority religious groups found safe haven in Muslim lands from Christian persecution. Muslim Sharia (holy law), based in the prescriptions of the Qur'an, guaranteed the safety and freedom of religious minorities. The Qur'an clearly and unequivocally states, "There shall be no compulsion in religion" (2:257). Under Muslim

Sharia, as long as a subjugated people declared allegiance to the Muslim state and paid an annual tax, they were legally considered *dhimmis* (protected people) who could freely practice their religion and be governed by their own religious law in their private lives. Many minorities in the Byzantine Empire only too gladly exchanged Christian rule for Muslim rule. "Islam proved more tolerant than imperial Christianity, providing greater religious freedom for Jews and indigenous Christians. Under Muslim rule, most local or indigenous Christian churches, persecuted as schismatics and 'heretics' by the 'foreign' Christian orthodoxy of their rulers, could practice their faith."[6]

This is evidenced above all in the city of Jerusalem, holy to all three faiths. Under Byzantine Christian rule, Jews were greatly persecuted. But, as scholar Karen Armstrong notes in her wonderful book *Jerusalem: One City, Three Faiths,* when the Muslims took control of Jerusalem:

> The Muslims . . . established a system that enabled Jews, Christians, and Muslims to live in Jerusalem together for the first time. Ever since the Jews had returned from exile in Babylon, monotheists had developed a vision of the city that had seen its sanctity as dependent upon the exclusion of outsiders. Muslims had a more inclusive notion of the sacred, however: the coexistence of the three religions of Abraham, each occupying its own district and worshipping at its own special shrines, reflected their vision of the continuity and harmony of all rightly guided religion, which could only derive from the one God.[7]

The best-known, glowing example of successful intermingling of cultures can be seen in the flourishing of Jewish thought and culture in Andalusian Spain under the Muslim Ummayad dynasty from 711–1492. A rare harmony and mutual respect that developed there among Jews, Christians, and Muslims resulted in a flourishing culture that gave the West some of its most important philosophers, such as the great Jewish philosopher, Maimonides (1135–1204). This rich blending of cultures produced a golden age of research and learning that could have ushered in the Renaissance centuries earlier, had this early experiment in cultural interaction been allowed to continue. Córdoba became the largest and richest city in western Europe. The Moors established thriving universities in Andalusia that cultivated scholarship and brought together the greatest achievements of all the civilizations they had encountered. During this period Muslim and Jewish scholars played a major part in reviving and advancing Western astronomy, medicine, philosophy, and mathematics.

In hindsight, we can say that the Spanish Reconquista by Christian forces was a tragic loss for western culture and progress, and unnecessarily extended the Dark Ages in western Europe. In Palestine, the Crusades were tragic not only for Muslims and Jews, but for Christian minorities as well:

> One unintended result of the Crusades was the deterioration of the position of Christian minorities in the Holy Land. These minorities had rights and privileges under Muslim rule, but after the establishment of the Latin Kingdom, they found themselves treated as "loathsome schismatics." In an effort to obtain relief from persecution by their fellow Christians, many abandoned their beliefs and adopted either Roman Catholicism, or—the supreme irony—Islam.[8]

To the east of Spain, however, in Septimania and Provence, the areas of southern France that in the High Middle Ages would be called the Languedoc, this earliest budding of a proto-Renaissance continued longer, but would also ultimately be crushed by Christian crusaders, which we will discuss when we consider Jewish Christian influence on the Cathars of southern France. Let us now examine the life and career of the prophet Muhammad, his influences, and the nature of his teaching that would eventually enable such cultural interaction.

THE PROPHET MUHAMMAD

Muhammad was born in the Arabian trade center of Mecca in 570 CE. In one of the greatest ironies in Western history, he was singularly responsible for preserving the Jewish Christian belief in the unity of God over Christian Trinitarianism and upholding Jesus as the Messiah in its original Jewish sense. The vast majority of Christians are completely oblivious to the fact that Muslims, following the teaching of their holy scripture—the Qur'an—highly honor and revere Jesus, considering him to be the last prophet sent by Allah* prior to Allah's calling of Muhammad as the final prophet. Muslims even believe in the virgin birth of Jesus, and an entire chapter in the Qur'an is devoted to the Virgin Mary.† Many contemporary Muslims in Palestine even celebrate Christmas with their Christian neighbors.

So, the question immediately needs to be raised: How did these beliefs about Jesus find their way into Muhammad's proclamation? Of course, the Muslim answer to this question is that the entire Qur'an is the word-for-word revelation of Allah to Muhammad. But putting Muslim theology aside in favor of a purely historical answer, the logical conclusion would seem to be that Muhammad received these ideas about Jesus from others before him who held such a Christology. And who could those others before him have been other than Jewish Christians? Laying aside the possibility of divine revelation, there is no other logical answer.

It is well known, based on the testimonies of those who knew Muhammad, as well as the personal testimony of Muhammad himself as recorded in the biographical writings called the Hadith,§ that from an early age Muhammad was deeply religious and ardently pursued theological and philosophical questions. His career as a caravan leader brought him into contact with many varieties of Jews and Christians, as well as Persian Zoroastrians, all of whom were monotheistic and with whom he eagerly pursued theological discussions and debate. "By Muhammad's time there were plentiful Jewish and Christian expatriate communities in Arab lands, who diffused their faith and observance among the Syrian Arabs who were intrigued and attracted by these monotheisms in the Roman world."[9] Many Jewish and Christian communities bordered northwestern Arabia and "Muhammad had himself traveled to Syria on business and

---

*Allah is an Arabic word that means "God." Christians sometimes mistakenly believe that Allah is a different God from the one they worship and do not realize that even Arabic-speaking Christians refer to God as Allah.

†Chapter 19 is entitled "Mary," the only woman mentioned by name in the Qur'an.

§Arabic for "traditions," traditional stories about the life of the prophet Muhammad.

numerous passages in the Koran attest his familiarity with both Judaism and Christianity."[10] The early Christian monastics known as the Desert Fathers had their enclaves in Egypt and the Arabian deserts, and were a huge influence on the mystical branch of Islam known as Sufism. The influence on Muhammad of all these contacts with monotheistic religions was such that by the time he was a young man, he had already come to accept that there was but one God—the God (in Arabic *al-Ilah,* derived as Allah)—and not the many individual tribal gods who engendered incessant intertribal battles that disturbed the peace-loving caravan leader.

From his contacts with Jews, Christians, and Zoroastrians, Muhammad also came to accept the belief in an *eschaton*—that Allah would one day bring the world to an end and judge all people according to their deeds. In light of this conviction, Muhammad became greatly concerned for the fate of his family, friends, and neighbors come Judgment Day. Muhammad greatly feared that Allah would consign their souls to hell because of their idolatrous worship, exemplified above all at the Kaaba in the heart of Mecca, an ancient Arabic shrine that was filled with idols, relics, and paintings of the many tribal gods.

The great turning point in Muhammad's life came in the year 610 when he received the first of many revelations while meditating in a cave on Mount Hira, just outside Mecca. From that point forward Muhammad publicly proclaimed his firm belief in the oneness of Allah and warned of divine condemnation of all idolaters who worshipped false gods and did not submit (*islam*) to the sovereign rule of Allah. As a result of his public proclamation Muhammad was forced to spend the next several years in hiding, for many threats were made on his life by his Meccan neighbors. Let us now examine the Muslim beliefs about Jesus that Muhammad proclaimed and which were recorded in the Qur'an, beliefs which are uncannily identical to the Christology of the Nazarenes and Ebionites.

JEWISH CHRISTIANITY IN THE QUR'AN

The following are a representative sampling of *ayahs* (verses) from the Qur'an that reveal a Christology that is clearly Jewish Christian, statements with which no Nazarene, Ebionite, or Elkesaite could have had any argument. We begin with a passage that clearly shows the roots of the Qur'an in the law of Moses:

> We* have revealed the Torah, in which there is guidance and light. By it the prophets who submitted to God judged the Jews, and so did the rabbis and the divines, according to God's Book, which had been committed to their keeping and to which they themselves were witnesses. (5:44)

The Qur'an firmly upholds the validity of the Torah, calling it "God's Book," as well as the legitimacy of the Hebrew prophets. In the next verse the Qur'an immediately goes on to assert that Jesus is in the line of the prophets and that his teaching confirms the Torah:

> After them [the Hebrew prophets], We sent forth Jesus son of Mary, confirming the Torah already revealed, and gave him the Gospel, in which there is guidance and light, corroborating what was revealed before it in the Torah: a guide and an admonition to the righteous. Therefore let those who follow the Gospel judge according to what God has revealed therein. (5:46–47)

The Qur'an also upholds the validity of the gospels, and asserts that they confirm the Torah. But this is where we also see a distinction between Torah and gospel—the Torah is the "judge" for the Jews as the gospel (the New Testment) is for the Christians. The Qur'an was given as the judge for the Muslims and is the final revelation from Allah, which confirms and corrects all revelation that has come before:

---

*In the Qur'an, as in the Old Testament (see Gen. 1:26, 3:22), Allah often speaks in the plural, which is most commonly explained by Jews and Muslims as God speaking to his court of angels, but commonly upheld in Christianity as evidence for the Trinity (Father, Son, and Holy Spirit, in one God).

> And to you [Muslims] We have revealed the Book with the truth. It confirms the Scriptures which came before it and stands as a guardian over them. (5:48)

Like the Ebionites, Muslims believe there are errors and distortions in the Torah as well as in the gospel, and thus the need for Allah's final revelation in the Qur'an.

What is perhaps most remarkable is the Qur'an's liberal teaching that each of the three communities has been assigned its own legitimate path:

> We have ordained a law and assigned a path for each of you. Had God pleased, He could have made of you one community: but it is His wish to prove you by that which he has bestowed upon you. Vie with each other in good works, for to God shall you all return and He will resolve your differences for you. (5:49)

Each community has been assigned its own law, and they are to strive with each other only in good works. There is certainly nothing here contrary to the Epistle of James. While God could have made one community out of them all, it is through their vying with each other in good works that their faith will be shown, and God will resolve all their theological differences in the end. If only all three communities had lived by this injunction! It is because of their common rootedness in God's written revelation that the Qur'an repeatedly refers to all three monotheistic communities as the "people of the book." Each community had received its own book and its own messenger—Moses, Jesus, or Muhammad:

> An apostle is sent to each community. When their apostle comes, justice is done among them; they are not wronged. (10:47)

> We raised an apostle in each community, saying: "Serve God and keep away from false gods." Among them were some to whom God sent guidance, and others destined to go astray. . . .
>
> The apostles we sent before you were but men whom We inspired

with revelations and with scriptures. Ask the People of the Book, if you know not. (16:36–44)

The continuity of Muhammad's revelation with the revelations granted the Jews and Christians is continually confirmed:

Say: "We believe in God and that which has been revealed to us; in what was revealed to Abraham, Ishmael, Isaac, Jacob, and the tribes; to Moses and Jesus and the other prophets by their Lord. We make no distinction among any of them . . . (2:136)

Of these emissaries We have exalted some above others. To some God spoke directly; others He raised to a lofty status. We gave Jesus, son of Mary, indisputable signs and strengthened him with the Holy Spirit. Had God pleased, those who succeeded them would not have fought against one another . . . But they disagreed among themselves; some had faith and others had none. (2:253)

This verse is keenly aware of the divisions among the People of the Book. But there are righteous people among all of the communities that comprise the People of the Book, irrespective of their particular sect:

Yet they are not all alike. There are among the People of the Book some upright men who all night long recite the revelations of God and worship Him; who believe in God and the Last Day; who enjoin justice and forbid evil and vie with each other in good works. These are the righteous men: whatever good they do, its reward shall not be denied them. God well knows the righteous. (3:113)

But there is a dividing line that distinguishes the righteous—the true believers—from the infidel. That dividing line is whether one truly understands the oneness of God and the nature of his prophets. What distinguishes those who have true faith from those who do not is their understanding of the nature of Jesus:

People of the Book, do not transgress the bounds of your religion. Speak nothing but the truth about God. The Messiah, Jesus son of Mary, was no more than God's apostle and His Word, which He cast upon Mary: a spirit from Him. So believe in God and His apostles and do not say: "Three." Forbear, and it shall be better for you. God is but one God. God forbid that he should have a son! (4:171)

There could be no clearer exhortation against the Christian Trinity. Any Ebionite could fully affirm these words of the Qur'an. The Qur'an clearly considers the words of the Nicene Creed, which calls Jesus "the only Son of God, eternally begotten of the Father" to be apostasy:

Say: "Praise be to God who has never begotten a son; who has no partner in His Kingdom; who needs none to defend Him from humiliation." Proclaim His greatness. (17:111)

Further, Mary is not the "Mother of God":

Unbelievers are those that say: "God is the Messiah, the son of Mary." For the Messiah himself said: "Children of Israel, serve God, my Lord and your Lord." He that worships other deities besides God, God will deny him Paradise . . .
    Unbelievers are those that say: "God is one of three." There is but one God. (5:72–73)

Muslims do believe that Jesus is the Messiah, but God is neither the Messiah nor the son of Mary. Simply put, Jesus is not God. To claim otherwise is to blaspheme the blessed memory of Mary:

They [the Christians] denied the truth and uttered a monstrous falsehood against Mary. (4:156)

In the Hadith, Muhammad himself issues a stern warning to Muslims against making a similar mistake in their understanding of him as a prophet:

Do not exceed the bounds in praising me, as the Christians do in praising Jesus, the son of Mary, by calling Him God, and the Son of God; I am only the Lord's servant; then call me the servant of God, and His messenger.[11]

And, finally, the last verses of the Qur'an make sure to reinforce this teaching: "God is One, the Eternal God. He begot none, nor was He begotten. None is equal to Him" (112:1–4).

There are other verses that could be cited, but this collection should suffice in conveying the Muslim understanding of God and Jesus as proclaimed by Muhammad. This teaching would not be disputed by Nazarenes or Ebionites. These verses could just as easily have come from the Gospel of the Hebrews as from the pages of the Qu'ran. The question we must now pause to ask is: How did this come to be? How did this clearly Ebionite understanding make its way into Islam? Was this, as all Muslims unwaveringly believe, a matter of divine revelation, or could there be a more mundane, historical explanation rooted in Muhammad's numerous contacts with Jews and Christians, as non-Muslim scholars believe?

JEWISH AND CHRISTIAN INFLUENCES ON MUHAMMAD

Whether the Qur'an was divinely inspired or influenced by Muhammad's contact with Christians and Jews has long been a source of controversy between Muslim and non-Muslim scholars. There have been three main theories among western scholars as to Muhammad's contacts and influences, epitomized by works such as Charles Cutler Torrey's *The Jewish Foundation of Islam*,[12] Richard Bell's *The Origin of Islam in Its Christian Environment*,[13] and Patricia Crone and Micheal Cook's theory of Samaritan influence in *Hagarism: The Making of the Islamic World*.[14] An important research paper presented at Princeton University back in the 1930s examined all three of these theories, as summarized in its title: "Jewish, Christian, and Samaritan Influences in Arabia."[15] Numerous works by Jewish and Christian scholars contain an anti-Muslim bias that affords Muhammad's message no originality at all, while many Muslim scholars go to the other extreme and downplay, or completely deny, Muhammad's contacts with Jews and Christians in order to uphold the complete originality and divine inspiration of his messages. Both sides tend to go to extremes and oversimplify matters. While among non-Muslim scholars there are three contenders as to influences—Jews, Christians, and Samaritans—a question that has only rarely been raised is whether any of the contacts Muhammad had were with *Jewish Christians.*

What we do know with certainty is that biographies of Muhammad written by Muslims do contain accounts of Muhammad's contacts with Christians and Jews. As in academic biblical studies, there has been much intra-Muslim scholarly dispute about the historical reliability of these accounts. Since there would seem to be no apologetic reason for these stories to have been invented, there is likely a core of historical truth to them. But the difficulty is in ascertaining the extent to which such encounters shaped Muhammad and, more controversially, shaped the teachings about Jesus found in the Qur'an.

The main source for knowledge of the life of Muhammad has been the *Sirat Rasul Allah* (The Life of the Prophet of God) written by Ibn Ishaq (died 767). This work records five instances of Muhammad having interactions with Christians. Most of Muhammad's encounters, whether known through such records or unknown to us, would have been with desert-dwelling monks in northern Arabia, all of whom would have had a somewhat unorthodox Christology by the standards of the Councils of Nicaea and Chalcedon. Many of these monks were fleeing persecution from the Orthodox Byzantine Church for their beliefs. Some of them had lingering Arian tendencies (that Jesus was not fully divine), while others tended toward monophysitism (that Jesus was so divine that he had no human nature at all).

Hans-Joachim Schoeps notes that many of the central doctrines of the Ebionites entered into Arabia via unorthodox Christian sects: "[T]he Arabian Christianity which Muhammad found at the beginning of his public activity was not the state religion of Byzantium but a schismatic Christianity characterized by Ebionite and Monophysite views. From this religion many beliefs flowed in an unbroken stream of tradition into the proclamation of Mohammed."[16] This "schismatic Christianity" of Arabia was commonly known as Nestorianism. Nestorian Christians believed that Christ exists as two persons, the man Jesus and the divine Son of God, or Logos, rather than as two natures (true God and true man) in one divine person. Thus, they do not believe that God suffered or died on the cross, for only Jesus in his human nature could suffer. This belief combines elements of Ebionite and Elkesaite theology. Nestorian beliefs are still found among contemporary Coptic Christians of Egypt.

One particularly intriguing encounter that Muhammad had with a heterodox Christian group took place not long after he received his first revelation in the year 610. Muhammad struggled mightily with the nature of these ecstatic revelatory experiences, in which he claimed he was visited by the angel Gabriel* and given the ability to memorize and recite the words of the angel, words that would become recorded in the Qur'an.† Early on Muhammad feared that he was going insane or being visited by a demon, but received assurance from his wife, Khadija, that Allah would not allow that to happen to one as devoted to God as he. In one particularly intriguing account in his biography, Ibn Ishaq tells how Muhammad also received assurance of the reality of his experiences from Khadija's cousin, Waraqa Ibn Nawful, whom Ishaq describes as "a Christian who had studied the scriptures and was a scholar."[17] This alone shows that Muhammad must have had extensive interaction with at least one very learned person about the teachings of Judaism and Christianity. But even more fascinating is Ishaq's description of Ibn Nawful as a man "who had become a Christian and read the scriptures and learned from those that follow the Torah and the gospel."[18] This description is highly intriguing. Does Ishaq mean that Ibn Nawful learned from both Jews and Christians, or from people who followed both the Torah and the gospel? If the latter was what he meant, it would give indisputable evidence that Ebionites still existed in Arabia in the late-sixth to early-seventh centuries.

---

*This is the same angel who made the annunciation of the birth of Jesus to Joseph and Mary in the New Testament Nativity stories.

†Muslims believe every word of the Qur'an to be the words of Allah given to Muhammad through the angel Gabriel.

MUHAMMAD AS THE TRUE PROPHET

One of the key links showing at least a theological connection between Muhammad and the Ebionites is the Ebionite acceptance of Jesus as the true prophet, which we put first in our list of core Ebionite doctrines in chapter 9. This understanding is based in this verse from Deuteronomy: "I will raise up for them a prophet like you from among their own people; I will put my words in the mouth of the prophet, who shall speak to them everything I command" (Deuteronomy 18:18). Hans-Joachim Schoeps notes the clear link here between Ebionite theology and Muslim theology: "The Ebionite conception of the True Prophet must have been directly operative in the proclamation of the prophet Muhammad himself . . ."[19] Schoeps notes how this conception of a series of true prophets is tied in with the core Jewish conception of God making covenants with the human race. While Islam does not emphasize God's covenant as Judaism and Christianity do, Schoeps notes that Muhammad saw himself as fulfilling the covenant that was made and renewed through the series of true prophets, and shows how this ties in with the universalism we saw is inherent in the Ebionite evangel:

> [B]ehind the Islamic idea of a series of prophets is a completely universal conception related to Ebionitism: the prophets are humanity's representatives, with whom God makes a covenant. Noah, Abraham, Moses, Jesus, and Muhammad are in the narrowest sense the contracting parties of the divine covenant. The truth of each earlier messenger—as the Elkesaites also believed—is taken up in the proclamation of the one who follows, so that Mohammed brings together all the truth conveyed through them.[20]

The fifth *sura* (chapter) of the Qur'an, (especially 5:48 and 5:49 quoted in the section above), "sounds like the extension of the Jewish Christian theology of the covenants to the population of Arabia through Muhammad, the new messenger of God."[21] Muhammad, as the prophet who brings the covenant to the people of Arabia, fulfills the role of

Abraham, who originally conveyed the covenant to the Jews. Both Abraham and Muhammad represent the universal nature of the covenant as relevant for all humanity: "Particularly important . . . is the fact that Abraham became for Islam the [Father] of all believers; neither Jew nor Christian, he serves as the link joining Jewish Christianity and Islam. The covenant with Abraham unites all believers at a stage *prior* to Torah and gospel. It was the reconstruction of this covenant that Muhammad saw as his task."[22]

The Qur'an clearly, as we saw in just the few verses quoted in the preceding section, upholds a universalistic conception of all believers under one God. This, I personally believe, is truly a fulfillment of the original Abrahamic covenant, which unequivocally states: "I will make of you a great nation, and I will bless you and make your name great, so that you will be a blessing . . . and in you all the families of the earth shall be blessed" (Genesis 12:2–3). These words could equally apply to Abraham, Jesus, or Muhammad. This universalism in the original covenant with Abraham is also found in the teachings of Jesus: "I have other sheep that do not belong to this fold. I must bring them also" (John 10:16). In his "great high priestly prayer" that Jesus prays before his betrayal and arrest in the Gospel of John, Jesus has one final wish: "I ask not only on behalf of these [his Nazarene disciples], but also on behalf of those who will believe in me through their word, that they may all be one" (John 17:20–21). As we shall see in the following chapters, there are those who have been forced to work underground to fulfill Jesus's final wish. In their quest they have above all upheld, as have both Ebionites and Muslims, the unity of God.

Let us summarize our findings with an extensive quote from the great scholar of Jewish Christianity, Hans-Joachim Schoeps, which highlights all that we have tried to express in this chapter (italics mine):

> In addition to the [Muslim] conception of the True Prophet . . . there is the doctrine of the absolute unity of God . . . excluding any kind of Trinity, which is just as characteristic of Mohammed as of Ebionitism. In the *Pseudo-Clementines* religion is defined as

follows: "This is religion, to fear him alone and to believe only the Prophet of Truth" (*Hom.* 7.8). This definition is so constructed that Islam could find in it its own confession of faith. According to Islam, Mohammed, as the Prophet of Truth, is the legitimate successor of Moses and Jesus in the mission of illuminating mankind. This extensive similarity in structure between Jewish Christianity and Islam explains why the population of the countries bordering Arabia, areas permeated with Monophysitism and Nestorianism, could so quickly become Mohammaden.

In addition to these, Islam took over a number of elements of the Jewish doctrine of the law *in the special form given them by Ebionitism.* This is true of the specifically Jewish rites of baptism and purification, and of the practice of directing prayers in a specific direction, originally northward, toward Jerusalem . . . A certain dependence upon Jewish Christianity may also be seen in the Mohammaden food laws, *which have their origins in the regulations of the Apostolic Decree.* . . . Later Islamic theologians also know a tradition of crude anti-Paulinism, which is quite in the temper of Jewish Christianity . . .

. . . Like the Ebionites, Mohammed wanted to correct the falsehoods which had crept into the law *and to effect a reformation to restore the original.* . . . And thus we have a paradox of world-historical proportions . . . the fact that Jewish Christianity indeed disappeared within the Christian Church, but was preserved in Islam *and thereby extended some of its basic ideas even to our own day.*[23]

Every one of these areas highlighted by Schoeps could be expounded upon in depth, but we have had to limit ourselves here to just the bare bones. A book about the many similarities between Jewish Christianity and Islam waits to be written, but the basic tenets of Jewish Christianity were preserved not only in Islam. In the chapters that follow we shall demonstrate that the universalistic tendencies of Jewish Christianity have been preserved in other places as well, in some rather unexpected places. It is fitting to close this chapter with the words of the other great scholar of Jewish Christianity, Hugh Schonfield, who wrote the following prescient words in 1936:

> With the rise of Islam the real work of Jewish Christianity in the East had finished. It had left in possession at least a faith in which the Unity of God was a fundamental principle and in which Jesus was recognized as a great and true prophet. The story is told of the [Byzantine] Emperor Heraclius (575–641), that being warned in a dream that his power would be destroyed by "the circumcised" he ordered the compulsory baptism of all the Jews in his realm: he did not realize that "the circumcised" were really the Arabs. From this time the future of Jewish Christianity lay in the West until the time of the Gentiles should be fulfilled.[24]

Let us now look to the West for the fulfillment of the time of the Gentiles.

12

FROM ELKESAITES
TO CATHARS
The Heresy Moves West

The meek shall increase their joy in the Lord, and the
poor men shall rejoice in the Holy One of Israel.

THE CATHARIST RITUAL (LATIN TEXT)[1]

In this chapter we shall fast forward several centuries, as well as move our
focus from the Middle East to the West, specifically to a region of southern France known in the High Middle Ages as the Languedoc, and a new
heresy that "infected" the region—Catharism, a movement partly influenced by the Jewish Christian sect of the Elkesaites. Along the way we
shall meet such interesting medieval heretics as the Messalians, Bogomils,
and Paulicians. Before looking west, however, we must first look to the
east to find the spiritual influence that would give rise to Catharism.

JEWISH CHRISTIANITY IN THE EAST

Some scholars believe that the Elkesaites, or at least their influence, survived longer than the Ebionites, much longer than has generally been
supposed, specifically in Persia. The Persian Shi'ite Muslim historian

Ibn al-Nadim, in his book *Kitab al-Fihrist,* written in 988, speaks of a sect in Persia called the Mughtasilah (washers), so-called, he says, because they washed all their food before eating it, though one wonders if the name originally referred to their ritual washings, as their name can also be translated as "practitioners of ablutions" (see chapter 10). Al-Nadim states that the great prophet whom they revered is named al-Hasi, "which means 'Elxai.'"[2] This gives convincing evidence of their descent from the Elkesaites. Additionally, they were reported to have a dualistic tendency in their teachings similar to that of the Elkesaites. The Mughtasilah are also called "Sabians" in some writings, which can be translated as "baptizers," and the Qur'an refers to Sabians in three places, listing them alongside Jews and Christians.[3] But the question is: How did Jewish Christianity makes its way as far east as Persia?

Hugh Schonfield tells us that in the sixth to seventh centuries, the "persecutions that had brought so many religious refugees to the northeast of Palestine in earlier times were now being repeated. This time . . . the Orthodox Christians were the persecutors, and a consequence was a new trek of the victims eastward to the territory of the more tolerant Persia of the Sassanian kings."[4] The Sassanid Empire, otherwise known as the Sassanian Dynasty, was the third Iranian dynasty and the second Persian Empire. It was a huge empire that encompassed what is today Iran, Iraq, Armenia, western Afghanistan, eastern Turkey, and parts of India, Syria, Pakistan, Caucasia, Central Asia, and Arabia. The Jews and Jewish Christians who made the trek east were, interestingly, taking the reverse route traveled by their ancestor Abraham and returning to the homeland of their great patriarch in southern Mesopotamia.*

The Sassanid Empire was the last great Iranian empire before the coming of Islam. As the Muslims conquered all of the Middle East, it was not overly difficult for the Jewish sectarians to accept their new rulers. As we saw in the last chapter, Muslim rulers were quite tolerant, and there was much in the new religion of Islam that was quite Jewish in nature; in

---

*According to Genesis 11:31, Abraham originally lived in Ur, the capital of Mesopotamia and cradle of civilization.

fact, Jewish Christian in nature—the belief in the unity of God and in Jesus as a prophet. But before the coming of Islam, the religious tolerance of the Sassanid rulers provided a welcome respite from the persecution that the Jewish Christians faced in the environs of Palestine from the Byzantine Orthodox Christians. Dr. Yuri Stoyanov writes:

> [T]he second Sassanid King of Kings, Shapur I (240–72), followed a generally tolerant and indeed syncretistic religious policy. . . . He forbade the Magian establishment to persecute the other faiths in the Sassanid empire and even patronized the founder of a new universalist but essentially Gnostic religion, Mani. . . . It was under Shapur's patronage that Manichaeism thrived and began its grand expansion in Asia and Europe.[5]

One of the major changes that came over Jewish Christianity in the east was this: "Political Messianism was now largely replaced by a Spiritual Messianism."[6] In other words, the messianic longing for Jesus to return to rule over a Kingdom of God on earth was replaced by a more gnostic spirituality in which the messianic longing was for the soul's release from this physical world in order to return to the Kingdom of God that lies beyond the physical. In the view of the Elkesaites, which was the dominant form of Jewish Christianity in the east, Jesus came to give us the necessary spiritual knowledge (gnosis) concerning our plight in this evil material world and how to attain salvation from it.

LINGERING VESTIGES

There are several other groups that shared an admixture of Jewish Christian and Gnostic beliefs and practices and set the stage for the rise of the Cathars, and who actually still exist today; they are the only contemporary groups that can legitimately be traced directly back to the earliest Jewish Christians. The first is the Nusairiyeh, "a mysterious people found mainly in Syria, whose ancestors belonged to the region south of the Lebanon."[7] A nineteenth-century explorer, Dr. William McLure Thomson, author of a hugely popular Victorian work, *The Land and the Book,* had personal encounters with the Nusairiyeh. Hugh Schonfield tells us:

> They were extremely evasive about their religion, and the good doctor could only gather that they claimed to be Christians, though not like others, *honoring Moses and Jesus.* Persecution by the followers of Islam had made them very wary. Their ceremonies were held in secret, and the author adds, "Should any of their number divulge their mysteries, he would be assassinated without remorse, mercy, or delay." . . . Their existence, as well as their name, remains . . . a link with the past which should not be ignored.[8] (Italics mine.)

This extreme desire to guard secrets can also be seen in the fraternal brotherhoods of the Knights Templar and the Freemasons, which we will discuss in the next chapters. Obviously, any heretical group that intends to continue their beliefs and practices in the face of severe persecution is going to resort to secrecy and threaten those who might divulge their secrets.

The other extant group that has obvious roots in Jewish Christianity is the Mandaeans, who are a greatly persecuted minority in Iraq today and who actually call themselves Nasoraeans! They live a rather miserable existence in the marshlands of the southern Euphrates River, where they were greatly persecuted under the regime of Saddam Hussein. The Iraq War has caused their dispersement and further reduced their numbers, and they are in grave danger of extinction.[9] What is most fascinating about the Mandaeans is that they maintain—and this is accepted by most scholars—that they are descendants of the followers of John the Baptist. To this day, they consider John to be the legitimate Messiah and denounce Jesus as a false Messiah. We know from the New Testament and other historical records that there was a certain amount of friction between the followers of John and the followers of Jesus, and some of Jesus's disciples were originally followers of John. The Mandaeans have also been hostile to the Jews throughout their history because they retain a memory of having been persecuted by them in the earliest days, as the Ebionites also were.

E. S. Drower (Lady Ethel Stefana Drower, 1879–1972), who was considered the primary specialist on the Mandaeans and the chief collector of Mandaean manuscripts, points out that they had a strict division between their laity and their priests:

> [T]hose amongst the community who possess secret knowledge are called *Nasuraiia*—Nasoreans (or, if the heavy s is written as z, Nazorenes). At the same time the ignorant or semi-ignorant laity are called "Mandaeans," *Mandaiia*—gnostics. When a man becomes a priest he leaves "Mandaeanism" and enters *tarmiduta,* "priesthood." Even then he has not attained to true enlightenment, for this, called "Nasiruta," is reserved for a very few. Those possessed of its secrets may call themselves Nasoreans, and "Nasorean" today indicates not only one who observes strictly all rules of ritual purity, but one who understands the secret doctrine.[10]

This twofold division of laity and priests is also seen in the Cathars, as we shall discuss. And again we encounter the keeping of secrets, which clearly is a necessity among persecuted groups. What else is fascinating is that the Mandaeans have three levels of initiation, as do the Freemasons in the basic three degrees of the Blue Lodges through which all initiates progress.

What is perhaps most important about the existence of the Mandaeans today is that they are truly the last surving Gnostic sect that can be traced back to antiquity. That they have survived two millennia in the face of ongoing persecution and repression is a remarkable testimony to their spiritual fortitude. Their existence is also a reminder that if such a group can continue to overtly exist, then surely it is possible for Jewish Christian theology to have survived through an undergound stream of influence on other groups, as we shall now begin to discuss.

CATHAR ROOTS

As we saw in chapter 10, Mani, the founder of Manichaeism, was brought up within a branch of the Elkesaite sect in the city of Babylonia, in the heart of ancient Mesopotamia. The sect was called the Mughtasilah by the Persian historian al-Nadim, but a Manichaean work refers to them by the Greek word Katharoi (pure ones), a piece of evidence connecting the Elkesaites to the Cathars of the High Middle Ages. There is also a highly fascinating piece of information that may show a link between the Elkesaites in Mesopotamia and the Desposyni. Richard Bauckham, the Desposyni scholar par excellence, expounds on what he calls an "intriguing and neglected piece of evidence":

> In the list, given in medieval chronicles, of the early bishops of Ctesiphon-Seleucia on the Tigris, in central Mesopotamia, the three names following that of Mari, the late-first-century founder of the church, are Abris, Abraham, and Ya'qub (James). Abris is said to have been "of the family and race of Joseph" the husband of Mary, while Abraham was "of the kin of James called a brother of the Lord," and Ya'qub was Abraham's son. *These persons should certainly not be dismissed as legendary simply because of their alleged descent from the family of Jesus.* Claims that particular individuals were descendants of the family of Jesus are extremely rare in Christian literature. Such claims seem neither to have been made by historical individuals without foundation, nor to have been attributed to legendary figures. So this feature is by no means obviously legendary. The name Abraham was not very common, but is by no means unknown, among Jews of that period; while James, of course, was both a common Jewish name and a family name, borne not only by the Lord's brother, but also by a grandson of Jude. Only if the three names had been Abraham, Isaac, and Jacob would we have been justified in suspecting them!
>
> ... The medieval chroniclers did have access to good older sources. Abris, Abraham, and Ya'qub may not have been precisely bishops of Seleucia, but that they were Christian leaders in some capacity in that area in the second century seems entirely possible. The suggestion of a kind of dynastic succession is also strongly in favor of the historicity of the tradition, for it resembles the way leadership of the

Church had passed down in this family in Palestine, where James was succeeded in Jerusalem by his cousin Symeon and the grandsons of Jude are found presiding over the churches. . . .

The large Jewish diaspora in Mesopotamia and the close links between it and Palestinian Jews means that there is nothing impossible in the idea that some of the desposynoi, in the late-first or early-second century, should have travelled there as missionaries and remained as church leaders.[11] (Italics mine.)

What is especially intruiging about this account is that the city of Seleucia was not far at all from Babylonia in central Mesopotamia. That Desposyni were leaders of the Elkesaites in Mesopotamia, and that Mani had inter-action with the Desposyni is not at all impossible; in fact, it is probable.

The Elkesaites, like the Mandaeans to this day, wore white robes and performed baptisms. But Mani came to feel that the Elkesaites' emphasis on ritual ablutions was too preoccupied with the body, so he broke away to start his own religion, Manichaeism, which would at one point challenge Catholic Christianity for the hearts and minds of the followers of Jesus. Like Muhammad, Mani considered himself a prophet who was a succesor to the prophetic missions of Buddha, Zoroaster, and Jesus. He called him-self the "apostle of light" and began his mission along with three other former Elkesaites. Unlike most Jewish Christian groups, however, Mani accepted, and was greatly influenced by, Paul's writings (which we now know show a Gnostic influence[12]), and this caused Mani to be rejected by the Elkesaites. But Mani's teachings would become quite influential among Gentile Christians, and would extend to almost every corner of the Roman Empire, becoming especially prominent in Egypt and Syria.

Manichaeism was essentially a *dualism,* which, as we saw in chap-ter 10, is also the essential feature of Gnosticism. As the native French expert on the Cathars, Jean Markale, states, "Manichaeism, a branch of Gnosticism, formed the most perfect example of dualistic heresy while becoming itself a veritable religion with its own rites and dogmas. The name . . . now designates anything that stems from a fundamental oppo-sition between two principles."[13] Like Gnosticism, all dualist religions believe that there are two opposing forces of good and evil in the universe and that the physical world is a creation of the evil Demiurge. While this latter belief may at first sound nonsensical to modern ears rooted in the Judeo-Christian tradition, there is an underlying logic to dualism that greatly appealed to the ancient mind. Jean Markale provides an excellent exposition on the inherent appeal of dualism:

> All [western] religions, all theological systems have established as a postulate the existence of an infinitely wise, infinitely good god, and it is not comprehensible why all at once this good god may commit evil, or at least permit the parallel existence within or by him of an infinitely intelligent, inifinitely evil being [Satan].
>
> All the theologians . . . have collided . . . with this fundamental problem that has haunted humans ever since they became aware of their condition: the problem of the existence of evil. . . .
>
> So what is evil and why do the gods tolerate its existence? It is generally accepted that the suggestion of a principle of absolute good immediately leads to the suggestion of its opposite. To our logical thinking, the principle of good cannot be conceived without its counterpart, the principle of evil. The main difficulty is in knowing which . . . is subordinate to the other, unless they are equals. This is how a doctrine was created that could be described as dualism.[14]

One of the most astute theological answers to the problem of evil that has ever been devised came from Catharism, and contributed to its great appeal and success. It is a remarkable combination of western dualism and eastern metaphysics that owes a great debt to Manichaeism.

The best scholarly account of dualism in Europe is, without doubt, that of Dr. Yuri Stoyanov of the Warburg Institute at London University, who wrote the groundbreaking book, *The Other God: Dualist Religions from Antiquity to the Cathar Heresy,* published by Yale University Press. I am indebted to Dr. Stoyanov's work for much of the material presented in this chapter. The original title of the first edition of his book, published by Penguin, was *The Hidden Tradition in Europe: The Secret History of*

Medieval Christian Heresy. Dr. Stoyanov makes an important statement in the preface of the second edition:

> The title of the first edition . . . alluded to a medieval heretical . . . notion that European dualist heresy derived from a tradition that was "hidden" or "concealed" and transmitted in secrecy from late antiquity onward. In the Catholic/Orthodox view this tradition was mostly recognized as Manichaeism . . . *whereas according to the dualist heretics it was the tradition of the early Christian apostles before it became corrupted by the Church.*[15] (Italics mine.)

We have seen this claim of apostolic rootedness made before by the Nazarenes and Ebionites. And indeed, dualism is present in much of the New Testament, especially in the Gospel of John and in Paul's letters, which speak of Satan as the "lord of this world" and present the great hope of those who follow Jesus as leaving this evil world behind, which is clearly the goal of the Manichaeans and their theological heirs, the Cathars.

Another key belief of the gnostic dualist tradition is that a succession of redeemer figures have come here to give the souls trapped in physical bodies the gnosis of their plight. These prophet-redeemers go all the way back to Adam and include Seth, Enoch, Noah, Abraham, Zoroaster, Buddha, and Jesus. "As in other Gnostic schools, in Manichaeism Jesus Christ remained a divine being who did not assume a material body, and whose incarnation, Passion, death, and Resurrection were only in appearance."[16] The idea that Jesus's death on the cross was in appearance only can also be found in Islam, as evidenced in the Qur'an: "They denied the truth and uttered a monstrous falsehood against Mary. They declared: 'We have put to death the Messiah, Jesus son of Mary, the apostle of God.' They did not kill him, nor did they crucify him, but they thought they did" (4:156–57). This again reveals the cross-cultural influence of both gnostic and Jewish Christian beliefs.

Like the Mandaeans, the Manichaeans were divided into two groups: the "elect" and the "listeners." The elect were those entrusted with the furthering of Mani's mission, and they were bound to a strict asceticism, including vegetariansim and celibacy. The far more numerous listeners were not held to these strict standards and could live a regular life. This same twofold division, with the same characteristics, can be seen in the Cathars, who were divided into the *perfecti* (the perfect) and the *credentes* (believers).

THE HEIRS OF MANICHAEISM

There are three medieval sects that have been identified as direct heirs of Mani's movement and forerunners of the Cathars—the Paulicians, the Messalians, and the Bogomils. The Paulicians emerged in Armenia in the sixth century. Armenia, which had been partitioned between Byzantium and Sassanid Persia in the late fourth century, provides us with another important link to James the Brother of Jesus. Today, in the old city of Jerusalem, one of the four quarters into which the city is divided is the Armenian Quarter, and their main church is the Cathedral of St. James, which, while named for James the son of Zebedee, contains many fascinating relics of James the Brother of Jesus. The Armenian Christians claim that their cathedral is built over James's home in Jerusalem, and, as noted earlier, that they have a replica of the original throne of James. They also claim that James's remains lie buried beneath their main altar (see plates 28–32).

Armenia has the distinction of being the very first Christian nation, having adopted Christianity as their state religion in 301 CE. The Armenians were among the very first Christians to take up residence in Jerusalem after the partitioning of their country between the Byzantine Empire and Sassanid Persia in 389. They defied the authority of Constantinople and remain to this day a Monophysite branch of Christianity (believing that Jesus had only one divine nature). So it is perhaps not unexpected that Armenia became a refuge for Gnostic Christian sects. The Paulicians, a Gnostic/Manichaean Christian group, first appeared in Armenia in the seventh century and flourished between 650 and 872 CE. According to medieval Byzantine sources, the group's name was derived from the third-century Bishop of Antioch, Paul of Samosata. Paul vigorously opposed the formalism of the Church and believed he had been called to restore the pure Christianity of St. Paul. He founded his first congregation in Armenia around the year 650. While quite unlike Jewish Christians, in that they revered St. Paul, what is intriguing about the Paulicians is that the most in-depth study that has been done on their origins concludes that they orginally held to a Jewish Christian view of adoptionism, as did all of early Armenian Christianity.[17]

Another group that influenced the Cathars was the Gnostic/dualist Messalians, who emerged in northeastern Mesopotamia and penetrated into Syria and Asia Minor by the late fourth century. By the eleventh century they were closely associated with the Bogomils. Both the Paulicians and Messalians were forcibly resettled in the Balkans during the eighth century by Byzantine forces, creating a Balkan homeland for heresy on the border between Roman Catholicism and Eastern Orthodoxy.

The Bogomils, the third related group that influenced the rise of the Cathars, are another Gnostic dualist sect. Named after a priest named Bogomil, Bogomilism was a synthesis of Armenian Paulicianism and the Bulgarian Slavonic Church reform movement that emerged in Bulgaria between 927 and 970 and spread into the Byzantine Empire, Serbia, Bosnia, Italy, and France. Scholars believe that Bogomil essentially synthesized elements of the Paulicians and the Messalians into a new and quite influential Gnostic movement. Bogomilism became so powerful and influential that, "in Bosnia and Serbia . . . it maintained itelf so effectively that it frequently figured as the offical State religion . . ."[18] Orthodox Church authorities denounced Bogomilism as a mingling of the beliefs of the Paulicians, Messalians, and Manichaeans.[19] The Bogomils taught that Christ's suffering and death were illusory, and they thus rejected the veneration of the cross because it had no salvific meaning, salvation coming instead through the gnosis of the plight of the human soul, a primary characteristic of the later Cathars. It is quite interesting, as we shall see in the next chapter, that one of the charges brought against the Knights Templar by the Inquisition is that they repudiated the cross.

There is clearly a "cross-pollination" of ideas going on among these related heretical groups. As Yuri Stoyanov states: "There remains . . . the intriguing possibility of an early intercourse between eastern and western heretics prior to the first serious outbreak of heresy in western Christendom."[20] That "first serious outbreak of heresy" was Catharism, a heresy so poweful and influential that the Catholic Church would launch a crusade to eradicate it—the only crusade ever launched by the Church against its own people.

THE RISE OF THE CATHARS

The doctrines held by the Cathars are believed to have come into southern France via trade routes with the Balkans. Indeed, the Cathars were found not only in the Languedoc, but also in northern Italy, along with the Paulicians and Bogomils; and in the Rhineland, where Catharism is believed to have originated. Scholars are in agreement that Catharism can first be identitified in Cologne in the mid-twelfth century, in northern Italy in the mid- to late-twelfth century, and shortly thereafter in France, particularly southern France, where it would reach its peak. One Italian Cathar bishop of the town of Concorezzo, who was ordained by a Bogomil bishop in Bulgaria, has the telling name of Bishop Nazarius. After his ordination, Nazarius brought back with him an important Bogomil tract that would have a huge influence on the Cathars in the Languedoc, the *Liber Secretum* (Secret Book), the only surving Bogomil tract.[21]

Two preeminent Medieval historians, Walter L. Wakefield and Austin P. Evans, authors of the classic reference *Heresies of the High Middle Ages,* give the following account of the rise of Catharism in Cologne:

> The first solid evidence of a new "heresy" . . . one that was to outdo all others in challenging the orthodox Church, comes from Cologne in 1143. There . . . were found persons who claimed, because they followed the apostolic tradition, to constitute the only true church. They were, in their own words, "apostles, Christ's poor," owning nothing, laboring only for daily sustenance, divorced from the world by their perseverance in prayer and fasting. They . . . spurned milk

and foods born of coition, replaced the Catholic sacraments with their own rites of blessing bread at meals and baptism by the imposition of hands. Their church, they said, was worldwide, having persisted in Greece and other lands from the days of the apostles.[22]

What is fascinating is that this could well be a description of the beliefs and practices of the Ebionites, and as for the claim that their church had persisted in Greece, we have the report of Epiphanius that there were still Ebionites on Cypress in the late-fourth century. Yuri Stoyanov notes that the Cathars' claim of apostolic succession was not just made in words, but in the way they lived their lives: "To their followers and sympathizers the Bogomil and Cathar *perfecti* did indeed seem like 'living icons' of genuine, apostolic Christianity, guardians and repositories of the authentic teaching of Christ secretly revealed to his disciples and transmitted in secrecy thereafter . . ."[23]

If Bogomilism and Catharism are indeed descended from earlier Jewish Christianity, how had the heresy reached Europe, particularly the Rhineland? Wakefield and Evans give the following answer:

One suggested [explanation] is that the persecution of Bogomils in Constantinople in 1143 accelerated a dispersion already stimulated by their missionary spirit. More than a century later, an inquisitor would recount how the heresy spread from Bulgaria to Constantinople, thence to Bosnia, and soon afterward, by the medium of returning crusaders, to France. . . . Perhaps the first crusaders had made contact with heretics in the East and carried back some of their ideas.[24]

The idea that the crusaders picked up heretical beliefs is one we shall take up in the next chapter. By the time Jewish Christianity reached the Balkans and eastern Europe, the pure water of the underground stream was being mixed with Gnostic and Manichaean tributaries, as we have seen. Wakefield and Evans provide a related metaphor for what was happening, which picks up the theme of this book:

Heresies spread throughout Europe but not even the greatest of them was homogeneous or monolithic, for in different areas varying emphases, different tenets and forms of organization came into being. The metaphor which might be used to describe this phenomenon is not of a river confined to one great channel, but of a delta where a dozen channels diverge.[25]

The waters of this delta would, however, later converge again in Catharism, as Yuri Stoyanov summarizes:

The diffusion of the dualist tradition in western Europe reached its climax in the growth of an organized and widespread Cathar movement in northern Italy and southern France. Contemporary Catholic accounts often refer to the crucial impact of Balkan dualism on its formation. Modern theories may differ in their estimation of the chronology and the scale of Bogomil influence on original Catharism, but invariably confirm its vital role in providing a new, dualist framework for western heretical and heterodox currents.[26]

The Cathars, as well as their predecessors, the Paulicians and Bogomils, were all great missionaries, and it is undisputed that the roots of Catharism are to be found in the Bogomils. Indeed, the Inquisition regarded the Bogomils as "the souce of all dualist churches in Europe."[27] The main evidence for this is their structure: "In their mature form both Bogomilism and Catharism were divided into two main classes, the elite grade of the perfecti and the lesser grade of the believers, beneath which there apparently existed another introductory and looser class—the listeners."[28] Along with these divisions were a set of ritual initiations, as seen in all secretive groups. And though the Cathars were great preachers and evangelists, they were secretive about their rituals and innermost doctrines; indeed, they had to be.

While some scholars are skeptical of lines of direct transmision between heretical groups over many centuries, the late Sir Steven Runciman, considered the preeminent historian of the Middle Ages, argued for a "tradition of dualism stemming from the Gnostics and the Manichaeans in two streams, one through the Paulicians, another through the Messalians, which join again in the Bogomils of the Balkans and thus continue to . . . the Cathars of Europe."[29] While it is all too easy to be skeptical of such claims of direct descent, Wakefield and Evans emphatically note, "The basic reason for insisting that connections do exist is the similarity of later sects to earlier ones, despite an intervening span of many years . . . between . . . Gnostics and Messalians, Paulicians, and Bogomils."[30] Wakefield and Evans sum up the line of transmission succinctly: "The Cathars were the heirs of the Bogomils, who were the heirs of the Manichaeans."[31] As to how these ideas found their way to southern France, Wakefield and Evans explain that ". . . ideas carried westward from the Balkans by missionaries, merchants, or crusaders returning home gave definition and formal structure to some of the already existing dissenting groups and produced the Catharist heresy . . ."[32] Indeed, the Knights Templar, the famed "warrior monks" of the Crusades, hailed from France and established one of their main bases in the Languedoc. The sober and reasoned assesment of such eminent scholars as Wakefield, Evans, and Runciman provides us with sure footing for the claims we will make in the chapters that follow.

CATHAR THEOLOGY 101

Before we look in more depth at Cathar beliefs and practices, we should take note of their name: Cathar comes from the Greek *katharoi,* which means "the pure ones," and is related to the modern word "catharsis," meaning a purification or "purging." It is my personal belief that the name may at least in part refer to the Cathars' desire to purge or purify themselves of Catholic doctrines that they felt were Hellenistic and pagan in nature. It is interesting that, like the Ebionites, the Cathars claimed they were the true heirs of a succession from the original apostles and believed that Rome and Byzantium had corrupted the original purity of Jesus's message. "Cathars regarded themselves as the true Church of God, which over the centuries had preserved the teachings of Christ and the baptism that he had given to the disciples."[33]

The name Cathar was not one the group chose for themselves, but was applied to them by admiring outsiders. They preferred to call themselves by the French *Bon Hommes et Bonnes Femmes* (good men and good women). It is fascinating to note that the Ebionites were sometimes called by a similar title of honor—the Tobim, or Agathoi, which means the "good ones."[34] The Cathars were also called Albigensians, and the Crusade that was launched by the Church of Rome to eradicate them is called the Albigensian Crusade. This name comes from a town in the Languedoc called Albi, located to the northeast of Toulouse. The name Albigensian is a misnomer, however, since Albi was by no means a center of Catharism; the name was applied because a major debate between Catholic priests and Cathar leaders was held in Albi. Thereafter, it was a commonplace that the Cathars supported the "Albigensian doctrine."

A handful of primary sources for Cathar beliefs and practice have been preserved. These have been collected in Wakefield and Evans's invaluable *Heresies of the High Middle Ages.* One of these documents is the *Cathar Ritual,* which gives invaluable insights into their primary religious practices. The *Cathar Ritual* is clearly derived from a very similar Bogomil liturgy that apparently came from the Paulicians, to whom it was transmitted by the third-century Catholic sect of Novatians. The Novatians, interestingly, also called themselves *katharoi*.[35] The main Cathar text that has been preserved clearly reveals the dualist underpinning of Cathar theology: *The Book of Two Principles.* Like all dualists, the Cathars believed there were two opposing forces of good and evil in the universe, and that the physical world of evil and suffering was created by Satan, whom they called Rex Mundi, or king of the world. One thing that distinguished the Cathars from other gnostic groups is their identification of the Judeo-Christian figure of Satan as the Demiurge. Because the Cathars held that matter and flesh were intrinsically evil as the creation of Satan, like the Ebionites (but for different reasons) they denied the physical incarnation of Jesus and repudiated the idea that atonement could be found in Jesus's crucifixion.

As far as their Christology, the Cathars combined a gnostic view with the adoptionist view of the Elkesaites and Ebionites. The Cathars believed that Jesus was a spirit who had voluntarily come into the physical world, and because he did not have a physical body, he did not actually suffer or die on the cross. They thus rejected the sacrament of the Eucharist. They especially embraced the more gnostic-flavored Gospel of John, which, interestingly, does not have an account of the Last Supper and the institution of the Eucharist. The Cathars also rejected the Trinity because it equated Jesus with the Old Testament God, and they rejected veneration of the cross because it was a material instrument of the forces of evil. "As a church . . . the Cathars set themselves in forthright opposition to the Roman Catholic organization, which, being of this world, in their eyes represented the prince of this world, the devil."[36] This idea is also rooted in the Bogomils, who likewise "renounced all Church services, the veneration of the cross, the cult of relics, and the efficacy of the Eucharist and baptism."[37]

While it may come as a surprise to many people today who think that anti-Catholicism began with the Protestant Reformation in the 1500s, there were fierce iconoclastic Christian reformers at least four hundred years before Luther, who rose up to protest the widespread degeneracy of the Catholic clergy and bishops in the late Middle Ages. Yuri Stoyanov gives this summary:

In the early twelfth century the popular success of the wandering preachers, with their yearning for piety, voluntary poverty, and an evangelical life, was coupled with the rise and spread of new and more vigorous reformist . . . movements often led by charismatic figures like . . . Henry the Monk in France. Inspired by apostolic ideals, heretical preachers and reformists attacked the Church hierarchy, sacraments, and corruption. Particularly zealous among them was the apostate monk Henry, who, having plunged the northern French city of Le Mans into anticlerical strife in 1116, moved to stir more antiecclesiastical agitation in the country of Toulouse, which embraced most of the Languedoc. There he encountered around 1133–4 another spirited and even more extreme preacher, Peter of Bruis, who rejected church buildings, the Old Testament, and the cult of the Cross, which was denounced as the instrument of Christ's torture and death. Peter urged his followers to revenge the torments and death of Christ by breaking and burning crosses . . .[38]

What is quite interesting about the rejection of the cross is that, as we shall see in the next chapter, one of the main charges the Inquisition would level against the Knights Templar was spitting on the cross as part of their initiation ceremony.

Like all gnostic groups, the Cathars believed that within each person there was a divine spark that had emanated from the supreme God like sparks from a bonfire. Using another analogy, Jean Markale points out that the Cathars, who elevated the Gospel of John with its image of Jesus as the light of the world above the other gospels, emphasized that God was "eternal and incorruptible light, from which derived all that existed":

> Thus, all transpired as if the original light had spread around itself, creating and shaping forms that, although each had [its] own distinguishing features, necessarily retained a particle of the luminous energy that prompted their existence. This creation theory could therefore be compared to the very scientific theory of the Big Bang, the initial explosion that gave birth to the universe. . . . In this gigantic explosion, the particles that were dispersed through space were not created ex nihilo, for they belonged to the original mass . . . So the Cathars came back to the Gnostic theory of emanation. Creation . . . was inseparable from the creator, just as the rays of the sun were inseparable from the sun itself; its creatures emanated from the original light.[39]

These sparks or emanations from God originally existed in the nonmaterial heavenly world, but were now trapped by Satan in this lower physical world in corrupt bodies of flesh. Yuri Stoyanov elaborates:

> The God of Light . . . created his heavenly people, comprising the [nonmaterial] body, soul, and spirit, the spirit being outside the body and serving as the custodian of the soul. Satan was believed to

have been envious of the God of Light, and having ascended into his sublime heavens he led astray the souls created by the good God and lured them to earth and the "murky clime." When Satan ascended into the heavens with his legions, war ensued in heaven and he was defeated by the archangel Michael and his hosts, as recounted in Revelation. Upon his expulsion from heaven Satan entrapped the deceived souls in the prison of the body; Jesus's mission was to deliver these souls from Satan's enslavement.[40]

As in the eastern religions, salvation comes through freeing the soul from its present entrapment in matter. The release of the soul was obtained through attaining the proper knowledge (gnosis) of our soul's predicament, as in some forms of Hinduism and Buddhism. In Hinduism the release of the soul is called *moksha;* in Buddhism, *nirvana.* In all forms of Christianity it is called "salvation." Also, like the eastern religions, the Cathars believed in the ongoing reincarnation of the soul. If gnosis could not be attained in this life, one's soul would reincarnate to try again. In Buddhism, whoever attains this salvific knowledge has attained enlightenment and becomes a *buddha,* an "enlightened being." In Catharism, those who attained gnosis of their metaphysical plight and achieved salvation from it were the perfecti; those who had yet to attain salvation were credentes.

One became a perfecti through a ritual called the *consolamentum,* which was a reunification of the earthbound soul with the heavenly body from which it had been torn. Stoyanov explains:

> Only through the consolamentum could the imprisoned soul receive back its heavenly custodian spirit and when, in the last days, all the ensnared souls would achieve their penance they would ascend back to their heavenly abodes and regain their heavenly bodies. This was deemed to be the resurrection of the dead in the Scriptures, not the resurrection of physical bodies but of spiritual bodies.[41]

The consolamentum was the only Cathar sacrament; in fact, it was considered a baptism in the Holy Spirit, as Wakefield and Evans explain:

Christ had granted to his Church the power to forgive sins through prayer and baptism in the ceremony by which one entered the company of true Christians, a baptism in the Holy Spirit. It could be received only by those who had faith, and thus was denied, generally but not invariably, to children. Baptism, called the consolamentum, brought forgiveness of the great sin which the soul had incurred in its fall from heaven, and a return of the guiding spirit, which had been lost . . . The rite of the consolamentum was a simple one, having, in fact, considerable likeness to baptism in the early church. How it survived or was recreated is not known, although the Cathars surely obtained its chief features from the Bogomils.[42]

The soul's fall from heaven is the Cathar version of original sin. The consolamentum was the equivalent of receiving the baptism of the Holy Spirit, absolution of sin, and ordination all in one, and those who received the consolamentum formed a kind of Cathar priesthood. After receiving the consolamentum the perfecti lived a life of strict asceticism, renouncing all worldy goods except for life's barest necessities. Reminiscent of the early Nazarene community, the perfecti surrendered all their worldly goods to the community. They wore simple black or blue robes and undertook the life of wandering monks, dedicating themselves to good works, prayer, and spreading the faith through preaching. As in Buddhism, the main life mission of the perfecti was to show others the way that leads to salvation.

The ritual for administering the consolamentum has been preserved in Latin and Provençal, the main language of the Provence region of southern France. These two different versions were "certainly formulated under Bogomil influence . . . and they present some obvious parallels to early Christian baptism."[43] Wakefield and Evans sum up the essential features:

When perfected Cathars imposed their hands on the body of the initiate while the Gospel was held over his head, their prayers were believed to win him forgiveness for the sin committed at the fall from heaven, as well as for his transgressions in this earthly life. Released from the power of the evil god, his soul would regain its guiding spirit and would find the way of return to its heavenly home. It was not easy to attain this consecrated state nor to follow the way of life required during the remaining bodily existence on earth. Like a catechumen of the early church—Catharist practices reflect the ancient usage—a believer had to undergo a period of probation, normally at least a year, during which he was instructed in the faith and disciplined in a life of rigorous asceticism. . . . This preliminary rite brought him to the [Cathar] Church; he might then proceed, either at once or after further probation, to the consolamentum, which would effect the complete spiritual transformation. Thereafter, the Christian renounced the material world and accepted a strict moral and ethical code. His life was to be spent in imitation of the apostles. He was to return good for evil in every circumstance and suffer without retaliation the persecution which must be endured by every true follower of Christ. To kill, to lie, to make an oath was to commit mortal sin. . . . Meat, eggs, and cheese . . . must not be used. Obeying these injunctions, the Cathar was assured that on the death of his body, his soul would be released from its material prison and would find salvation.[44]

Unlike the perfecti, the credentes, who made up the vast majority of the Cathars, were not expected to live such a strict, ascetic lifestyle. As we can see, there are some fascinating commonalities between the beliefs and practices of the Cathar perfecti, the Ebionites, and especially the more gnostic Elkesaites. These linkages were "transmitted somehow to the medieval dualists from early eastern, probably Syrian Christianity."[45] One other intriguing link is the Cathar "Eucharist," which, like the Ebionite Eucharist, "was a mere remembrance of table-fellowship with Jesus and replaced the cup of blood with a cup of water."[46] The Cathars rejected the Catholic Eucharist because it was a reenactment of sacrifice. The Cathar rejection of sacrifice is another telling link that takes us back to the Ebionites, and like the Ebionites, they thus rejected false texts in the Old Testament, primarily those commanding sacrifice, as Yuri Stoyanov explains:

> While charting the feats of Satan as the Lord of the Old Testament, the Cathar accounts are as explicit as those of the Bogomils, recounting that Satan sent prophets to men and through their prophecies precipitated animal sacrifices, the blood offerings through which he was honored as god. . . . In one Cathar version [of the Flood story] it was the "Holy God" who saved Noah and "all living creatures" from Satan's flood.[47]

Such interpretations of the Old Testament made sense of what is still today a confusing portrait of a supposedly good and loving God in the Old Testament. As an ordained minister, I have many times seen average Christian laypeople who are quite confused as to how to reconcile the vastly differing images of God in the Old and New Testaments. So, historically, the development of the dualist belief that the God of the Old Testament and the God of the New Testament were two different gods was inevitable. While it may not seem so to us today, to anyone in the Middle Ages who was literate and able to read the Bible, Gnosticism and dualism seemed quite logical, especially in the terrible world of suffering that was the Middle Ages, a time when the devil was semingly everywhere. "Catharist dualism . . . was simply a natural development from belief in the devil, who assumed vast importance for Christians throughout the Middle Ages."[48]

The fact that the nature of God in the Old Testament seems so completely at odds with the God of love and forgiveness that Jesus proclaimed is what initially led the early Christian Bishop Marcion (ca. 85–160) to reject the Old Testament. Marcion's Gnostic form of Christianity became so popular that it rivaled emerging Catholicism, which led to Marcion's excommunication by the Church of Rome around the year 144. More than a millennium after Marcion, Gnosticism and dualism still held huge appeal, and the rapidly growing popularity of Catharism would lead not merely to excommunication for the Cathars, but to their extermination.

THE NEED FOR CRUSADE

Ironically, what eventually brought the Church of Rome to launch a crusade to wipe out the Cathars was the sect's great success. The perfecti were marvelous, inspiring preachers because they were quite literate. They "lived with books, for they attracted members from the social classes apt to be literate. There are references to their own schools as well as their practice of sending qualified persons to study at the great universities."[49] Zoé Oldenbourg, author of the classic account of the Albigensian Crusade, *Massacre at Montségur,* states, "What is quite certain is that the Cathars were great preachers . . . On several occasions we see them taking part in theological debates, or attending meetings at which their learned doctors argue with bishops and legates."[50] The high value placed on education and learning in the Languedoc led to another budding pre-Renaissance environment, similar to what unfolded in neighboring Spain under the Muslims. Yuri Stoyanov gives this summary:

> By the end of the twelfth century Catharism was already well established in Languedoc, where it secured the favor not only of much of the rural aristocracy but also of great . . . nobles. In contrast to the prevalent climate in western Europe, Languedoc society was markedly more tolerant and cosmopolitan and had also attained a high degree of prosperity. With its distinctive and diverse culture, Languedoc was a prominent center of the twelfth-century "renaissance" and the cradle of troubador lyric poetry, which flourished under the patronage of the noble courts . . .[51]

It has been said that if the Albigensian Crusade had not curtailed the Cathar experiment, the Renaissance may have begun in France a couple of centuries before the Italian Renaissance. It is little known that at the time Tolouse, the main center of Catharism, was the third-largest city in Europe after Venice and Rome. The most brilliant intellectuals in Europe were flooding into Tolouse because of the spirit of intellectual freedom that existed there. As in Spain under the Muslims, the Jews enjoyed a time of little-known freedom and prosperity, and their culture contributed to the high culture of the Languedoc. We will learn more about the Jewish influence in the area and its influence on the rise and fall of the Knights Templar at the beginning of the next chapter.

By the late twelfth century the majority of people in the Languedoc were credentes, including many noble families and royal courts. Catharism had almost completely replaced the Catholic Church in southern France at a time when the Catholic clergy were widely despised as corrupt. It was mainly due to the neglect of their superiors that the Catholic clergy were in such a terrible state. Many were poor and illiterate, forced into a life of corruption in order to survive, and provided poor role models for the people. Others lived luxurious and decadent lifestyles. The Cathar perfecti, on the other hand, were eloquent in their preaching, upstanding in their lifestyle, and won the admiration and devotion of both nobles and commoners. Another important factor in the popularity of the Cathars was their great devotion to Jesus: ". . . one thing beyond any doubt is the fact that the Cathars always displayed a devotion to the person of Christ such as no Catholic could exceed: we can argue with anything except (in this sense) their Christianity."[52]

The rapid growth and popularity of Catharism in the heart of Catholic Europe became more than the Church of Rome could bear. Zoé Oldenbourg puts it thus:

> It was no longer a matter of local or individual manifestations of independence [from the Church]; a rival religion, no less, had planted itself in the very heart of Christendom and was gaining ground fast—largely by presenting itself as the one true Faith. The traditional means of persuasion which the Church employed against her straying flock, here ran into an absolutely immovable brick wall. These heretics were no longer dissident Catholics; they drew their strength from their consciousness of belonging to a faith that had never seen eye to eye with Catholicism, and was more ancient than the Church itself.[53]

Oldenbourg notes that some historians do not consider Catharism to be a Christian heresy, but a separate religion altogether, though Oldenbourg corrects this notion: "It might be more accurate to say that it had nothing in common with the Christianity that ten centuries of Church history had produced. The Cathar religion was indeed a heresy, one which can be dated back to a time when the Church's doctrines had not yet hardened into dogma."[54]

With the Cathars we come as close to the original Nazarene piety and devotion as subsequent history has seen. Dr. René Weis of the University College, London, gives this wonderful summary of what makes Catharism stand out in history:

> Among medieval heresies Catharism stands out as the most striking and anachronistic. Here was a dissident faith with, at its doctrinal core, gentleness and the promise of universal redemption. It was inspired by the New Testament, and it was Christ and his Disciples whom the spiritual leaders of the Cathar Church, the so-called Perfects or Good Men, emulated. The Cathars' opposition to all forms of killing extended to human and animal life alike, and like Christ, they intended to forgive those who persecuted them. To encounter such a philosophy in the long-distant past is in itself surprising; to learn that in thirteenth-century Languedoc it inspired tens of thousands of ordinary men and women to risk their lives is astonishing. The popular perception of the Middle Ages is of a cruel and benighted period in which the Church held absolute sway . . . Catharism, on the other hand, has become a beacon of light in that darkness through providing a moral and spiritual model whose idealism has rarely been matched in the history of Europe.[55]

The Cathars apparently possessed ancient documents from the time of the Nazarenes, as evidenced by their writings. Oldenbourg explains:

> [T]he Cathars declared themselves the heirs of a tradition that was older than that held by the Church of Rome—and, by implication,

both less contaminated and nearer in spirit to the Apostolic tradition. . . . And it looks as though this claim was at least partially justified. The Catharist Ritual . . . demonstrates, as Jean Guiraud proves in his magnum opus on the Inquisition, that this Church undoubtedly possessed certain most ancient documents, which were directly inspired by the traditions of the Primitive Church.[56]

One is forced to wonder if what the Cathars possessed was not the actual *Didache,* for as Oldenbourg goes on to specify:

> In fact . . . by a comparison of initiation ceremonies among Cathars with the Baptism of the Catechumens in the Primitive Church—the parallelism between the two traditions is so consistent that it could not conceivably be due to mere coincidence. . . . The admission of a catechumen into the Primitive Church was at all points identical with that of a Cathar postulant into his new faith.[57]

It is also interesting that the believers who were candidates to become perfecti were called "living stones in the temple of God"; and the Knights Templar, who took their name from the temple of Solomon, had a major base in the Languedoc, where many of their leaders had connections. The Templars pointedly did not take part in the Albigensian Crusade, as Yuri Stoyanov notes:

> The Albigensian Crusade was vigorously promoted in northern France and in the early summer of 1209, northern feudal lords and prelates mustered a formidable army at Lyons. Yet the military orders of the Templars and the Hospitallers did not play an active military role in the crusade, which, in the case of the Templars, was bound to attack some of their patrons, who were renowned Cathar supporters . . .[58]

The Albigensian Crusade was fought mainly by the armies of the king of northern France, who had long desired to bring the Languedoc under his control; the papal Crusade against the Cathars presented a golden opportunity. Pope Innocent III, whose ongoing diplomatic and evangelistic efforts to convert the Cathars met with little success, had been considering using force against them. He was given the perfect excuse in the year 1208 when a papal legate, Pierre de Castelnau, who had been sent to try to persuade Count Raymond VI of Toulouse to rein in the Cathars, was murdered (allegedly by an agent of the Count of Toulouse). It took little urging on the Pope's part to rally the northern nobles to send an army into the Languedoc to eradicate the Cathars once and for all. Innocent III officially declared a crusade against the Cathars in the year 1209, offering the lands of the schismatics to any French nobleman willing to take up arms. The Albigensian Crusade went on for twenty years until 1229, by which time an estimated million people had died—most of the population of southern France—not all of them Cathars and, in fact, many of them Catholics. The oft-heard quote that sums up the cruel and barbaric nature of the Albigensian Crusade is that of the papal legate Arnald-Amalric, who, when asked how to distinguish the Cathars from the Catholics, is reported to have replied, *"Tuez-les tous; Dieu reconnaitra les siens"* (Kill them all; God will look after his own).[59] The need to ferret out the Cathars and interrogate those who were captured played a major role in the creation and institutionalization of the Medieval Inquisition.

The final climax of the crusade was the famous siege of the high mountain fortress of Montségur, where a little more than two hundred of the remaining Cathars put up their last stand. Hopelessly outmatched by ten thousand French troops surrounding them below, the siege of Montségur is similar to the last stand of the Jewish freedom fighters at Masada that ended the first Jewish War, except that the Cathars were not soldiers and were unarmed. As food and water ran out, the Cathars were given the choice to recant or be burned alive. None accepted the offer of clemency. As the last Cathars were dragged down the high cliffs to the pyre waiting below, legend has it that all went smiling and singing hymns into the roaring flames. If the legend is true, they were no doubt thinking of the words from the First Letter of Peter: "In this you rejoice, even if now for a little while you have had to suffer various trials, so that the genuineness of your faith—being more precious than gold that . . . is tested by fire—may be found to result in praise and glory and honor when Jesus Christ is revealed" (1 Peter 1:6–7). Shortly before surrendering, those who had not yet received the consolamentum received it. For the Cathars, their funeral pyre represented their final purification, their salvation from the evil world ruled by Rex Mundi.

There is also the report, not legendary, that four of the Cathars had escaped the night before, carrying down the sheer face of the cliff in pitch-blackness the legendary Cathar "treasure" that had been holed up in the fortress. While there has been much speculation as to the nature of this treasure, it would seem that the only treasure valuable to an ascetic community like the Cathars would be their scriptures and religious texts. That the Cathars would have gone to extraordinary lengths to save their writings we know to be likely from the famous examples of the Dead Sea Scrolls hidden by the Essenes at Qumran, and the cache of gnostic texts buried in the sands at Nag Hammadi in Egypt by Gnostic Christians in order to preserve their treasured writings from the flames of the enemy.

We now turn to another story of Christians who were declared heretics, who did in fact have an enormous monetary treasure that was spirited away before the fires of the Inquisition could be lit. And, like the Cathars, their greatest treasure may not have been monetary. The fascinating story of the legendary and infamous Knights Templar provides many interesting theological links between the early Jewish Christianity of the Nazarenes and Ebionites, the later Gnostic Jewish Christianity of the Elkesaites and Cathars, and the modern rituals of the fraternal order of Freemasons. As we shall see, the underground stream would continue to flow despite the best efforts of the Crusade and Inquisition to dam it up.

13

HERESY IN HIGH PLACES
The Rise and Fall of the Knights Templar

Now King Hiram of Tyre sent his servants to Solomon . . .
for Hiram had always been a friend to David. Solomon
sent word to Hiram . . . "I intend to build a house for the
name of the Lord my God . . . Therefore command that
cedars from the Lebanon be cut for me."

1 KINGS 5:1–6

It must be said up front that when one invokes the name of the Knights Templar, in the scholarly world there will be a raising of eyebrows and a rolling of eyes. The Poor Fellow-Soldiers of Christ and of the Temple of Solomon, commonly known as the Knights Templar or the Order of the Temple, operative from 1119 to 1307, are the most famous of the Western Christian military orders, which also include the Knights Hospitaller and the Teutonic Knights. In their distinctive white mantles with a prominent red cross, the Templars were among the most skilled fighting units of the Crusades. Renowned for their military prowess and bravery on the battlefield, following the Crusades the Templars became the most infamous of the Christian military orders. Partly due to charges of heresy that resulted in their forced dissolution and the burning of their leaders at the stake in the year 1307, over the centuries so many legends have accrued around them that bringing up the Templars among academics today is akin to raising the topic of UFOs or Bigfoot. In the late Middle Ages the Grail legends associated the Templars with the discovery of the Holy Grail. Today, stories continue to be written associating the Templars with all manner of things; most recently Dan Brown's *The Da Vinci Code* characterized them as guardians of a bloodline descended from Jesus and Mary Magdalene.

This is all a shame, for there is a genuine historical mystery surrounding the rise and fall of the Templars, one that needs more attention from scholars. After studying the Templars for the past twenty-five years, I would here like to put forth my own theory as to what exactly the Templars were and why such legends have accrued around them. But first, a brief historical sketch of their story is in order.

TEMPLAR ORIGINS

The origin and mission of the Knights Templar is inextricably linked with the city of Jerusalem. After Christian forces captured Jerusalem from the Muslims in the year 1099, for the first time in many centuries Christian pilgrimage to the Holy City was big business, and along with it, so was banditry. According to the standard history, around the year 1119 two veterans of the First Crusade, a French knight of royal blood, Hugh de Payens, and his relative, Godfrey de Saint-Omer, hatched a plan to create an elite corps of knights dedicated to protecting the pilgrimage route from the port city of Jaffa to Jerusalem. The plan was for the knights all to take monastic vows, and several of the original nine members were already Cistercians; in fact, one of them, André de Montbard, was the uncle of St. Bernard of Clairvaux, who helped form the Cistercian order of monks. The nine founding knights were almost all from noble families, old Burgundian and Flemish families based in and around the city of Troyes in Champagne. Dr. Karen Ralls, a current Templar specialist, notes the following pertinent facts: "Champagne (old Burgundy) was the headquarters of this early group of interrelated families, dubbed the 'Troyes fraternity' by some. It was at this court that . . . medieval author Chrétien de Troyes wrote his famous Grail romances."[1]

These original nine knights presented themselves and their services to King Baldwin II of Jerusalem, who was so enthusiastic about their plan that he immediately offered them his own quarters at the Al-Aqsa Mosque on the Temple Mount, formerly the site of King Solomon's stables, as their headquarters (see plates 3 and 9). It was from this hallowed ancient site that they took their name—The Poor Fellow-Soldiers of Christ and of the Temple of Solomon. They were the "poor" fellow-soldiers because, like all monastics, they took a vow of poverty, captured in their official symbol, which shows two knights mounted on a single horse. They were, in Hebrew, *ebionim*. But though each knight swore to lead an ascetic life, thanks to donations of land and money pouring in from admiring supporters, the Order as a whole would become the wealthiest organization in medieval Europe after the Church of Rome.

It was thanks to their most enthusiastic supporter, St. Bernard of Clairvaux, who drew up the guiding rule for the Order, that the Templars won the official approval of the Pope at the Council of Troyes in the year 1129. Bernard wrote a famous letter of endorsement, "In Praise of the New Knighthood," in which he "elevated the Knights Templar order above all other orders of the day . . . This letter established the image of the Templars as a fierce spiritual militia for Christ."[2] Bernard saw the Templars as a new species of "warrior-monks." The major Templar historian, Malcolm Barber, characterizes their mission statement this way: "Strong warriors, on the one hand, and monks waging war with vice and demons on the other . . . these men had no dread of death, confident in the knowledge that in the sight of the Lord they would be his martyrs."[3]

Having won papal approval, the Templars began wearing their white habits, which would later carry the famous equal-armed red cross, added as a symbol of martyrdom. With the great success of the early Crusades and the rapidly growing reputation of the Templars, donations increased by leaps and bounds. Their power particularly increased in 1139, when Pope Innocent II issued a papal bull declaring that the Templars could pass freely between countries, were exempt from all local and national taxes, and were not answerable to any king or secular authority, but to the Pope alone.

TEMPLAR INFRASTRUCTURE

Though its initial mission was defensive in nature, as the Order and its military prowess grew, the Templars became a frontline group in the Crusades. One of their most famous victories was at the Battle of Montsigard in 1177, where five hundred Templars routed Salah al-Din's army of some twenty-five thousand soldiers. As they grew ever larger and more powerful, a huge infrastructure became necessary to support the warrior knights. In their prime, relatively few members of the Order were soldiers; the majority worked in a support role managing their huge financial resources and real estate holdings. The Templars would actually establish the world's first international banking system, as well as a construction program that financed and built fortresses and churches throughout Europe and the Middle East. As one historian puts it, "The Templars . . . with their vast revenues from land holdings in Europe and the Levant [the lands of the eastern Mediterranean] began a veritable building boom."[4] I believe it is the Templar building program that would later give rise to the modern brotherhood of Freemasons, as we will discuss in the next chapter.

The Templars were so trusted that many noblemen who participated in the Crusades turned complete control of their assets over to the Templars while they were away. The Templars are credited with developing the first rudimentary checking system, as many people who journeyed to the Holy Land would deposit all of their wealth in the nearest Templar preceptory and be issued letters of credit that could be redeemed at other preceptories.

Over the two hundred years of their existence, the Templars acquired numerous large tracts of land, which they used for all types of agriculture; in fact, at one point they owned the island of Cypress. They built fortresses and churches, owned and managed many businesses and manufacturing companies, had a fleet of ships, and were involved in exporting and importing. It could truly be said that by the time of their demise they had become the world's first multinational corporation.

A FALL FROM GRACE

As with any powerful entity, the more powerful the Templars became, the more resentment developed against them, especially since many of the Templars grew haughty and arrogant and fell away from their monastic vows. To "drink like a Templar" became a popular saying. The acclaim the Templars enjoyed had always come primarily from their great success in the Crusades. When the Muslims recaptured the Holy Land, much of the blame for its loss fell on the Templars. With their military campaigns at an end, the Templars concentrated their efforts on their many businesses and farms located throughout Europe. As they were still exempt from all local laws and oversight, many local nobles and rulers grew resentful, even fearful, when the Templars began to express interest in establishing their own monastic state, possibly on Cypress or in France, as the Teutonic Knights had already done in Prussia and the Hospitallers had done on the island of Rhodes.

With no more need for large orders of Crusader knights, in the early 1300s the new Pope, Clement V, began urging the Templars and the Hospitallers to merge, something neither group was at all enthusiastic to do. In a formal meeting that Clement held with the Templar grand master, Jacques de Molay, in 1307 to discuss the situation, another problem was raised. Several years earlier an ousted Templar had brought charges of heresy against the Order. Clement asked King Philip IV (Philip "the Fair") of France to help with the investigation. Philip was deeply in debt to the Templars due to loans he had taken out with them to finance his war with England, and he saw an opportunity to get out of his debt. As resentment toward the Templars grew, rumors began circulating about their engagement in heretical practices, particularly in their secret initiation ceremony. While Pope Clement believed all of the accusations to be false, Philip insisted otherwise and pressured Clement to take action against the Templars. Clement was old and ailing and fearful of Philip, who had brought about the downfall of the previous Pope, Boniface VIII, on grounds of papal corruption. Philip was, therefore, bold enough to take matters regarding the Templars into his own hands. He issued secret orders for all the Templars in France to be arrested.

On the morning of Friday, October 13, 1307 (the date has given rise to speculation that this is the origin of the Friday the 13th superstition), all the Templars in France who could be rounded up were arrested, including the grand master, Jacques de Molay. They were charged with all manner of heresies and sordid practices, and were tortured. After obtaining many confessions under torture, Philip was able to compel Clement to issue a papal bull ordering the arrest of all Templars in Europe and the seizure of their assets. No other European leader was as anxious as Philip to take action against the Templars, and in many countries only a few arrests were made and token trials held. Under further pressure from Philip, in 1312 Clement issued a papal bull officially dissolving the Order.

The final end came when the elderly grand master, Jacques de Molay, and his second in command, Geoffrey de Charney, who had both confessed to most of the charges under torture, retracted their confessions and were therefore declared lapsed heretics. As such, they were burned together at the stake in Paris on March 18, 1314. Later legend would have it that as he was being consumed by the flames, de Molay cried out for God to bring divine retribution upon his accusers. It is a fact that Clement died of natural causes within a month (though it must be noted that he was sick and elderly), and Philip died before the end of the year in a hunting accident.

Today, the official position of the Roman Catholic Church is that the Templars were innocent victims of the machinations of Philip IV and his dominating influence over Clement. Just recently, in 2001, a document surfaced in the Vatican Secret Archives which is the official record of the trial of the Templars. The so-called Chinon Parchment is said to have been stored in the wrong place in 1628. The document shows that Clement V formally absolved the Templars of all charges against them in 1308, four years before he officially disbanded the Order.

ASSESSMENT

While most historians have tended to agree with the Church's assessment that the Templars were innocent of all charges, it is my personal belief that the Templars did indeed hold to certain heretical beliefs and practices, some of which were part of the belief structure of their founders. We need to keep in mind that the founders lived just north of the center of Catharism, as well as right in the center of a large Jewish population in central France. I believe that they held to some Cathar beliefs and most likely picked up other heretical beliefs during their sojourn in Palestine, especially through their interaction with Muslims, with whom they did not always have adversarial relations and whom the Templar leaders came to admire.

To present my evidence for all this, let us first examine the main charges leveled against the Templars. Many of these are clearly spurious—charges of sodomy, worshipping a cat, and engaging in witchcraft, all pretty much standard charges against heretics in the Middle Ages—but others give one pause, especially if one is aware of Ebionite and Cathar theology. The following are the most pertinent:[5]

- The Templars denied Christ in their reception ceremony or soon after. They also spat and trampled on the cross.
- They did not believe in the Mass or in other sacraments. Their priests did not say the words of consecration over the host.
- They were told that the Templar masters could absolve their sins, implying that they had no need of a priest.
- They exchanged kisses on various parts of the body, the navel and base of the spine being favorites.
- They were not allowed to reveal to anyone what happened in the reception ceremony.
- They venerated an idol, a bearded male head, sometimes called Baphomet. Each of them wore a cord around his waist that had touched the idol.
- They met at night and in secret.

It is interesting that many of these charges are similar to the charges that had been leveled against the Cathars less than a century earlier: They rejected the cross, they kept their ceremonies secret, they did not believe in the Mass or the sacraments of the Church. The fact that many

Templars lived in the Languedoc and received support from the nobility there, in addition to the fact that they had given only nominal support to the Albigensian Crusade, makes it not at all outside the realm of possibility that their Christianity was closer to Catharism than to Catholicism. Even such a respected medieval scholar as Sir Steven Runciman concurs: "It may be that the secret practices of the Templars . . . were partly based on dualist ideas and usages. . . ."[6] This is indeed evidenced by the first three charges above, which could just as well have been leveled against the Cathars, or the Ebionites for that matter. Even the charge of exchanging inappropriate kisses (allowing for inevitable lurid exaggeration) is explainable by the original Jewish Christian practice of the Nazarenes, who exchanged a kiss of peace to conclude their worship services.

Sir Steven Runciman, considered by many the preeminent historian of the Crusades, clearly demonstrates that the Cathar practices have their roots in the early church. What he says could apply equally well to the Templars and would explain all the major charges brought against them (allowing, of course, for exaggeration and embellishment). The bracketed amendments are mine to show how all of this could equally apply to the Templars:

> The Ritual Feast of the Cathars (which involved a simple breaking-of-bread ceremony) is, if we equate the Perfect [or a Templar priest] with the early Christian priest, exactly the same as the Early Christian Communion Feast. The Kiss of Peace terminated Early Christian services as it did those of the Cathars [and perhaps Templar services and rituals] . . . The *consolamentum* in its two aspects was closely akin to adult baptism administered by the early church to the dying and to the ordination or initiation into its ministry [Templar initiates were becoming monks]. The very details of the service are similar. In the early church (as was the case with a prospective Cathar *perfectus*) the catechumen was tested by a long and stern probationary period . . . The actual ordination [and perhaps Templar initiation] was identical, consisting of the laying on of hands and of the Gospel upon the catechumen's head. . . .

> [When] polemical churchmen in the Middle Ages denounced
> the heretics for maintaining a class of the elect or perfect, they were
> denouncing an Early Christian practice [likewise in the case of
> Templar initiation], and the heretical initiation ceremony that they
> viewed with so much horror was almost word-for-word the ceremony
> with which early Christians were admitted to the Church.[7]

Runciman sums up the similarities between Cathar practices and those of
the early church in words that could equally apply to the Templar rites:
"Such similarity cannot be fortuitous. Obviously the Cathar Church had
preserved, only slightly amended to suit its doctrines of the time, the services extant in the Christian Church during the first four centuries of its
life."[8] The Templars would also certainly have amended their practices to
suit their particular needs.

Further confirmation that the Templars had a Jewish Christian understanding of Jesus comes from the Templar trials held in England, where
English Templars also confessed to being told to deny the efficacy of the
cross. English records give the name of the first Templar in England to
confess to heretical practices—Stephen de Stapelbrugge. He reported that
during his induction he was shown a crucifix and told he must deny that
"Jesus was God and man and that Mary was his mother," and ordered to
spit on the cross.[9] This gives us independent confirmation that what the
French Templars confessed to was indeed part of their belief. Further, de
Stapelbrugge said that the Order's beliefs originated in the Agen region
of France, Agen being one of the hotbeds of Catharism. Another English
Templar, Thomas Tocci de Thoroldeby, said that a former Templar master
in England, Brian de Jay, had said "Christ was not true God, but a mere
man."[10] The treasurer of the temple in London, John de Stoke, testified
that the Templar grand master, Jacques de Molay, had told him to believe
in "the great omnipotent God, who created heaven and earth, and not in
the crucifixion."[11] The British researchers who present this evidence from
England comment on de Stoke's testimony: "This is not even Cathare
[*sic*]: for the Cathares, God the creator was evil. It could be construed
as more or less orthodox Judaism or Islam; and certainly, during years of

activity in the Holy Land, the temple had absorbed a good deal of both Judaic and Islamic thought."[12]

Here a word also needs to be said about the Templars alleged worship of a bearded idol named Baphomet. In April of 2009, the Vatican made the stunning announcement that a document was found in the Vatican Secret Archives that convincingly shows that the Templars had been in possession of the Shroud of Turin* for more than a hundred years. Dr. Barbara Frale, who discovered the document, is the same researcher who found the Chinon parchment in which the Pope declared the Templars absolved of all charges. Frale is convinced that the Templars' veneration of the Shroud fully accounts for the charge against them of worshipping a bearded male head. If this is indeed the case, then the charge that the Templars called this idol Baphomet is spurious.

But there is an explanation for how the charge of worshipping Baphomet came to be. Many authors have speculated on the meaning of the name, but the answer is rather obvious. The name occurs repeatedly in the French *chansons de geste*, medieval poetic tales of great warriors that were often sung by the French troubadours—the famous wandering minstrels of the Languedoc. The chansons de geste included many stories of the Crusaders battling the Saracens (a common term for the Muslims at the time of the Crusades), and Baphomet occurs as the name of one of the gods of the Muslims. Most scholars are "generally agreed that 'Baphomet' is a [French] corruption of the name 'Mohammed,' and this is linguistically probable."[13] It is possible that the charge of worshipping Baphomet derived partly from the Templars' great regard for Muhammad, whose theology, they came to discover, closely matched their own. Karen Armstrong, in her wonderful history of Jerusalem, notes the friendships that were formed between Muslim leaders and the Templars. She tells of one particular relationship that the Templars forged with a Syrian Muslim diplomat, which illustrates the depth of the bond between Templars and Muslims:

---

*The Shroud of Turin is a controversial Catholic relic, a linen cloth that many faithful believe to be the burial shroud of Jesus, on which the faint image of a crucified man can be seen that perfectly matches the gospel accounts of how Jesus was crucified.

One of the [Muslim] diplomats . . . the Syrian prince Usamah ibn Mundiqh . . . had made friends with the Templars in Jerusalem, and whenever he visited them in the Aqsa* they put a little oratory at his disposal. One day, when he was praying facing Mecca, a Frank [Frenchman] rushed into the room, lifted Usamah into the air, and turned him forcibly toward the east: "This is the way to pray!" he exclaimed. The Templars hurried in and took the man away, but as soon as their backs were turned, the same thing happened again. The Templars were mortified. "He is a foreigner who has just arrived today from his homeland in the north," they explained, "and he has never seen anyone pray facing any direction other than east. . . ."

Increasingly the Kingdom of Jerusalem was torn by an internal conflict between those Franks who had been born in Palestine and . . . could, like the Templars in this story, understand the Muslims' point of view and wanted to establish normal relations with their neighbors; and the newcomers from Europe, who found it impossible to tolerate another religious orientation.[14]

At the very least, this story illustrates the Templars' openness to Muslim beliefs and practices.

The fact that the Templars took as their headquarters in Jerusalem the al-Aqsa Mosque and did not tear it down as a pagan shrine, but in fact renovated and expanded it, is significant. It is also significant that the mosque is directly opposite the Dome of the Rock, the third holiest site for Muslims in the world today. An interesting fact about the Dome of the Rock is that ". . . a great majority of the Arabic calligraphy that can be seen on its inside walls refers to both Muhammad and Jesus Christ, the latter being referred to as 'the Shadow of God.' The Dome of the Rock is as much dedicated to Islam as it is dedicated to Christianity, but this is Christianity in its purest form . . . where the deeds of men are remembered but where only God is worshiped."[15] As one Christian scholar puts it: "By

---

*The al-Aqsa Mosque was the main Muslim mosque the Templars had taken over for their headquarters in Jerusalem.

the time the Crusaders arrived in Jerusalem, it appears, Christians no longer cared who built the Dome of the Rock, or when it was done. What
mattered was that the temple—whether the work of Jews, Christians, or
Muslims—sat on a holy site sanctified by the Bible . . ."[16]

Just to the east of the Dome of the Rock stands the smaller "Dome
of the Chain," which the Knights Hospitaller converted into a chapel
dedicated to James the Brother of Jesus before the arrival of the Templars,
since it was known that James had been martyred not far from this
site (see plate 10).[17] Living in the midst of these Jewish, Christian, and
Muslim holy sites must have had a great spiritual impact on such devout
men as the Templars. In fact, it may be no accident that they ended up
having their headquarters on the Temple Mount. Hugh de Payens and the
founding knights may have had prior interests in the Temple Mount that
were the real reason for their coming to Jerusalem. The Templars' very
name shows their devotion to the temple, but no scholars have stopped to
ask the obvious question of why Christian monastics would be so infatu-
ated with the *Jewish* temple. The original nine knights may have gone to
Jerusalem on a spiritual quest.

THE RIDDLE OF TEMPLAR ORIGINS

Many writers have commented on the fact that the stated reason for
the creation of the Templars—patrolling and protecting the pilgrimage
route to Jerusalem—does not make sense when one takes into account
that although they would have needed to expand their ranks in order to
carry out such a task, the original nine knights made no effort to do so
until almost ten years after their founding. It also seems odd that King
Baldwin would immediately turn over his own residence at the al-Aqsa
Mosque to them upon their arrival in Jerusalem. These inconsistencies in
the traditional story of their origins have given rise to all kinds of speculation as to what the Templars were really doing. One of the most popular
alternative theories is that they were intent on finding some holy artifact,
such as the Ark of the Covenant or the Holy Grail, and conducted excavations under the site of the temple. Dr. Karen Ralls, who has written the

most evenhanded account examining all of the conflicting theories, puts it this way: "That the first nine Templar knights, during the order's initial nine years, may have been engaged in other activities besides assisting pilgrims should at least be considered, since the evidence that they were assisting pilgrims full time is as scanty as the evidence that they were digging for something."[18]

I believe we can get some clues as to the real goals of the Templars by taking a closer look at the backgrounds of the founding knights. First of all, the nine founding knights all hailed from the area of Champagne, just north of the Languedoc, and several were related to each other. "The Order thus began as very much a 'family affair' of certain old Burgundian and Flemish families, based around the area of Troyes in Champagne, originally part of Burgundy."[19] The pieces all fall into place when we realize that Burgundy was a center of Judaism in the Middle Ages. Dr. Arthur Zuckerman of the Reconstructionist Rabbinical College in Philadelphia has done extensive and detailed research showing that the area of Burgundy was a Jewish "princedom" from 768–900 CE, the only time after their expulsion from Judea in the early second century that the Jews had their own self-governed land. Zuckerman also shows that even prior to the wars with Rome, southern France had been a center of the Jewish Diaspora. According to Dr. Zuckerman a remarkable thing was happening in central and southern France in the Middle Ages:

> The primary concern of the church councils meeting in France during the sixth century seems to have been the protection of Christians against Jewish influence, rather than the restriction of Jewish rights . . . These decisions reflect the close social relations existing between Jews and Christians and a notably high status of the Jews . . . Mixed marriages were a frequent object of attack, so was conviviality generally between the two communities, which extended apparently also to the Christian clergy. . . . Several church councils report Jews even in judgeships and administrative posts. Many church canons fixed severe penalties for conversion or circumcision of Christian slaves, which speaks for the permanent nature of their service . . .[20]

The time period when the Jews had their own independent princedom in France was the time of the Carolingian Dynasty (ca. 580–876). The greatest of the Carolingian kings was Charlemagne, who founded the Holy Roman Empire in the year 800. The great influence of Judaism in Charlemagne's domain is demonstrated by the conversion of the court chaplain of Charlemagne's successor, King Louis I, to Judaism in the year 839. This explains a lot about the existence of Catharism in the area, for as Dr. Yuri Stoyanov shows over and over again in *The Other God,* in the lands where Cathars, Bogomils, and Paulicians were found, so, too, were large populations of Jews. As mentioned earlier, this Jewish influence also contributed to a Renaissance-like environment in central and southern France in the High Middle Ages, as it had in Muslim Spain. Not only did Judaism and Christianity richly interact in medieval France, but Muslim scholarship was embraced as well. Zoé Oldenbourg elaborates on the high culture of southern France:

> [T]he townships of the South attained an opulence which the North had every reason to envy. There was no comparison between Paris and Toulouse . . . imagine just how magnificent these cities must have been in their heyday—great centers of religious and cultural development, where business, industry, and every sort of craft and art flourished. The larger ones could boast schools of medicine, philosophy, mathematics, and astrology . . . At Toulouse, the course on Aristotle embodied various recent discoveries made by Arab philosophers . . .
>
> Regular contact with the Moslem world had been established very early on, mainly through the medium of Arab merchants and doctors, who reached Languedoc either from the East or across the Pyrenees [from Spain]. The infidel could no longer be regarded as a natural enemy. The Jews, who formed a large and powerful community in every major business center, were not debarred from public life . . . Their doctors and savants were held in high regard by the general populace throughout the cities of the area; they had their own schools, where they gave free courses of lectures . . . Catholic students had no objection to attending such lectures. . . . The

influence of Jewish and Moslem apocryphal writings was widespread among the clergy, and even reached the common people.[21]

Any seeming idiosyncrasies in the origin and mission of the Knights Templar make much more sense when put in the context of the environment from which their founders came. Karen Ralls points out this pertinent fact about the city that was the birthplace of the founding Templars:

> Troyes was also the birthplace of one of the most brilliant Jewish intellectuals in Western European history—Rabbi Solomon ben Isaac, affectionately known as Rabbi Rashi. He was a frequently honored guest at the court of Hughes I [Count of Champagne, 1102–1125, when the Templars were formed], a court known to have been a haven for Jews and other non-Catholics who fled persecution. Rabbi Rashi started his famed Kabbalistic school, also based at Troyes, in 1070.[22]

The Muslim Sufis,* who were found in large numbers in Spain, also migrated east and had an influence in Hughes's court:

> Following the fall of the Umayyad Spanish caliphate, a western trend of Sufism was taken to the South of France and introduced to the courts of the counts of Toulouse, who were originally dependents of the Muslim court of Cordoba. Later, that eastward trend was taken to the court of the Count of Champagne and amalgamated within the teaching of its kabbalistic school, itself an offshoot from a Jewish kabbalistic school in southern France.[23]

In sum, it would seem that the original nine Templar knights, who were all highly educated, went to the Holy Land with great respect for, and interest in, both Jews and Muslims, as well as in religious esoterica. It

---

*The Sufis, commonly known as "whirling dervishes," comprise a mystical branch of Islam that incorporates dancing and spinning into worship practice as a way of achieving mystical ecstasy and union with God.

explains why they were not at all averse to taking as their headquarters a Muslim mosque; and not only did they not raze it, but expanded it, and took a keen interest in the Temple Mount.

TEMPLAR EXCAVATIONS?

The Templars believed, as do most scholars today, that the Dome of the Rock was built over the site of the Holy of Holies of the temple, and that the al-Aqsa Mosque was built on the site of King Solomon's palace. Whether the latter is true or not, there were large underground Herodian vaults beneath the al-Aqsa Mosque that the Templars used to stable over a thousand of their horses, believing that they were Solomon's legendary stables. Here is one current scholar's assessment:

> The Crusaders considered the Haram [Arabic for the Temple Mount] a sacred place, even though the great platform had been built by a Jewish king, Herod the Great, and all its structures had been built by Muslims. Almost from the beginning of Christian rule over Jerusalem, Crusader texts and maps refer to the Dome of the Rock as the Templum Domini (Temple of the Lord) and to the Al-Aqsa Mosque as the Templum Salomonis (Temple of Solomon). This is in remarkable contrast to the earlier period of Byzantine rule, when the Christians left the Temple Mount in neglect. Why the sudden interest?[24]

The latter question is the prime question. The Templars did indeed take a great (and perhaps not sudden) interest in the Temple Mount. Perhaps their interest was tied to their ecumenical outlook:

> Construction of the Dome of the Rock in Jerusalem began in 687 CE to be finished and dedicated in 691 CE. No one had seen anything quite like it. What is not known to most Christians is that the greater part of the Arabic calligraphy on the walls mainly refers to Koranic passages relating to Jesus, so as to commemorate the

location of the city that witnessed the climax of Jesus's teaching. The Dome of the Rock not only emphasizes Islam's link to Christianity but is also concerned with reintroducing Jesus's ethnic birthright as a Jew. It is the first building with the concept of ecumenism, in which the three main spiritual faiths are celebrated as one.[25]

But the Templars' interest was assuredly not just theological or academic:

> The earliest Crusader accounts indicate that the contents of the biblical Tabernacle would soon be found within the Dome of the Rock. Fulcher of Chartes, for example, the chaplain of Jerusalem's first Crusader king, Baldwin I (1100–1118), describes the Europeans' reaction to the rock in the midst of the Temple:
>
> > "They claimed to know by divination that the Ark of the Covenant of the Lord with the urn and with the tablets of Moses were enclosed and sealed in it . . ."
>
> Other writers state that the seven golden lamps of the temple, the rod of Aaron, the altar of Jacob, the head of Zechariah, and the urn of manna were physically present in the Templum Domini.[26]

If it was generally believed that such relics were still underground waiting to be found, it is to be expected that someone with the financial resources would soon go looking.

It is interesting that while historians generally dismiss the idea that the Templars performed any excavations under the Temple Mount, archaeologists have generally accepted that they did, based on the findings of the first and only modern excavations done in that specific location. The Warren Expedition, begun in 1867 by Captain Charles Wilson of the British Royal Engineers and his chief excavator, Colonel Charles Warren, carried out the most extensive excavations under the Temple Mount that have ever been performed. Warren's team discovered remnants of a lance, a spur, a sword, and a Templar cross,[27] sure evidence the Templars at least explored old shafts and cisterns under the Temple Mount, whether or not they did their own actual digging.

In 1968 noted Israeli archaeologist Meir Ben-Dov was able to revisit Warren's work. He writes the following about a long tunnel that some writers call the "Templar tunnel," because it has an entrance outside the Temple Mount and goes directly underneath Solomon's stables:

> The tunnel leads inward for a distance of about thirty meters from the southern wall before being blocked by pieces of stone debris. We know that it continues further, but we had made it a hard-and-fast rule not to excavate within the bounds of the Temple Mount, which is currently under Moslem jurisdiction. . . . The tunnel was indeed built by the Crusaders . . . the Temple Mount served as military headquarters for the Templars.[28]

It is not known how far this tunnel extends. All that can be said with certainty is that if the tunnel continues in a straight line it does indeed pass directly beneath the Dome of the Rock.

It is certainly fun to speculate as to all manner of things that the Templars might have found during their time at the Temple Mount, and the writing of books on such speculation has become a bit of a cottage industry. It is my own feeling that the Templars probably found next to nothing in the way of treasures from the temple, since we know from the famous bas-relief carved on the Roman Arch of Titus that the Romans had already helped themselves to all the valuable artifacts. If the Templars found anything of historical importance, it may have been in the form of scrolls and codices. In the light of the many serendipitous, accidental manuscript discoveries in the last century, it is not at all unlikely that the Templars, if they indeed engaged in excavations, may have found buried manuscripts. And if they found anything akin to the Dead Sea Scrolls or Gnostic writings, this could only have furthered their already heretical theological notions. It is a fact that the Templars were in possession of religious relics, as most monastic communities were. They carried a purported piece of the "true cross" into battle with them, and were in possession of the head of St. Euphemia, which may have been a source of the charges that they worshipped a disembodied head, though we now know that this charge likely came from them having the Shroud of Turin, which may have been folded up to only show the head.

TEMPLAR BUILDERS AND MASONS

With their extensive financial resources, the Templars financed numerous building projects in the Holy Land and throughout Europe, many of which are still standing. Pope Innocent II granted the Templars the right to build their own churches in 1139. Characteristic of their building design are round churches, built to resemble the Church of the Holy Sepulchre in Jerusalem, where it is traditionally believed that Jesus was crucified and buried. They also built octagonal-shaped buildings, which, it has rarely been noted, were likely patterned on the famous octagonal shape of the Dome of the Rock. The Templars enlisted master craftsmen and masons in their renovations of the al-Aqsa Mosque and "the craftsmanship was of a high standard. The sculpture in particular, with a characteristic 'wet-leaf' patterning, shows an imaginative blend of Byzantine, Islamic, and Romanesque style."[29] A German monk by the name of Theodoric was an eyewitness to the splendor of the Templars' work. In 1174 he wrote: "On the other side of the [Mosque], the Templars have built a new house, whose height, length, and breadth, and all its cellars and refectories, staircase, and roof, are far beyond the custom of this land. Indeed its roof is so high that, if I were to mention how high it is, those who listen would hardly believe me."[30] Unfortunately, this magnificent building was destroyed by the Muslims during renovations on the Temple Mount in the 1950s.

While many historians reject the notion that the Templars were themselves trained masons or builders (believing that they always hired construction workers), it is a fact that the Templars had their own sub-order of mason brothers, as evidenced in their Rule Number 325: "No brother should wear leather gloves, except the chaplain brother . . . And the mason brothers may wear them sometimes, and it is permitted them because of the great suffering they endure and so that they do not easily injure their hands; but they should not wear them when they are not working."[31] This clearly belies the claims of some modern skeptics who deny that the Templars built anything themselves. It also gives us our first evidence of a link with the later brotherhood of Freemasons.

In chapter 7 we discussed the building on Mt. Zion known as the Cenacle, or upper room, which was the synagogue and headquarters of the Nazarenes (the Jerusalem Church). What is little recognized is that the existing building is entirely the work of the Templars, who obviously took a great interest in this site. As Father Bargil Pixner explains:

Once the Crusaders arrived in Jerusalem, they found that a Byzantine church called Hagia Sion (Holy Zion) on today's Mt. Zion . . . had been destroyed. In a better-preserved annex south of the church, they discovered what has been identified as David's tomb . . .

For the Crusaders, however, David's tomb was less important than another tradition, that this sanctuary was a site associated with . . . the Last Supper.[32]

On the south part of the ruins of the Hagia Sion, the Crusaders built a new church, which they named St. Mary of Mt. Zion, in memory of the tradition that Mary had lived on Mt. Zion after the resurrection . . . and had also died there. . . .

Thus it was the Crusaders who first included the walls of the ancient Judeo-Christian synagogue, which had become the Church of the Apostles, into their own basilica.

Above the remaining walls of the Church of the Apostles, the Crusaders built a second floor, which may have been the actual site of the upper room. This room is still visited today by Christian pilgrims. . . .

When the Crusaders were forced to leave Jerusalem after their defeat at the Horns of Hattin near Tiberias in 1187 CE, they entrusted their church on Mt. Zion to Syrian Christians.[33]

It is interesting that the Templars entrusted the church to Syrian Christians. Why? It is likely not coincidence that Syria had been one of the centers of Jewish Christianity, and the Templars were probably aware of the Jewish Christian nature of this important building. The Muslims were also obviously aware of the importance of this building, for they would later take it over and basically leave it as the Crusaders had renovated it, except for the addition of a *mihrab,* a niche on the south wall indicating the direction of Mecca (see plate 13). It is thus obvious that the Muslims held prayer services in this *Christian* building!

It could be objected that it was not the Templars but the Knights Hospitaller who conducted these renovations, as they were also known to have been present on Mt. Zion. I believe I can demonstrate that it was indeed the Templars. In the picture section I have included photos that I took in the summer of 2008 of Crusader carvings on the walls and ceiling of the Cenacle (see plates 15–18). On the ceiling apses are two medallions carved with symbols associated with the Templars—the Agnus Dei, depicting Jesus as the victorious Lamb of God; and the Lion of Judah, a symbol of Jesus's Jewish ancestry. On the walls I also found faint, but clearly recognizable pieces of Crusader graffiti: two roughly carved shields, one showing crossed battle axes, the other a shield that shows a coat of arms very similar to that of Jacques de Molay, the last Templar grand master. Individually, these carvings could be associated with other crusading orders, but in combination the odds increase that they are Templar in origin.

THE TEMPLARS AND THE GRAIL

It is titillating to speculate about interesting finds the Templars may have made as they conducted renovations on the most sacred site of the upper room. Karen Armstrong notes one significant discovery that has been recorded: "While they were restoring this chapel, the Crusaders made a discovery that they did not know quite how to deal with. One of the old walls fell in to reveal a cave, containing a golden crown and scepter."[34] Could this have been a relic of James or Symeon? I leave it to the reader to conjecture. Recall that the Armenian Cathedral of St. James is just around the corner from the Cenacle, which the Armenian Christians claim was built over James's house, where they claim James's body is buried under the main altar, and where they have a replica of the throne of James.

While we are speculating, it is also interesting to consider that if the legendary Holy Grail were to be found anywhere, it would not be buried beneath the Temple Mount, but surely here at the site of the upper room. There was great interest in the Holy Grail myth during the Crusader era, and the Grail was already associated with the Templars in the twelfth century. The first Grail romance, *Le Conte du Graal,* was written in 1180 by Chrétien de Troyes. Note well the author's name—Chrétien came from the same area as the nine founding Templars. In another of the famed Grail romances, *Parzival,* Wolfram von Eschenbach speaks of the Templars guarding the Grail Kingdom. Based on these popular stories, the legend developed that during their sojourn in Jerusalem the Templars must have excavated for relics, found the Grail, and then protected this greatest of all secrets and holiest of all relics with their lives.

And now we turn to another group that has its roots in the building trades and who are best known in the public mind today for their keeping of secrets—the brotherhood of Freemasons. I believe that it is not just coincidence that both the Knights Templar and the brotherhood of Freemasons are rooted in, and centered on, the Jerusalem Temple. So, too, were James the Brother of Jesus and the Nazarenes.

14

FROM JESUS TO FREEMASONRY

The Founding Fathers and the Building of a New Jerusalem

I have other sheep that do not belong to this fold. I must bring them also . . .

JESUS (JOHN 10:16)

While I am not myself a Freemason, I have had a longstanding interest in Freemasonry and have done quite a bit of research into its historical origins over the past twenty-five years. I have come to the conclusion that there is a definite link between the theology of earliest Jewish Christianity and the rituals and teachings of Freemasonry. I posit that Freemasonry has somehow preserved in its rituals and teachings the core essence of Nazarene and Ebionite theology.*

---

*In this chapter I am most indebted to the assistance of Master Mason Brian Fegely for the supporting evidence he shared with me of the ideas I am putting forth in this chapter.[1] Brian and I are in disagreement, however, on how original Jewish Christianity evolved into Freemasonry. Brian is completely disdainful of any link between the Knights Templar and Freemasonry, while I personally believe strongly that the Templars are the prime connecting link.

MASONIC THEOLOGY

One of the most obvious pieces of evidence for my claim is that, for a group that was founded by Christians and still today has a large Christian majority, belief in the divinity of Jesus is not a requirement. There is nothing in Masonic ritual that a Jew or Muslim would find offensive. In fact, Freemasonry is one of only a few international organizations that welcomes people of all religions. The *only* requirement to be a Freemason is that one believe in a Supreme Being.* However, one is never asked to declare what his particular beliefs about the Supreme Being are. The Supreme Being can be understood as Jesus by a Christian, Allah by a Muslim, or Brahman by a Hindu. In its rituals and writings Freemasonry refers to God in neutral terminology as the Great Architect of the Universe.

A "volume of the sacred law" is always among the standard furnishings of a Masonic lodge room, and while this is commonly the Bible, in lodges with members of other religions, it is not uncommon to have scriptures of other religions placed alongside the Bible. A lodge is the basic organizational unit of Freemasonry. Blue Lodges, also known as "Craft Lodges," confer the three basic degrees of Freemasonry—Apprentice, Fellow Craft, and Master Mason. It is interesting that Masonic lodges have also been commonly referred to as Masonic "temples."

Today there are approximately five million Freemasons in the world and Freemasonry is found in almost every nation, though it is telling that Freemasonry is outlawed in many Muslim nations for being a Zionist organization. Some radical Muslims argue that Freemasonry promotes Jewish interests and that one of its aims is to destroy the al-Aqsa Mosque so that the Temple of Solomon can be rebuilt.[2]

The generally accepted definition of Freemasonry among Freemasons is that it is "a system of morality veiled in allegory and illustrated by symbols." In pursuit of this ideal, Freemasonry, which is commonly referred to by Freemasons as "the craft," uses the symbols of masons' tools, such

---

*This requirement has gone by the wayside in some branches of European Freemasonry, such as French Freemasonry, where atheists can become members.

as the square and compass, in an allegorical retelling of the story of the building of King Solomon's Temple that is meant to inculcate the building of straight and upright moral character. In Freemasonry, as in Jewish Christianity, deeds are more important than any particular expression of faith. "What good is it . . . if you say you have faith but do not have works? Can faith save you?" (James 2:14).

Many times in recent decades, Masonic leaders, in response to charges and accusations against the lodge, have denied that Freemasonry is a religion and emphatically stated that it is not a substitute for religion. But as a professor of religion, I can categorically state that Freemasonry clearly meets every criteria of the definition of a religion (at least a Western religion). Freemasonry requires belief in a Supreme Being, has a set of rituals designed to cultivate the improvement of the morals of its followers, and provides a way to attain salvation of one's soul (there is a clear belief in resurrection expressed in the primary rituals of the first three degrees of the Blue Lodge). One of the most popular Masonic writers today, Dr. Robert Lomas, after exploring the origins and meaning of Freemasonry in a number of bestselling books, has concluded that the primary purpose of Masonic ritual is to enable the participant to come to grips with the ultimate questions of life and death: "After a long and interesting journey, I have now arrived at a surprising conclusion. I believe that Freemasonry has preserved one of the oldest religious stories . . . a myth that dramatizes the idea that death is a part of life, and is something that humans must learn to accept."[3] Lomas also says that this is the ultimate purpose of Masonic ritual: "Over the ages, the Craft has evolved and refined its ritual forms to help its followers find answers to such questions [as] . . . how we should react to the knowledge of our own inevitable death, and what is the purpose of life?"[4]

The first question a new candidate is asked in the entrance ritual for the first degree of Masonry is this: "In whom do you put your trust?" The prescribed and only accepted answer is: "In God." To answer "Jesus" would not be acceptable. The candidate is later asked by the worshipful master, "From whence come you, and whither are you traveling?" At this point the senior deacon answers for the candidate, "From the west, and traveling toward the east." The worshipful master then asks, "Why leave you the west and travel toward the east?" The prescribed answer is, "In search of light."[5] It is interesting that the Letter of James refers to God as the "Father of lights, with whom there is no variation or shadow due to change" (James 1:17); and the favorite gospel of the Cathars, the Gospel of John, calls Jesus "the true light" (John 1:9). The questions and answers that are the first part of Masonic initiation exhibit Jewish Christian and gnostic theology, not necessarily orthodox Christian theology.

But how did Jewish Christian theology make its way into Freemasonry? I believe it came through the Knights Templar, who had been uniquely exposed to both Cathar and Muslim theology. We have seen how a gnostic form of Jewish Christian theology came to be preserved in Catharism and how this may have influenced the Knights Templar. I believe the main connecting link between the Nazarenes, the Templars, and Freemasonry is the Jewish temple. The temple was the focal point of the Nazarene community under James. The temple was where the Nazarenes continued to worship, and it is where James was martyred. The temple remained the center of Nazarene worship not only because of its historical and religious significance, but especially because it was the site of the expected Parousia of Messiah Jesus.

THE TEMPLE AND THE LODGE

One obvious connection between the Templars and Freemasonry is that the original group of nine crusader knights from France called themselves "The Poor Fellow-Soldiers of Christ and of *the Temple of Solomon*." All Masonic ritual is centered on the building of Solomon's Temple, allegorized as a spiritual temple. In Masonic ritual and symbolism the *pillars* of the Temple play a central role. I do not believe it is coincidence that James, Peter, and John were referred to, even by Paul, who was often at odds with them, as the "pillar apostles" (Galatians 2:9). Speaking of Paul, one of his major goals, as we saw, was to take up a collection for "the poor" in Jerusalem, a self-designation of the Nazarenes. The Templars called themselves the "*Poor Fellow-Soldiers of Christ*." Freemasons also call themselves "fellows" and have a great interest in helping the poor through their many charities.

It would seem that the original nine Templars, all from the area of Troyes, were not granted a base at the site of Solomon's Temple on a whim. As we saw, Troyes was the birthplace of one of the most brilliant Jewish intellectuals in European history, Rabbi Solomon ben Isaac, who was frequently an honored guest at the court of Hughes I—a court that was a haven for Jews and non-Catholics fleeing persecution. The Jews had previously had their own princedom in this very area. Just to the south, the Languedoc, home of the Cathars, would become one of the main bases of the Templars after their return from Palestine. Based on all of this circumstantial evidence, I believe it is possible that the Templars originally went to Jerusalem with an agenda to find records and relics of Jesus's family and the Nazarenes. It is interesting that the ritual of the branch of Freemasonry known as the Holy Royal Arch, which we shall discuss shortly, centers around the finding of a precious object beneath the Holy of Holies. As we have seen, there is solid archaeological evidence that the Templars explored tunnels under the Temple, and may have done their own tunneling.

Not long after their establishment in Jerusalem, the Templars quickly became the wealthiest and most powerful group in medieval Europe after the Church of Rome. While it was their power and wealth that led to their ultimate demise, it was something else too—*claims of heresy*—which are a matter of historical record. As we saw, while fighting the Muslims, the Templars also enjoyed good relations with them and became enamored of their advanced culture and learning. Additionally, the Muslims have a Jewish Christian understanding of Jesus, due to Muhammad's contact with Ebionites in Arabia.

Finally, the legendary first Freemason, Hiram Abiff, who plays a central role in Masonic ritual, was killed with a blow to the head at the Temple. One version of the death of James says that he was clubbed on the head after being pushed from the pinnacle of the Temple. These are just some of the many curious links between the Nazarenes, the Templars, and the Freemasons. While there are clearly many theological links between Jewish Christianity and Masonic ritual, the main obstacle one faces in forging a link *historically* between the first-century Nazarenes and modern Freemasonry is the problem of the "chain of transmission." How do you get from a first-century movement in Palestine to a movement that (ostensibly) began in eighteenth-century Europe?

THE MYSTERY OF MASONIC ORIGINS

I think it is obvious that Freemasonry did not just appear out of thin air, fully formed, when the Grand Lodge of England was established on June 24, 1717, and publicly announced its existence, which is generally considered the official beginning of Freemasonry. The Grand Lodges of Ireland and Scotland were established in 1725 and 1736, respectively, and the Grand Orient de France in 1728. While these dates are generally accepted as the official commencement of Freemasonry in Europe, obviously there had to have been predecessor bodies. How else can one explain these various lodges arising at almost the same time in different locales? It is a fact that the Templars had bases in all these locales.

According to the standard history accepted by most Masons today, Freemasonry arose from obscure and murky beginnings in the late-sixteenth to early-seventeenth centuries in Scotland and England. Historical records indicate that there were proto-Masonic lodges in Scotland in the late-1500s and in England in the mid-1600s. A poem known as the "Regius Manuscript" is generally considered to be the first Masonic document, and it has been dated around 1390. It is called one of the "Old Charges" or "Gothic Constitutions" of the Masons from the time when they were a craft guild. Modern Freemasonry is called "speculative" Masonry to distinguish it from original "operative" Masonry. According to Masonic tradition, medieval stonemasons met and shared meals in a "lodge" at a building site.

Although many competing claims have been made, no one is precisely sure how Freemasonry began. One of the most authoritative volumes that has ever been written—*The Craft,* by John Hamill, librarian and curator of the United Grand Lodge Library and Museum in London—opens with these words: "When, why, and where did Freemasonry originate? There is one answer to these questions: We do not know, despite all the paper and ink that has been expended in examining them."[6] Some Freemasons, mostly in earlier times, have claimed that the roots of Freemasonry are to be found in the masons who built King Solomon's Temple, a claim that is rejected by all Masonic historians today.

There are currently two competing theories regarding the historical origins of Freemasonry. The first asserts that the Masons evolved out of the Knights Templar. Officially, Freemasonry has increasingly distanced itself from this claim, perhaps out of embarrassment. The generally accepted theory among most Freemasons today, and certainly the one accepted by almost all historians, is that Freemasonry is an outgrowth of the medieval trade guilds. Here is a succinct summary of what can be called the "standard theory":

> [I]n the Middle Ages guilds were predominant in many trades, serving as a combination of union, technical school, benevolent society, and guarantor of professional standards. Because the medieval world was focused on the sacred, the guilds had a spiritual element as well; they resembled religious fraternities. Some of them, including the trade guilds of France, known as the *compagnonnages,* even transmitted a kind of initiatic wisdom.
>
> The Masons were among these guilds. They differed from most guilds in [that] . . . the nature of their work ensured that masons would spend more time traveling from job to job than would men of most trades. This made it necessary to create certain signs and words by which a mason could make himself known in a strange city.[7]

On the surface this would seem to provide a logical answer to the question of Masonic origins, but there are some serious and insurmountable problems with it. The first is the purported need for secret signs and words to recognize a fellow mason. Surely a skilled mason could demonstrate his skill and knowledge at any job site anywhere, or simply carry written references. The need for secret signs and words in a medieval trade guild makes little sense. How could one ensure that they would be universally recognized? What umbrella organization could standardize them? In addition, why would stonemasons have the need for secret oaths in which they ask for the most bloodcurdling things to come upon themselves if they reveal the secrets with which they have been entrusted? The nature of these infamous oaths, which are an integral part of Masonic ritual, has become one of the prime areas of criticism by those opposed to Freemasonry.

The need to keep secret the various signs (gestures), handshakes (grips), and code words of each degree of Freemasonry is referred to as the Masonic "obligations." One must know them to gain admittance to a lodge of which one is not a member. All Masons are required to take oaths that they will not reveal these secrets under risk of some truly gruesome penalties. While these penalties are considered symbolic and have never to anyone's knowledge been applied, it is rather curious that they exist at all. Here is part of the oath that the candidate for the first degree of Entered Apprentice recites:

> I . . . most solemnly and sincerely promise and swear that I will always hail, ever conceal, and never reveal any of the arts, parts, or points of the hidden mysteries of ancient Free Masonry . . . binding myself under no less penalty than that of having my throat cut across, my tongue torn out by its roots, and my body buried in the rough sands of the sea, at low water mark, where the tide ebbs and flows twice in twenty-four hours, should I ever knowingly violate this my Entered Apprentice obligation.[8]

In the second degree of Freemasonry, that of Fellow Craft, one variation of the penalty invoked is this: ". . . binding myself under no less penalty than of having my breast torn open, my heart plucked out and placed on the highest pinnacle of the temple, there to be devoured by the vultures of the air . . ."[9] Two items of note here: first, *James was thrown to his death from the pinnacle of the temple.* Second, *Solomon's* Temple, which is the temple invoked over and over again in Masonic ritual, *did not have any pinnacles;* but the *second* temple (Herod's Temple) did. It was Herod's Temple, not Solomon's Temple, that the Knights Templar were familiar with and, as we shall see, it is actually Herod's Temple that is being described in Masonic ritual and symbol.

The prime question we must ask about the bloody penalties invoked *in the earliest stages* of Masonic initiation is simply: Why? Why the need? The need for secrets signs and words and bloodcurdling oaths makes no sense for a trade guild, but it certainly does for a group with heretical beliefs who are in fear for their life and on the lam from the Catholic Church, as the Templars were.

Most historians have simply assumed that any remaining Templars who had been freed from prison, or never arrested, were absorbed into their rival organization, the Knights Hospitaller. The Hospitallers were granted legal rights to all Templar properties that had not been taken over by government fiat, and indeed, some Templars did join their old rivals. But certainly not all. Noted historian Edward Burman presents the following eye-opening facts:

> [H]ow many of the 14 or 15,000 Templars of all ranks . . . were given their freedom after Pope Clement's 1312 constitution? How many had survived Philip the Fair's onslaught? The answer must be: most of them. Thousands. Retellings of the legend often give the impression that *all* members of the Order of the Temple died between 1307 and 1312, or were at least imprisoned for life. The truth was quite different . . . Ironically, there is no need to fabricate stories of dramatic escapes or local survivals in order to sustain continuation myths. There really were a lot of ex-Templars around: some repentant, some camouflaged, and some still proud of their own and the Order's past—like many old soldiers.[10]

That such a widespread and powerful group as the Templars would not have made some concerted effort to continue meeting and to preserve their traditions is inconceivable to me. The ongoing underground existence of the Templars after their official dissolution has been historically established by a remarkable amateur historian, the late John J. Robinson, in his bestselling book, *Born in Blood*. Here is Robinson's summation at the end of his book:

We have seen that there are only two organizations that have found their principal identifications in the Temple of Solomon: Freemasonry and the Crusading Order of the Temple. The great mass of circumstantial evidence has clearly indicated that the common identification was no mere coincidence, but rather that the secret organization was born in the ashes of the public organization that had been condemned by both the church and state in an era of the most brutal bodily punishments. The only way the hunted Templars could continue to stay in contact with each other and help each other was in the darkest secrecy. That state of secrecy required no great adaptation for the Templars, to whom secrecy was part of their vows and of their Rule. Every Templar was subject to swift punishment if he revealed any portion of the Rule of the Order, or any part of the proceedings of their chapter meetings, which were kept secret by means of guards stationed outside the meeting room, their swords at the ready.[11]

To this day, whenever a lodge meeting is held, an officer called the "Tyler" guards the door and examines visitors. The term "Tyler" likely comes from the French *tailleur,* whence comes the English word "tailor." In French, tailleur literally means "cutter" (of cloth). In French Freemasonry there is a legend of a man named Maitre Jacques Le Tailleur de Pierre, who was one of the architects of Solomon's Temple. Pierre is French for Peter, and recall that Jesus gave this name to the apostle Simon as a nickname that means "rock" (*petros,* in Greek). Jacques is James in English. So Maitre Jacques Le Tailleur de Pierre literally translates as "Master James the cutter of rock." Master James was a mason!*[12] Further, the Old Testament says that the two main pillars at the entrance of Solomon's Temple were called Jachin and Boaz, and were built by King Hiram of Tyre (1 Kings 7:13–21). These two pillars are found in all Masonic lodges. Boaz means "strength" and Jachin means "founding." Is it coincidence that Jesus's brother James

---

*It is interesting that in the New Testament, while Jesus and his father are called "carpenters" (Mark 6:3, Matt. 13:55), the Greek word is *tekton,* which can also be translated as "builder" or "mason." Jesus and Joseph may have been workers in stone rather than wood.

was the founder and one of the "pillars" of the Jerusalem Church? It is also a fact that many of these double pillars were built by the Templars on the Temple Mount, as one scholar of the Holy Land notes:

> One pervasive motif used by the Crusader sculptors is the braided double column. This motif, which is found in both Byzantine and Romanesque art, was associated with the bronze pillars, called Jachin and Boaz, that Solomon erected at the portal of the first Temple . . . Many pairs of such columns appear as spolia* in the extant gates and fountains of the Haram [Temple Mount]. These braided columns were probably used as supports for cloisters on the Temple Mount, perhaps . . . the Templars' court at the Templum Salomonis. Their association with King Solomon . . . asserted the Christians' claim to be legitimate successors of ancient Israel.[13]

Not all of this circumstantial evidence linking the Templars with Freemasonry can simply be coincidence. Although the majority of Masonic scholars shun the idea, after twenty-five years of research, the explanation of Masonic origins that makes the most logical sense to me—because it ties together the most loose ends—is the Templar theory. I have come to believe that the majority of Masonic historians are in denial of this because so many legends and hysterical claims have accrued around the Templars and Freemasonry, and Masonic leaders yearn to have their fraternity taken seriously by academics.

Those who scoff at any link between the Templars and Freemasonry point to the seemingly insurmountable gap of four hundred years that exists between the time of the Templar suppression in 1307 and the founding of the Grand Lodge of England in 1717. But the gap is not as large as it seems. It is accepted that proto-lodges existed in Scotland in the late-1500s and that proto-Masonic documents existed in the late fourteenth century, so the gap can be narrowed to less than a century. John J. Robinson also points to an enigmatic event in English history that deci-

---

*Spolia refers to reused materials from a former structure.

sively suggests ongoing underground activity of the Knights Templar—the Peasant's Rebellion of 1381:

> It may seem that there is a great leap from the Templar suppression in 1307 to the public revelation of Freemasonry in 1717, with no evidence of any Masonic existence within that four-hundred-year span, but that is not true. Evidence does exist, but since no historian even suspected a Masonic connection, much of that evidence has been passed over . . . Consider . . . the Peasant's Rebellion of 1381, with its hints of Masonry and its Templar-related mysteries, such as the concentration of the vicious attacks on the property of the Hospitallers; the incredibly easy seizure of the Tower of London for no known purpose but the murders of the archbishop of Canterbury and the prior of the Hospitaller order; the special protection of the central Templar Church as the rebels burned down all the buildings around it. Then there is the haunting evidence of rebel leaders who confessed to being members of a Great Society, which no historian has ever attempted to define. Once the origin of Masonry in the fugitive Templars' secret society is accepted, it is easy to conclude that the Great Society . . . was the direct descendant of the Templar fugitives and the predecessor of the secret society of Freemasonry.[14]

Robinson also points to another telling connection between the Templars and Freemasonry:

> Another [Masonic] mystery that found a solution in the Order of the Temple was the "clothing" of Freemasonry. The primary item, of course, is the Masonic apron, the first item received by the Entered Apprentice at his initiation . . . in ancient Masonry . . . [it] was an untrimmed white lambskin tied around the waist. This lambskin has been proclaimed by Masonry to be a badge of innocence and purity . . .
>
> . . . It may be remembered that [the Templar] Rule forbade any personal decoration except sheepskin, and further required that the

Templar wear a sheepskin girdle about his waist at all times as a reminder of his vow of chastity . . .[15]

Today, many different symbols and decorations may be sewn onto the Masonic apron. One with particular significance as a link with the Templars is the *tau* cross,* worn on the aprons of those Masons who have progressed to the Royal Arch branch of Freemasonry (see plate 20).

THE HOLY ROYAL ARCH

Technically, there is no degree in Freemasonry higher than that of the Master Mason, the third degree. There are, however, "appendant bodies" that confer other degrees, the best-known of which is the Scottish Rite, in which one can progress up to the thirty-third degree. These are not considered higher degrees, but supplementary to the Master Mason degree. One appendant body that has interesting connections to the Knights Templar is the Holy Royal Arch, which, in some countries, is part of the "York Rite."

In England in 1751, a rival body to the Grand Lodge, with ties to the lodges of Ireland and Scotland, called itself the Ancient Grand Lodge of England. The "Ancients" claimed to preserve older traditions than the Grand Lodge, one of which was the Holy Royal Arch, the full formal title of which is: "The United Religious, Military and Masonic Orders of the Temple of St. John of Jerusalem, Palestine, Rhoades and Malta." The Holy Royal Arch, usually shortened to simply "Royal Arch," is the most widespread of the higher degrees of Freemasonry in the world, and is often called the "completion of the Master Mason degree."[16] The rituals of the Royal Arch revolve around the rebuilding of Solomon's Temple following the Babylonian Exile. There is also an offshoot of the Royal Arch called "Cryptic Masonry," which deals with the legends of a crypt discovered under

---

*Tau is the nineteenth letter of the Greek alphabet. It resembles a T, usually with expanded ends and base. Some scholars believe this was the actual shape of the cross on which Jesus was crucified.

Solomon's Temple during its rebuilding. Some researchers have claimed that the rituals of Royal Arch and Cryptic Masonry are reenactments of the most important discovery of the Templars—the finding of scrolls when they excavated under the Temple Mount.[17]

What is most intriguing about the Royal Arch branch of Freemasonry is its main symbol—three interconnecting tau crosses. The tau cross is believed by some scholars to be the actual shape of the cross on which Jesus was crucified, rather than the traditional Latin or Christian cross. But what is most significant for a connection between Freemasonry and the Knights Templar is that the shape of Herod's Temple (not the original Temple of Solomon) is a tau (see plate 35).[18] And again, it is *Herod's* Temple with which the Templars were most acquainted. Karen Ralls make this interesting observation:

> Supporters of the theory that Gothic architecture may have had Templar origins—or, at the very least, input—point out that shortly after the Templars returned from the Holy Land (in late 1127), an extraordinary transformation began to take place in Europe. In addition to the Gothic cathedrals beginning to appear in France, some of the Templars' own buildings had interesting architectural designs. The plan of the Temple Church in London, for instance, is based on the Tau cross. . .[19]

It is also interesting that Freemasons who are part of the Holy Royal Arch are also eligible to join the Knights Templar branch of Freemasonry. It is a fact that already in the 1700s this branch of Freemasonry identified itself with the original Templars and began to incorporate their symbols and legends into its rituals. The Knights Templar are one of a number of Masonic bodies that today call themselves "commemorative orders," and while they officially disclaim any actual descent from the original Knights Templar, many of the members of this order do believe otherwise. In the United States there is even a youth organization for children of Freemasons called the Order of DeMolay, named after the martyred Templar grand master, Jacques de Molay.

BUILDING A BRIDGE

There is, finally, one other pertinent fact that requires explanation: How does one explain the fact that Freemasonry arises in so many different places in Europe (Ireland, Scotland, England, and France) at almost exactly the same time? It is a fact that the Templars had bases in all these places. And it is also a fact that one of the main occupations of the Templars wherever they existed following their return from the Crusades was the construction of buildings, especially churches.

In the two main theories of Masonic origins—the standard theory and the Templar theory—perhaps the truth, as always, lies somewhere in the middle. The origins of Freemasonry *are* to be found in the medieval trade guilds; and the roots of the medieval trade guilds are to be found largely in the construction projects sponsored and financed by the Knights Templar. This is the main thesis of what I have found to be the best academic book ever written on the origins of Freemasonry—*The Secret History of Freemasonry: Its Origins and Connection to the Knights Templar,* by Paul Naudon. Originally published in France in 1991, this book was little known in English-speaking countries until recently, because it was only translated into English in 2005. Naudon is in a unique position to write about the origins of Freemasonry because he is a law scholar and a high-ranking Freemason, having held the positions of grand prior of the Gauls (Rectified Scottish Rite) and state minister for the supreme council of the ancient and accepted Scottish Rite.* By utilizing church records of medieval Paris, Naudon conclusively shows that the vast majority of medieval stonemasons lived and worked on Templar properties. In fact, he says, "[T]here are no profound traces of masons and carpenters having settled *outside* the boundaries of the [Templars'] former jurisdiction."[20] (Italics mine.)

Naudon also demonstrates that the ultimate roots of Freemasonry can be traced back as far as the Roman *collegia*—colleges of artisans that existed in many parts of the world, including Arabia. Here are Naudon's main points:

---

*Though called the Scottish Rite, this branch of Freemasonry has its origin in France.

From a chronological perspective, the most certain sources of Freemasonry have emerged as the following:

1. The Roman *collegia,* the remnants of which remained in the West following invasions and survived in the East as institutions discovered by the Crusaders at the end of the eleventh century.
2. The ecclesiastical associations of builders formed by the bishops of the Early Middle Ages, especially the Benedictines, the Cistercians, and the Templars.
3. Trade-based freemasonry, which was born under the aegis of these associations and followed the form of lay brotherhoods or guilds.[21]

Naudon notes that these collegia of builders and craftsmen were quite numerous in the parts of France from which the original Templars hailed.[22] This would explain the Templars' great interest in sponsoring construction projects, and why so many of their buildings are found in France. "From the twelfth century on [the Templars] were involved with the organization of lay communities of builders that enjoyed specific franchises, earning them the name *francs métiers* [free craftsmen] . . ."[23] Templar-sponsored building associations became very attractive: "In this insecure time, tradesmen flocked to the [Templar] commanderies, where, in addition to its powerful protection, the Temple offered to its operatives considerable advantages, including the right of asylum, the right of franchise, and fiscal privileges."[24]

Naudon does make an emphatic disclaimer, however: "It should be clearly stated . . . that this does not mean I believe modern "speculative" Freemasonry is a direct survival of this vanished Order [of the Templars]."[25] What Naudon is saying is that while the building projects of the Templars gave rise to the trade guilds of "operative" masons that would in turn give rise to modern "speculative" Freemasonry, there is no *direct* bridge from the Templars to Freemasonry. This is a point that needs to be emphasized in regard to the entire enterprise of this book: There is no *direct* connection between the Nazarenes, with whom this book started, and the Cathars, Knights Templar, and Freemasons. However, as I hope I have demonstrated in these pages, there are indisputable *theological* connections between these groups for which there must be indirect historical connections. For the past two thousand years an underground stream of alternative Christian belief has ebbed and flowed, branched and twisted, and risen to the surface at various times in often surprising ways. That stream still continues to flow.

Finally, Paul Naudon shows that trade guilds were also to be found in the Muslim world, specifically in an offshoot of the Shi'ite sect called the Karmates:

> . . . Karmatism is characterized by the organization of labor and groups of workers into professional corporations . . . which seem to have been in existence since the tenth century and were connected with religious brotherhoods . . .
>
> The kinship of these professional brotherhoods with the Christianized collegia of the late Roman Empire is obvious. *Among their members could be found not only Arabs but converts—mainly Christians and Jews. . . .*
>
> The Karmati movement . . . stands out both religiously and philosophically in its introduction to Islam of basic foreign . . . elements *through an esoteric method of initiation based on reason, tolerance, and equality . . . the Karmates facilitated ties among all races and castes.*[26] (Italics mine.)

It is this universalism, the desire for unity, that we have encountered over and over again in all the Jewish Christian sects we have studied in these pages—in the Nazarenes, Ebionites, Elkesaites, Cathars, Templars, and ultimately in Freemasonry. It is quite fascinating that this desire for universal unity and brotherhood has been at the core of Freemasonry ever since its inception.

A leader of early French Freemasonry, Chevalier Andrew Michael Ramsey has been a source of much controversy in Freemasonry due to a speech he gave in 1737, which is the earliest assertion that Freemasonry is descended from the Templars. While most Freemasons dismiss Ramsey's claim as his own fabrication, what is not commented on very often are some of his other statements, which, for the time, were far more controversial. The following is a summation of Ramsey's main points, which he made at the age of seventy:

1. The Crusaders created the Order of Freemasonry in the Holy Land during the period of the Christian Wars in Palestine.
2. Its objective was to unite the individuals of every nation and to restore the temple in the city of Jerusalem and maintain and extend the true religion there.
3. The Masonic mystery is a continuation of the old religion of Noah and the patriarchs.[27]

It is the universalism of the latter two statements that is remarkable. While Ramsey's claim that the Crusaders created Freemasonry can be dismissed, there is indeed a remarkable universalism found in the Knights Templar branch of Freemasonry. Consider the following statements made in the ritual of Templar Masonry:

No man truly obeys the Masonic law who merely tolerates those whose religious opinions are opposed to his own. Every man's opinions are his own private property, and the rights of all men to maintain each his own are perfectly equal. Merely to tolerate, to bear with an opposing opinion, is to assume it to be heretical and assert the right to persecute, if we would, and claim our [tolerance] as merit.

The Mason's creed goes further than that; no man, it holds, has any right, in any way, to interfere with the religious belief of another. It holds that each man is absolutely sovereign as to his own belief . . . Masonry is the handmaid of religion. The Brahmin, the Jew, the Mahometan, the Catholic, the Protestant—each professing his peculiar religion, sanctioned by the laws, by time, and by climate— may retain [his] faith, and may yet be [a Mason].

Masonry teaches, and has preserved in their purity, the cardinal tenets of the old primitive faith . . . [that] are the foundation of all religions. Masonry is the universal morality which is suitable to the inhabitants of every clime—to the man of every creed. . . .[28]

These are remarkably inclusive statements, especially for the time at which they were written. It is a universalism that is also found in the Gospel of John, where Jesus says, "I have other sheep that do not belong to this fold. I must bring them also . . ." (John 10:16), and where Jesus prays, "I ask not only on behalf of these, but also on behalf of those who will believe in me . . . that they may all be one" (John 17:20–21).

Something else highly fascinating is found in Chevalier Ramsey's third statement above, in which he says that Freemasonry is a continuation of the "old religion of Noah." The Masonic *Book of Constitutions* from 1738 contains this intriguing statement: "A mason is obliged by his tenure to observe the moral law like a true Noahid . . . and to the three great articles of Noah . . ."[29] This statement bears the utmost import for showing a connection between Freemasonry and Jewish Christianity. As we saw in chapter 4, a Noahid was a Gentile convert to Judaism who, while not being circumcised, was obligated to follow the Noahide Laws cited in the holiness code found in chapters 17–18 of the book of Leviticus—not to worship idols, not to engage in sexual immorality, and not to eat meat with blood in it. What is especially telling is that in the fifteenth chapter of the book of Acts, in the so-called Apostolic Decree written at the Jerusalem Council, James cites these Noahide Laws as being the only Jewish laws binding on Gentiles who become followers of Jesus.[30] The founding documents of Freemasonry *cite these same laws* as being binding on those who become Freemasons. These are laws that originally united Jews and Gentiles. And, remarkably for the time, Freemasonry began accepting Jewish members as early as 1723.[31]

It is hard to believe that all of this is coincidence. Somehow, Freemasonry has preserved the core teachings of Jewish Christianity. While not everyone will agree with the theory I have presented in this book as to the line of transmission that brought these ideas into Freemasonry, somehow these core Jewish Christian laws and ideals, as well as the universalism seen in the Abrahamic Covenant and in the teachings of Jesus and Muhammad, made their way into Freemasonry. These same ideals would also make their way into the founding documents of a new nation born of the principle that "all men are created equal."

BUILDING A NEW JERUSALEM

In the Covenant that God made with Abraham God promised, "I will make of you a great nation, and I will bless you . . . and in you all the families of the earth shall be blessed" (Genesis 12:2–3). There is only one international entity in modern times that has worked to fulfill this lofty universalism—Freemasonry. And there is one country that has built this radical universal ideal into its constitution—the United States of America. It is no coincidence that Freemasonry and the United States were both founded at the peak of the European Enlightenment. Many of the Founding Fathers of the United States were Freemasons who looked upon America as a "New Jerusalem," a land chosen by God, a shining beacon on a hill, that would lead the world into a new age of universal peace and enlightenment.

The prophet Isaiah was the first to hold up a radical universal ideal for the New Jerusalem that he prophesied God would build at the end of the age:

> *Nations shall come to your light,*
> *and kings to the brightness of your dawn.*
> *Lift up your eyes and look around;*
> *They all gather together, they come to you . . .*
> *. . . the abundance of the sea shall be brought to you,*
> *the wealth of the nations shall come to you.*
> *A multitude of camels shall cover you,*
> *the young camels of Midian and Ephah;*
> *all those from Sheba shall come. . . .*
> *All the flocks of Kedar shall be gathered to you,*
> *The rams of Nebaioth shall minister to you;*

> *they shall be acceptable on my altar,*
> *and I will glorify my glorious house.* (Isaiah 60:3–7)

What is most remarkable about this passage is that Midian, Ephah, Sheba, Kedar, and Nebaioth are all *Arab* tribes! The statement that their offerings would be accepted on God's altar and that their offering would glorify the temple in the New Jerusalem is an astoundingly inclusive vision.

Those who drew up the Declaration of Independence and the Constitution of the United States of America shared such a radical inclusiveness in their dreams for the new nation. It is a fact that two, and possibly three of the members of the committee of five that drafted the Declaration of Independence were Freemasons. Benjamin Franklin and Robert Livingston were active Freemasons, and Roger Sherman is believed to have been a Mason, though this is not confirmed. The other two members, Thomas Jefferson and John Adams, were not Freemasons, although they certainly shared the same Enlightenment Era ideals. Of the fifty-six signatories of the Declaration of Independence, nine were definitely Freemasons, and another ten possibly so. These included Benjamin Franklin, George Washington, and the congressional president, John Hancock. Some Masonic researchers have made the claim that the Declaration of Independence is a Masonic document, or was heavily influenced by Freemasonry. While this cannot be supported, the U.S. Constitution was inarguably heavily influenced by Masonic ideals:

> Except in some of its rhetoric and phraseology, the Declaration of Independence . . . could not be called a Freemasonic document.
>
> The Constitution of the United States, on the other hand, in a very real sense, can. By the time the [Constitutional] Convention assembled to devise the Constitution, Freemasonic influences had prevailed and were unequivocally dominant. . . .
>
> In its final form, of course, the Constitution was a product of many minds and many hands, not all of them Freemasonic. . . . But there were ultimately five dominant and guiding spirits behind the Constitution—Washington, Franklin, [Edmund] Randolph,

Jefferson, and John Adams. Of these, the first three were not only active Freemasons, but men who took their Freemasonry extremely seriously—men who subscribed fervently to its ideals, whose entire orientation had been shaped and conditioned by it. And Adams's position, though he himself is not known to have been a Freemason, was virtually identical to theirs. When he became president he appointed a prominent Freemason, John Marshall, as first chief justice of the Supreme Court. . . .

. . . The new republic, when it emerged with the Constitution, conformed to their ideal image, and that image reflected the ideals of Freemasonry.[32]

While Thomas Jefferson was not present at the Constitutional Convention (he was overseas, serving as Minister to France), his shadow loomed large over the proceedings. Although Jefferson was not a Freemason, he certainly shared, in fact, embodied, their ideals, as evidenced in a piece of legislation he had championed:

In 1779, Jefferson proposed a bill that would guarantee complete legal equality for citizens of all religions, and of no religion, in his home state of Virginia. Jefferson's was the first plan in any of the thirteen states to call for complete separation of civil and religious authority . . . Virginia stood alone in marshaling a legislative majority that, as Jefferson observed, "meant to comprehend, within the mantle of its protection, the Jew and the Gentile, the Christian and the Mahometan, the Hindoo and infidel of every denomination." It is impossible to overstate the importance of Virginia's 1786 Act for Establishing Religious Freedom, for, much to the dismay of religious conservatives, it would become the template for the secularist provisions of the federal Constitution.[33]

This piece of legislation was ultimately the template for the "wall of separation" between church and state enshrined in the first amendment to the Constitution. While James Madison was the primary architect of the Constitution, the Bill of Rights was almost entirely Jefferson's idea. The wording of Virginia's Act for Establishing Religious Freedom is uncannily close to the wording found in the Masonic Constitution, cited above, making it easy to see why some have claimed that Jefferson was a Freemason. As one expert on the Founding Fathers, Dr. Robert Hieronimus, said, "In essence Jefferson was espousing the foundational philosophy of Freemasonry . . ."[34]

Dr. Hieronimus has written a remarkable book—*Founding Fathers, Secret Societies*—that shows how the Masonic goals of a universal brotherhood are built into both our founding documents, as well as our national mottos and symbols found on the Great Seal of the United States—*E Pluribus Unum:* Out of many, one; and *Novus Ordo Seclorum:* A new order of the ages. Also found on the Great Seal is the controversial "All Seeing Eye of God" within a triangle, one of the main symbols of Freemasonry. What is less well known about the All Seeing Eye is that it is associated with James the Brother of Jesus. The All Seeing Eye in a triangle is the main symbol of the Armenian Church in Jerusalem and is prominently displayed at their Cathedral of St. James (see plates 33 and 34). In the Sermon on the Mount in the Jewish Christian Gospel of Matthew, Jesus says, "The eye is the lamp of the body. So if your eye is healthy, your whole body will be full of light" (Matthew 6:22). And, as we saw, the letter of James calls God the "Father of lights, with whom there is no variation or shadow due to change."

On the Great Seal, the All Seeing Eye of God shines it rays upon an unfinished pyramid, which has often been interpreted as symbolizing the incompleteness, but perfectibility of our nation and of every person, which is the goal of Freemasonry. In Freemasonry the human being "is the true temple of God, for which Solomon's Temple is a symbol."[35] Paul Naudon asserts that the symbolic and allegorical rituals of Freemasonry bring the highest philosophical, theological, and ethical ideals down to a level that can be internally grasped by all:

In order to grasp these things, which touch on the Absolute, there is no need to employ the abstract vocabulary of philosophers. . . . No other initiatory path has managed better to express the inexpressible. The medieval freemason, the builder of cathedrals, never viewed himself as anything more than the [imager] of an infinitely more elevated work: the Temple of the Eternal One who dwells within Man, the Heavenly Jerusalem, symbol of the universality of all men belonging to all times and races, temples of Immortality and Perfection.[36]

Is this not the task to which Jesus originally called us? "Be perfect, therefore, as your heavenly Father is perfect" (Matthew 5:48).

The Founding Fathers held out a great hope that the United States would be the incubator that would make this lofty goal possible. Both Jefferson and Franklin wanted to root our nation in the ethics of the *Jewish* Jesus, *not* the Christian Jesus. In 1816 Jefferson wrote what he called "a wee-book," *The Morals and Life of Jesus of Nazareth,* in which he set out to answer his many critics who questioned his Christianity. He called it "a document in proof that *I am a real Christian,* that is to say, a disciple of the doctrine of Jesus . . ."[37] As is well known, Jefferson was a deist through and through, as were most of the Founding Fathers, and did not believe that God ever intervened in the working of his creation, and therefore denied the possibility of the miraculous.* Jefferson literally took scissors and paste to the New Testament in order to create his own account of Jesus that he called "The Philosophy of Jesus," which he described in a letter to John Adams as "the most sublime and benevolent code of morals which has ever been offered to man."[38]

FRANKLIN'S JEWISH CHRISTIANITY

Benjamin Franklin clearly shared Jefferson's sentiments. According to Franklin biographer, Walter Isaacson, "Franklin showed little interest in organized religion and even less in attending Sunday services. Still, he continued to hold some basic religious beliefs, among them 'the existence

---

*The God of Deism has sometimes been referred to as the "watchmaker God," who, like a watchmaker who creates a perfect timepiece, does not need to open up his perfect creation to make adjustments.

of the deity' and that 'the most acceptable service of God was doing good to man.' He was tolerant toward all sects, particularly those that worked to make the world a better place."[39] Like presidents Washington, Adams, and Jefferson, Franklin's personal religion was "a virtuous, morally-fortified and pragmatic version of deism."[40]

When one looks at what Franklin wrote on religion and Christianity (which is surprisingly little for such a voluminous writer and reporter), what is striking is Franklin's upholding of "works righteousness" over "faith alone." While he was definitely a child of the Enlightenment, Franklin was no son of Luther. In his writings he raised a number of objections to the Calvinist theology of the Puritans back in his native Boston, as well as that of the Presbyterians in his adopted home of Philadelphia. These objections were all centered on his belief that salvation came through good works, and not through faith in Jesus alone as Protestant Christianity emphasized. One exception to Franklin's criticism of the proclamation of Calvinist preachers was the Rev. Samuel Hemphill, one of the only pastors Franklin would go to hear. Hemphill was a Presbyterian minister from Ireland who got in trouble for preaching the doctrine of good works in Philadelphia. When Hemphill was put on trial by the local Presbyterian synod for heresy, Franklin came to his defense in a fictional dialogue he wrote for his *Pennsylvania Gazette*. It is fascinating that here Franklin lifts up the Sermon on the Mount, in which the Jewish nature of Jesus's teaching shines through. Franklin asks:

> What is Christ's sermon on the mount but an excellent moral dis-course, towards the end of which, (as foreseeing that people might in time come to depend more upon their *faith* in him, than upon *good works,* for their salvation) he tells the hearers plainly, that their saying to him *Lord, lord* (that is, professing themselves his disciples or *Christians*) should give them no title to salvation, but their *doing* the will of his father; and that though they have prophesied in his name, yet he will declare to them, as neglecters of morality, that he never knew them. . . .[41]

Franklin then goes on to assess the proper place for faith:

... Faith is recommended as a means of producing morality: our savior was a teacher of morality or virtue, and they that were deficient and desired to be taught, ought first to *believe* in him as an able and faithful teacher. Thus faith would be a means of producing morality, and morality of salvation. But that from such faith alone salvation may be expected, appears to me to be neither a Christian doctrine nor a reasonable one. . . . Faith in Christ . . . may be and is of great use to produce a good life, but that it can conduce nothing toward salvation where it does not conduce to virtue, is, I suppose, plain from the instance of the devils, who are far from being infidels, *they believe,* says the scripture, *and tremble.*[42]

Here Franklin is tellingly citing the Epistle of James (2:19), which he is fond of quoting:

St. James, in his second chapter, is very zealous against these criers-up of faith, and maintains that faith without virtue is useless, *wilt thou know, o vain man, says he, that faith without works is dead; and, show me your faith without your works, and I will show you mine by my works.* Our savior, when describing the last judgment, and declaring what shall give admission into bliss, or exclude from it, says nothing of *faith* but what he says against it, that is, those who cry *lord, lord,* and profess to have believed in his name, have no favor to expect on that account; but declares that 'tis the practice, or the omitting the practice of the duties of morality, *feeding the hungry, clothing the naked, visiting the sick,* etc. In short, 'tis the doing or not doing all the good that lies in our power, that will render us the heirs of happiness or misery.[43]

The obviously Jewish Christian nature of Franklin's theology is quite remarkable. What is even more remarkable is that Franklin clearly shared the Ebionite view that it was the Church begun by Paul that fostered apostasy from the true teachings of Jesus, and he asserts that the Reformation was actually not so reforming:

The apostasy of the church from the primitive simplicity of the gospel, came on by degrees; and do you think that the reformation was of a sudden perfect, and that the first reformers knew at once all that was right or wrong in religion? Did not Luther at first preach only against selling of pardons, allowing all the other practices of the Romish church for good? He afterwards went further, and Calvin, some think, yet further. The Church of England made a stop, and fixed her faith and doctrine by 39 articles; with which the Presbyterians not satisfied, went yet farther; but being too self-confident to think, that as their fathers were mistaken in some things, they also might be in some others; and fancying themselves infallible in *their* interpretations, they also tied themselves down by the Westminster confession. . . . And if any doctrine then maintained is, or shall hereafter be found not altogether orthodox, why must we be forever confined to that, or to any, confession?[44]

The open-minded, liberal thinking that Franklin displays here is remarkable. Of course, most Christians today are completely unaware of Franklin's views, as well as the views of the other Founding Fathers on religion. It is sobering to think that in today's evangelical and fundamentalist religious climate in the United States, great leaders like Franklin, Jefferson, and Washington would have no chance of being elected to public office! Consider what Franklin once said about Islam and Christianity:

. . . if the Presbyterians in this country, being charitably inclined, should send a missionary to Turkey, to propagate the gospel, would it not be unreasonable in the Turks to prohibit his preaching? . . .

And if the Turks, believing us in the wrong, as we think them, should out of the same charitable disposition, send a missionary to preach Mahometanism to us, ought we not in the same manner to give him free liberty of preaching his doctrine?

. . . In the present weak state of human nature, surrounded as we are on all sides with ignorance and error, it little becomes poor fallible man to be positive and dogmatical in his opinions. No point of faith is so plain, as that *morality* is our duty, for all sides agree in that. A virtuous heretic shall be saved before a wicked Christian: for there is no such thing as voluntary error. Therefore, since 'tis an uncertainty till we get to heaven what true orthodoxy in all points is . . . I hope . . . that we shall as heretofore unite again in mutual *Christian Charity.*[45]

What is plainly on display here is Franklin's remarkable religious tolerance, and it is no accident that this ideal became enshrined in the U.S. Constitution. And there can be little doubt that the breeding ground for this tolerance was the Masonic lodge. Franklin's biographer, Walter Isaacson, calls Franklin an "apostle of tolerance":

The most important religious role Franklin played—and it was an exceedingly important one in shaping his enlightened new republic—was as an apostle of tolerance. He had contributed to the building funds of each and every sect in Philadelphia, including £5 for the Congregation Mikveh Israel for its new synagogue in April 1788, and he had opposed religious oaths and tests in both the Pennsylvania and federal constitutions. During the July 4 celebrations in 1788, Franklin was too sick to leave his bed, but the parade marched under his window. For the first time, as per arrangements that Franklin had overseen, "the clergy of different Christian denominations, with the rabbi of the Jews, walked arm in arm."[46]

Franklin could have received no better send-off as he prepared to depart this world. And at the end of his life Franklin was also able to share his personal beliefs about Jesus. One month before he died, the president of Yale University, the Rev. Ezra Stiles, wrote to Franklin asking him specifically about his understanding of Jesus. Franklin wrote back:

You desire to know something of my religion. *It is the first time I have been questioned upon it.* . . . Here is my creed: I believe in one God, creator of the universe. That he governs it by his providence.

That he ought to be worshipped. That the most acceptable service we can render to him, is doing good to his other children. That the soul of man is immortal, and will be treated with justice in another life respecting its conduct in this. These I take to be the fundamental principles of all sound religion, and I regard them as you do, in whatever sect I meet with them.

As to Jesus of Nazareth, my opinion of whom you particularly desire, I think the system of morals and his religion as he left them to us, the best the world ever saw, or is likely to see; but I apprehended it has received corrupting changes, and I have with most of the present dissenters in England, some doubts as to his divinity: though it is a question I do not dogmatise upon . . . I see no harm however in its being believed, if that belief has the good consequence as probably it has, of making his doctrines more respected and better observed . . .[47]

While little is known about the personal religious beliefs of Franklin's fellow Mason, George Washington (who was much more circumspect than Franklin), it is known that while he regularly attended services with Martha, he would always leave before Holy Communion, which is surely indicative that his own beliefs about Jesus were the same as those of Franklin and Jefferson.

APOSTOLIC CHRISTIANITY

While they probably did not consciously realize it, Jefferson, Franklin, and Washington were stepping back beyond the Christian Jesus to return to the Jewish Jesus. They were actually fulfilling what the Protestant Reformation had attempted, but ultimately failed to do—return to pure apostolic Christianity. In the prophetic words of Hugh Schonfield:

What the Protestants could not readily detect was that the . . . Church had not started to go wrong in the fourth century. The process had begun in the first century AD with the movement of [Jewish] Christianity into association with an alien [Hellenistic] religious environment. To an appreciable extent Protestantism was only reverting to an earlier and less contaminated phase of the process of Gentilisation. It was not capable of going behind it, or seeing any necessity to do so, since it was imagined that through the New Testament contact had been made with the original content of the Christian faith. To advance further, toward the questioning and repudiation of second-century Christianity, was not possible before the dawn of the Age of Reason and the arrival of Unitarianism . . .[48]

It was actually Freemasonry, as much as, or more than, the Unitarian movement, that made this possible.

I want to be clear that I am not a Freemason, and I am certainly not trying to elevate Freemasonry to some exalted status as the preserver of pure apostolic Jewish Christianity, or saying that the roots of our nation are purely Masonic, but I would agree with this assessment of the outcome of the American Revolution: "The republic which emerged from the war was not, in any literal sense, a 'Freemasonic republic' . . . but it did embody those ideals; it was profoundly influenced by those ideals; and it owed much more to those ideals than is generally recognized or acknowledged."[49] In the end, Freemasonry was just one rivulet of the underground stream that was surfacing at the time of the Enlightenment:

[I]t was not just Freemasonry in itself . . . It was also an ambience, a mentality, a hierarchy of attitudes and values for which Freemasonry provided a particularly efficacious conduit. The Freemasonry of the age was a repository for an imaginatively stirring and potent idealism, which it was able, in a fashion uniquely its own, to disseminate. Most colonists did not actually read Locke, Hume, Voltaire, Diderot, or Roussseau . . . Through the lodges, however, the currents of thought associated with such philosophers became universally accessible. It was largely through the lodges that "ordinary" colonists learned of the lofty premise called "the rights of man." It was through the lodges that they learned the concept of the perfectibility of society. And the New World seemed to offer a species of blank slate; a species of laboratory in which social experiment was possible and the principle enshrined by Freemasonry could be applied in practice.[50]

The underground stream of Jewish Christianity that led to Freemasonry broke above ground at a time of enlightenment such has never since been seen. It was a time profoundly influenced by the recapturing of Jewish and Jewish Christian thought. While Israel was always the smallest of countries, the religious genius of the Hebrew prophets made an incalculable contribution to western civilization all out of proportion to its size. The overarching theme of the Hebrew Bible is that God has made a covenant with the people of Israel that will ultimately bring blessings to all the people of the world. This is also the theme of the New Testament, which one-third of the people on earth today claim to follow. A large majority of Americans have always claimed that the United States is a Christian nation founded on Judeo-Christian principles; but in recent times, American Christians have largely abandoned these founding principles. American Christians have lost sight of the core principles of our Founding Fathers. Christians have lost sight of the core teachings of Jesus the Nazarene. The pristine waters of original Jewish Christianity have been tainted by a misguided and bigoted Christian fundamentalism that would horrify the Messiah, Jesus. We have lost the inclusive, salvific universalism that goes all the way back to the Abrahamic Covenant and was enshrined in the life and sacrificial death of the one who willingly died on a cross so "that they may all be one."

If we can recapture and return to the original teaching of Jesus, James, and the Nazarenes, if we can recover the spiritual vision of the American Founding Fathers, there may yet be hope for reconciliation among Christians, Jews, and Muslims throughout the world, and the Prince of Peace—Messiah Jesus—may yet return to his rightful throne in a New Jerusalem.

NOTES

INTRODUCTION

1. According to a bibliography compiled by researcher Paul Smith (www.priory-of-sion.com), almost three hundred books on this topic have been written since 1982.
2. *Jewish Christianity Reconsidered* (Minneapolis: Fortress, 2007); see especially chapter 1 by Matt Jackson-McCabe, "What's in a Name? The Problem of 'Jewish Christianity,'" and the comments by F. Stanley Jones on p. 287.

CHAPTER 1. AN UNHERALDED FAMILY

1. See especially the works of Margaret Starbird listed in the bibliography.
2. Richard Bauckham, *Jude and the Relatives of Jesus in the Early Church* (London: T&T Clark, 1990), 8–9.
3. Ibid., 9, note 14.
4. For a succinct summary of the issues see the late Roman Catholic scholar Raymond E. Brown's invaluable little book, *The Virginal Conception and Bodily Resurrection of Jesus* (New York: Paulist Press, 1973).
5. James D. Tabor, *The Jesus Dynasty: The Hidden History of Jesus, His Royal Family, and the Birth of Christianity* (New York: Simon & Schuster, 2006), see especially chapter 8.
6. Eusebius, *The History of the Church,* revised edition, trans. by G. A. Williamson (London: Penguin, 1989), 79.
7. Bauckham, *Jude and the Relatives of Jesus,* 6.
8. Jeffrey J. Bütz, *The Brother of Jesus and the Lost Teachings of Christianity* (Rochester, Vt.: Inner Traditions, 2005), see especially chapter 2.
9. Eusebius, *History of the Church,* 21–22.

10. Hugh Schonfield citing Lukyn Williams in *Those Incredible Christians* (New York: Bantam, 1969), 123–24.

11. Eusebius, *History of the Church,* 95.

12. Malachi Martin, *The Decline and Fall of the Roman Church* (New York: Bantam, 1983), 30–31.

CHAPTER 2. "WHO DO YOU SAY THAT I AM?"

1. Albert Schweitzer, *The Quest of the Historical Jesus* (New York: Macmillan, 1962), book jacket notes.

2. Ibid., 232.

3. Ibid., 4.

4. Ibid., 5.

5. Ibid., 5.

6. Ibid., 4.

7. Ibid., 370–71.

8. N. T. Wright, *Jesus and the Victory of God: Christian Origins and the Question of God,* vol. 2 (Minneapolis: Fortress, 1996), 28.

9. Ibid., 56–57.

10. Ibid., 81.

11. Ibid., 95–97.

12. Ibid., 84–86.

13. Schweitzer, *The Quest of the Historical Jesus,* 311.

14. Ibid., 312.

15. Wright, *Jesus and the Victory of God,* 5–6.

16. David R. Catchpole, *The Quest for Q* (Edinburgh: T. & T. Clark, 1993), 279.

CHAPTER 3. IN THE BEGINNING

1. James D. Tabor, *The Jesus Dynasty: The Hidden History of Jesus, His Royal Family, and the Birth of Christianity* (New York: Simon & Schuster, 2006), 144–48.

2. Hyam Maccoby, *The Mythmaker: Paul and the Invention of Christianity* (New York: Barnes & Noble, 1986), 126–27.

3. James D. G. Dunn, *Unity and Diversity in the New Testament: An Inquiry into the Character of Earliest Christianity* (Philadelphia: Trinity Press, 1990), 239.

4. Bart D. Ehrman, *Lost Christianities: The Battles for Scripture and the Faiths We Never Knew* (New York: Oxford, 2003), book jacket notes.

5. See Numbers 15:38–39, Matthew 9:20–22, Luke 8:43–48.

6. See Acts 1:15.

7. See Jeffrey J. Bütz, *The Brother of Jesus and the Lost Teachings of Christianity* (Rochester, Vt.: Inner Traditions, 2005) for a full exposition of these ideas, particularly chapters 4, 5, and 8.

8. Matthew 2:23, 26:71; Luke 18:37, 24:19; John 18:5, 18:7, 19:19; Acts 2:22, 3:6, 4:10, 6:14, 22:8, 24:5, 26:9.

9. Hugh Schonfield, *The Pentecost Revolution: The Story of the Jesus Party in Israel, A.D. 36–66* (London: MacDonald, 1974), 278.

10. Tabor, *The Jesus Dynasty*, 55.

11. Schonfield, *The Pentecost Revolution*, 112.

12. Robert Eisler, *The Messiah Jesus and John the Baptist according to Flavius Josephus' recently rediscovered "Capture of Jerusalem" and other Jewish and Christian sources* (London: A. H. Krappe, 1931), 539–40.

13. S. G. F. Brandon, *Jesus and the Zealots* (Cambridge, England: Scribners, 1967), 96–99.

14. Huston Smith, *The World's Religions: Our Great Wisdom Traditions* (New York: HarperSanFrancisco, 1991), 332.

CHAPTER 4. THE CALIPHATE BEGINS

1. See Acts 15 and 21 and Galatians 2. This evidence is discussed at length in Bütz, *The Brother of Jesus and the Lost Teachings of Christianity*, chapters 3–5.

2. Clement of Alexandria, *The Stromata*, VI, 5.

3. Schonfield, *The Pentecost Revolution*, 124.

4. See Wilhelm Schneemelcher, ed. *New Testament Apocrypha* Vol. II, Rev. ed. (Louisville: Westminster John Knox, 2003), 493.

5. Translated from the Latin by Robert E. Van Voorst, *The Ascents of James: History and Theology of a Jewish-Christian Community* (Atlanta: Scholars Press, 1989), 73–74.

6. Ibid., 21.

7. Hans-Joachim Schoeps, *Jewish Christianity: Factional Disputes in the Early Church* (Philadelphia: Fortress, 1969), 42–45.

8. *The Panarion of Epiphanius* Book I, trans. by Frank Williams (Leiden: Brill, 1997), 30.16.6–8.

9. Schneemelcher, *New Testament Apocrypha* Vol. II, 494.

10. Schonfield, *The Pentecost Revolution*, 130–31.

11. Eusebius, *The History of the Church*, 44.

12. Schneemelcher, *New Testament Apocrypha* Vol. II, 496–97.

13. Albert Schweitzer, *The Mysticism of Paul the Apostle,* trans. by William Montgomery (London: A & C Black, 1931), 156.

14. See my fuller discussion in *The Brother of Jesus and the Lost Teachings of Christianity,* 90–95.

15. Schonfield, *Those Incredible Christians,* 118–19.

16. Ibid., 119–20.

17. Epiphanius, *The Panarion,* 29.3.9–29.4.4.

18. Eusebius, *The History of the Church,* 7.19.1.

19. www.armenian-patriarchate.org (accessed July 24, 2009).

20. Schonfield, *Those Incredible Christians,* 120.

21. Ibid., 120.

CHAPTER 5. JAMES VERSUS PAUL

1. See especially chapter 2.

2. Michael Goulder, *St. Paul versus St. Peter: A Tale of Two Missions* (Louisville: Westminster John Knox, 1994), 2–3.

3. James D. G. Dunn, *Unity and Diversity in the New Testament: An Inquiry into the Character of Earliest Christianity* (Philadelphia: Trinity Press, 1990), 254.

4. Ibid., 256.

5. See Bauckham, "James and the Jerusalem Church," *The Book of Acts in Its Palestinian Setting,* vol. 4 of *The Book of Acts in Its First Century Setting* (Grand Rapids: Eerdmans, 1995), 478.

6. Ralph P. Martin, *James,* Word Biblical Commentary, Vol. 48 (Waco, Tex.: Word Books, 1998), xl–xli.

7. Hugh J. Schonfield, *The History of Jewish Christianity: From the First to the Twentieth Century* (London: Duckworth, 1936), 45–46.

CHAPTER 6. STORM SIGNALS

1. Schonfield, *The History of Jewish Christianity,* 30–31.

2. Eisler, *The Messiah Jesus,* 540.

3. Epiphanius, *Panarion,* 29.4.2–4.

4. Eusebius, *History of the Church,* 2.23.

5. Schonfield, *The Pentecost Revolution,* 148.

6. Josephus, *Antiquities of the Jews,* 20.9.2.

7. Josephus, *Antiquities,* 20.8.5–6.

8. Ibid., 20.9.1.

9. John Dominic Crossan, *Jesus: A Revolutionary Biography* (New York: HarperSanFrancisco, 1994), 134–35.
10. Eusebius, *History of the Church,* 2.23.11–18. See *The Brother of Jesus and the Lost Teachings of Christianity* chaper 6 for a fuller exposition.
11. Ibid., 2.23.24–25.
12. Ibid., 2.23.24.
13. Ibid., 3.13.11.
14. Ibid., 4.22.4.
15. Bauckham, *Jude and the Relatives of Jesus in the Early Church,* 17.
16. Tabor, *The Jesus Dynasty,* 165.
17. John McHugh, *The Mother of Jesus in the New Testament* (Garden City: Doubleday, 1975), 234–54.
18. Tabor, *The Jesus Dynasty,* 164.
19. Bauckham, *Jude,* 85–87.
20. Josephus, *Antiquities,* 20.11.1.
21. Eusebius, *History of the Church,* 3.5.3.
22. Epiphanius, *Panarion,* 29.7.7–8.
23. Ibid., 30.2.7–9.
24. Schonfield, *The History of Jewish Christianity,* 49.
25. See Simcha Jacobovici and Charles Pellegrino, *The Jesus Family Tomb* (New York: HarperSanFrancisco, 2007).
26. Jacobus de Voragine, *The Golden Legend: Readings on the Saints,* Vol. 1 (Princeton: Princeton University Press, 1995), 374–82.
27. Josephus, *Wars of the Jews,* 3.7.9.

CHAPTER 7. AFTERMATH

1. Schonfield, *Jewish Christianity,* 56.
2. While this book was in its final stages, a book by Barrie Wilson, professor of humanities and religious studies at York University, Toronto appeared: *How Jesus Became Christian* (New York: St. Martin's Press, 2008). This is an invaluable work for providing the layperson with an understanding of the exact nature of Jesus's Jewish teachings and the beliefs and practices of the original Nazarenes.
3. Origen, *De Principiis,* 4.38 and *Contra Celsum,* 2.1.
4. Eusebius, *History of the Church,* 3.32.
5. Ibid., 4.22.
6. Irenaeus, *Adversus Haereses,* 1.26.
7. S. G. F. Brandon, *Jesus and the Zealots: A Study of the Political Factors in Primitive Christianity* (Cambridge, England: Charles Scribner's Sons, 1967), 208–17.

8. Gerd Lüdemann, *Opposition to Paul in Jewish Christianity*, trans. by M. Eugene Boring (Minneapolis: Fortress Press, 1989), 200–211.

9. Schoeps, *Jewish Christianity*, 22, footnote 7.

10. Josephus, *Antiquities*, 20.256.

11. Tabor, *The Jesus Dynasty*, 188.

12. Schoeps, *Jewish Christianity*, 27.

13. This text has been studied extensively by Samuel Krauss, *Das Leben Jesus nach Jüdischen Quellen*. Cited in Schonfield, *The Pentecost Revolution*, 234–35.

14. Epiphanius, *Panarion*, 30.6.9.

15. Schonfield, *The Pentecost Revolution*, 234.

16. Ibid.

17. Epiphanius, *On Weights and Measures*, 14–15.

18. Eusebius, *Demonstratio Evangelica* 3.5, cited in *Patristic Evidence for Jewish Christian Sects*, ed. by A. F. J. Klijn and G. J. Reinink (Leiden: E. J. Brill, 1973), 139.

19. Cited in Bargil Pixner, "Church of the Apostles Found on Mt. Zion," *Biblical Archaeology Review*, May/June 1990, 26.

20. All the information that follows is taken from the remarkable article written by Bargil Pixner, "Church of the Apostles Found on Mt. Zion," *Biblical Archaeology Review*, May/June 1990.

21. Ibid., 28.

22. Eusebius, *Demonstratio Evangelica*, cited in ibid.

23. Eucherius, cited in Pixner, ibid.

24. Cited in Pixner, ibid.

25. Ibid., 30.

26. Ibid.

27. Eusebius, *History of the Church*, 7.19.

28. James Tabor, *The Jesus Dynasty*, 206–7.

29. In Eusebius, *History of the Church*, 3.32.

30. Julius Africanus, *Epistle to Aristides*, 5.

31. Schonfield, *The Pentecost Revolution*, 289–90.

32. Ibid., 293–94.

33. Ibid., 294.

34. Ibid., 279.

35. Ibid., 283–84.

36. Richard Bauckham, *Jude and the Relatives of Jesus*, 62–64.

37. Ibid., 64–66.

38. Schoeps, *Jewish Christianity*, 25–26.

39. Ibid., 25, footnote 10.

40. Eusebius, *History of the Church,* 3.20.

41. Anonymous manuscripts (Paris MS 1555A) trans. by Richard Bauckham, *Jude and the Relatives of Jesus in the Early Church,* 97.

42. Bauckham, *Jude and the Relatives of Jesus in the Early Church,* 104–5.

43. Eusebius, *Church History,* 3.32.

44. Ibid., 4.5.

45. Schonfield, *History of Jewish Christianity,* 60.

46. James Tabor, *The Jesus Dynasty,* 291.

47. Bauckham, *Jude and the Relatives of Jesus,* 73.

48. Epiphanius, *Panarion,* 66.21–22.

49. Bauckham, *Jude,* 76.

50. Tabor, *Jesus Dynasty,* 291.

51. Ibid., 292.

52. Justin Martyr, *The First Apology,* 31.

53. Schoeps, *Jewish Christianity,* 28.

54. As quoted in Schoeps, *Jewish Christianity,* 33–34.

55. Jerome, *Epistle to Augustine* (Letter 112), trans. by Carolinne White, *The Correspondence (394–419) between Jerome and Augustine of Hippo* (New York: The Edwin Mellen Press, 1990).

CHAPTER 8. THE EBIONITE EVANGEL

1. Johannes Weiss, *Earliest Christianity,* trans. by F. C. Grant (New York: Harper & Row, 1959), II, 716.

2. Schoeps, *Jewish Christianity,* 28.

3. Epiphanius, *Panarion,* 30.18.1.

4. Schoeps, *Jewish Christianity,* 29–30.

5. Eusebius, *History of the Church,* 5.9.

6. Aaron Milavec, *The Didache: Text, Translation, Analysis, and Commentary* (Collegeville, Minnesota: Liturgical Press, 2003), xiii.

7. Ibid., ix.

8. *Catholic Encyclopedia,* 1913, s.v., "Didache."

9. Translation by Milavec, *The Didache,* 3.

10. Ibid., 39–40.

11. Ibid., 69.

12. Eusebius, *History of the Church,* 3.25.

13. Ibid., 3.27.

14. Talmud, Shabbat, 116a.

15. Justin Martyr, *Dialogue with Trypho the Jew,* cited in Schonfield, *History of Jewish Christianity,* 73.

16. Schonfield, *The History of Jewish Christianity,* 73.

17. *The Anchor Bible Dictionary,* s.v., "The Gospel of the Nazoraeans," by William L. Peterson (New York: Doubleday, 1992), 4:1051.

18. Schoeps, *Jewish Christianity,* 14.

19. Jerome, *Commentary on Matthew,* 12, 13.

20. Jerome, *Against the Pelagians,* 3.2.

21. Cited in Epiphanius, *Panarion,* 30.13.4.

22. Ibid., 30.13.7.

23. Jerome, *Commentary on Isaiah,* 11.2, trans. by Schonfield, ibid., 82.

24. Origen, *Commentary on Matthew,* 15.14, trans. by Schonfield, ibid., 83.

25. Epiphanius, *Panarion,* cited in ibid., 84–85.

26. See Matthew 10:5 and 15:24. See further my discussion in *The Brother of Jesus and the Lost Teachings of Christianity,* 172–74.

27. Jerome, *Lives of Illustrious Men,* 2.

28. Eusebius, *History of the Church,* 2.1.2–5.

29. Hugh Schonfield, *The History of Jewish Christianity,* 76.

30. Babylonian Talmud: Tractate Abodah Zarah, 16b.

31. Talmud, Shabbat, 116a, cited in Schonfield, *The History of Jewish Christianity,* 77.

32. Talmud, Abodah Zarah 27b, cited in ibid., 79.

33. Talmud, Shabbat, 14b, cited in ibid.

34. Epiphanius, *Panarion,* 30.9.3.

35. Ibid., 30.9.5.

36. See Richard Bauckham, *Jude and the Relative of Jesus,* 115 for a fuller discussion.

37. Ibid., 116.

38. The following information is gleaned from ibid., 121–23.

39. Martyrdom of Conon 4:2, cited in Bauckham, *Jude,* 122. Conon's belief in Jesus as "God over all things" reveals that he is not an Ebionite per se, but part of an offshoot branch called the Elkesaites, who came to accept the divinity of Jesus.

40. Bauckham, *Jude,* 122.

41. B. Bagatti, *Excavations in Nazareth,* Vol. 1, cited in *The Anchor Bible Dictionary,* s.v., "Nazareth," by James F. Strange (New York: Doubleday, 1992), 4:1050.

42. Bauckham, *Jude,* 124–25.

CHAPTER 9. EBIONITE THEOLOGY

1. For the discussion of the various Jewish Christian sects that follows, the most helpful reference is A. F. J. Klijn and G. J. Reinink, *Patristic Evidence for Jewish Christian Sects*. Supplements to Novum Testamentum, Vol. XXXVI (Leiden: E. J. Brill, 1973). I am also especially indebted to Keith Akers, author of a landmark work on Jewish Christianity: *The Lost Religion of Jesus: Simple Living and Nonviolence in Early Christianity* (New York: Lantern Books, 2000). Keith graciously shared with me his yet-unpublished manuscript, *The First Followers of Jesus*. This has the most edifying discussion of the various Jewish Christian sects I have come across, and helped sharpen my thinking greatly. Keith wonderfully simplifies a good deal of the confusing debate about these groups among scholars. Much of the discussion that follows was influenced by Keith's helpful analysis.

2. Justin Martyr, *First Apology to the Greeks,* 21–23.

3. Hans Joachim Schoeps, *Jewish Christianity: Factional Disputes in the Early Church,* translated by Douglas R. A. Hare (Philadelphia: Fortress, 1969), 18.

4. Schonfield, *The Pentecost Revolution,* 283.

5. Irenaeus, *Against Heresies,* 1.26.

6. Hippolytus, *Refutation of All Heresies,* 7.33 and 10.21.

7. Epiphanius, *Panarion,* 28.1.3.

8. Klijn and Reinink, *Patristic Evidence,* 68.

9. Eusebius, *History of the Church,* 6.17.

10. Schonfield, *The History of Jewish Christianity,* 95.

11. Klijn and Reinink, *Patristic Evidence,* 53–54.

12. Ibid., 68.

13. Epiphanius, *Panarion,* 19.2.1.

14. Akers, *The First Followers of Jesus.*

15. Ibid.

16. See Isaiah 42:1–4; 49:1–6; 50:4–11; 52:13–53:12.

17. Schoeps, *Jewish Christianity,* 67.

18. Ibid.

19. Ibid.

20. Ibid., 68.

21. Ibid.

22. Hippolytus, *Refutation of All Heresies,* 7.34.1.

23. Schoeps, *Jewish Christianity,* 64.

24. Ibid., 72.

25. See Matthew 4:6; John 12:31; 2 Corinthians 4:4.

26. Schoeps, *Jewish Christianity,* 101.

27. Ibid., 102.

28. Ibid.

29. Ibid.

30. Epiphanius, *Panarion,* 30.22.4, 30.16.4–5, trans. by Bart Ehrman, *Lost Scriptures,* 114.

31. See *The Lost Religion of Jesus: Simple Living and Nonviolence in Early Christianity.*

32. Schoeps, *Jewish Christianity,* 100.

33. Ibid., 101.

34. Epiphanius, *Panarion,* 30.18.17–19.

35. Schoeps, *Jewish Christianity,* 76.

36. Ibid., 76–77.

37. Ibid., 78.

38. Ibid.

39. Ibid., 77–79.

40. Ibid., 80.

41. Ibid., 81.

42. Ibid., 82.

43. Ibid., 103.

44. Ibid., 106.

45. Ibid.

46. Ibid., 108–9.

47. Epiphanius, *Panarion,* 30.36.

CHAPTER 10. FROM EBIONITES TO ELKESAITES

1. Epiphanius, *Panarion,* 30.

2. Schonfield, *The History of Jewish Christianity,* 90.

3. Ibid.

4. Justin Martyr, *Dialogue with Trypho the Jew,* 47.

5. Origen, *Against Celsus,* 5.61.

6. Eusebius, *History of the Church,* 3.27.

7. Ibid.

8. Ray Pritz, *Nazarene Jewish Christianity: From the End of the New Testament Period Until Its Disappearance in the Fourth Century* (Jerusalem: The Magnes Press, 1992), 28.

9. Epiphanius, *Panarion,* 29.5.4.

10. Ibid., 29.1.2–3. See the fuller exposition of the account of James's martyrdom in *The Brother of Jesus and the Lost Teachings of Christianity.*

11. Ibid., 29.7.8.

12. Ibid., 30.2.8.

13. Ibid., 29.7.3.

14. Ibid., 29.7.5.

15. Klijn and Reinink, *Patristic Evidence for Jewish Christian Sects,* 50.

16. Ibid.

17. Schonfield, *The History of Jewish Christianity,* 91.

18. Barrie Wilson, *How Jesus Became Christian* (New York: St. Martin's Press, 2008), 182.

19. See Anthony J. Saldarini, *Matthew's Jewish-Christian Community* (Chicago: University of Chicago Press, 1994).

20. Wilson, *How Jesus Became Christian,* 184.

21. Ibid., 186.

22. Schonfield, *The History of Jewish Christianity,* 91.

23. Ibid.

24. Ibid., 93.

25. Ibid., 94.

26. Eusebius, *History of the Church,* 10.1.

27. Schonfield, *The History of Jewish Christianity,* 97.

28. Ibid., 98.

29. Ibid., 113.

30. Hippolytus, *Refutation of All Heresies,* 9.13–17, 10.25, 29.

31. Keith Akers, *The First Followers of Jesus,* part 3, chap. 9, footnote 3.

32. Epiphanius, *Panarion,* 19.2.3–4.

33. Gerard P. Luttikhuizen, *The Revelation of Elchasai: Investigations into the Evidence for a Mesopotamian Jewish Apocalypse of the Second Century and Its Reception by Judeo-Christian Propagandists* (Tübingen: Mohr Siebeck, 1985), 190–92.

34. Epihanius, *Panarion,* 19.1.4., 19.5.4.

35. Ibid., 19.2.1.

36. Schonfield, *The History of Jewish Christianity,* 114.

37. Epiphanius, *Panarion,* 19.1.7.

38. Ibid., 19.5.4–5.

39. Ibid., 53.1.1.

40. Ibid., 19.1.8.

41. Keith Akers, *The First Followers of Jesus,* part 3, chap. 9.

42. Hippolytus, *Refutation of All Heresies,* 9.14.1.

43. See Mark 8:27–28 and parallels, where the disciples say that some of the Jews believe that Jesus is a reincarnation of one of the prophets.

44. Schonfield, *The History of Jewish Christianity,* 114.

45. Ibid., 115.

46. *Pseudo-Clementine* "Homilies" 2.15 in Wilhelm Schneemelcher, ed., *New Testament Apocrypha,* Vol. II, trans. by R. McL. Wilson (Louisville: Westminster John Knox, 2003), 511.

47. Schonfield, *The History of Jewish Christianity,* 116.

48. Baring Gould, *Lost and Hostile Gospels,* cited in ibid., 117.

49. Epiphanius, *Panarion,* 30.22.4, trans. by Bart Ehrman, *Lost Scriptures,* 14.

50. Hippolytus, *Refutation of All Heresies,* 9.8.

51. Yuri Stoyanov, *The Other God: Religious Dualism from Antiquity to the Cathar Heresy* (New Haven: Yale University Press, 2000), 102.

52. This has been established through the recently deciphered *Cologne Mani Codex.* See Stoyanov, *The Other God,* 353, footnotes 68 and 70.

CHAPTER 11. JEWISH CHRISTIANITY IN ARABIA

1. Pritz, *Nazarene Jewish Christianity,* 76.

2. Schoeps, *Jewish Christianity,* 29.

3. Richard Fletcher, *The Cross and the Crescent: Christianity and Islam from Muhammad to the Reformation* (New York: Viking, 2003), 8.

4. Marcus N. Adler, *The Itinerary of Benjamin of Tudela: Critical Text, Translation and Commentary* (New York: Phillip Feldheim, Inc., 1907), 70–72.

5. Muhammad al-Shahrastani, *The Book of Religious and Philosophical Sects,* ed. William Cureton (Piscataway, N.J.: Gorgias Press, 2002), 167.

6. John Esposito, Darell Fasching, Todd Lewis, *World Religions Today,* 2nd ed. (New York: Oxford University Press, 2006), 212.

7. Karen Armstrong, *Jerusalem: One City, Three Faiths* (New York, Ballantine Books, 2005), 245.

8. Ibid., 232.

9. Fletcher, *The Cross and the Crescent,* 8.

10. Ibid., 9.

11. Abdullah and Al-Suhrawardy, *Sayings of Muhammad,* 60; cited in Philip Novak, *The World's Wisdom: Sacred Texts of the World's Religions* (New York: HarperSanFrancisco, 1994), 320.

12. Charles C. Torrey, *The Jewish Foundation of Islam,* 2nd ed. (New York: KTAV Publishing, 1967).

13. Richard Bell, *The Origin of Islam in Its Christian Environment* (London: Routledge, 1968).

14. Patricia Crone and Michael Cook, *Hagarism: The Making of the Islamic World* (London: Cambridge University Press, 1977).

15. Joshua Finkel, "Jewish, Christian, and Samaritan Influences on Arabia," in W. C. Shellabear, E. E. Calvarly, et al, eds., *The MacDonald Presentation Volume: a Tribute to Duncan Black MacDonald* (Princeton: Princeton University Press, 1933), 147–66.

16. Schoeps, *Jewish Christianity,* 136–37.

17. Alfred Guillame, *The Life of Muhammad* (London: Oxford University Press, 1955), 83.

18. Ibid., 107.

19. Schoeps, *Jewish Christianity,* 138.

20. Ibid., 138–39.

21. Ibid., 138.

22. Ibid.

23. Ibid., 139–40.

24. Schonfield, *The History of Jewish Christianity,* 120.

CHAPTER 12. FROM ELKESAITES TO CATHARS

1. Taken from Walter L. Wakefield and Austin P. Evans, *Heresies of the High Middle Ages: Selected Sources Translated and Annotated* (New York: Columbia University Press, 1969), 468.

2. Klijn and Reinink, *Patristic Evidence for Jewish-Christian Sects,* 65.

3. Qur'an 2:62, 5:69, 22:17.

4. Hugh Schonfield, *The Essene Odyssey: The Mystery of the True Teacher and the Essene Impact on the Shaping of Human Destiny* (Great Britain: Element, 1984), 88.

5. Stoyanov, *The Other God,* 101–2.

6. Schonfield, *The Essene Odyssey,* 89.

7. Schonfield, *The Pentecost Revolution,* 283.

8. Ibid.

9. For more information about their situation today and to find out how to support this endangered people, go to the website of the Mandaean Associations Union: www.mandaeanunion.org.

10. E. S. Drower, *The Secret Adam: A Study of Nasoraean Gnosis* (Oxford: Clarendon Press, 1960), ix.

11. Richard Bauckham, *Jude and the Relatives of Jesus in the Early Church,* 68–70.

12. See Elaine Pagels, *The Gnostic Paul: Gnostic Exegesis of the Pauline Letters* (Harrisburg: Trinity Press International, 1992).

13. Jean Markale, *Montségur and the Mystery of the Cathars,* trans. by Jon Graham (Rochester, Vt.: Inner Traditions, 2003), 140–41.

14. Ibid., 114–19.

15. Stoyanov, *The Other God,* xi.

16. Ibid., 110.

17. Nina Garsoian, *The Paulician Heresy: A Study of the Origin and Development of Paulicianism in Armenia and the Eastern Provinces of the Byzantine Empire* (The Hague: Mouton, 1967), 183–85.

18. Zoé Oldenbourg, *Massacre at Montségur* (London: Phoenix Press, 2000), 31.

19. Stoyanov, *The Other God,* 162.

20. Ibid., 165.

21. Ibid., 199.

22. Walter L. Wakefield and Austin P. Evans, *Heresies of the High Middle Ages: Selected Sources Translated and Annotated* (New York: Columbia University Press, 1969), 26.

23. Stoyanov, *The Other God,* 260.

24. Wakefield and Evans, *Heresies of the High Middle Ages,* 27.

25. Ibid., 29.

26. Stoyanov, *The Other God,* 184.

27. Ibid., 166.

28. Ibid., 165.

29. Wakefield and Evans, *Heresies of the High Middle Ages,* 17.

30. Ibid.

31. Ibid., 22.

32. Ibid., 19.

33. Ibid., 43.

34. Schoeps, *Jewish Christianity,* 12.

35. Stoyanov, *The Other God,* 391, footnote 121.

36. Wakefield and Evans, *Heresies of the High Middle Ages,* 43.

37. Stoyanov, *The Other God,* 170.

38. Ibid., 188.

39. Markale, *Montségur and the Mystery of the Cathars,* 206–7.

40. Stoyanov, *The Other God,* 275.

41. Ibid.

42. Wakefield and Evans, *Heresies of the High Middle Ages,* 43.

43. Stoyanov, *The Other God,* 170.

44. Wakefield and Evans, *Heresies of the High Middle Ages,* 465.

45. Stoyanov, *The Other God,* 195

46. Schoeps, *Jewish Christianity,* 62.

47. Stoyanov, *The Other God,* 273.

48. Oldenbourg, *Massacre at Montségur,* 39.

49. Wakefield and Evans, *Heresies of the High Middle Ages,* 64.

50. Oldenbourg, *Massacre at Montségur,* 33.

51. Stoyanov, *The Other God,* 192.

52. Oldenbourg, *Massacre at Montségur,* 41.

53. Ibid., 29.

54. Ibid.

55. René Weis, *The Yellow Cross: The Story of the Last Cathars 1290–1329* (New York: Alfred A. Knopf, 2001), xxiii.

56. Oldenbourg, *Massacre at Montségur,* 42.

57. Ibid., 43.

58. Stoyanov, *The Other God,* 205.

59. Oldenbourg, *Massacre at Montségur,* 116.

CHAPTER 13. HERESY IN HIGH PLACES

1. Karen Ralls, *The Templars and the Grail: Knights of the Quest* (Wheaton, Ill.: Quest Books, 2003), 37.

2. Ibid., 9–10.

3. Malcolm Barber, *The New Knighthood: A History of the Order of the Temple* (Cambridge: Cambridge University Press, 1994), 44.

4. Warren T. Woodfin, "The Holiest Ground in the World," in *Crusaders in the Holy Land: The Archaeology of Faith,* ed. by Jack Meinhardt (Washington, D.C.: Biblical Archaeology Society, 2005), 19.

5. The list is adapted from Malcolm Barber, *The Trial of the Templars* (Cambridge: Cambridge University Press, 1978), 248–50.

6. Steven Runciman, *The Medieval Manichee: A Study of Christian Dualist Heresy* (Cambridge: Cambridge University Press, 1999), 179.

7. Ibid., 164–73.

8. Ibid., 164.

9. Richard Barber, *The Knight and Chivalry,* cited in Michael Baigent and Richard Leigh, *The Temple and the Lodge* (New York: Arcade Publishing, 1989), 58.

10. Baigent and Leigh, *The Temple and the Lodge,* 59.

11. Ibid.

12. Ibid.

13. Sharan Newman, *The Real History Behind the Templars* (New York: Berkley Books, 2007), 338.

14. Armstrong, *Jerusalem: One City, Three Faiths,* 288–89.

15. Prince Michael of Albany and Walid Amine Salhab, *The Knights Templar of the Middle East* (San Francisco: Weiser Books, 2006), 73.

16. Woodfin, "The Holiest Ground in the World," in *Crusaders in the Holy Land,* 13.

17. Ibid., 281.

18. Ralls, *The Templars and the Grail,* 33.

19. Ibid., 30.

20. Arthur J. Zuckerman, *A Jewish Princedom in Feudal France 768–900* (New York: Columbia University Press, 1972), 5.

21. Oldenbourg, *Massacre at Montségur,* 24–25.

22. Ralls, *The Templars and the Grail,* 38.

23. Michael of Albany and Walid Salhab, *The Knights Templar of the Middle East,* 69.

24. Woodfin, "The Holiest Ground in the World" in *Crusaders in the Holy Land,* 10–11.

25. Michael of Albany and Walid Salhab, *The Knights Templar of the Middle East,* 34.

26. Woodfin, "The Holiest Ground in the World" in *Crusaders in the Holy Land,* 13–14.

27. Ralls, *The Templars and the Grail,* 145.

28. Meir Ben-Dov, *In the Shadow of the Temple,* trans. by Ina Friedman (New York: Harper & Row, 1985), 347.

29. Ibid., 282.

30. John Wilkinson, Joyce Hill, and William F. Ryan, eds., *Jerusalem Pilgrimage 1099–1185* (London: Hakluyt Society, 1988), 294.

31. Judi Upton-Ward, trans. and ed, *The Rule of the Templars: The French Text of the Rule of the Order of the Knights Templar* (Woodbridge, Suffolk: Boydell Press, 1992), 91.

32. Bargil Pixner, "Church of the Apostles Found on Mt. Zion," in *Crusaders in the Holy Land: The Archaeology of Faith,* ed. by Jack Meinhardt (Washington, D.C.: Biblical Archaeology Society, 2005), 63.

33. Ibid., 71–72.

34. Armstrong, *Jerusalem,* 286–87.

CHAPTER 14. FROM JESUS TO FREEMASONRY

1. Brian is past master of Montgomery Lodge #19 (Pennsylvania), a member of the Keystone Royal Arch Chapter #3, and charter member and presenter of the Pennsylvania Lodge of Research. A truly top-notch amateur historian, Brian contacted me shortly after my first book on James was published to share with me his conviction that Freemasonry was descended from James and the Nazarenes, something I had already been suspecting. I am thankful for the verification of my suspicions that Brian has provided.

2. www.islamonline.net (accessed July 24, 2009).

3. Robert Lomas, *Turning the Templar Key: The Secret Legacy of the Knights Templar and the Origins of Freemasonry* (Beverly, Mass.: Fair Winds Press, 2007), 331.

4. Ibid., 337.

5. Malcolm C. Duncan, *Duncan's Ritual of Freemasonry* (New York: David McKay Company, 1976), 30–32.

6. Cited in John J. Robinson, *Born in Blood: The Lost Secrets of Freemasonry* (New York: M. Evans & Company, 1989), 199.

7. Richard Smoley, *Forbidden Faith: The Gnostic Legacy from the Gospels to The Da Vinci Code* (New York: HarperOne, 2006), 141.

8. Duncan, *Duncan's Ritual of Freemasonry,* 34–35.

9. Ibid., 65.

10. Edward Burman, *Supremely Abominable Crimes: The Trial of the Knights Templar* (London: Allison & Busby, 1994), 259.

11. Robinson, *Born in Blood,* 277.

12. I am most indebted to Master Mason Brian Fegely for sharing this information with me. He considers this one of the prime connecting links between James the Brother of Jesus and Freemasonry.

13. Woodfin, "The Holiest Ground in the World," in *Crusaders in the Holy Land: The Archaeology of Faith,* 20.

14. Robinson, *Born in Blood,* 281–82.

15. Ibid., 238–39.

16. S. Brent Morris, *The Complete Idiot's Guide to Freemasonry* (New York: Alpha Books, 2006), 92.

17. See Christopher Knight and Robert Lomas, *The Hiram Key: Pharaohs, Freemasons, and the Discovery of the Secret Scrolls of Jesus* (New York: Barnes & Noble Books, 1998).

18. Again, I am indebted to Brian Fegely for this insight.

19. Ralls, *The Templars and the Grail,* 65.

20. Paul Naudon, *The Secret History of Freemasonry: Its Origins and Connection to the Knights Templar,* trans. by Jon Graham (Rochester, Vt.: Inner Traditions, 2005), 140.

21. Ibid., 2.

22. Ibid., 15.

23. Ibid., 35.

24. Ibid., 82.

25. Ibid., ix.

26. Ibid., 73–74.

27. Adapted from Lomas, *Turning the Hiram Key,* 111.

28. Cited in ibid., 338.

29. Cited in Naudon, *The Secret History of Freemasonry,* 261.

30. See my previous book, *The Brother of Jesus and the Lost Teachings of Christianity,* 76–77.

31. Naudon, *The Secret History of Freemasonry,* 250.

32. Baigent and Leigh, *The Temple and the Lodge,* 259–60.

33. Susan Jaccoby, *Freethinkers: A History of American Secularism* (New York: Owl Books, 2004), 19.

34. Robert Heironimus, *Founding Fathers, Secret Societies* (Rochester, Vt: Destiny Books, 2006), 170.

35. Naudon, *The Secret History of Freemasonry,* 227.

36. Ibid., 273.

37. Cited in Joseph B. Ellis, *American Sphinx: The Character of Thomas Jefferson* (New York: Vintage Books, 1998), 309.

38. Ibid., 257.

39. Walter Isaacson, ed. A Benjamin Franklin Reader (New York: Simon & Schuster, 2003), 38.

40. Ibid., 39.

41. The Pennsylvania Gazette, April 10, 1735, cited in ibid., 102.

42. Ibid., 102–3.

43. Ibid., 103–4.

44. Ibid., 105.

45. Ibid., 105–6.

46. Isaacson, *A Benjamin Franklin Reader,* 376–77.

47. Ibid., 378.

48. Schonfield, *Those Incredible Christians,* 235.

49. Baigent and Leigh, *The Temple and the Lodge,* 219.

50. Ibid., 211.

BIBLIOGRAPHY

Adler, Marcus N. *The Itinerary of Benjamin of Tudela: Critical Text, Translation and Commentary.* New York: Phillip Feldheim, Inc. 1907.

Africanus, Julius. *Epistle to Aristides.* The Early Church Fathers on CD-ROM. Salem, Ore.: Harmony Media, 2000.

Akers, Keith. *The Lost Religion of Jesus: Simple Living and Nonviolence in Early Christianity.* New York: Lantern Books, 2000.

————. *The First Followers of Jesus.* Unpublished manuscript.

Al-Shahrastani, Muhammad. *The Book of Religious and Philosophical Sects.* Edited by William Cureton. New York: Gorgias Press, 2002.

Anchor Bible Dictionary. 6 vols. New York: Doubleday, 1992.

Ariarajah, S. Wesley. *Not Without My Neighbor: Issues in Interfaith Relations.* Geneva: WCC Publications, 1999.

Armstrong, Karen. *Muhammad: A Biography of the Prophet.* New York: HarperSanFrancisco, 1992.

————. *Jerusalem: One City, Three Faiths.* New York: Ballantine Books, 2005.

Arndt, William F., and Wilbur F. Gingrich. *A Greek-English Lexicon of the New Testament and Other Early Christian Literature.* 2nd ed. Chicago: University of Chicago Press, 1979.

Baigent, Michael, and Richard Leigh. *The Temple and the Lodge.* New York: Arcade Publishing, 1989.

Barber, Malcolm. *The New Knighthood: A History of the Order of the Temple.* Cambridge: Cambridge University Press, 1978.

————. *The Trial of the Templars.* Cambridge: Cambridge University Press, 1978.

Bauckham, Richard. *Jude, 2 Peter.* Word Biblical Commentary, vol. 50. Waco, Tex.: Word Books, 1983.

————. *Jude and the Relatives of Jesus in the Early Church.* London: T&T Clark, 1990.

————.ed. "James and the Jerusalem Church." In *The Book of Acts in Its Palestinian Setting*, vol. 4 of *The Book of Acts in Its First Century Setting.* Grand Rapids: Eerdmans, 1995.

——. *James: Wisdom of James, Disciple of Jesus the Sage.* New Testament Readings Series. London: Rutledge, 1999.

Bauer, Walter. *Orthodoxy and Heresy in Earliest Christianity.* Edited by Robert A. Kraft and Gerhard Krodel. Translated by Philadelphia Seminar on Christian Origins. Philadelphia: Fortress, 1971.

Baur, Ferdinand Christian. *Paul: The Apostle of Jesus Christ, His Life and Work, His Epistles and His Doctrine,* Vol. 1. 2nd ed. Revised by A. Menzies. London: Williams and Norgate, 1875.

Bell, James B. *The Roots of Jesus: A Genealogical Investigation.* Garden City, N.Y.: Doubleday, 1983.

Bell, Richard. *The Origin of Islam in Its Christian Environment.* London: Routledge, 1968.

Ben-Dov, Meir. *In the Shadow of the Temple.* Translated by Ina Friedman. New York: Harper & Row, 1985.

Blinzler, Josef. *Die Brüder und Schwestern Jesu.* Stuttgarter Bibelstudien, Vol. 21. Stuttgart: Verlag Katholisches Bibel Werk, 1967.

Brandon, S. G. F. *Jesus and the Zealots: A Study of the Political Factors in Primitive Christianity.* Cambridge, England: Scribner, 1967.

Brown, Raymond E. *The Virginal Conception and Bodily Resurrection of Jesus.* New York: Paulist Press, 1973.

——. *The Community of the Beloved Disciple: The Life, Loves, and Hates of an Individual Church in New Testament Times.* New York: Paulist Press, 1979.

——. "Not Jewish Christianity and Gentile Christianity, but Types of Jewish/ Gentile Christianity." *Catholic Biblical Quarterly* 45 (1983): 74–79.

Brown, Raymond E., and John P. Meier. *Antioch and Rome: New Testament Cradles of Catholic Christianity.* New York: Paulist Press, 1983.

Bruce, F. F. *Peter, Stephen, James, and John: Studies in Early Non-Pauline Christianity.* Grand Rapids: Eerdmans, 1979.

Burman, Edward. *Supremely Abominable Crimes: The Trial of the Knights Templar.* London: Allison & Busby, 1994.

Bütz, Jeffrey J. "The Quest for James the Brother of Jesus: A Survey of the Literature and Analysis of Its Implications." S.T.M. Thesis. Lutheran Theological Seminary at Philadelphia, 2002.

——. *The Brother of Jesus and the Lost Teachings of Christianity.* Rochester, Vt.: Inner Traditions, 2005.

Carroll, Kenneth L. "The Place of James in the Early Church." *Bulletin of the John Rylands Library* 44 (1961): 49–71.

Catchpole, David R. "Paul, James and the Apostolic Decree." *New Testament Studies* 23 (1976–77): 428–44.

——. *The Quest for Q.* Edinburgh: T & T Clark, 1993.

Catholic Encyclopedia. www.catholic.org/encyclopedia/ (accessed July 24, 2009).

Chilton, Bruce, and Craig A. Evans, eds. *James the Just and Christian Origins.*

Supplements to *Novum Testamentum*, Vol. XCVIII. Leiden: E. J. Brill, 1999.

Chilton, Bruce, and Jacob Neusner, eds. *The Brother of Jesus: James the Just and His Mission*. Louisville: Westminster John Knox, 2001.

Clement of Alexandria. *The Stromata*. The Early Church Fathers on CD-ROM. Salem, Ore.: Harmony Media, 2000.

Coggins, R. J., and J. L. Houlden, eds. *A Dictionary of Biblical Interpretation*, s.v., "Judaizers," by James D. G. Dunn. Philadelphia: Trinity, 1990.

Crone, Patricia, and Michael Cook. *Hagarism: The Making of the Islamic World*. London: Cambridge University Press, 1977.

Crossan, John Dominic. "Mark and the Relatives of Jesus." *Novum Testamentum*, 15 (1973).

———. *The Historical Jesus: The Life of a Mediterranean Jewish Peasant*. New York: HarperSanFrancisco, 1991.

———. *Jesus: A Revolutionary Biography*. New York: HarperSanFrancisco, 1994.

Daniélou, Jean. *The Theology of Jewish Christianity*. The Development of Christian Doctrine Before the Council of Nicaea, Vol. 1. Translated and edited by John A. Baker. Chicago: Henry Regnery, 1964.

De Voragine, Jacobus. *The Golden Legend: Readings on the Saints, Vol. 1*. Translated by William Granger Ryan. Princeton: Princeton University Press, 1995.

Dictionary of Paul and His Letters. s.v., "Judaizers," by W. S. Campbell. Downers Grove, Ill.: InterVarsity Press, 1993.

Drower, E. S. *The Secret Adam: A Study of Nasoraean Gnosis*. Oxford: Oxford at the Clarendon Press, 1960.

Duncan, Malcolm C. *Duncan's Masonic Ritual and Monitor or Guide to the Three Symbolic Degrees of the Ancient York Rite and to the Degrees of Mark Master, Past Master, Most Excellent Master, and the Royal Arch*. 3rd ed. with additions and corrections. New York: David McKay Co., orig. pub. 1976.

Dunn, James D. G. *Unity and Diversity in the New Testament: An Inquiry into the Character of Earliest Christianity*. 2nd ed. Philadelphia: Trinity Press, 1990.

———. *The Partings of the Ways: Between Christianity and Judaism and Their Significance for the Character of Christianity*. Philadelphia: Trinity Press, 1991.

Eck, Diana L. *A New Religious America: How a "Christian Country" Has Become the World's Most Religiously Diverse Nation*. New York: HarperSanFrancisco, 2001.

Ehrman, Bart D. *Lost Christianities: The Battles for Scripture and the Faiths We Never Knew*. New York: Oxford University Press, 2003.

———. *Lost Scriptures: Books That Did Not Make It into the New Testament*. New York: Oxford University Press, 2003.

Eisenman, Robert. *James the Brother of Jesus: The Key to Unlocking the Secrets of Early Christianity and the Dead Sea Scrolls*. New York: Penguin, 1997.

Eisler, Robert. *The Messiah Jesus and John the Baptist*. London: A. H. Krappe, 1931.

Elliott-Binns, L. E. *Galilean Christianity: Studies in Biblical Theology.* Chicago: Alec R. Allenson, 1956.

Ellis, Joseph B. *American Sphinx: The Character of Thomas Jefferson.* New York: Vintage Books, 1998.

Epiphanius. *The Panarion.* Translated by Frank Williams. Leiden: E. J. Brill, 1997.
———. *On Weights and Measures.* The Early Church Fathers on CD-ROM. Salem, Ore.: Harmony Media, 2000.

Esposito, John, Darell Fasching, and Todd Lewis. *World Religions Today.* 2nd ed. New York: Oxford University Press, 2006.

Eusebius. *The History of the Church.* Rev. ed. Edited and translated by G. A. Williamson. Harmondsworth: Penguin, 1989.

Finkel, Joshua. "Jewish, Christian, and Samaritan Influences on Arabia." In *The MacDonald Presentation Volume: a Tribute to Duncan Black MacDonald.* Edited by W. C. Shellabear and E. E. Calvarly. Princeton: Princeton University Press, 1933.

Fitzmyer, Joseph A. *The Acts of the Apostles.* The Anchor Bible. Garden City, N.Y.: Doubleday, 1998.

Fletcher, Richard. *The Cross and the Crescent: Christianity and Islam from Muhammad to the Reformation.* New York: Viking, 2003.

Funk, Robert W., Roy W. Hoover, and the Jesus Seminar. *The Five Gospels: The Search for the Authentic Words of Jesus.* New York: HarperSanFrancisco, 1997.

Gardner, James. *Jesus Who? Myth vs Reality in the Search for the Historical Jesus.* Booklocker.com, Inc., 2006.

Garsoian, Nina. *The Paulician Heresy: A Study of the Origin and Development of Paulicianism in Armenia and the Eastern Provinces of the Byzantine Empire.* The Hague: Mouton, 1967.

Georgi, Dieter. *Remembering the Poor: The History of Paul's Collection for Jerusalem.* Nashville: Abingdon, 1992.

Goddard, Hugh. *A History of Christian-Muslim Relations.* Chicago: New Amsterdam Books, 2000.

Goulder, Michael. *St. Paul versus St. Peter: A Tale of Two Missions.* Louisville: Westminster John Knox, 1994.

Griffiths, Paul J. *Problems of Religious Diversity.* Malden, Mass.: Blackwell, 2001.

Guillame, Alfred. *The Life of Muhammad.* London: Oxford University Press, 1955.

Harris, Stephen L. *Understanding the Bible.* 6th ed. Boston: McGraw-Hill, 2003.

Heironimus, Robert. *Founding Fathers, Secret Societies.* Rochester, Vt.: Destiny Books, 2006.

Hick, John. *God and the Universe of Faiths.* New York: St. Martin's Press, 1973.
———. *A Christian Theology of Religions: The Rainbow of Faiths.* Louisville: Westminster John Knox, 1995.

Hick, John, and Paul F. Knitter, eds. *The Myth of Christian Uniqueness: Toward a Pluralistic Theology of Religions*. Maryknoll, New York: Orbis Books, 1987.

Hill, Craig C. *Hellenists and Hebrews: Reappraising Division Within the Earliest Church*. Minneapolis: Fortress, 1992.

Hippolytus. *Refutation of All Heresies*. The Early Church Fathers on CD-ROM. Salem, Ore.: Harmony Media, 2000.

Irenaeus. *Against Heresies*. The Early Church Fathers on CD-ROM. Salem, Ore.: Harmony Media, 2000.

Isaacson, Walter. *A Benjamin Franklin Reader*. New York: Simon & Schuster, 2003.

Jaccoby, Susan. *Freethinkers: A History of American Secularism*. New York: Owl Books, 2004.

Jackson-McCabe, Matt, ed. *Jewish Christianity Reconsidered: Rethinking Ancient Groups and Texts*. Minneapolis: Fortress Press, 2007.

Jacobovici, Simcha, and Charles Pellegrino. *The Jesus Family Tomb: The Discovery, the Investigation, and the Evidence That Could Change History*. New York: HarperSanFrancisco, 2007.

Jerome. *Against the Pelagians*. The Early Church Fathers on CD-ROM. Salem, Ore.: Harmony Media, 2000.

———. *Commentary on Matthew*. The Early Church Fathers on CD-ROM. Salem, Ore.: Harmony Media, 2000.

———. *Epistle to Augustine*. The Early Church Fathers on CD-ROM. Salem, Ore.: Harmony Media, 2000.

———. *Lives of Illustrious Men*. The Early Church Fathers on CD-ROM. Salem, Ore.: Harmony Media, 2000.

Josephus, *Antiquities of the Jews*. Translated by William Whiston. *The Works of Josephus*. New updated edition. Peabody, Mass.: Hendrickson, 1987.

———. *Wars of the Jews*. Translated by William Whiston. *The Works of Josephus*. New updated edition. Peabody, Mass.: Hendrickson, 1987.

Khalidi, Tarif. *The Muslim Jesus: Sayings and Stories in Islamic Literature*. Cambridge, Mass.: Harvard University Press, 2001.

Klijn, A. F. J., and G. J. Reinink. *Patristic Evidence for Jewish-Christian Sects*. Supplements to *Novum Testamentum*, Vol. XXXVI. Leiden: E. J. Brill, 1973.

Knight, Christopher, and Robert Lomas. *The Hiram Key: Pharaohs, Freemasons, and the Discovery of the Secret Scrolls of Jesus*. New York: Barnes & Noble Books, 1998.

Knitter, Paul F. *Jesus and Other Names: Christian Mission and Global Responsibility*. Maryknoll, N.Y.: Orbis Books, 1996.

———. *Introducing Theologies of Religions*. Maryknoll, N.Y.: Orbis Books, 2002.

The Koran. Translated with notes by N. J. Dawood. New York: Penguin, 1999.

Lightfoot, J. B. "The Brethren of the Lord." In *The Epistle of St. Paul to the Galatians*. Grand Rapids: Eerdmans, 1967.

Lomas, Robert. *Turning the Templar Key: The Secret Legacy of the Knights Templar and the Origins of Freemasonry.* Beverly, Mass.: Fair Winds Press, 2007.

Longenecker, Richard N. *The Christology of Early Jewish Christianity.* Studies in Biblical Theology, Second Series, Vol. 17. London: SCM, 1970.

Lüdemann, Gerd. *Opposition to Paul in Jewish Christianity.* Translated by M. Eugene Boring. Minneapolis: Fortress, 1989.

Luttikhuizen, Gerard P. *The Revelation of Elchasai: Investigations into the Evidence for a Mesopotamian Jewish Apocalypse of the Second Century and Its Reception by Judeo-Christian Propagandists.* Tübingen: Mohr Siebeck, 1985.

Maccoby, Hyam. *The Mythmaker: Paul and the Invention of Christianity.* New York: Barnes & Noble, 1986.

Mack, Burton L. *A Myth of Innocence: Mark and Christian Origins.* Philadelphia: Fortress, 1988.

MacNulty, W. Kirk. *Freemasonry: Symbols, Secrets, Significance.* London: Thames & Hudson, 2006.

Markale, Jean. *Montségur and the Mystery of the Cathars.* Translated by Jon E. Graham. Rochester, Vt.: Inner Traditions, 2003.

Martin, Malachi. *The Decline and Fall of the Roman Church.* New York: Bantam Books, 1983.

Martin, Ralph P. *James.* Word Biblical Commentary, Vol. 48. Waco, Tex.: Word Books, 1988.

Martin, Raymond. *The Elusive Messiah: A Philosophical Overview of the Quest for the Historical Jesus.* Boulder, Colo.: Westview Press, 2000.

Martyr, Justin. *Dialogue with Trypho the Jew.* The Early Church Fathers on CD-ROM. Salem, Ore.: Harmony Media, 2000.

——. *The First Apology.* The Early Church Fathers on CD-ROM. Salem, Ore.: Harmony Media, 2000.

McLaren, James S. "Ananus, James, and Earliest Christianity. Josephus's Account of the Death of James." *Journal of Theological Studies,* 52:1 (2001): 1–25.

Meier, John P. *A Marginal Jew: Rethinking the Historical Jesus.* Vol. 2: *Mentor, Message, and Miracles.* The Anchor Bible Reference Library. New York: Doubleday, 1994.

Meyer, Marvin W. *The Secret Teachings of Jesus: Four Gnostic Gospels.* Translated by Marvin W. Meyer. New York: Vintage, 1986.

Michael of Albany and Walid Amine Salhab. *The Knights Templar of the Middle East.* San Francisco: Weiser Books, 2006.

Milavec, Aaron. *The Didache: Text, Translation, Analysis, and Commentary.* Collegeville, Minn.: Liturgical Press, 2003.

Millar, Angel. *Freemasonry: A History.* San Diego: Thunder Bay Press, 2005.

Morris, S. Brent. *The Complete Idiot's Guide to Freemasonry.* New York: Alpha Books, 2006.

Munck, Johannes. *Paul and the Salvation of Mankind.* London: SCM Press, 1959.

Naudon, Paul. *The Secret History of Freemasonry: Its Origins and Connection to the Knights*

Templar. Translated by Jon E. Graham. Rochester, Vt.: Inner Traditions, 2005.

Newman, Sharan. *The Real History Behind the Templars*. New York: Berkley Books, 2007.

Novak, Philip. *The World's Wisdom: Sacred Texts of the World's Religions*. New York: HarperSanFrancisco, 1994.

Oldenbourg, Zoé. *Massacre at Montségur*. London: Phoenix Press, 2000.

Origen. *Against Celsus*. The Early Church Fathers on CD-ROM. Salem, Ore.: Harmony Media, 2000.

———. *De Principiis*. The Early Church Fathers on CD-ROM. Salem, Ore.: Harmony Media, 2000.

Osiek, Carolyn, and David L. Balch. *Families in the New Testament World: Households and House Churches*. The Family, Religion, and Culture Series. Louisville: Westminster John Knox, 1997.

Pagels, Elaine. *The Gnostic Gospels*. New York: Vintage, 1979.

———. *The Gnostic Paul: Gnostic Exegesis of the Pauline Letters*. Harrisburg: Trinity Press International, 1992.

Painter, John. *Just James: The Brother of Jesus in History and Tradition*. Minneapolis: Fortress, 1999.

Peake, A. S. *Paul and the Jewish Christians*. Manchester: Manchester University Press, 1929.

Pegg, Mark Gregory. *A Most Holy War: The Albigensian Crusade and the Battle for Christendom*. New York: Oxford University Press, 2008.

Pixner, Bargil. "Church of the Apostles Found on Mt. Zion." *Biblical Archaeology Review* (May/June 1990): 17–34, 60.

Pritz, Ray. *Nazarene Jewish Christianity: From the End of the New Testament Period Until Its Disappearance in the Fourth Century*. Jerusalem: The Magnes Press, 1992.

Ralls, Karen. *The Templars and the Grail: Knights of the Quest*. Wheaton, Ill.: Quest Books, 2003.

Ridley, Jasper. *The Freemasons: A History of the World's Most Powerful Secret Society*. New York: Arcade Publishing, 2001.

Robinson, J. M., ed. *The Nag Hammadi Library in English*. New York: Harper & Row, 1988.

Robinson, John. *Born in Blood: The Lost Secrets of Freemasonry*. New York: M. Evans & Company, 1989.

Rodkinson, Michael L., trans. *Babylonian Talmud*. www.sacred-texts.com/jud/talmud.htm (accessed July 24, 2009).

Rubenstein, Richard E. *When Jesus Became God: The Struggle to Define Christianity during the Last Days of Rome*. San Diego: Harcourt, 1999.

Runciman, Steven. *The Medieval Manichee: A Study of Christian Dualist Heresy*. Cambridge: Cambridge University Press, 1999.

Saldarini, Anthony J. *Matthew's Christian-Jewish Community*. Chicago Studies in the History of Judaism. Chicago: University of Chicago Press, 1994.

Sanders, E. P. *Jesus and Judaism*. Philadelphia: Fortress, 1985.

Schmithals, Walter. *Paul and James*. Studies in Biblical Theology No. 46. Translated by D. M. Barton. London: SCM Press, 1965.

Schneemelcher, Wilhelm, ed. *New Testament Apocrypha*, Vol. 1. Rev. ed. Translated by R. McL. Wilson. Louisville: Westminster John Knox, 2003.

———. *New Testament Apocrypha*. Vol. 2. Rev. ed. Translated by R. McL. Wilson. Louisville: Westminster John Knox, 2003.

Schoeps, Hans-Joachim. *Jewish Christianity: Factional Disputes in the Early Church*. Philadelphia: Fortress, 1969.

Schonfield, Hugh J. *The History of Jewish Christianity: From the First to the Twentieth Centuries*. London: Duckworth, 1936.

———. *Those Incredible Christians*. New York: Bantam, 1969.

———. *The Pentecost Revolution: The Story of the Jesus Party in Israel, A.D. 36–66*. London: MacDonald, 1974.

———. *The Essene Odyssey: The Mystery of the True Teacher and the Essene Impact on the Shaping of Human Destiny*. Great Britain: Element, 1984.

Schweitzer, Albert. *The Mysticism of Paul the Apostle*. Translated by William Montgomery. London: A & C Black, 1931.

———. *The Quest of the Historical Jesus: A Critical Study of Its Progress from Reimarus to Wrede*. New York: Macmillan, 1962.

Scott, J. J. "James the Relative of Jesus and the Expectation of an Eschatological Priest." *Journal of the Evangelical Theological Society* 25 (1982): 323–32.

Segal, Alan F. "Jewish Christianity." In *Eusebius, Christianity and Judaism*. Edited by Harold W. Attridge and Gobei Hata. Detroit: Wayne State University Press, 1992.

Shanks, Hershel, and Ben Witherington III. *The Brother of Jesus: The Dramatic Story and Meaning of the First Archaeological Link to Jesus and His Family*. New York: HarperCollins, 2003.

Silberman, Neil Asher. *The Hidden Scrolls: Christianity, Judaism, and the War for the Dead Sea Scrolls*. New York: G. P. Putnam's Sons, 1994.

Smith, Huston. *The World's Religions: Our Great Wisdom Traditions*. New York: HarperSanFrancisco, 1991.

Smoley, Richard. *Forbidden Faith: The Gnostic Legacy from the Gospels to the Da Vinci Code*. New York: HarperCollins, 2006.

Spong, John Shelby. *Why Christianity Must Change or Die: A Bishop Speaks to Believers in Exile*. New York: HarperSanFrancisco, 1999.

Starbird, Margaret. *The Woman with the Alabaster Jar: Mary Magdalen and the Holy Grail*. Rochester, Vt.: Bear & Company, 1993.

———. *The Goddess in the Gospels: Reclaiming the Sacred Feminine*. Rochester, Vt.: Bear & Company, 1998.

———. *Mary Magdalene, Bride in Exile*. Rochester, Vt.: Bear & Company, 2005.

Stevenson, J., ed. *A New Eusebius: Documents Illustrating the History of the Church to AD 337*. Rev. ed. London: SPCK, 1987.

Stoyanov, Yuri. *The Other God: Religious Dualism from Antiquity to the Cathar Heresy.* New Haven: Yale University Press, 2000.

Strayer, Joseph R. *The Albigensian Crusades.* Ann Arbor: The University of Michigan Press, 1992.

Swidler, Leonard, ed. *Toward a Universal Theology of Religion.* Maryknoll, N.Y.: Orbis Books, 1987.

Tabor, James D. *The Jesus Dynasty: The Hidden History of Jesus, His Royal Family, and the Birth of Chrisitanity.* New York: Simon & Schuster, 2006.

Theissen, Gerd, and Annette Merz. *The Historical Jesus: A Comprehensive Guide.* Minneapolis: Fortress, 1998.

Torrey, Charles C. *The Jewish Foundation of Islam.* 2nd ed. New York: KTAV Publishing, 1967.

Upton-Ward, Judi, trans. and ed. *The Rule of the Templars: The French Text of the Rule of the Order of the Knights Templar.* Woodbridge, Suffolk: Boydell Press, 1992.

Van Voorst, Robert E. *The Ascents of James: History and Theology of a Jewish-Christian Community.* Atlanta: Scholars Press, 1989.

Wakefield, Walter L., and Austin P Evans. *Heresies of the High Middle Ages: Selected Sources Translated and Annotated.* New York: Columbia University Press, 1969.

Wansbrough, Henry. "Mark III.21—Was Jesus Out of His Mind?" *New Testament Studies* 18, 1972.

Weeden, Theodore J. *Mark: Traditions in Conflict.* Philadelphia: Fortress, 1971.

Weis, René. *The Yellow Cross: The Story of the Last Cathars 1290–1329.* New York: Alfred A. Knopf, 2001.

Weiss, Johannes. *Earliest Christianity.* Translated by F. C. Grant. New York: Harper & Row, 1959.

White, Carolinne. *The Correspondence (394–419) between Jerome and Augustine of Hippo.* New York: The Edwin Mellen Press, 1990.

Wilkinson, John, Joyce Hill, and William F. Ryan, eds. *Jerusalem Pilgrimage 1099–1185.* London: Hakluyt Society, 1988.

Williams, Frank, ed. *The Panarion of Epiphanius.* Book I. Translated by Frank Williams. Leiden: Brill, 1997.

Wilson, Barrie. *How Jesus Became Christian.* New York: St. Martin's Press, 2008.

Witherington III, Ben. *Jesus the Sage: The Pilgrimage of Wisdom.* Minneapolis: Fortress, 1994.

Woodfin, Warren T. "The Holiest Ground in the World." In *Crusaders in the Holy Land: The Archaeology of Faith.* Edited by Jack Meinhardt. Washington, D.C.: Biblical Archaeology Society, 2005.

Wright, N. T. *Jesus and the Victory of God: Christian Origins and the Question of God,* Vol. 2. Minneapolis: Fortress, 1996.

Zuckerman, Arthur J. *A Jewish Princedom in Feudal France 768–900.* New York: Columbia University Press, 1972.

INDEX

BOOKS OF RELATED INTEREST

The Brother of Jesus and the Lost Teachings of Christianity
by Jeffrey J. Bütz

Founding Fathers, Secret Societies
Freemasons, Illuminati, Rosicrucians, and the
Decoding of the Great Seal
by Robert Hieronimus, Ph.D. with Laura Cortner

Secret Societies of America's Elite
From the Knights Templar to Skull and Bones
by Steven Sora

Secret Societies
Their Influence and Power from Antiquity to the Present Day
by Michael Howard

The Secret History of Freemasonry
Its Origins and Connection to the Knights Templar
by Paul Naudon

Montségur and the Mystery of the Cathars
by Jean Markale

The Secret Society of Moses
The Mosaic Bloodline and a Conspiracy Spanning Three Millennia
by Flavio Barbiero

The Secret Doctrine of the Kabbalah
Recovering the Key to Hebraic Sacred Science
by Leonora Leet, Ph.D.

INNER TRADITIONS • BEAR & COMPANY
P.O. Box 388
Rochester, VT 05767
1-800-246-8648
www.InnerTraditions.com

Or contact your local bookseller